SILENT MOMENTS IN EDUCATION

COLETTE A. GRANGER

Silent Moments in Education

An Autoethnography of Learning, Teaching, and Learning to Teach

UNIVERSITY OF TORONTO PRESS
Toronto Buffalo London

© University of Toronto Press 2011
Toronto Buffalo London
www.utppublishing.com
Printed in Canada

ISBN 978-1-4426-4320-8

Printed on acid-free, 100% post-consumer recycled paper with
vegetable-based inks.

Library and Archives Canada Cataloguing in Publication

Granger, Colette A., 1956–
Silent moments in education: an autoethnography of learning, teaching,
and learning to teach / Colette A. Granger.

Includes bibliographical references and index.
ISBN 978-1-4426-4320-8

1. Psychoanalysis and education.   2. Teaching – Pyschological aspects.
3. Teacher-student relationships.   4. Learning, Psychology of.   I. Title.

LB1092.G73 2011   370.15   C2011-902770-4

University of Toronto Press acknowledges the financial assistance to its
publishing program of the Canada Council for the Arts and the Ontario
Arts Council.

 Canada Council   Conseil des Arts
for the Arts   du Canada

 ONTARIO ARTS COUNCIL
CONSEIL DES ARTS DE L'ONTARIO

University of Toronto Press acknowledges the financial support of the
Government of Canada through the Canada Book Fund for its publishing
activities.

For Emma and Paul,
always

For Alberto,
remembered always

And for B M L,
some other way

Contents

x   Contents

Acknowledgments

A long car trip punctuated by rest-stops and rainstorms, side-tracks and torn maps, flat tires and static on the radio: it is an obvious metaphor for the making of a book, but it captures something of the feeling of interminability that makes a writer wonder at times how much further the destination can be. And then suddenly, we arrive.

For their important contributions to this process I thank those anonymous reviewers whose thoughtful comments added to my own learning and thinking, and facilitated the publication of the manuscript. I am also indebted to the following people at University of Toronto Press: Virgil Duff (now retired), Anne Laughlin, Brittany Lavery, Doug Richmond, and Shoshana Wasser, and to freelance copyeditor Robyn Gallimore for her attention to the manuscript. Any remaining errors are mine.

This book began as a doctoral dissertation at York University. I am grateful to my supervisor, Alice Pitt, for her trust in my very personal academic project, her rigorous intellectual mentoring, and the splendid and compassionate gift of breathing space when I needed it. I thank the members of my dissertation and examining committees, Chloë Brushwood Rose, Susan Ehrlich, Susan Ingram, and Karen Krasny, for their generous and thought-provoking responses to the work. I owe a particular debt of gratitude to my external examiner, Janet Miller of Columbia University, whose careful and sensitive reading attended to important personal and private tensions inhering in the study, as they do at times in all our work. And to the Canadian Association for Teacher Education I express gratitude for honouring my study.

That's the formal part. But in travelling the road from dissertation to book I have also benefited more informally from the theoretical insights, humour and laughter, late-night phone calls, and home-cooking – and in some cases all these things at once – of friends and colleagues in the academic community in addition to those named above: Deborah Britzman, Trent Davis, Don Dippo, Cara Ellingson, Lisa Farley, Karleen Pendleton Jiménez, R.M. Kennedy, Heather Lotherington, Rebecca Luce-Kapler, Sara Matthews, Linda Radford, Lorin Schwarz, Jordan Singer, Aparna Mishra Tarc, Leanne Taylor, and Deirdre Whitfeld. I am also very grateful to my friends of many years: Kathy Bates, Gina Bell, Lucy Bowers, Ann Breen, Donna Dwan, Elaine Edgely, Julia Keeling, Judy Newman, Anita Thachuk, and Peter Thachuk.

I come, last but never least, to my family. To Emma Quarter and Paul Quarter, and to Manuel Mendelzon and Martin Mendelzon, whose father, Alberto Mendelzon, we sadly lost in 2005, go my love and deep appreciation for your patience, humour, support, and company along the way. This book belongs to each of you.

I am grateful for the financial assistance for my work provided by a Social Sciences and Humanities Research Council of Canada doctoral fellowship (award no. 752-2000-1837), as well as for a doctoral scholarship from the International Order of Daughters of the Empire.

An earlier and shorter version of Chapter 5, titled 'On (not) representing sex in preschool and kindergarten: a psychoanalytic reflection on orders and hints,' was published in February 2007, in the Taylor & Francis journal *Sex Education: Sexuality, Society and Learning* 7(1), 1–15.

SILENT MOMENTS IN EDUCATION

Prologue

First Circumnarrative: The Sun

> It matters to stumble after.
> ... It matters in this time of not-yet sight
> that some skin cells seem sensitized to light.
> — Joy Kogawa, *Itsuka*

It is not a straight line.

January 2006
If an ending is also a beginning, can a beginning be also an ending? And can there be a place where we are neither beginning nor ending, but waiting to do both? I have been wandering around in academic limbo for some time now. For well over two years I have done virtually no work. This time has divided itself roughly into two not-quite-equal parts: caring for a terminally ill loved one, and mourning the death and the permanent absence of that beloved.

Still, it seems as if it might be time to begin, stumbling.

November 2005
Five months after the death of my partner, Alberto Mendelzon, I drive from Toronto to Ottawa to take his place in a ceremony inducting him into the Royal Society of Canada. With me are his sons and my own two children. Our little trip is bittersweet: the five of us joke about the recitations of inductees' (to us strange and even incomprehensible) scientific accomplishments, and roll our

eyes at the dinner speeches, but we feel sadness and regret and loneliness too, because the one to whom all of it would have meant the most is not with us.

The day after the ceremony we drive home, five hours through cold, rainy, late-autumn weather. Our spirits are low. But about halfway home, as we come over the crest of a high hill and see a valley spread out below us, its forest stark and leafless, I catch my breath as the sun breaks through the clouds, just for a moment, and turns the trees' dark wetness to silver. And in that moment, I feel a lifting, a sense of light not just around me but in me. It is not quite a new beginning, not yet, but there is the possibility of beginning.

March 2006
This is taking longer than I expected. I have begun to move forward, but slowly: I am not finished grieving. I know this because, in the way of such things, there are days of feeling quite well, of believing not only that a life less marked by absence might be possible but that I may actually be capable of beginning to live that life. On these days I can read, and think, and even write, at least a little. But there are other days, of a crippling, bewildered hollowness that cannot find its own expression in words and that refuses to let words express anything else either: days passed numbly with memories necessary but painful – the same letters read and reread, the same music played over and over, and conversation, silent and impossible yet imperative, with the one who is gone.

Introduction

I hope the usefulness of what I am embarking upon
lies partly in inviting round the table . . . guests who should
talk to one another but have not yet managed to do so.
                                    – Harold Rosen, *Speaking from Memory*

There was nothing he could do to contravene the certainty
that awaited him: a whole solid clock-ticking afternoon
buried alive in the dark, lonely den
with that goddamned book.
                                    – Carol Shields, *Happenstance*

Silent Moments

A four-year-old kindergarten pupil is silently, utterly obedient, even
when faced with disagreeable demands from the teacher. A secondary
school student feels drawn to a specific subject area, but vehemently
refuses to enrol in a course with a particular teacher, despite warnings
that this decision could preclude continuing in a beloved discipline.
A university student, despite being familiar with the texts the course
addresses and interested in its concepts, sits at the computer for days
on end, producing nothing, as the due date for the final paper rapidly
approaches. A preservice teacher is eager and obliged to gain practical
experience, but owing to a conflicted relationship with a supervising
teacher finds herself unable to use her new knowledge and skills in a
practicum classroom. An experienced educator, usually confident and
at ease in the classroom, suddenly feels lost, unanchored, cast adrift by

the demands of a new technology she is required to use. Adults in a dance class find their own movements strangely inhibited as a young child moves with abandon among them.

At first these events seem quite unconnected, but for the relationship each of them bears, in one way or another, with education. There are other similarities they share, however. First, despite their disparity, each of them implies something about individual identity on one hand and a relationship on the other, a relationship perhaps between facets of identity, or between individuals, or among individuals, institutions, and ideas, all within the context of education. Second, each encapsulates the notion of some form of difficulty with or breakdown in learning or meaning, and concomitantly in relationship: a moment when an individual learner or teacher – or something inside of that individual – gets stuck, freezes, becomes paralysed, is in one sense or another rendered silent. Third, although each is quite particular in its circumstances and enactment, all are arguably emblematic of broader and deeper difficulties, breakdowns, or silences within the likewise broad and deep world and work of education. Finally, and most significantly in this context, all of these events are autobiographical artefacts of my own educational history.

I grew up in southern Ontario, Canada, attending public elementary and secondary schools in the 1960s and early 1970s, the elder of two daughters who, like almost all of our counterparts, spoke the dominant language (English) and identified as 'white,' although our ethnic heritage (Franco-Manitoban/Aboriginal on the paternal side, and Hungarian/German on the maternal) made us slightly exotic in what were then almost exclusively Anglo-Irish semi-rural and suburban communities. I was a strong student in academic terms, and but for one brief period when I was 12 and my parents' marriage was coming to an end, and another when, as a grade 11 student, I insisted on dropping English (the first 'silent moment' I speak of in this book), I caused little trouble. At parents' night meetings my teachers occasionally suggested that my talking tended to distract others, but by and large I was considered an exemplary student: in the report-card vernacular of the time, an 'asset to the class.'

Occasional bouts of classroom chatter notwithstanding, life at school, and even more at home, was marked mostly by containment and silence. Worries were held in; high grades were the goal; 'being good' – in the form of unquestioning obedience – was key. I remember being worried when I had to ask questions in class about things I ought already to have known, and anxious about what would be said at home when a test had come back with a grade lower than A-plus. I recall sneaking out of bed early on dark winter mornings to finish homework I did not want my parents to see for fear of their criticism, and attending class with colds and flu that might have kept other students home, because in my family illness meant weakness and less-than-perfect school attendance was unthinkable.

Perhaps unsurprisingly, under all this surface acquiescence, trouble was brewing. Following secondary school, persuaded by a scholarship (and a grateful, financially strapped mother), I finished a year of university. But by the end of it I was sure that my relationship with education at all levels, and indeed with educators (by that time both my parents had become teachers), was over: I would never return to school. Aside from a few language courses, and a nursing program at a polytechnic that I began but did not finish, I kept that vow for 20 years. By then my own marriage was ending and my children were in school. Influenced, however ironically, by my parents' career choices and by dominant discourses of teaching as appropriate 'women's work' (along with the nursing program I had already tried and rejected), I decided that acquiring an undergraduate degree, and subsequently a primary teaching qualification, would lead to a career that would let me support my family.

Extreme difficulties in the practicum portion of that Bachelor of Education program led to a change in plan. Those difficulties – the 'silent moments' that inform Part 3 of this book – led to my work over the past 10 years in post-secondary teaching, educational research, and graduate studies, and ultimately to the doctoral dissertation that has become this book. Above all they led to my ongoing scholarly interest in moments within education when what is supposed to happen does not happen: when curriculum or pedagogy is resisted, refused, denied; when learners become stuck, frozen, or paralysed; when the self, as learner or teacher, grows silent.

The events enumerated at the start of this introduction are examples of such moments, each of which I either experienced personally or witnessed firsthand at some point during the almost 30 years I have spent in primary, secondary, and tertiary educational settings. Together, they are the kernels of lived experience that have become the empirical jumping-off points for this autoethnographic study. My descriptions of the events and their accompanying difficulties endeavour to articulate those silent memories, while my analyses explore and work with what the events, difficulties, memories, silences – and ultimately the speaking – evoke, provoke, resist, and refuse.

From a more abstract vantage point, the study arises from and works with questions about those and other moments, and about larger issues of identity, difficulty, and relationship in education. How do we, as individual learners and teachers, make relations with ourselves and one another, with knowledge, and with ideas? What is at stake in these relations and in the identities that emerge through and from them? How, and why, might they at times break down? Can they be remade? How might they be remembered, thought and rethought, theorized and re-theorized, over time and in light of their own reiterations, transformations, re/in/con/versions, evolutions, even revolutions? In tending to these questions my work moves along some complexly interconnected routes: my remembered experiences as learner, teacher, and researcher in education as well as my evolving relationships (also as learner, teacher, and researcher) with discourses and literatures that consider such experiences. What deepens my curiosity about the questions is the sense that they are rendered difficult to answer by the multiple tensions, silences, and breakdowns embodied within the moments which they are asking about.

In my earlier work on second language learning (Granger, 2004), which theorized silence as a presence rather than an absence, psychoanalytic theory was my hermeneutic of choice for reading language learners' narratives about silence, and silence within those narratives, as possible manifestations of intrapersonal loss, conflict, or anxiety experienced by some second language learners for whom acquiring a new language might also mean acquiring, or making, a new self. This book expands that concept of silence outward from language-related identity issues to other points within the educational sphere at which ruptures occur and inaugurate yet other silences. In viewing these silences as manifestations of intrapersonal difficulties, disruptions or breakdowns that may have been utterly unspeakable at the time of their occurrence, and in some cases for many years afterwards, it melds together the three components – the 'silent moments' themselves, my questions about the making and breaking of pedagogical relations, and my relationship with theories that invite thinking about both moments and questions – which constitute the set of preoccupations informing this book.

My task, then, is to engage different kinds of silence, literal and metaphorical, that gesture to, implicate, or are symptomatic of particular kinds of difficulty or disruption in the work of learning, teaching, and learning to teach. I wish not to flatten their distinctions, but rather to invoke their commonalities: to consider how such difficulties challenge, resist, or even rupture the wishes and the work of education, writ both small and large, that a protracted conceptual and theoretical conversation with them might invite. This conversation maintains my previous work's primarily psychoanalytic orientation to reading and interpreting the experiences and their silences, and to exploring the questions, but supplements it with elements of critical and feminist discourse analysis.

Of course mine is not the only possible conversation that might be had within the realm of education. The moments I remember, the ways I remember them, and my theorizations and interpretations of them are all informed by multiple factors. First, there is my socio-cultural position as a white, heterosexual, dominant-language-speaking woman who came of age in a part of the world much less diverse than it is today, and in a historical moment in which much of the diversity that did exist – ethnic, linguistic, sexual – was flattened by discourses that denied difference and privileged the trope of 'equal treatment for all' (Harper, 1997a, p. 198).[1] Perhaps this positioning has to do with why my work, while it does engage questions of marginalization and equity, does so from a rather different vantage point than is usual in a North American (and specifically Canadian) context at the beginning of the twenty-first century. But that was not a choice; this book would be less authentic were I to don a cloak of marginalization of a kind and degree that I have not experienced.

My memories and interpretations, and my approach in this work, are additionally informed by my history as an adult learner, and by the discourses and conceptual/interpretive frameworks (primarily psychoanalytic theory and, to a lesser extent, critical discourse analysis) which I bring to bear on both the memories and their interpretations. More particularly, I trace my introduction to this orientation to a little paper by British psychoanalyst Winnicott (1963b), which I first read during those months in a teacher education program when my difficult practicum experience came close to convincing me that I did not belong in education at all.

'Sum, I am,' with its doubly meaningful title, addresses the issue of individuation, of the moment when an individual comes to understand him- or herself as separate from other individuals. It also pointed me in the direction of a way of thinking about individuals in relation with others, and with the world, that satisfied my disinclination to flatten either individuals or relations to sets of characteristics attributable to groups or categories. Again, perhaps this was due to my feeling some-how marginal in spite of not belonging to an identifiable marginalized group. In addition, however, while I knew the tremendous importance of identifying, understanding, and working to change the social fac-tors and processes that privilege some and subordinate others, ap-proaches to doing so which appeared to reduce human experience to categories always seemed to me to be missing part of the puzzle: namely, that part that dealt with how individuals live, and move, and have their being within, or outside of, those categories.

'*Sum,* I am' was my introduction to psychoanalytic theory. And in-deed, while I do work with several other theories, it is no great stretch to read the conversation that forms these chapters as primarily compris-ing manifestations *in* psychoanalytic theory, *of* psychoanalytic theory, *in* and *of* particular times and places, all of which are at once both socially informed and idiosyncratic. In the process of manuscript review pre-ceding the publication of this book, one reader pointed out that 'these interpretations could only have been made by this particular author.' In some ways this is true of all books, but it struck me as very important, because it spoke to that uniqueness that lies at the heart of all our ways of being: each set of experiences is unique in its combination of time and place, inner perspective and outer context, and the individual re-sponses to those factors of the self that is doing the experiencing.

My own combination of influences and responses to experience has informed my choice of what book to write and how to write it. Paradoxically, however, it is also the reason why these were, in a sense, not choices at all. For if it is true, as that reader said, that I am the only author who could have written this particular book, it is also the case that this is the only book I could have written at this point in my own history.

So no, this book is not the only possible conversation. But it is one conversation. And, if all goes well, perhaps it will invite others.

Conceptual Framework: If It's Not One Thing, It's an Other

While it is crucial to recognize that the story these pages tell is em-phatically not the only story that can be told, the point also bears mak-ing that sometimes one person's remembered story, or interpretation of that story, can inform and even nourish another's memory, story, or interpretation, even if on their surfaces they are quite distinct. This is my first wish: that the moments I recall, narrate, and interpret may open up possibilities for others to think in similar ways about different moments in education, or in different ways about similar moments, or even about different moments in different ways – because sometimes, there are surprises.

Teaching and learning, within an institution peopled by diverse individuals and beset by multiple demands and worries (from the pedagogical to the philosophical, the economic to the ethical, the political to the logistic to the technical), can be an intricate and opaque affair. These concerns imply multiple vantage points that are not unfamiliar to educators. Yet despite theorists' efforts to highlight these various preoccupations, much of current Western education, from curriculum documents to classroom practices, from preschools to universities and even to teacher preparation programs, persists in conducting itself as if such difficult moments were unheard of, progress and success were certain and unequivocal, and the uniform linear development of a homogeneous generation of learners were guaranteed – or, at the very least, that any detours along that presumed straight road of development were predictable, and could be either pre-empted or easily remedied by use of the correct strategy.

Perhaps we should not be surprised by this. Epistemologies informing present-day Western education have, for the most part, long understood progress in general as a steady and incremental journey toward a specific goal, and have privileged predictability and measurability along with Newtonian/Cartesian concepts of the rational, the empirical, and the scientific (see Mitrano, 1981; Britzman, 1998). Alongside this, the myth that education's goals represent consensus among interested parties (including governments, school boards, teachers, students, and communities) has persisted even when those goals either undergo significant change or compete with other goals (Prentice, 1977; Egan, 1997; Labaree, 1997). Only recently has this myth been met with postmodern and deconstructionist challenges (Taubman, 1992; Doll, 1993; Britzman, 1998; Pinar, Reynolds, Slattery, & Taubman, 2000; Pitt, 2003).

There are, for example, individuals and groups that dedicate themselves to promoting and implementing constructivism, learner autonomy, student-centred learning, and the like, along with feminist, antiracist, and anti-homophobic discourses and practices, all informed by an overarching ethic of care (see Noddings, 2003; Todd, 2003a), which direct themselves toward social change and the democratic participation of those involved in education. But the hegemonic work of social and cultural reproduction which education performs, arguably both deliberately and by default, has kept responses to these challenges significantly at bay (Cuban, 1986, 2001; Bourdieu & Passeron, 1990; Britzman, 1991). The visible structures, overt dynamics, and observable practices of mainstream schooling have changed less, and more slowly, than might have been anticipated (Cuban, 1993b; Aronowitz & Giroux, 1993; Giroux & McLaren, 1994; Apple, 1996).

Hegemony notwithstanding, given the call to attend to all of education's participants in ethical and caring ways, it seems both curious and difficult to reconcile that an institution which on one hand traditionally favours the observable and the measurable and, on the other, explicitly dedicates itself to the success of all those it seeks to serve, should resist, and effectively keep silent about, what to the participant and even to the casual onlooker is evident: education does not proceed in a straight line. Though we might be forgiven for wishing that it did, or imagining or pretending that it does, if we visit a classroom even briefly, converse with a teacher struggling with a new curriculum, or recall moments when our own learning was sidetracked by theoretical, technological, or personal vicissitudes, we are compelled to recognize that our wish is probably futile, our pretence likely in vain.

For an ethical response to any difficulty to be attainable, education must recognize that that difficulty might be something more and other than a readily observed, easily overcome blip in an otherwise smooth learning curve. The idea that the difficult not only resides in specific subject matter, government policy, or institutional processes, but also lives in and acts upon (and at times silences) the psyche of the individual participant in education, points to the usefulness of studying those intrapersonal dynamics, and the moments where they fall silent, as a way to begin, ethically and with care, to respond to and work with the larger scenes – and the larger silences – of education.

This can mean trouble though, for while educators want to respond ethically and with care to students' difficulties and worries, it is not always easy to know what those difficulties and worries are. It is even harder to act ethically in responding, for example to a breakdown in meaning, when the possibility of breakdown is itself not acknowledged (Britzman, 1998). The problem of precisely knowing or clearly understanding another's difficulty, of hearing and responding fully to another's silence, is part of the more fundamental problem of that Other's alterity.

Knowing the Other may be more than a mere problem: it may be quite impossible. Working closely with Levinas's idea (1987, p. 83) that the 'Other as Other is not only an alter ego ... [but also, precisely,] what I myself am not,' Todd (2003a, p. 3) understands the Other's difference as 'absolute' and the Other as 'infinitely unknowable.' Still, Todd argues (p. 9), we must not be discouraged by this. For it is precisely the unknowability of the Other, in her words the nonreciprocity and fundamental strangeness that inevitably characterize and circumscribe self-other relations, which can give rise to the possibility for an ethical engagement with that Other, provided we give up the too-easy and even misguided belief that learning about other people is sufficient to generate an ethical response to them and, more generally, to difference itself. At the very least, it seems, such learning about can, in a Levinasian conceptualization, be only part of what constitutes an ethical response, since learning about or knowing about an 'unassimilable and unknowable alterity' (p. 9) can only ever be partial at best.

Learning *about* is insufficient: we must also learn *from*. Todd cites Freud (1919), Phillips (1998), and Britzman (1998) on the importance of distinguishing between the two processes. Britzman, Phillips, and Todd find psychoanalytic theories instructive for developing ways to learn from others, and Todd (2003a, p. 10) specifically identifies the encounter with otherness as both prerequisite to meaning-making and conducive to 'connections, disjunctions and ruptures' in the self. The qualities of the *encounter with* an Other and a *learning from* that Other may not be altogether oppositional, particularly if we consider that connections can form out of what is disjointed, that a rupture can become an opening, that meaning might be made from a breakdown in meaning. And in that sense, perhaps learning *from* another might engender learning, in the form of insight (literally, seeing-in), *about* one's self.

This may seem an obvious notion, but aspects of it are neither straightforward nor simple. My work is emphatically not a declaration that either the story of one individual's learning or the silences within that story can be extrapolated to another's. Even less does it claim that what can be interpreted from one story (or its silences) can be applied to all. To pretend that would be arrogant and, in light of the foregoing brief discussion of alterity, patently false. I share the view that each of us is other to, and in important ways unknowable by, one another. What is more, I contend, following the lead offered by psychoanalysis, that in profound ways we are unknown and unknowable even to ourselves. This idea, of the self's imperfect accessibility to itself, locates itself centrally in psychoanalytic theory's foundational concept of the unconscious; its paradoxical nature is summed up in Lacan's view that the self is 'other to itself' (Fink, 1995, p. 7).

But how are we to move from the self as *other to itself*, in important ways silent to itself, unknown and not-quite-knowable, to a consideration of those deeper silences, those perplexing larger unknowns? Perhaps a partial answer to that question lies within a curious double paradox: first, of trying to know that Other's interiority, which in the end is simply not knowable; and second, of the ways learning from others might disrupt the likewise not-fully-known and not-quite-knowable self. Todd takes the view that it is

> precisely because the Other is seen to be that which disrupts its coherency [that] the subject tumbles into uncertainty, its past strategies for living challenged by the very strangeness of difference itself ... In gaining insight, one risks altering the very parameters of self-perception and one's place in the world, and risks losing, therefore, one's bearings and conventions. (2003a, p. 11)

If this is so, and if, as Todd further maintains, 'the encounter with otherness becomes the necessary precondition for meaning and understanding' (2003a, p. 10), it may be that the personal (Pitt, 2003) and the anecdotal (Gallop, 2002) can help us. At least that is my second wish, an expansion of the first, as I offer my personal and my anecdotal: my silences made them (or allowed them to) speak. I take the position here, similar to my claim in the second language learning context, that autobiographical writing, and particularly autoethnography, can raise opportunities for thinking about how individual silences might resonate with larger institutional and cultural ones. Specifically, just as the manifest content of any story leaves something out, 'knowing' (or thinking we know) leaves out what is not and cannot be known, including, obviously, whether or not that unknown might itself be of use. Tolerating *not-knowing* might thus allow us to *think* – about, with, and through our questions.

The Shape of the Study: 'Every Moment Is Two Moments'[2]

The structure, content, and goals of this book are informed by the dual route I have taken in arriving at it: silent moments from my life in education, and the close reading-, thinking-, and working-through of those moments. These components work side by side and together in what is remembered and narrated, and in the larger silences in and around these moments and memories. More specifically, I start with narratives of moments which vary in content and in form: a somewhat unconventional mix of journal entries and remembered experiences, personal observations and communications, classroom 'texts,' and artefacts of several kinds, all chosen for their evocative, even provocative, qualities.

Moments, stories, and silences constitute both text and context, and the book as a whole, with its aim of expanding and deepening thinking about intrapersonal, interpersonal, cultural, and institutional relations, is a circuitous and sometimes even messy engagement that doubles back upon itself again and again in a mutually recursive conversation between the personal on one hand and the culture of education on the other.

This introduction is bracketed by the first and second of what I am naming *circumnarratives*: short passages describing events outside the strict boundaries of the study but which nevertheless affect and guide what goes on within it. Here the form of my work resonates somewhat with that of Fowler (2006), who intersperses chapters about narrative research with tales of 'difficulty in teaching' that she calls *internarratives* (p. vii), as well as with that of Miller (2005), who follows Richardson (1997) in layering *interludes* between her chapters which 'explore and highlight the situated nature of knowledge-making that the process of rereading one's work compels,' and consider questions of ambivalence about the chapters themselves (Miller, 2005, pp. 9–10). While this book does not constitute a 'rereading' in precisely the same sense as Miller's, the work of turning and returning between the present and the past, and the relationship between events internal and external to the self, are cornerstones of my thinking.

The circumnarratives serve personal and methodological aims. They mark the idiosyncratic methodology that I develop, set out, and use, informing a significant part of my work's context. My reluctance to leave them out is supported by Behar's (1996) and Pelias's (2004) notions of heartfelt methodologies and by Fowler's contention that narrative can be 'a starting point for authentic research' (2006, p. 8), as well as for getting at 'untold and darker stories that need to emerge and be examined' (p. 27). Fowler distinguishes between such darker stories and the 'happier' (often fictional) tales of teaching that dominate, for instance, Hollywood's vision of education. My circumnarratives are not fictional, and they are not explicitly about teaching or learning, but I include them as *circum-* (or *meta-*)[3] level meditations on the processes of thinking about ideas, and about the work of writing, and equally as phenomenological reflections on real-life events that inform, interfere with, disrupt, and yet potentially enrich both the processes and the ideas.

The book is divided into three parts. Taken together, the chapters of Part 1 contextualize the whole work, and in particular its principal theme of silence, in terms of literature on ethnography, autoethnography, discourse analysis, and psychoanalytic theory. They also engage conceptual questions about the multiple, inconstant dynamics of forgetting and remembering, the partiality of narrative, and the complex pushes and pulls of the personal in academic writing to underscore the importance of finding ways of working with and through silence. These discussions are interwoven with a personal story, told several ways, which drives the making of a methodology for reading silence even as it explores the application of that methodology: two strands moving in a kind of hermeneutic choreography.

Chapter 1 traces a path through ethnography and autoethnography as research genres, and discourse analysis and psychoanalysis as hermeneutic frameworks, to arrive at my concept of *psychoanalytic autoethnography* as a methodological/interpretive process for reading personal narratives of difficult moments or silences. This is followed by a short, 'bare-facts' story of a refusal to learn – the book's first 'silent moment' – and a brief overview of branches of discourse analysis that invite thinking about what is both present in and absent from narratives of educational experience.

In Chapter 2, I recast a new version of those 'facts' from a different angle, in the light of Foucauldian and feminist theories of discourse. Raising the idea of recursion to consider how stories of experience, and reflection on them, can mutually inform and help to evolve one another, I call on psychoanalytic theory as a hermeneutic within the autoethnographic framework and use concepts of deferred action, repression, and memory to examine how moments are recalled, retold, worked through, reworked, and remade, again and again. This chapter also uses my narrative to introduce the notion of the personal in research, as well as some of the complex aspects of autobiography and memory that unsettle questions about the value to research of narrative generally, and autoethnography in particular.

Thus the first two chapters are a stepping-off point for discussing process, structure, and informing concepts. The third chapter follows Althusser and Balibar (1972, p. 28), offering a symptomatic reading that 'divulges [what is] undivulged' in a third articulation (or *re*-articulation) of the same narrative. In consultation with its psychoanalytic underpinnings – the interruptions of trauma, repression, desire denied – this reading works outward from my story's idiosyncrasies to reflect on how desire in education is made from longings that contain, but are not fully contained by, genitally focused sexuality. This chapter, indeed all of Part 1, addresses thinking about desire in teaching and learning by showing how a learner's response to the traumatic disruption of desire, in the form of denial or repression, can work unconsciously to thwart personal and institutional objectives and to keep at bay both the curriculum and knowledge of the self and its desires in ways that seem counterproductive but are psychically crucial.

In Part 2, following the third circumnarrative, I shift the choreography of methodologies onto two stages in my theatre of reading-and-interpretation. The narratives of Chapters 3 and 4 comprise several texts which embody silences of various kinds. Each recounts or represents moments in educational contexts; all connect with broad educational concerns. Together they function as inaugural points for a twofold discussion comprising a critical discourse analysis and a psychoanalytic conversation: between relevant concepts, stories of silent moments, and the large pedagogical issues to which both are connected.

In Chapter 4 I move the theme of desire explored in Part 1 onto new terrain, to work with psychoanalytic considerations of curiosity and sexuality vis-à-vis the role of the unconscious in bringing desire to the forefront in an educational context, despite efforts and mandates on the part of the institution to bury that desire. I invoke several pedagogical texts, or moments, that embody different silences, first asking why young children's curiosity about their bodies poses a difficulty for education such that curricula and practice endeavour, however ineffectually, to silence that curiosity. Beginning with social constructs of children's sexuality and sexual curiosity followed by a critical reading of related developmentally appropriate practice discourse, I turn to Freudian concepts of polymorphous perversity, pleasure and unpleasure, repression, and defence against curiosity, to argue that children's unconscious wishes and desires, silenced in (and not consciously remembered by) adults, may return to make themselves heard from within those silent gaps. I then reflect on how, through this return, education and educators might be inviting in precisely the childhood curiosity they seem to want to shut out.

Chapter 5 considers a kind of silence inaugurated by educational changes such as those demanded by new technologies. Here I reflect on my own experiences and those of some teachers I have come to know through research, examining from a critical sociological standpoint some of the changes to teachers' work imposed by mandates for computer use. Looking next at how discourses of education create and reinforce the teacher's position as classroom locus of knowledge and power, I show how computers can alter both the nature of the teacher's work and her sense of herself-as-a-teacher. Finally, I reflect on how computers and the relation of teachers and students to them embody a particular set of implications in which the psychical and the professional knit together and inform one another. I take up psychoanalytic notions of transference and the Lacanian mirror stage to read the computer itself as an artefact that can silence and dislocate the teacher and disrupt her relationship to her students, and the call to use it as embodying the demand that the teacher 'translate' herself in ways potentially threatening to her identity.

Following the fourth circumnarrative, Part 3 returns to some of the worries about writing the self raised in Part 1, expanding them into a self-referential meditation on the writing process. It then moves that meditation and its informing events into the uncertain world of the student teacher, for if practising teachers at times have trouble with multiple demands to change their practices and their selves, the trouble is doubled for those learning to teach. The student teacher – even the name is contradictory – is 'neither here nor there' and at the same time both here *and* there: teaching and learning, instructing and being instructed, talking and listening, assessing and being assessed. Despite efforts of teacher education programs, the individual learning to teach may be caught in a moment that is intense, complex, and ambiguous, and which embodies unique silences informed by that ambiguity.

In these chapters I look behind the difficulties to ask – Why are they difficult? And what are the qualities of the silences that serve as responses to the difficulties? Chapter 6 offers a theoretical speculation on difficult moments in the process of learning to teach, beginning with some of the preconceptions that student teachers bring with them to their preservice programs. It continues with a Foucauldian reading of the complex power relations that inhere in teacher education, and more specifically in divisions between teachers and learners, theory and practice, and old and new theories. This is followed by a psychoanalytic speculation in which I suggest that learning to teach parallels the second-language learning process, in that both may be marked by a partial inability to define, articulate, position, or express a self. I then invoke the concepts of mourning, melancholia, and object- and ego-splitting as ways to think about the psychical losses and silences that can accompany the gains inherent in the process of learning to teach.

Chapter 7 shifts to the landscape of a particular classroom, beginning with a meta-level reflection on the psychoanalytic concept of the split-off intellect and an examination of how that concept has informed my own thinking and my work within, and outward from, my silent moments. I offer an autoethnographic case study, using narratives and textual artefacts from my practice-teaching experience as a locus for a twofold reading of the complexities of my relationship with my practicum host teacher. The first level of analysis explores the dynamics of that relationship using Foucauldian concepts such as discipline, authority, and resistance. The second part looks at some of the ways psychoanalytic notions of transference and (re)translation invite a consideration of interpersonal dynamics inside the practicum classroom. I use my experience to consider how those dynamics might echo other earlier ones, notably in the mother/child dyad, and to offer new ways to think about the complex silence of the student teacher as a kind of hyphenated individual caught in the liminal space of learning to teach.

Three parts; seven chapters; many moments. This work invites recognition of some of the psychical complexities and costs, as well as the benefits, of various pedagogical relationships. My goal is to contest assumptions that those relationships are constant, transparent, and straightforwardly understood, and to suggest that part of their significance and their usefulness may at times rest in the very opacity of their silences. My proposition is that education, rather than simply attempting to conquer or eliminate those silences, might do well to make the time and take the care to work ethically and compassionately with, in, and through them.

Onward: let us begin.

PART 1

Second Circumnarrative: The Wind

June 2006
On an early summer day, at the point in the distinct but inseparable processes of grieving a loss and creating a project, when I know that for pragmatic reasons I must try to shift the balance away from the former and toward the latter, I read, for the umpteenth time, my dissertation proposal. And as I do, to my great surprise I feel an excitement rising in me. This excitement is physical, visceral. It begins in the soles of my feet, moves up my legs, vibrates through my thighs. At the core of me it is a kind of trembling that is almost (almost?) sexual, a warm shivering feeling similar to what we sometimes call spring fever. Spring has passed, both this year and in my life's seasons, but this feeling calls to mind birdsong and green-budding trees, and a light, mild breeze touching the skin as it blows through a window finally open after a long winter. It is, and it is more and other than, the awakening of an intellectual interest that has been, for a time, in hibernation. It's a kind of falling in love, again, with ideas. Or perhaps with the idea of ideas, the possibility of loving ideas – the idea that an idea might be something to love. It is a feeling that lets me imagine I can do this work. But like any new love, it invites a surrender that could end with a broken heart.

I am reading work by Pelias [2004], that puts into text and context his wish to write in ways that are something 'more than making a case, more than establishing criteria and authority, more than what is typically offered up' [p. 1]. He locates this wish in the body – by turns desiring, messy, consuming, curious, weeping, playful – and especially in the heart, so typically missing from academic discourse and wounded in that absence. His is a 'methodology of the heart.'

And I am reading work by Behar [1996], who writes partly about mourning a death, and partly about anthropology's work, within and outside that mourning, as spanning 'the border between the private and the public' in ways that let mourners 'honor the dead [and] never walk on their tombs if we can help it' [p. 173]. Hers is an 'anthropology that breaks your heart.'

A methodology of the heart; an anthropology that can break hearts.

Where, I wonder, shall we look for a methodology that can heal the heart that is broken?

1 Thinking about Facts: Ethnography, Autoethnography, Discourse Analysis, Psychoanalysis

Scientific method per se does not make it possible
for the mind to transcend the skin.

> – Art Bochner, *It's about Time*

Ring the bells that still can ring
Forget your perfect offering
There is a crack in everything
That's how the light gets in.

> – Leonard Cohen, *Anthem*

The Facts

They seem straightforward enough.

> *I attended secondary school in Ontario from 1969 to 1974. In the curriculum then
> in effect, English became non-compulsory after Grade 11. I did not like English, so
> although I had been informed of the consequences, I chose to stop taking it.*

These facts are where I am choosing, for now, to begin my story. It is
not so easy to determine what the beginning actually is, what the facts
really are. There is more than one beginning, and there are many facts.
Beginnings are more than moments in time. They are events in thinking, places in thought. They embody intentions and decisions, and
moments of consolidating intentions, and other moments when intentions fall apart and reconfigure themselves. So this is just one possible

beginning for this theoretical project, this piece of work which starts years after-the-fact. Or after the facts; those specific facts; that particular version of the facts. Reader, you are warned. Things could get messy.

Am I alluding already to multiple versions of the facts? Am I getting ahead of myself? Well, the self (and the facts) to which I am alluding are not yet visible to the reader, and they are only somewhat more available to me. This is not quite the moment for revelation. What it is the moment for, and this page the place for, is a sharing of intentions. Here is a place of intent.

Like Derrida (1982, p. 1), I will speak of a letter. Not precisely as he speaks, however. Derrida's letter 'a' – phonetically written in standard French and English as /a/ and /eɪ/ respectively – is reminiscent, in Canadian English, of the interrogative '*eh?*: différAnce, read differently. For my part I speak of a kind of 'letter of intent': letters (and words, and ideas, and thoughts) of intention that I make, in tension. My intention at this juncture is to trace a historical and conceptual path toward the methodological framework I have developed for this study, and which I am naming *psychoanalytic autoethnography*. I start by contextualizing the ways I have combined, adapted, and appropriated research and hermeneutic methods, tracing the process that has brought me to my intended structure at more or less the same time that I outline and illustrate the structure itself. As I say, it could all get messy.

Sure enough, at once I am brought up short. I search for a metaphor, an analogy, something that will set out my overarching vision of how this methodological map ought to look, indeed of how it *must* look, if it is to persuade the reader to think a little differently about some of my (and education's collective) worries.

Each year as a child I visited my paternal grandmother in Winnipeg. There, a favourite activity was to help her with her knitting. My grandmother, having lived through the Great Depression, wasted nothing: this particular task consisted of unravelling old sweaters, mittens, and scarves so that the yarn could be knitted into something new. Particularly enthralling for me were the argyle, fair-isle, and other patterned sweaters I would separate into different-coloured strands of yarn and wind into new balls, to be reworked in novel combinations into new garments. This metaphor for both my methodology and its devising fits for the moment as comfortably as . . . well, as an old sweater. But this does not mean that the methodology, once made, will suit every project or every researcher – even 'one size fits all' never really does. Still, some of it might settle onto some shoulders, if all goes well to be worn for a while or, in the way of such things, unravelled and reworked into still another methodological garment.

The several strands are ethnography and its progeny autoethnography, critical discourse analysis, and psychoanalytic theory. The latter two I will use to consider silences, and silencings, that seem both to inform and to be embodied in the particular remembered moments-of-silence in education my narratives relate.

The silent moments offer both evidence of, and a point of departure for thinking about, three things: the wish for a direct route to pedagogical success; the futility of that wish; and the frequent denial by educational discourses of that futility. But to make this claim is to invite some practical questions. How might we consider difficult moments in education – moments when its work is interrupted, when teaching and learning fail to meet institutional, curricular, or individual goals, when tensions within individuals, or between individuals and knowledge, ideas, or institutions become difficult or even intolerable – when one of the most salient characteristics of such moments is silence? How can we invite silence into the conversation? These are questions of both methodology and interpretation. First, how to join small silences with large difficulties? And second, having done that, how to think about them? To respond to the first of these questions, I begin with ethnography.

Ethnography: Ways to Write about Things

The words of others help here – first, the Greeks: ethnos (nation) and graphia (writing). Much later comes Malinowski, for whom ethnography aims 'to grasp the native's point of view, his relation to life, to realize his vision of the world' (Malinowski, 1922, p. 25). Later Western understandings are of a research method useful for producing '"theoretical", "analytical" or "thick" descriptions ... [which] remain close to the concrete reality of particular events [while revealing] general features of human social life' (Hammersley, 1992, p. 12); or a 'cultural translation ... [in which] a surplus of difference always remains, partly created by the process of ethnographic communication itself' (Marcus, 1994, p. 566).

These definitions conceive of ethnography as a manifestation in anthropology (and the social sciences more generally) of what Rosenwald and Ochberg describe as a movement from 'realism to narrativity' (1992, p. 2). Early conceptions of ethnography, grounded in positivist-empiricist notions of validity in research, which saw it as a scientific means of describing cultures that led ultimately to full 'insider' knowledge and understanding, have given way to two interrelated postmodern views. First, a socially constructed reality can never be fully captured by positivist methods (see Clifford & Marcus, 1986). Second, such methods are themselves social constructions: even 'scientific' descriptions incorporate culturally based, non-neutral interpretation in which the researcher is implicated. Thus, ethnography recognizes the complex relationships between what people do and what they say about what they do, alongside the social nature of behaviours and, in Marcus's reiteration, the intractability of difference – an acknowledgment framed by a different disciplinary orientation in Todd's (2003b) discussion of Levinasian alterity.

This shift has come about partly because documenting and attempting to make sense, from the perspective of the ethnographer's own culture, of data from societies and cultures deemed 'alien, foreign, and strange' (Denzin, 1997, p. 17) demand something more than hypothesis-testing: something Agar (1986, p. 12) describes as 'an intensive personal involvement, an abandonment of traditional scientific control, [and] an improvisational style.' This near-renunciation of received views of science amounts to a seismic shift in ethnography's terrain, as reflected in a collection of papers co-edited, as it happens, by Marcus along with Clifford (Clifford & Marcus, 1986), and originating in a 1984 seminar (1986, p. vii) focusing on the construction of ethnographic texts qua texts. Clifford's introduction to this volume frames it as a *de*-construction of views of ethnography as a science of objectivity, transparency, and the unmediated reportage of experience (p. 2), returning to the reader a process that is 'actively situated *between* powerful systems of meaning. It poses its questions at the boundaries of civilizations, cultures, classes, races and genders. Ethnography codes and recodes. . . . It describes processes of innovation and structuration, and is itself part of these processes' (Clifford & Marcus, 1986, pp. 2–3; italics in original).

For these authors, ethnographic data are not merely collected but actually constructed through researchers' participation in what they are studying; similarly, ethnographic writing is not merely the factual reporting of some phenomenon, but also, at least partly, its discursive construction. And indeed, the reality was ever thus – what is absent from earlier thinking about ethnography is not the researcher's implication in what is being studied, but the *recognition* of that implication.

That ethnography has come to view itself through this self-implicating lens is not to say, however, that there is consensus on what it is or ought to be, either within or outside the academy. As *New York Times* writer Zalewski (2000) summarizes:

> Disputes within anthropology have a way of becoming blood feuds. Virtually all of the field's leading figures have been struck by poison arrows. Margaret Mead? Dupe! Franz Boas? Spy! Colin Turnbull? Hoaxer! Marshall Sahlins? Imperialist! Indeed, the excessive ferocity of anthropological warfare has fractured the discipline and tarnished its public image. It's become the academic equivalent of 'The Jerry Springer Show.'

Zalewski's comment points to debates within the field that are not only healthy but essential. Hammersley's *What's Wrong with Ethnography?* (1992) examines its ambivalent status: widely used and generally accepted as legitimate, but simultaneously challenged both as to the kinds of representation it offers (also addressed in Clifford & Marcus, 1986), and also, more significantly here, on its implicit connections 'between facts and values, and between researchers and practitioners' and its perceived 'failure to contribute to practice' (Hammersley, 1992, pp. 1–2).

Ethnographic work has continued to take different forms and directions, and there are many new ethnographies. Bochner and Ellis (1999, pp. 485–8) see in critiques of ethnography a tendency to 'oppositional rhetoric' aimed at achieving 'a singular and dominating perspective.' Enumerating within ethnography dichotomous *sides* (modernist/postmodernist, empirical/interpretive, objective/subjective, scientific/artistic) and *turns* (interpretive, linguistic, constructionist, rhetorical, narrative, to which I add the explicitly autobiographical), they call for ethnographic dialogue that 'signal[s] the death of singularity, clos[es] the book on the notion that one size fits all.' Their plea is for a research genre that recognizes its own 'vexing differences' and attends to them through dialogue that aims not to flatten but to understand and be enriched (pp. 486–7).

The turns in orientation Bochner and Ellis observe, as well as the conceptual shift from positivism to interpretation and from assumed objectivity to acknowledged implicatedness (see Lather, 1986; Spigelman, 2001), are synopsized in the introduction to Denzin's anticipatory volume subtitled *Ethnographic Practices for the 21st Century* (1997, p. xiii). That work sees ethnography as 'dialogical ... [in that] the voices[1] of the other, alongside the voices of the author [sic], come alive and interact with one another.' Here is the suggestion that the dialogic is an inescapable component of ethnography. Denzin further summarizes postmodern ethnography as producing messy, co-constructed, experimental, and/or autobiographical (1997, p. xvi) texts, or, presumably, combinations of these characteristics. I concur with Denzin, as well as with Bochner and Ellis's tongue-in-cheek contention (1999, p. 490) that 'what would be remarkable would be to ... say, "Look at all the changes in the world, but ethnography, well that is one thing that has stayed the same!" ' Indeed, I plan to make some adjustments to it myself.

Ethnography has been much used in educational research. In fact, assert Spindler and Spindler (1992, p. 62), it has come to 'supplant as well as supplement the broader concerns of an anthropology of education.' But again, we can not presume philosophical and methodological homogeneity. Qualities Preissle and Grant enumerate as characteristic of educational ethnography's multiple tensions – between description and evaluation, practice and theory, 'what is and what ought to be' (1998, p. 9) – include views of education as constituted not just of formal schooling, but of multiple kinds of relevant encounter; diverse and divergent orientations toward both mainstream and marginalized communities, institutions, and practices; and multi- and interdisciplinary research as product and researchers as persons.

Researchers as persons; research as personal; the personal in research: Malinowski is a case in point. It was not until I read Behar's (1999) paper on ethnography as a 'second-fiddle genre' that I happened upon what was for me a startling piece of information about the 'father' of ethnography. Some 25 years after his death Malinowski's widow published his *Diary in the Strict Sense of the Word* (1967), a personal journal from his seminal (1922) research in the Trobriand Islands. Less savoury aspects of Malinowski are manifested in the *Diary* – 'ugly smutty things he wanted to say about the (black) natives and his own [sometimes homosexual] desires that he could not say aloud, in polite (white) [and presumed heterosexual] company' (p. 473). Writes Behar on the consequences of this 'inescapable truth':

> The unspeakable ... was to be inscribed in the ethnographer's diary, and kept secret from the natives ... and discussed only in hushed whispers with the colleagues back home. And so, the legacy of the Diary, which is inseparable from the very birth of ethnography, is ultimately a legacy of shame – of Malinowski's shame. Our shame too, for we cannot ignore our complicity with the history that makes us ethnographers. (Behar, 1999, pp. 473–4)

Elsewhere Behar (1996, p. 19) refers to being 'taught to maintain the same strict boundary Malinowski had kept between his ethnography and his autobiography.' My view is that the *Diary* – as a counterpoint to his 'official' study of the Trobrianders – constitutes a kind of autoethnography such that the boundary Behar refers to is artificial, perhaps even impossible. I am bolstered in this view by Crawford's assertion (1996, p. 158) that 'the ethnographer is unavoidably in the ethnography one way or another, manifest in the text, however subtly or obviously,' and to an even greater degree by Cohler and Cole (1996, p. 68), who contend that a significant connection between Malinowski's use of psychoanalytic concepts in his ethnographic work and the 'reflexive perspective' of his diary actually 'points the way toward a psychoanalytic ethnography.'

Autoethnography's response to ethnography's question, Where ought the boundary between researcher and researched to fall?, refuses the idea of a boundary altogether. The related questions, What is absent from ethnography? and What is it that, even if present, is unnoticed and thereby rendered silent? are thus also partially answered by the exemplar of Malinowski's *Diary*, for it contains the personal voice and the history that appear to be absent from, or silent in, his other work. This element of the personal in autoethnography makes explicit the idea that ethnography is, to some degree at least, always already autoethnographic.

Autoethnography: The Researcher as One of Those Things

While current thinking about ethnography goes some significant distance toward recognizing the nebulousness of boundaries between researcher and subject, its offshoot autoethnography makes this recognition explicit by embracing and acting upon the notion of researcher as both subject and object of the research. Autoethnography, broadly defined, is thus the study of a culture, cultural group, community or institution, such as education, by a 'full insider' (Ellis & Bochner, 2000, p. 739). It '*(re)position[s] the researcher* as an object of inquiry who depicts a site of personal awareness; it utilizes the self-consciousness ... to reveal subjectively and imaginatively a particular social setting' (Crawford, 1996, p. 167; my italics).[2] By turns both autobiographical and ethnological, it may emphasize one or more segments of its tripartite name: the research and writing process, the culture or institution being examined, or the individual engaged in it (Reed-Danahay, 1997, p. 2). It connects the personal and the social through narratives that illumine relations between them. Here I offer a doubling of Crawford's repositioning: relocating that repositioning to study an individual for hints about the culture or institution she participates in.

In an article detailing the expansion of ethnography practices since its early days, Adler and Adler (1999) point to the work of Riemer (1977) and Hayano (1979) as paving the way for the ethnographer to 'fess up' to being 'a "true" member of the setting' (Adler & Adler, 1999, p. 444). This notion illustrates two important qualities of autoethnography which emblematize postmodern epistemological discourses more generally: the questioning of assumptions regarding the necessity, and indeed the possibility, of complete objectivity in research and, more centrally here, challenges to the trope of a 'coherent, individual self' (Reed-Danahay, 1997, p. 2).

Autoethnography's methodological variations have encompassed the biographical, the feminist, and the experiential, and it has found its way into sociology, anthropology, and communication studies. And while for some it includes genres otherwise referred to as 'narratives of the self, ... critical autobiography, ... ethnographic poetics, ... [or] lived experience narratives' (Ellis & Bochner, 2000, pp. 739–40), to name but a few, for others it is understood as a sub-category of narrative ethnography or postmodern ethnography:

> Autoethnography is an autobiographical genre of writing and research that displays multiple layers of consciousness, connecting the personal to the cultural. Back and forth ethnographers gaze, first through an ethnographic wide-angle lens, focussing outward on social and cultural aspects of their personal experience; then, they look inward, exposing a vulnerable self that is moved by and may move through, refract, and resist cultural interpretations. (Ellis & Bochner, 2000, p. 739)

But for all the progressive possibilities it ushers in, autoethnography has felt the burn of heated debate (see, for example, Ragan, 2000; Banks & Banks, 2000), including allegations that it is undependable and untrustworthy (Holt, 2003), narcissistic and excessively introspective (see Sparkes, 2000; Fowler, 2006), even, possibly, grossly self-indulgent (see Coffey, 1999, p. 132). For some, the autoethnographic writer may simply be *too* present within a text, and if ever it were possible to ascertain 'just the facts,' an autoethnography might be understood as the least likely place for that to happen. Behar (1996, p. 12) explains that the problem for some critics is 'the insertion of personal stories into ... paradigms [which] ... have traditionally called for distance, objectivity and abstraction.' In summarizing that for these critics 'the worst sin [is] to be "too personal",' and in further illuminating some of the ways in which the personal is, often unavoidably and even relentlessly, implicated in 'the facts,' she contests the very possibility of research ever being objective. I agree with her view, and with Brodkey's related contention that research has an obligation to refuse the kinds of totalizing claims that belie the reality of all theorizing as 'both an *incomplete* and an *interested* account of whatever is envisioned' (Brodkey, 1996, p. 8; italics in original). Might autoethnography offer a possible, if partial, answer to some silent moment in ethnography – when ethnography asks, explicitly or implicitly: Where does the researcher end and the research begin? Can an ethnography, or indeed an anthropology, be made which is not in some way personal? Ought we even to try? And why does it matter?

Autoethnography contests the modernist ideas that researcher and subject, or object, of research are distinct from one another in an absolute sense, as well as the notion that interpretation is a neutral exercise producing transparent knowledge and objective truth. In addition, '[by a]dding the voice, the story, the field experiences of the researcher as data, autoethnography re-focuses the direction of ethnographic inquiry from a unilateral gaze outward at others to either an internal gaze into the self or a multidirectional analytical gaze into self and other simultaneously' (Hausbeck & Brents, 2003, p. 8).

This turning inward of the researcher's gaze might be what Crawford (1996, p. 167) characterizes as a means 'to minimize the hubris of traditional ethnographic research' and thereby soften the tendency of such research to exoticize some cultural 'other.' Thus might autoethnography fill in some of the silent spots in ethnography; for in its turning and returning, focusing and re-focusing, it broadens and deepens the possibilities for ethical and responsible engagement among participants in cultures, institutions and other settings, large and small.

Brodkey's educational autoethnography (1996) acknowledges – as does Pratt (1999) – that part of the genre's usefulness is its ability to facilitate the realization of a 'singular self . . . in writing that challenges received categories' (Brodkey, 1996, p. 28). Nevertheless, Brodkey herself favours it for its 'potential for social change rather than any psychological benefits that may accrue' (1996, p. 28). For me, psychological (or in psychoanalytic terminology *psychical*) benefits and social change are inextricably connected. For although we may rightly be cautious of the notion that one individual's experiences can be extrapolated to an entire community or culture, it is possible that in reading about and reflecting on individual experience we might expose possibilities previously unconsidered, ultimately benefitting both education (the social) and the individual participant in it (the psyche).

In research, a personal story can be a place where the approach to implication and possibility begins, but must not become the place where it ends. And so, because I am mindful both of the call to use personal narrative to move thinking along (Pitt, 2003) and of the caution to avoid self-indulgence (Grumet, 1990), while autoethnography serves as a collecting place for my personal stories, my narratives of silent moments, it is also a connecting place for the larger education-related concerns for which those narratives can be read as metonymic markers.

This work is thus necessarily both speculative and partial given two premises that underpin it: the first, poached from Ellis and Bochner (2000) and from psychoanalysis (Freud, 1948; Winnicott, 1990; Phillips, 1999), that there is a relationship between the personal and the cultural; and the second (more exclusively the domain of psychoanalytic theory), that the personal – the subjectivity, the interiority of the individual – is never fully knowable by that individual or by any other, much less by the culture or the researcher, however hard they might try to give voice to it. There is an important distinction to be drawn here between interpretation, which says that one thing *is* because another thing *is,* and speculation, which says that one thing *might be* partly because another thing *is,* or *might be,* or *might have been.* It is a distinction between extrapolation, which projects and concludes, and something we might conceptualize as a kind of theoretical or contemplative interpolation, a tentative 'placing between' of implication and possibility.

It might seem intuitive, in comparing ethnographies conducted by outsiders with autoethnographies, that the latter should offer greater potential for knowing some categorical, identifiable truth of an individual or a culture. But this is plausible only if we accept the notion that individuals' motivations, beliefs, understandings, and so on are always transparent and fully accessible, that is, if we are confident of a direct and unmediated relationship between what the autoethnographer does, and what she says, and what she knows about what she does and says. Such confidence would, however, be misplaced in a poststructural moment. For if we are sure of anything it is, paradoxically, that there is very little of which we can be absolutely sure. We must look further to uncover, so far as it is possible, why we say and do what we say and do.

This, then, is my response to the first part of my methodological-hermeneutic question: How then can I make these concerns (and these silences) speak to one another? To respond to the second part – How shall I think about what they say? – I call on discourse analysis and on psychoanalytic theory to anchor my discussion of these moments and the larger silences they instantiate.

Critical Discourse Analysis and Psychoanalytic Theory: Ways to Think about Things

A cartoon is tacked to the wall of my little office. I do not know its origin; it has been photocopied several times and the artist's name is now illegible. It shows a meek, hesitant Everyman, who has just entered an anteroom through a door that bears a sign marked *IN*. There is a second door in the wall opposite. The sign on it reads *IN DEEPER*. The cartoon, a metaphor for the psychoanalytic process, also serves as a kind of adumbration for my work here: getting deeper in – to silence, to breakdowns in meaning and learning, to some of what is troubled by, and troubling in, education. My 'way in' begins with critical discourse analysis; my way 'in deeper' is through psychoanalytic theory. I name this methodological process *psychoanalytic autoethnography*.

First, critical discourse analysis: the kind of critical reading of discursive texts[3] described by Fairclough (1995, 2003) as working to illumine those relationships between language, power, and ideology which may not be readily observable in texts that typically constitute or reproduce what Lather calls 'totalizing, universalizing "metanarratives" and the humanist view of the subject that undergirds them' (1991, p. 5).

Part of ethnography's work is to shine a light on the ongoing, if implicit, presence of such metanarratives. However, that is just one of the methodological issues at play here, related but not mutually isomorphic, each embodying its own silences. It is not just a question of what method we use to collect data – or what data we choose to privilege, or what interpretive method we choose, or even whether we openly acknowledge our own implication in those choices. In a postmodern, poststructuralist world, where every choice is made from a particular position and every position is multiply informed, there simply can be no straightforward interpretation, no 'objective' observer, no 'unbiased' researcher, no 'neutral' set of facts. Interpretation is always undertaken from some perspective or other.

Gone are the days when a single 'native point of view' or 'vision of the world' (Malinowski, 1922) could be assumed. As methods for producing ethnographic data have evolved, so have methods for reading and interpreting: for making ethnography, in other words, out of ethnographic data. This is, of course, not purely coincidental. Poststructural ethnographers swim in the same theoretical waters as other critical social theorists, such that in education, for instance, the reconceptualization of curriculum as interpretable text (Pinar, Reynolds, Slattery, & Taubman, 2000) is a reflection of larger societal movements. One such shift runs, vis-à-vis interpretation, from origins in Saussurean linguistics through conversation analysis to critical discourse analysis, including the feminist and Foucauldian.

The claim of early structural linguistics, rooted in the work of de Saussure (1983 [1907]), was that spoken and written texts are grounded in a single codified system that renders meaning universal within a language and equivalent across languages. Structural linguistics evolved into the structuralism of the 1960s, which saw linguistic events as facilitated by structures (Macdonell, 1986) that, among other things, make for coherence and relevance in conversation, and determine participants' understanding of such matters as turn-taking and non-verbal signals (Coulthard, 1985; Remlinger, 2005). Arising out of structuralism, speech act theory (Austin, 1962; Searle, 1969; Pratt, 1977) posits linguistic utterances as both descriptive and performative. In this paradigm language (in speech of all kinds as well as in literary texts) is always being used to do something – for Austin (1962) it does three somethings, which he terms locutionary, illocutionary, and perlocutionary. Speech act theory has been critiqued, however, for focusing too narrowly on speech as the act of an individual agent unbound by social determination or delimitation (Dillon, 2005); Esterhammer and Robinson (2005) call on Bourdieu (1982) to argue that speech act theorists fail to recognize 'the performative [as] effective only when, and because, it is authorized by a power that comes from outside language.'

Poststructuralist thinking frames textual and other discourses as both performative (in that they reflect an already-present individual) and 'constructive phenomena, shaping the identities and practices of human subjects' (Luke, 1997, p. 51). The analysis of discourse involves, in addition to a description of its structures, an examination of 'a variety of contextual factors [that reveal] ... specific social relationships between the interlocutors' (Coulthard, 1985, p. viii). What is crucial is the understanding that meanings are located not in words themselves, not even in language, but in 'the concrete forms of differing social and institutional practices' (Macdonell, 1986, p. 12).

Thus have analyses of linguistic texts been at least partially relocated in discourse writ large. Discourse includes language, but also encompasses all communicative social action or practice (Fairclough, 1989; Dillon, 2005). It thus spreads wider and runs deeper than words and the rules, patterns, syntactic structures, and systems of their combination. Words are important. But speech is informed by, and varies according to, social context: Gee, who reflects on 'whos-doing-whats' with language, posits: ' Each human being creates complex meanings in language, but each of us is so good at finding meanings that we are often too quick to attribute meanings to others that are rooted more in our own cultures, identities, and fears than they are on a close inspection of what the other person has said or written' (2005, p. xii).

We are also very good at leaving things out: Gee's 'whos-doing-whats' with language are also whos-*not*-doing-whats, or whos-doing-*not*-whats, or whos-doing-*whatnot:* other things beyond what we might seem, either to ourselves or to others, to be doing. Our silences are as complex and at least as articulate as what we actually say – indeed, often more so.

Responding to the question of what is left out by a focus on language, in the sense of the-words-said (or written), is critical discourse analysis, with its ability to illuminate some of the shadows in a text, and listen to some of its silences.[4] It does this by refusing to limit interpretation to 'just words' and by favouring multi-faceted, deeper, more open readings which consider the power dynamics that hover outside texts, reside in the relations between those who make and those who interpret them, and ultimately infiltrate text, maker, and interpreter. A theory of discourse thus encompasses, in Dillon's summary, 'a theory of power, legitimacy, and authority' (2005, p. 211). The fact of these multi-level, many-angled relationships between makers and takers of discursive texts charges us with considering their qualities, along with their social contexts, as a crucial part of our work with the texts themselves. It is at just this methodological juncture that critical discourse analysis finds its home, as an approach to research variously articulated as a perspective (van Dijk, 1993) or a program (Wodak, 1997) which directs itself at the social contexts in which discourse is produced and interpreted, as well as at the relations between those contexts.

Associated questions that arise alongside the recognition of these relations are approached in distinct ways by different thinkers, including those interested in race relations (van Dijk, 1993) and the social and power structures of capitalism (Fairclough, 1995, 2003) and patriarchy. Feminist theorists Lakoff (1975), Spender (1980), Hollway (1984), and Tannen (1991) examine how language can exploit women and reinforce inequitable power structures, in particular through discriminatory valuations of gender differences in communication style. They argue that an explicitly feminist hermeneutic is needed in order to challenge hegemonic assumptions about gender relations more specifically than discourse analysis has heretofore done. Still, there is no single feminist ethnography. In contending that all research models are in one way or another deficient and that none of them, especially standing alone, can promise particular results, Bloom (1998, p. 153) asserts that 'feminist methodology is alive with contradictions, ambiguities and nonunitariness [which] must be seen to offer open, partial, situated and fluid guidelines to research practitioners.'

Critical discourse analysis is thus more than a single approach to research. Yet its many iterations share – not only with each other but with critical theories across the social sciences (Bhabha, 1994; McWilliam, 1995; Lather, 2001; Todd, 2003b; Freire, 2005 [1970]) – deep concerns with social inequities, and with the role of discourse in producing and reproducing such inequities, as well as urgent calls to expose and challenge them and ultimately to improve the lives of their victims, by 'expos[ing] and explor[ing] the top-down processes of domination' (Wooffitt, 2005, p. 139). If discourse analysis in general responds to the question, What have we here?, critical discourse analysis may offer an answer to an extended version of that question, about the specific societal *what* that is created and recreated, reflected and reinforced, by a particular text: a point on which conversational analysis, and earlier discourse analysis, with their tendency to focus more exclusively on the structures and forms internal to the text, can be seen as silent.

Given that they both arose from a historical moment in anthropological, linguistic, and educational research when questions about colonialism and ethnocentrism (in anthropology), communicative competence, elitism and 'grammaticality' (in linguistics), and hegemony vs. threats and challenges to it (in cultural and educational studies) were flying fast and furious, the relation between critical discourse analysis and current approaches to (auto)ethnography seems both non-accidental and non-trivial. Similarly, my two threads – autoethnography as methodological framework and critical discourse analysis as hermeneutic – now begin to wind themselves back together again in ways relevant to my methodological and interpretive direction.

As an approach to interpretation, critical discourse analysis allows a questioning of the assumptions on which interpretations, and perhaps even data, are founded. It works to exhume previously buried motives that undergird a theoretical position, a research method, or the shaping of a text as well as its overarching and enabling discourse. It.tries to understand the conditions that ground an issue and to pose questions that might help locate that issue in ways that reveal what is hidden in its construction *as* an issue – the hegemonic structures and discourses that make ethical engagement such a problem, particularly, as numerous theorists charge us with recognizing, in education (Noddings, 1992; Behar, 1996; A. Luke, 1996; Bailey, 1997; Britzman, 2003; Pitt, 2003; Todd, 2003a; and others).

Foucault offers a conceptualization and analysis of discourse which are prominent and revolutionary enough to have received, along with those of fellow philosopher and deconstructionist Derrida (1976, 1982), their own category under the larger umbrella of critical discourse analysis (Fairclough & Wodak, 1997; Luke, 1997; Ehrlich, 2001; Wooffitt, 2005). For Foucault discourse is comprised of interconnected systems of knowledge and power whose structures trump the agency of participating individuals, preceding and constituting (rather than merely reflecting) speaking subjects and their beliefs. In the Foucauldian paradigm, discourse informs, forms, and perpetuates particular identities, 'disciplining' individuals into ways of being and relating that are grounded in power. Power, in turn, exists only as a dynamic (Foucault, 1980a): mutable and never static; informed by and lying in close relationship with knowledge. Discourse, or more specifically a 'political technology of the body' (1977a, p. 26), is an externally and internally functioning means by which bodies are disciplined and identities made.

Educational researchers are often charged with analysing the discursive development and maintenance of hegemonic power structures and relations, but do not always answer the call. It would not, of course, be accurate to say that no attention at all has been paid to these matters: A. Luke (1996, p. 10) does enumerate multiple studies in which notions of voice, subjectivity, and discourse have been investigated (in relation to the education of females and minorities, teacher education, and knowledge construction) in both traditional texts and classroom interactions. Luke acknowledges that attempts to reframe educational research as discourse have endeavoured to 'move beyond descriptive research and to use discourse analysis to critique and challenge dominant institutional practices.' But he is not quite satisfied. His explanation:

These ethnographies and case studies all use broad, interpretive approaches to analysis, drawing content-level themes from transcripts. So while there is a good deal of Foucault-inspired talk about discourse in

recent educational research, instances in which it is translated into detailed analysis of discourse use in local sites ... are few and far between.
(A. Luke, 1996, pp. 10–11)

Critical analyses of local texts-and-contexts of education may cast revealing light on the hegemonic structures hidden in them. And well
might teachers and learners (and education as a whole, and indeed
society at large) profit from readings that challenge common-sense
understandings and naturalized assumptions by aiming, as Luke
(following Parker, 1992) contends, 'to reinforce scepticism toward
the transparency of talk, interview data, and recounts as unproblem-
atic sources of information about "reality" and "truth," "intent" and
"motivation"' (A. Luke, 1996, p. 9). Indeed, my view is that such readings are crucial for uncovering how education and its discourses deal
with questions of silence, and for helping to expose how the thinking
of individual participants in education, about its difficulties and the
silences (in and of doctrine and practice) that surround those difficulties, is informed by cultural and discursive hegemonies. Ultimately,
insights gleaned through these analyses may serve to bring the idea
of social situatedness into relation with the notion of the personal
and, in the present case, with the autoethnographic. Thus feminist
and Foucauldian orientations each play a role in what happens in the
following pages. At the same time, I believe that no single approach
can tell the whole story. These analyses, however illuminating, are
themselves partial; they can hardly claim to be otherwise given their
provenance.

If the personal is political, the political is also personal: in examining
the ways discourse positions its participants it is necessary to look also
at those participants. While I recognize the importance of (and undertake) discourse analyses of my autoethnographic data in order to expose
troubled and troubling aspects of education as both an institution and a
set of relations, I aim additionally to push Ellis and Bochner's acknowledgment of 'multiple layers of consciousness' in autoethnography (2000,
p. 739) a little further, not only to consider the several *conscious* ways in
which we can and do make relations between individual experiences
and the culture in which those experiences take place, but also to work
with that part of the mind that is *other than* conscious – to address the
contextual interplay both between individuals and the culture that constitutes them, and also among those individuals, the culture as a whole,
and the psychical dynamics that interact with both.

Thus I arrive at psychoanalytic theory. For while critical *discourse analysis* brings the social to the personal, psychoanalysis, used as an *analytic discourse*, brings the personal, and particular ways of thinking about the personal, to the social. And although these two frameworks may initially seem opposed to each other, when triangulated with autoethnographic data in the form of personal narratives and their silences, they actually share some qualities: both understand that description is always partial and knowledge and understanding are perpetually incomplete and imperfect; both refuse transparency, read between lines, and attend – albeit in different ways and from different angles – to silence.

The very large question of how to think about silence, as a quality shared by apparently disparate kinds of difficulty, separates itself into several strands: What is silence? Are all silences the same? How does one become silent? Why should silence be a response to difficulty? How can a narrative be silent, and how can a narrative *about* silence speak? Might silence be a means to what Lionnet (1991, p. 175) conceives as autoethnography's end: the opening of 'a space of resistance between the individual *(auto-)* and the collective *(-ethno)* where the writing *(-graphy)* of singularity cannot be foreclosed'? And if so, how can we listen to and interpret such silences? What might they have to tell us?

While critical discourse analysis and psychoanalysis offer significant opportunity for contemplation, reflection, and speculation on these questions, psychoanalytic theory, in my view, is especially useful, for it takes as its very project the work of getting inside what we think we know and moving behind what we know we think. It works intentionally with what is unsaid, or not clearly said, or only hinted at, attends consciously to what is unconscious, and thinks deliberately about the parts of individuals' lives that are not deliberate. Generally, in this context, while critical discourse analysis considers how hegemonic power structures work to subordinate and silence individuals and groups, and how those individuals and groups respond to those imposed silences, psychoanalytic theory wonders, additionally, what the individual is using silence to do. Here my concern is those moments when education's work stumbles or becomes stalled, when relations among teacher, learner, knowledge, and institution are somehow disrupted. This concern is not in itself unique. What is particular to this study, though, is the notion that my narratives embody silences both rooted in and characterized by several kinds of difficulty, which are at once both socially informed and psychical in nature, and which come variously into play across different educational arenas. My claim is that they all (the experiences, the narratives of the experiences, their difficulties, and their silences) are, and continue to be, made and remade in constant relation with one another, both inside and outside the individual, as well as in the space between the psychical inner world of the individual and the outer social world of education.

Two points bear raising here. First is the positivist critique (or from another perspective, the postmodernist acknowledgment) that ethnography and autoethnography are always already interpretive, their data selectively collected and conclusions made via a mediating discourse that is itself socially constructed (Clifford & Marcus, 1986; Denzin, 1997; Ellis & Bochner, 2000). If this is so even partially – and to argue otherwise would be difficult – we must attend to those discourses. Differentiating psychoanalytic theory from 'purer' social constructionist theories of identity (Mead, 1934; Burkitt, 1991) is the claim that while the continual making and remaking of an individual's psyche, or self, takes place in relation with the material world outside that self, there exists a de facto individual, an *inside* informed by its own multiple components as well as by the world *outside* itself (Winnicott, 1965; Pitt, 2000): the psychoanalytic egg to social constructionism's chicken.

Second is the view, sometimes used to reject ethnography, that as a methodology it tells more about the researcher than the researched (see Kapferer, 1988). Naturally it would be troubling for research to claim an objectivity it lacks. But what can this criticism mean when the researcher *is* the researched? Again, given psychoanalytic theory's interest in seeing inward as well as outward, it resounds as a useful method for thinking about this meta-level issue, about questions raised by autoethnographic narratives in general, and about worries inherent in the difficult moments in teaching and learning that I explore. My claim is that it is crucial to look not only at the interpretation and its socially based mitigating and mediating factors, but also at the one interpreting, and at the psychically based factors influencing that individual.

Still, introspection is itself no easy exercise, since, for psychoanalysis, 'inner' life is not fully accessible to consciousness. 'We may know what is on our minds, but not what is on the other minds inside us' (Phillips, 1999, p. xx). Central to this work, therefore, is the understanding that 'thinking is but a snare and a delusion unless the unconscious is taken into account' (Winnicott, 1945, p. 169), even if it is 'an awful nuisance to the thinkers-out' (p. 171).

While he attributed the discovery of the unconscious to philosophers and poets, Freud laid early claim to that component of the mind, with its instincts, desires, pleasures, and unpleasures, as carrying a force that is primary, ongoing, and persistent though hidden. Psychoanalytic approaches, attending both to inside/outside relations and to relations between distinct elements of the inside, which coexist but are largely unaware of each other, might thus enrich autoethnographic analyses. If in the past one of ethnography's worrying aspects has been a tendency to assume that proximity equates to understanding – 'I know because I was there' – which autoethnography might recast as 'I know because I am I,' and critical discourse analysis might reframe as 'I know, or do not know, in these ways and for those reasons,' psychoanalysis might have its own peculiar way of disrupting this presumption:

I *do not* know because I am I; I do not know because I am *not* I;

I *do not know because I am always already both I and not-I.*

Yet if it is a central tenet of psychoanalytic theory that in the normal course an individual does not have conscious access to the unconscious, how can we come to know it at all?

For psychoanalysis, the qualities and vagaries of the unconscious mind are revealed through dreams, in parapraxes (jokes, slips of the tongue, forgetting) and, of course, through the therapeutic relationship. But Markham (1999, p. 63) reminds us that while at times the analytic relation embodies pedagogical characteristics, and (following Lacan, 1950) while psychoanalytic theory may be useful for rethinking matters, we must not conflate the two. This means, among other things, that a psychoanalytic approach of the kind I am undertaking, which is emphatically *not* a psychoanalysis, must be done scrupulously, and with caution. And so, in using psychoanalytic theory as a hermeneutic, I am mindful of Felman's empathic reminder that 'the lesson to be learnt about pedagogy from psychoanalysis is not "the *application* of psychoanalysis to pedagogy" [but] the *implication* of psychoanalysis in pedagogy and of pedagogy in psychoanalysis' (1982, pp. 26–7; italics in original). My goal is to offer speculative readings of my autoethnographic narratives, of the large difficulties and silences writ more broadly across education of which those moments are emblematic, and of the connections between the two: not to supplant other analyses, but to listen to silence's hints and take up those hints in ways that help develop wise and ethical responses to them.

Worth emphasizing too is that the idea of the unconscious is itself not inconsistent with social constructionist views of personhood. Put in terms of my study, this means that although the constructions of, for example, *teacher* and *learner* may come about in social settings both within and outside education, all these contexts are always populated by individuals (Burkitt, 1991; Harré, 1993): someone exists who is doing the constructing. And so even as we make our way through a world populated by others and which, in acting upon us, continually makes and remakes us, it is worth reiterating: some 'inside' thing exists that is being made and re-made and that inside-self and the outside-world are in relation to each other.

Each of these relations – the intra-personal relationship of one part of the self to another (Phillips's 'other minds inside us' relating with *other* 'other minds,' also inside us), and the inside/outside connection between self and world – is complex, for each moves and shifts, over and over. Social constructions have histories that influence the construction of the individual; the individual has a history which affects the relation of that individual to the social. Other concepts drawn from psychoanalysis, such as deferred action and the return of the repressed, are particularly important for thinking about the connections, changing yet persisting through time and space, between my own 'silent moments' and their narration on one hand, and their larger counterparts on the other, as well as about the ways they inform each other in a multilayered and mutually recursive dialogue.

In light of all this, the following chapter presents a reworked version of 'the facts' of my story, offering Foucauldian and feminist readings of them. And then, given the partiality of that interpretation, I offer my own *IN DEEPER:* my *psychoanalytic-autoethnographic* approach to interpretation that endeavours both to fill in some of the silences left by discourse analyses and to tolerate (because that interpretation too can only ever be partial) some of the silences that persist, behind all speech and beyond any reading.

2 Thinking about Stories: Narrative, Memory, Psychoanalytic Theory

Thinkers within the scholarly community . . . do not split their work from their lives . . . [but] seem to want to use each for the enrichment of the other. . . . What this means is that you must learn to use your life experience in your intellectual work.

    – C. Wright Mills, *The Sociological Imagination*

This memory of myself is carefully staged.

    – L. Brodkey, *Writing Permitted in Designated Areas Only*

The Field Notes

Here is another version of the story of dropping English: a fictive reconstruction and expansion, shifted into third-person, of the 'facts' set out at the beginning of Chapter 1.

From the notes of a secondary school guidance counsellor:

Date: June 1972
Student: Colette Granger
Grade: 11
Purpose of appointment: Grade 12 timetable

Everything in order. Grade 12 option sheet signed by mother. Student wants to drop English. I told her this was unusual, because
(a) many Grade 11 girls want to drop math, but English is usually one of their favourite courses
(b) she has always had high marks in English

Student replied somewhat belligerently that she hates English and always has, has only been waiting for the moment (Grade 12) when it is no longer compulsory. Says she knows she'll never want to take English in university. Her selections for next year are French, German, Latin, history, theatre arts, world religions, but also math and chemistry. Nearly all university-bound students take English, and I told Colette that she could be making a mistake, since sciences and math are not her strongest subjects and she probably won't want to study those in post-secondary. But she insisted that she knows what she wants, has her mother's permission. I had no choice but to sign the sheet, though I suggested she think about it. She told me firmly she would 'never' change her mind about this.

Reading the Field Notes: Critical Discourse Analysis

Let me reiterate, for I do not wish to mislead: the above transposes into a fictive third-person narrative the autobiographical moment summarized at the beginning of the previous chapter; the 'report' is a retroactive theoretical reconstruction of an event in my school life. However, while I am mindful of the view that narrative (like ethnography) not only reflects but also constructs the reality it purports to represent (Rosenwald & Ochberg, 1992; Elliott, 2005), my aim here is to use the narratives as stepping-off points rather than moments of arrival – and arguably, for 'better' rather than 'worse' interpretations (Riessman, 1993). It becomes less important that these are not actual notes of the particular 'real-life' guidance counsellor with whom I met the day I decided to drop English. Nor is it especially relevant whether such notes actually exist, or indeed ever existed. What matters is that the notes *might have existed*: the text tells a story, or rather a version of a story, 'that is possible, not one that is necessary' (Ellis, 1993, p. 725). And so, while the memory on which I base this version of 'the facts' is explored more fully in the following chapter, I present this variant, first to illustrate the rather obvious point that the event the 'notes' refer to is bound to be interpreted differently by different readers, and second as an object for analysis in Foucauldian and feminist terms, and reflection on those analyses.

So how might a Foucauldian reading of these notes look? My interpretation turns on three concepts at play within them: power dynamics, knowledge, and the body. The counsellor is institutionally and discursively constructed as an authoritative subject by education's institutional 'régimes of truth' (Foucault, 1980a, p. 133). He is also constructed as an adult, both by society and by his institutional employer. The student is positioned opposite him by these and other discourses, although her status is complex: she is a student, and thereby subject to the authority of the school; but in addition she is an adolescent in a 'liminal state,' transitional and difficult to define precisely, which renders her 'dangerous and need[ing] to be controlled' (Ehrensal, 2003, p. 123).

In addition to these constructions into which counsellor and student must fit, and onto which attach particular kinds and degrees of power (more on this below), the exercise of power is for Foucault closely connected with, and in fact preceded by, knowledge. For power exists only as a dynamic – in action as informed by knowledge (1980a). It is a *doing* rather than a *having*. Thus, we might read the notes above as demonstrating how the counsellor's professional knowledge gives him specific permission to judge, and to attempt to influence, the student: the counsellor 'knows' that this particular student is academically successful in humanities, but not sciences, that she is making an atypical choice for a girl, and that the combination of her choices and her academic strengths and weaknesses may later put her at an educational disadvantage.

The counsellor's professional knowledge gives him more than mere permission, however. It gives him power, and with that power an obligation. He is a counsellor, required to counsel: he reminds the student of the potential consequences of the choice she insists on making. In relation to him, the student seems to have no power other than that which is bestowed on her.

But things are not quite so straightforward. There are rules, policies, discourses that circumscribe the power, and simultaneously the powerlessness, of both participants in this moment. This is key, for both knowledge and power dynamics move and shift, 'embedded in that set of relationships between social agents who may variably exercise or resist' them (Wooffitt, 2005, p. 199).

Or indeed, exercise *and* resist. The student, by failing to cooperate and do what 'good' adolescents/students do, resists relegation to the category of girls-who-like-English, or more generally, to the category of 'good student.' That is, she refuses to be 'disciplined' in the Foucauldian sense. Yet just as the counsellor knows and enforces the rules, the student knows them too, and conforms – by waiting until it is 'legal' to drop English and providing the requisite documentation. Her cooperation, though, is strategic, not capitulatory: she cooperates *in order to* resist, follows the law the better to break it, thereby refusing to be the 'docile body,' 'manipulated, shaped, trained, which obeys [and] responds' (Foucault, 1977a, p. 136), that prevailing discourses of education and of gender expect her to be. Thus the larger context of student-meeting-counsellor can be understood as a kind of procedural tennis match – serve, rally, return – in which one individual's knowledge and power are played against another's.

Discourse in the form of a 'political technology of the body' (Foucault, 1977a, p. 26) works on and in individuals to discipline them as particular *kinds* of body, 'defined and constructed both in generic categories (e.g., as "children" and "teachers") and in more specialized and purposive historical categories (e.g., as "professionals," "adolescents," "linguistic deficit," "preoperational")' (Luke, 1997, p. 51), Or, here, as student and counsellor. This happens partly through the privileging of institutional documentation and record-keeping within institutions, as the 'body is the inscribed surface of events (traced by language and dissolved by ideas)...[and] totally imprinted by history' (Foucault, 1984b, p. 83). The particular roles of counsellor and student are tattooed on them by the institution, and tacitly understood by themselves, each other, and others not present at the meeting – her parents, his supervisors, the Board of Education, society at large.

It thus becomes irrelevant whether the counsellor may himself have liked high-school English, or found it pointless, or whether he perhaps admires the girl for her willingness to risk the consequences of an apparently unorthodox choice. In current parlance, *he is what he is* – that is, what the various discourses have constructed and identified him as: the knowing, professionally designated adult. She too is constructed and identified: as intelligent and capable, but nevertheless naïve, inexperienced, and needing guidance. And, she is a girl; girls like studying English; she ought to like studying English. Indeed, it may be only the primacy of another's authority (the parent who signed the permission form) that stops the counsellor from interceding further. In this sense both counsellor and student bodies are, in Foucauldian terms, de-centred and fragmented, subjugated by their discursive construction as particular kinds of body in ways that preclude their acting as other kinds.

The construction of the student as a gendered being is also an important part of this scenario, which a more pointedly feminist reading might angle a little differently. Traditional feminist discourse analyses have focused on speech and conversation style (Wooffitt, 2005),[1] although in educational (and other) contexts work has been done on gender and language as social practice. This work is summarized by Remlinger (2005, p. 114) as considering turn-taking strategies, including 'interruption, questions and conversational development' in addition to those in phonological and lexical domains. Here we are not dealing with actual speech, which might lend itself more readily to such an analysis: here, where the 'notes' are a kind of fictionalized back-formation, my analysis is offered as a theoretical illustration of possibility, as what Turkle has called an 'object to think with' (1985, p. 22). My reading calls on the notion of language and gender as performance (Butler, 1990; Remlinger, 2005); more precisely, in this hypothetical text-and-context, on whether and how the counsellor's documentation might 'reinforce and challenge beliefs, values, and attitudes' (Remlinger, 2005, p. 116) concerning *the female student* as a discursive construction.

On a lexical level, the qualifiers *many, usual,* and *usually* suggest that the writer is working from specific normative views about girls in general, to which, however, this particular girl does not conform. Second, the phrase *but also* (in listing the student's chosen courses) sets the sciences apart from the humanities, reinforcing the meta-level assumption made explicit in the warning that dropping English could be 'a mistake' and that the science subjects are surprising or even inappropriate choices – for a girl. Granted, the text juxtaposes the issue of grades with this presumption, but I suggest that the juxtaposition too is fraught with presumption. It is unclear, for example, whether the student's science grades are actually too low to allow her to study sciences in university, or simply lower than her grades in other subject areas. What is more, the point might be altogether irrelevant if girls are simply not expected to study sciences.

Other lexical choices offer points for analysis. The counsellor describes the student as firm, belligerent, and insistent, which arguably has the effect of reinforcing gender stereotypes by alleging that this young woman exceeds or contravenes them. A feminist analysis might thus ask whether these attitudes of firmness, insistence, and belligerence are remarked on because they are remark*able,* their contravention of stereotypes atypical. There is no single answer to this question. But to view it from another side, we might further speculate whether it would have been recorded had the student in this hypothetical scenario burst into tears, in a fashion more normatively 'feminine.' Or conversely, we might wonder whether, had the student been a boy, crying would have been remarked on in the 'notes,' and firmness and insistence left out.

The question of lexical choice raises another point. For Gal 'the control of discourse or of representations of reality occurs in social interaction, located in institutions, and is a source of social power.' (1991,

p. 177). In my vignette any notes the counsellor made would become the official record of the meeting such that the student's participation would effectively have no existence outside that document, thereby silencing her, or at least those aspects of her that the meeting, and the documentation, did not address.

I must acknowledge here that as a female I have likewise privileged the (male) adult in this scenario. That is, in this fictionalized account of a moment in my own educational life, I have given power and privilege to the counsellor, allowed him to 'speak,' and kept myself silent. Part of the reason for this is that my memory of this appointment is vague, but other factors may also be implicated in my failure to allow myself full license – even in a speculative, narrative sense – to use my own voice to relate the event. My narrative may be inhibited by what Kadar (1992b, 155) calls an 'imperative to mask the self, or pretend one has lost it in a third-person narrative.' And that imperative to conceal may be grounded in a worry about my ability to command what Miller terms 'the sanctioned merits of schooling' (2005, p. 103).

Here is what I mean. In the story entitled 'Mr Brucker's good girl,' Miller (2005) analyses a relationship with one of her early teachers, in which important lessons about 'connections, conversations, and new ways of being in the world' were countered by 'official' discourses requiring her 'to impersonate the patriarchal inflections found in others' words, to speak in the modulated serious tones of others' understandings, to memorize others' stories, to replicate others' knowledges.' She comments that in her 'ironic desire to please, to receive authorization, [she] effectively denied or erased parts of [her] self' (2005, p. 103). Her words resonate, albeit uncomfortably, with my choice regarding who 'speaks' in the reconstructed 'notes' of the counsellor: Miller's appraisal implicitly queries the extent to which the reconstruction hints at my worries and doubts about the academic legitimacy of my own personal narratives, as a 'way in' or 'in deeper' to this project. For I too seem to have denied or erased parts of my self, at least for the moment, by using the traditional (patriarchal) institutional discourse, which privileges the 'professional' counsellor's right to speak, and thereby to erase, for now at least, the voice of the student subordinated to that discourse.[2]

Everything said is something else left unsaid; every question posed is another unasked. Sometimes even a question that is asked seems to slide by. Here, our partly fictional guidance counsellor wonders why someone who has always excelled in a particular subject area is choosing to abandon it, but he does not pursue this question, perhaps because

he is invested in normative discourses of gender, institutional procedure, and academic 'excellence' which announce what is expected even
as they create the expectation. The question is worth considering nonetheless: what might resisting the discourses, refusing the expected, do
for this student? Or, put slightly differently, what might this student be
using the unexpected to do?

Let us remember, the socially constructed individual subject is not
without agency, will, creativity. Bloom's analysis of women telling, retelling, and analysing 'their life experiences against the backdrop of the
prevailing discourses that seek to silence them' (1998, p. 64) argues implicitly for an individual subject capable of resisting and analysing such
discourses. More explicitly, in distinguishing agency from autonomy in
a reading of Foucault, Bevir (1999, p. 68) cites the fact that not everyone
in the same social structure performs identically as evidence for 'an un-
decided space in front of these structures where individuals decide what
beliefs to hold and what actions to perform.' Much social constructionist
theory follows similar lines, from Mead's claim that 'the self . . . arises in
the process of social experience and activity, that is, develops in a given
individual as a result of his relations to that process' (1934, p. 199) to
Harré's view that we are both 'products of social process' and makers of
meaning 'built to be capable of autonomous action' (1993, p. 3).

I am here offering speculative readings of equally speculative 'field
notes.' Need that be a problem? These retroactively constructed and
explicitly fictive 'notes' are obviously not an ethnography; even if they
were a historical artefact, such as the actual notes from a counsellor's
record of his appointments with students, they would still not constitute an ethnography. At most they might be a fragment of data, an ethnographic snapshot which, in combination with many other snapshots,
could be used 'to describe and interpret cultural behavior' (Wolcott,
1987, p. 43) in the development of an ethnographic study.

I have those limitations in mind as I reiterate the two very specific
purposes of my speculation: one, to offer a textual locus for my discussion of Foucauldian and feminist discourse analyses; and two, to give,
through a reading of the text, an opening to think about its absences – its
silences. Where Chapter 1's just-the-facts version of the incident illustrates even in (or because of) its brevity the relatively thin possibilities for interpretation or reflection, and concomitantly the large gaps
in 'facts-only' narratives generally, this second version offers a starting
point for a discussion of what *it* in turn lacks: the voice, thoughts, affect
of its main actor. In a word . . .

The Personal

With its multiple connotations, implying transformative power (Gallop, 1995, p. 3), a way to make meaning or relate to others (Pitt, 2003) – and of course the political[3] – 'the personal' is ubiquitous in poststructural research in numerous disciplines. And personal writing, itself called by many names including life writing, personal narrative, and life testimonial (Kadar, 1992), has of late made inroads into multiple research areas. In sociology this turn evokes 'feeling and participatory experience as dimensions of knowing' (Ellis, 1993, p. 726) in ways that imply self-representation as a highly credible means of understanding the social (Denzin, 1997; Richardson, 1997; Maines, 2001). In anthropology it may inform traditional narratives of 'the Other,' with diaries, novels, letters, and other textual forms that describe fieldworkers' experience (Cole, 1992, pp. 114–15). In women's studies, it 'problematizes the notion of Literature' (Kadar, 1992a, p. 12; italics in original) and carves out space for individuals and groups 'previously silenced ... at the margins of an otherwise hegemonic discourse' (Kadar, 1992, p. 81). In educational research, it is an important locus for thinking about teacher education and development (Goodson, 1992; Carter & Doyle, 1996).

The epigraph to this chapter – Mills's directive to allow the personal to help the professional along (1961, pp. 195–6) – is taken up by Neumann (1998) in an essay reflecting on how learning about her father's life as a Holocaust survivor has influenced her academic work. Her questions speak to this relationship: 'How are the personal and the professional intertwined? How much of our "selves" is inextricably bound into our work? How much of our selves should we purposefully let into our work?' (Neumann, 1998, p. 427).

They are tricky questions. The call to 'get personal' that Church names, in her (1995) study of social relations among former psychiatric patients, as a kind of special permission to write one's life into research, is a seductive luxury but one that is fraught with potential pitfalls. This is because it is also 'vital intellectual work [that] celebrates survivor voice while moving the "observer" directly into view in the knowledge construction process' (Church, 1995, p. 5). While the inclusion of the personal in autoethnography (and often too in ethnography) is deliberate, if – as Rosen (1998, p. 1) alleges – we are all autobiographers whether or not we have consciously tried to write our life stories, we should not be surprised that when it comes to our work, even if its explicit focus is elsewhere, bits of us and of our lives creep into our narratives. The sense of inevitability in Richardson's (2001, p. 34) assertion that 'people who write are always writing about their lives . . . [and n]o writing is untainted by human hands' is echoed by Pitt (2003), who juxtaposes a caution against overusing personal narrative with a startled recognition of its frequent appearance in her own work.

The ubiquity of the personal demands that we ask, Is it useful? And how much is too much? One does not want to be sentimental to the point of untrustworthiness, as Spigelman (2001, p. 63) reports personal narrative is often perceived to be. And it is quite *un*helpful if, for instance, we allow the personal to 'foreclose rather than open discussion and debate' (Pitt, 2003, p. 5). With Pitt, I am 'suspicious' of unproblematized personal narratives offered as 'an explanatory device for understanding experience' (2003, p. 5). Equally, I am wary both of the 'patronizing sentimentality' that Grumet (1990, p. 324) suggests can result from the uninterpreted presentation of autobiographical narrative, and of the risks (professional and personal) of veering too close to the self-indulgent. Perhaps most importantly, I am mindful of the partiality of personal narratives, and of the fact that reading them is a similarly selective undertaking. At the same time, autobiographical approaches that incorporate, as Miller (1992, p. 508) recommends, 'situated analyses of specific contexts that influence the constructions and representations of self and other' and, more broadly, 'theorized and contextualized accounts of educational experience and practice' may inaugurate important challenges to positivist discourses in education. The notion of the autobiographical in general, and more specifically of the autoethnographic, resonates with my conception of silence as rich with implicative meaning rather than as merely empty space.

Claims that autobiographical writing is somehow truer and more illuminative than other genres seem to hinge on the presumption of an illuminable unitary self, a single 'honest truth' there for the telling. But the concept of the self as unified and unchanging over time and across contexts is widely rejected by postmodern thinking generally, and by poststructuralist and feminist theorists in particular (see Fischer, 1986; Norquay, 1990). Furthermore as Kermode (1995, p. 37) observes, 'the honest truth . . . is inaccessible; the minute you begin to write it you try to write it well, and writing well is an activity which has no simple relation to truth.'

Kermode's argument is about narrative form and discursive style. The other side of that coin is content. A short story by Borges and Casares (1999), about a country in which cartography is so precise that the only adequate map is scaled 'point for point' with the territory it represents, gestures poetically toward the futility of the goal of finding and telling the 'whole story' or the completely 'honest truth.'[4] First, the content of a life *is* that life, such that documenting its entirety would have to include thoughts formed and interrupted, words spoken and forgotten, deeds planned and either done or decided against, and would thereby take up more space and time than the life itself. Second, the life-writing process, if undertaken by the one living that life, would likewise have to be documented, as would that process of documentation ... and that one ... and that one ... and so on. Third, to anticipate my psychoanalytic punch line, even if all that documentation were logistically possible, none of us has full access to our own story. Even common sense understands that we don't know what we don't know or what we have forgotten, and while we may be fascinated by what we seem to have forgotten, attending to that fascination in specific, contextualized detail would seem to require remembering at least *something* about its context.

Britzman's (1991) ethnography of learning to teach follows Brodkey (1987) in cautioning against the assumption that an account of an experience can ever be isomorphic with that experience. The recounting of any story is always multiply delimited, on one hand by the teller's perspective and on the other by 'the exigencies of what can and cannot be told' (Britzman 1991, p. 13). Further, although an ethnographic narrative by its nature might appear to reify, in some discursive freeze-frame, a particular moment as emblematic of the life of a stable subject, that life in reality is composed of innumerable moments which are 'private, elusive, chaotic and unaccounted' (p. 61). The stable subject does not exist and never has. We are all living multiple stories, each characterized by interruption and contradiction, repetition and reworking, learning, and unlearning and relearning.

If personal narratives are always partial, reading them is likewise a selective undertaking. We must remind ourselves that as readers, our understandings of an ethnographic text, as of any other, are filtered through the lenses of our own elusive and perhaps inchoate lives: lenses that render the text even further removed from what it purports to narrate. And on reading goes, in a kind of interminable filtering, making what is always already partial more partial still, and simultaneously insinuating the reader into the text. The moments recollected, reconstructed, and read in the narrative are informed by all these vicissitudes, by all that they do not contain – by their silences. So while a narrative (or a thoughtful consideration of it) might cast light on some unspoken worry or other, we cannot and should not expect it to entirely explain that worry, for it cannot fully explain itself; not only is it partial, but it can only ever be partially useful. If we imagine that any autoethnographic text embodies the truth, the whole truth, and nothing but the truth about a culture, individual, or event, we are simply imagining too much of it.

All this is easy to forget, though, because the ethnography or other narrative seems to a listener or reader to be self-contained and complete – the whole truth: in Derridean terms, completeness and even objectivity are what is there to be read by virtue of their (performative) presence-in-the-sign. In the *difference* between researcher and researched Other lies the *deferred presence* (implicit-but-as-yet-unarticulated) of the researcher: a presence/present that is in text always already a past:

> The sign represents the present in its absence. It takes the place of the present. When we cannot grasp or show the thing, state the present, the being-present, when the present cannot be presented, we signify, we go through the detour of the sign. We take or give signs. We signal. The sign, in this sense, is deferred presence. (Derrida, 1982, p. 6)

What might narration be useful for if it is not identical to the experience it narrates, does not encapsulate the entirety of a life, or cannot be extrapolated to emblematize the lives or the truths of others, and if all of this partialness is rendered even more incomplete by the acts of reading and interpreting?

Well, here is a little twist. If an actual experience is always fuller than any account of it can be, it may also be that the account can paradoxically exceed – by being other to – the experience. Personal narrative or life writing is not made just from what is internal to the individual; nor, once made, does it remain there. Grumet (1990, p. 322) refers to personal writing as simultaneously inner and outer, personal and public. And her later (1992) discussion of 'inner temporality' further elucidates this surprising and complexifying phenomenon, wherein remembering events and narrating those memories embodies a 'double awareness of encounters in the world and of experience of those encounters extended through . . . inner time' (1992, p. 35). The doubling is doubled again when reading happens; even reading one's own personal writing constitutes a doubling of the self. Moreover,

> as the reader voluntarily re-creates that which the writer has disclosed, once again a fictive world is created, drawn from the substance of the

reader's experience and fantasy. Reading is one way of demonstrating the reciprocity of objectivity and subjectivity and their interdependence; it extends to the reader/researcher the artist's awareness that subjectivity transforms any objectivity it seeks to describe. (Grumet, 1992, p. 37)

By involving the reader, and everything that individual brings to a reading, an autobiographical or autoethnographic narrative is not only a field for the re-creation and re-enactment of past moments in the writer's and the reader's worlds, but a potentially rich breeding ground for ideas and questions: a place from which we begin to think ideas and theorize issues. Narrative offers fertile soil for what Gallop (2002, p. 2) calls anecdotal theory – a process and product that reads an account of an incident for potential theoretical insights. Such an approach can kindle important challenges to education's positivist discourses. Gallop argues for a focus on 'the theoretical moment' as a way 'to move toward an anecdotal relation to theory' (2002, p. 3) that may, by attending to the individual, the atypical, even (in a word that enters Gallop's lexicon by way of Derrida) the exorbitant (p. 8), subvert traditional regard for the typical in ways that facilitate challenges to the tendency of traditional academic research methods to privilege epistemologies that separate intellect from affect (Miller, 1988, p. 487).

To read is to interpret, deliberately or otherwise. In querying what we might ask interpretation to do in our research, Pitt (2003) resists the inclination to use it as an unambiguous tool for making meaning, either directly from experience or (in a poststructural world) indirectly from discourses of knowledge and power that imprint themselves on narrated experience. Refusing the notion of narrative as transparently representative of identity, and spurning the idea that discourse can tell the full story of *any* story, she arrives at the wish to allow narrative interpretation to 'move things along' (Pitt, 2003, p. 6). I am with Pitt here, in that just as Foucauldian, feminist, and other angles from which to read discourse can be useful and edifying, my use of the personal – in an autoethnographic mix of my narrated memories, diary and journal entries, and reflections on experience – is partly about the finding of the one hidden, about what Chambers (1998, p. 14) calls 'making a home' as teacher, learner, or worker.

True, my approach might make this work a little less academic in a traditional sense, a little more self-serving. But perhaps that is not all it does. The trick lies, I think, in refusing unproblematized, untheorized 'stories.' Here is what Miller (2005) says about what makes autobiographical work, particularly in education, both challenging and rich:

> To 'tell your story or my story' without challenging either language 'that unwittingly writes us,' or the self as singular, unified, chronological, and coherent, is to maintain the status quo, to reinscribe already known situations and identities as fixed, immutable, locked into normalized and thus often exclusionary conceptions of what and who are possible.
>
> Instead, addressing 'self' and autobiographical investigations of 'self' or 'woman' or 'teacher,' for example, as 'site(s) of permanent openness and resignifiability' opens up potential for accessing as well as creating new modes of speaking and writing into existence ways of being that are obscured, unknown, or simply unthinkable when one centered, self-knowing story is substituted for another. (p. 54)

The idea of openness is important here, because with openness can come insight – even if the Other (or indeed the self) is marked by unknowability (Todd, 2003a). I have suggested previously (2004) that psychoanalytic theory allows us to imagine that another's experience might be not identical to, but a little bit like, our own. I argue the same for narrative: not that readers will identify fully and absolutely with an experience or its narration, but that in it they might find a little something that resonates with another little something, and that invites them to recognize a *narrative* of education as a useful place to begin thinking about some of the larger somethings: education's big *questions*.

Narrative and Memory

Writing by Crawford, Kippax, Onyx, Gault, and Benton (1990) explores how events are remembered, deconstructed and reconstructed, and understood differently over time, and illuminates gaps between the one who experiences the event, the one who remembers, and the one who articulates the memory. At their most basic, these gaps are a function of the passing of time and the forgetting of detail. But I think there is more to it. Working in conversation analysis, Pomerantz (2005, p. 93) posits that reviewing (videotaped) events can help participants recall their feelings at the time of the events, and that recounting those recollections can fortify and extend memories of the events. However, she refuses the conclusion that such commentaries are clear windows to actual thoughts or emotions at the time of the original interaction, pointing out several factors that can interfere with accurate remembering: foreknowledge of the event's outcome; silence on aspects of the initial interaction perceived as sensitive or troubling; and the 'temptation [on a researcher's part] to treat the inferred interpretation, aim, or concern as stable and explanatory rather than as shifting, amorphous, or however else it may be manifest' (p. 112).

The personal is about narration. Narrating is about remembering. In a sense all speech is about remembering; even the microseconds between an event, an observation, or a thought and their articulation in speech or writing mark a spacing that reflects the translation of event or thought into memory.[5] And here I concur with Chambers's claim, echoing Grumet (1992), that 'in the act of remembering, we come face-to-face with at least two sides of ourselves: the self writing and the self who is remembered' (Chambers, 1998, p. 14). In this chapter's version of the 'dropping English' narrative, as well as the version appearing in the next chapter, I must attend to the fact that what I *think* I remember is filtered through multiple screens: the nearly 35 years that have passed, the transformation of the memory into a part of this project where I am using it to do certain things, and the reading I have done preparatory to interpreting. These several (of potentially many) layers of removal or distance from the actual events force us to acknowledge that there may be little value in positing a transparent and unitary set of meanings for them.[6]

Relatedly, in their writing not about difficult moments qua events, but about the difficulties that attach to the work of constructing narratives representing teaching and learning, Pitt and Britzman (2003) raise the crucial problem of time: 'Where does one situate the event that is experience? In the past that is narrated or in the presence of its interpretation?' (p. 759). I am not sure whether the more expected *present* was intended here (though it seems likely given that the following sentence refers to 'both positions of time'), but the appearance in the question of *presence*, a homophone of the plural *presents*, hints at a kind of temporal recursion[7] that nudges my own thinking along. For there are, by my count, two *presents* of interpretation (and indeed, two *pasts*) with a narrated version of any experience: the narrator's present in which the memory is narrated; the present in which that narration is read, or heard, and interpreted; the actual past event on which the narrative is based; and finally the narrative itself, which is *past* in relation to both reading and interpretation. The personal, and the writing, and reading, and interpretation in which it makes itself present, constitute ways of 'fixing' past events that refuse to solidify them. Grumet concludes her

(1992) essay on the existential and phenomenological foundations of autobiography by observing that 'autobiographical method may not effect the total reconciliation of objectivity and subjectivity in educational research, but it does commit us to acknowledge the paradox' (1992, p. 42).

Neumann's (1998) curiosity about the role of the personal in academic work relates even more directly to my ultimate aim of thinking about how education, by examining its silences (the personal *as* silenced; silences *of* the personal), can find ways to proceed that are ethical, beneficent, and generous. Neumann asks, 'How much of the other's experience can we know? How far can empathic imagination stretch?' (1998, p. 429). I ask, additionally, how much we can know of our own experience, as learners and as teachers. And, more importantly, how can we learn to tolerate what we cannot know about that personal – or those 'personals': our own and those of the others with whom we work and live?

Writing on *The Play of the Personal* Pitt (2003) turns her lens more directly to a psychoanalytic reading of the personal in education and educational research, looking this time at the Winnicottian notion, at first contradictory and even paradoxical, of the 'secret self' that, like a child playing hide-and-seek, finds it *'joy to be hidden but disaster not to be found'* (1963c, p. 186; italics in original). Pitt's question is, What do we use the personal to do? Her answer, in part, is that we use personal stories to make sense of ourselves and to make meaning, to help us relate to others, and to think about that relating. But, she says, there is 'something more' – the personal does not stand alone, but rather is profoundly *inter*personal. It is not constituted in one time or place in a static reduction of ingredients: it simmers along, occasionally boiling over, and is comprised of past events, processes undergone and underway, knowledge, learning, current and long-ago relationships with others, and former versions of itself. To Pitt's question, I add a corollary: *how* do we use it to do these things? And what will be our tool for this excavation?

Psychoanalytic Concepts: Another Way of Reading

Perhaps it seems contrived, given what I have just said about their interrelatedness, to separate the preceding sections on the personal and on narrative from each other and from this discussion of psychoanalytic ideas. Nevertheless, the same sense of artificiality follows me into this section, for psychoanalysis in clinical practice is both profoundly *about* the personal and conducted *through* narrative; it is through the sharing of personal story, however conceived, that the analysand achieves the 'talking cure' (Breuer & Freud, 1974[1895]) to which psychoanalysis aspires. The psychoanalytic encounter forms a dialogue between analysand and therapist; narrating the self implicates both narrator and reader – even if they are one. Still, for ease of reference, it makes sense to draw a line between these parts of my study, while recognizing that their boundaries are fuzzy and overlapping. Here I review some psychoanalytic concepts that are relevant to the difficult moments and silences I am engaging, as well as to my meta-level discussion: how do we think about the narratives, but also, what are we thinking about when we think about the narratives? And, what can we use the narratives to think about? – which after all is the whole point.

The Unconscious

Even those who refuse most of Freud's work accept that much goes on in our minds without our minds' conscious awareness of it: the processing of language; sensory perception; 'choices' about behaviour; associations with events or phenomena in the environment that trigger memories. But psychoanalysis conceptualizes the unconscious as both more general and more particular than that. At its very centre lies the idea that the human organism is a complex one, of which, in the ordinary course of existence, the individual subject only consciously knows, or ever can know, a very small portion. Almost everything else is part of what Freud's first topography named the system of the unconscious – a kind of vast mental chamber in which the self deposits, and holds, wishes and desires deemed unacceptable or intolerable to consciousness (Laplanche & Pontalis, 1973, pp. 474–5).[8] These contents are not accessible in the normal course, but they reveal themselves in the therapeutic encounter, in symptomatic manifestations such as neuroses, in dreams, and in parapraxes.

Generally, the unconscious is composed not of instincts, but of 'instinctual representatives' or 'wishful impulses' (Freud, 1915b, p. 186) which can be described first through what they lack: they do not know negation, doubt, or certainty, or care about reality (insofar as they can be said to 'know' or 'care about' anything); and they are not ordered, bound, or altered by the passage of time, which is constructed by the conscious mind. Second, these inhabitants of the unconscious combine ideational and affective elements, vary in strength, are governed exclusively by the pleasure and unpleasure principles, and aim perpetually to move into the conscious realm – a goal they achieve in multiple ways and to varying degrees.

Insistence in psychoanalytic thought on the power of the unconscious troubles the social constructionist waters in which it wades. Although I do not altogether reject claims that experience constitutes the individual subject (Scott, 1992, p. 25), I insist on the bi- (or indeed multi-) directionality of that constitutive process: we are made both from what is outside us and from what persists within – the 'old conflicts' that we are always reworking (A. Freud, 1974, p. 88). In fact, the branch of psychoanalytic thought named object relations theory marks relationship as foundational to and prominent in the work of making identity. Winnicott honours the view of identity development as beginning with the infant's coming to understand the separation of itself from its environment: a moment that inaugurates 'a complex interchange between what is inside and what is outside . . . [and which comes to be] the main relationship of the individual to the world' (1963a, p. 72).

Here, my returns to the moment of 'dropping English' are also returns to the narration of, and to the relations I make (or *my self* makes) with, that event. Pitt (2003, p. 7) reviews Lacan's assessment of Freud as having established psychoanalysis as a practice in order to 'avoid being affected' (cited in Felman, 1987, p. 23), on an unconscious level, by his patient's unconscious. What relationship is at play – or is refusing to play – when it is one's *own* unconscious that one is reading? What am I avoiding by using my own stories (other than the labour-intensive and ethically complex process of collecting others' stories)?

It is an odd idea, that we study a narrative in order to avoid being affected by it. But when it is one's own narrative, one is by definition already affected, by both its manifest content and its unconscious plotlines; attempting to exhume these may help lighten the weight of difficult stories. At the same time we must take care not to make that lightening the purpose of either narration or interpretation, for this is neither the confessional nor the couch. The goal here is not personal absolution or redemption, and it is not cure or mastery; it is especially not mastery. It is, rather, a way to let interpretation help us along in our thinking about the questions raised. Still, my concern about one question of return raises another: the psychoanalytic notion of the repressed and its return.

Repression

For Freud, the instincts represented within the unconscious precede the split between conscious and unconscious minds: in fact it is their repression (named *primal repression*) that causes the split (1915a, p. 148). Additional to this primal repression are subsequent repressions, where what is pushed down or away is what consciousness cannot tolerate: traumatic events that cannot be assimilated at the time of their occurrence because their impact on the psyche would simply be too debilitating. Psychoanalysis postulates that repression is enacted when the ego is terrified of a renewed fusion of its own carefully constructed organization with the chaos of the id,[9] whose demands it may be too fragile to repress. Here the unconscious performs a service, holding in abeyance what the conscious mind can neither tolerate nor work through in the moment (1915a).

The most significant aspect of the repressed is its persistence. Repressed instincts do not change or diminish with time: they are the psychical ghosts that haunt us, returning over and over with the aim of emerging into the conscious realm. The return comes about 'by more or less devious routes, and through the intermediary of secondary formations' (Laplanche & Pontalis 1973, p. 398) including dreams and the analytic process, during which, if all goes well, an analysand comes to regard his 'illness' (including obsessions, phobias, and repressed material) as a worthy enemy, 'a piece of his personality, which has solid ground for its existence and out of which things of value for his future life have to be derived' (Freud, 1914a, p. 152).

I contend that the repressed might also return in or as a consequence of narration, and that reading psychoanalytically allows the reader to recognize repressed elements and/or events that the narrator might be revealing, albeit unconsciously. The one remembering is not identical to the one narrating. Though the two may be closer in time than either is to the event itself – especially if the memory is of an event in the distant past – we must not forget that a narrator, 'in the present moment of the narration, possesses the knowledge that she did not have "then," in the moment of the experience' (King, 2000, p. 2). Yet somehow we imagine narrated memory 'as if the narrating "I" and the subject of the narration were identical' (p. 3).

Psychoanalysis demands that we articulate the discrepancy. For Freud there are two ways to consider the remembering process: as an 'excavation' of a past which may 'seem completely forgotten [but is] present somehow and somewhere, . . . [has] merely been buried and made inaccessible to the subject' (Freud, 1937b, p. 260), and which is retrievable in original form; and as a more ongoing reworking of an earlier self by a later one, in the time marked by what Freud named Nachträglichkeit, or 'deferred action' (Laplanche & Pontalis, 1973, p. 111).

Deferred Action

The fact that narrative is about events whose occurrence is not contemporaneous with, but rather prior to, the time of narration, raises a question: What – or perhaps who – is being interpreted? The one who actually experienced the events in some earlier time? The 'author' at the time of speaking or writing, who narrates and reconstructs events from memory? Or the way this author would be experiencing those events if they were occurring at the time of writing? That is, when I remember, whether I write or tell those memories (or indeed simply recall them), am I remembering the events *as they were*, or reconstructing them through hindsight?

Deferred action or Nachträglichkeit, also translated as 'afterwardsness' (Laplanche, 1999), is one response to these questions. It describes the 'after-the-fact' time of working through trauma. By definition trauma cannot be assimilated at the time of its occurrence; we can only even identify it in hindsight, after we have come to re-construct certain events as having been traumatic. Nachträglichkeit speaks both to the usefulness of engaging narrative psychoanalytically, as a way of getting behind the spoken and between the lines of the written, and to the importance of acknowledging that such an engagement works on two levels: that of the after-the-fact narrator, and that of the original participant in the unworked-through, and un-narrated, events.

The idea of a deferred engagement with an event or experience is important because of its implications in relation to the agent that undergoes, or undertakes, the deferred revision: the nachträglich reader. This point becomes particularly relevant in reading one's own narrative, for whatever discourse or method I use as a reader now (that is, the 'I' at the time of reading), I am not the same 'I' as the one who initially experienced the event.[10] Part of what this means is that there is more to every story – and part of the 'more' is in the storyteller and in the reader, each of whom also reads from a place in public and in private – historically, socially, and personally.

This notion of reworking or re-editioning the self (A. Freud, 1974) favoured by psychoanalysis, in which later versions of self embody all earlier ones, can thus be framed (like the perpetually self-re-informing *me/not-me* relations mentioned above) as another instance of a kind of recursion – or alternatively as a mise-en-abyme: that image within an image, story within a story, or dream within a dream (in visual art, literature, or film, respectively) that evokes a reflection or re-instantiation of itself. Most important for psychoanalysis is that each manifestation of 'self' contains material from former manifestations. The deferred reading of an event is thus both recursive and reflective, because the self doing the post facto reading is informed (and formed) by the self who originally experienced the event. Echoing Grumet (1992) and Chambers (1998) on the work of narration, King describes memory as 'a continuous process of re-remembering' in tripartite form: 'first, the event; second the memory of the event, and third the writing of (the memory of) the event' (King, 2000, p. 21). I add a fourth layer of recursion: {the reading of (the writing of [the memory of])} the event. Because the self remembering is already a revised self, it is almost a truism that the recording and even the remembering of an event are bound to 'reconstruct the events of a life in the light of "what wasn't known then," highlighting the events which are now [that is, in the moment of narration], with hindsight, seen to be significant' (King, 2000, p. 22).

Events are reconstructed. But so are memories. This should not surprise us, since if the unconscious mind is so powerful it makes sense that one of the things it has power over is memory: what we remember, how we remember it, in what detail, for how long. Psychoanalytic discourse invites thinking about the persistence of experiences and events both in and separate from conscious memory, and about the recounting of memory (to the self and to others), that may prove useful for thinking about these narratives and the larger questions toward which they gesture.

The Mystic Writing-pad

Psychoanalysis is committed to the idea that human development comprises a series of re-workings or 'new editions of very old conflicts' (A. Freud, 1974, p. 88). S. Freud (1924) illustrated this using, as a metaphor for the unconscious, the 'mystic writing-pad' – a child's toy made of a wax slab, overlaid with a transparent sheet of celluloid and a sheet of waxed paper. The writing-pad (in today's version, usually called a magic slate, the top sheet is plastic) functions as a paper pad, but with the added novelty of retaining traces of what has been written on it. Since the stylus leaves no deposit, no marks are visible on the celluloid (or plastic) when it is lifted, but traces remain on the wax below even when the pad is repeatedly overwritten. The combination of concealed and visible is made possible by the separate yet connected elements of lower wax pad and upper layers.

Perception in the human mind functions similarly. Consciousness (the mind's 'top layer') receives content but does not fully retain it; the unconscious holds traces of what was 'written' earlier and has a potentially infinite capacity to be rewritten upon. Thus, though in a given moment we are conscious of only a very small part of who we are, who we have been, and our attendant motivations, urges, and other psychical phenomena, in a crucial sense, all the rest is still present. No event is gone completely; nothing we experience, feel, or know is truly lost; we are always rewriting our psychical histories.

The writing-pad metaphor is imperfect, however, in at least two ways. While it is useful for understanding the recursive quality of unconscious processes that carry 'traces of the dynamics of earlier experience even as the earlier experience can be revised' (Pitt & Britzman, 2003, p. 758), a magic slate cannot spontaneously reproduce original writing, while memory can re-create in some sense the original experience that has been buried in the unconscious. In addition, as with the medieval palimpsest, in memory the erasure is never quite complete.[11] This is because the traces already in the unconscious have themselves some bearing on what is perceived and written on the top (conscious) layer. We might liken it to the writing on the celluloid layer of the mystic pad becoming a little wobbly due to grooves left in the wax below by previous writing: the topmost layer is thus not perfectly flat except at the start. We can see this demonstrated in the version of the 'dropping English' story in the following chapter: a version which for decades was unavailable to my conscious mind.

In postmodern terms, this written-on tablet, the unconscious, is itself a text, for Derrida 'a weave of pure traces, differences in which meaning and force are united – a text nowhere present, consisting of archives which are always already transcriptions' (1978, p. 211). This concept resonates with the Freudian 'screen memory,' which in contrast with the mystic writing-pad contains traces not of experience but rather of the *memory-of*-experience. Derrida is being quite psychoanalytical when he remarks: 'This is my starting point: no meaning can be determined out of context, but no context permits saturation. What I am referring to here is not richness of substance, semantic fertility, but rather structure: the structure of the remnant or of iteration' (1979, p. 81).

Each sign, each text, each scribble on the writing-pad has a context that works to determine and delimit its meaning. However, this context can never be completely isolated; it arises from previous scribblings, and it informs future ones.

Screen Memories

The mystic writing-pad metaphor deals with how we make and remake ourselves, with the ways who we *were* inform, resonate with, and echo in who we *are*. Repression has to do with how what we are is also what we are not. Freud's concept of the screen memory offers ways to think about how remembering, and the ways of telling that remembering, work with and against our conscious wishes.

Freud expresses curiosity, even astonishment, at individuals whose early memories are of 'everyday and indifferent events which could not produce any emotional effect even in children' (1899, p. 305). He goes on to say that analysis can often reveal details that have been 'omitted' from such an apparently trivial memory, thereby returning it to the realm of the significant (p. 306). Interesting here is the 'choice' of image, for which Freud credits two competing forces – an urge to remember *because of* the event's importance, and an unconscious resistance to designating significance that inaugurates repression. Together these result in a compromise to a 'mnemic image' or 'screen memory' (Freud, 1899, p. 307) that works in one of two directions: either an early memory screening a later one, or the reverse. In this psychical process, the collapse of a memory into its symbol or image (the screen) allows its retention while preventing the conscious attention that might cause a painful reliving of the trauma originally produced by the event being screened – a partial silence caused by what Freud calls the substitution of one psychical content for another (1899, p. 307). We can read my fictionalized counsellor's notes version (and even more the just-the-facts version) of my decision to drop English as the mnemic image which screens the fullness of the event giving rise to it. For many years after I dropped English, and despite the fact that I had taken, and thoroughly enjoyed, university-level English literature courses – I stuck to my story as originally 'written' – the screen memory. Only with my own analysis did I come to the fuller version set out in the next chapter. And with the fuller version came, and continues to come,[12] the interpretation.

Thinking about the moves memory makes helps us consider the question of empathy in the approach of teachers to learners. I am reminded of a connection Young-Bruehl makes, in a piece about empathic relations between a 'biographer and her subject' – between screen memories as 'complex condensations of experience' and a kind of empathy 'directed at the subject's life over time' which is 'particularly sensitive to turning points, junctures, moments of high density' (1998, p. 8). We can also engage Young-Bruehl's notion of empathy in relation with the other psychoanalytic concepts I have discussed, not in the sense that an educator can 'know everything' about the learner's life, but rather in the sense of recognizing and acknowledging that there *is* a life there, outside and beyond what can be consciously known or spoken, a life that in its partial silence might benefit from what Schafer (1992, p. 11) calls 'the open-minded questions, the mirroring questions, the benevolently interested questions: What have we here? How can we respond to it genuinely? How can we help it along?'

These questions are reflected in Paley's lament (2004, p. 47): 'The potential for surprise [in primary education] is largely gone. We no longer wonder "Who are you?" but instead decide quickly "What can we do to fix you?" ' I have sat in school staffrooms and heard that one child or another is behaving 'badly' because she or he is from a single-parent family, from a visible minority, too religious, not religious enough, religious in the wrong way, too poor, too rich, unloved, over-loved, spoiled, deprived, an only child, one of too many children. It can seem comforting to find easy causes, but the reality of each individual life is complex, and cheap explanations can cost dearly. Perhaps we can approach a more ethical understanding of learning, and of breakdowns in learning, by refusing those cheap explanations in favour of the recognition that both processes involve conscious and unconscious elements.

In speaking of symptoms as 'involuntary and disguised memories of desire, unsuccessful attempts at self-cure, the cure of memory' – which for him 'need to be forgotten' – Kermode protests that 'Freudian theories of memory cannot . . . be the friends of autobiography' (1995, pp. 41–2). I hope to encourage at least cordiality among the playmates in this theoretical sandbox: autobiography/autoethnography, psychoanalysis, education. Here is a place where they might join hands, if only for a moment: Agar (1986, p. 12) jokes that among ethnography's requirements is a need for the 'ability to learn from a long series of mistakes.' Psychoanalysis too learns from mistakes, such as mislaying, forgetting, and slips of the tongue. It learns that something is buried or repressed, and through its return, if all goes well, it learns something of what that buried material is.

Crucially, we must acknowledge that education, and educators, cannot know everything. One way psychoanalysis might help us live with that knowledge is in corroborating, from its own distinct vantage point, the poststructuralist understanding that context and meaning are only ever partial. That is, our knowledge and understanding can be fuller, but it can never be *full*. Learning to tolerate that is no small thing. Let us move to the third and (for now, at least) final version of the story of dropping English.

3 Field Notes, Felt-notes, Felt and Noted: Silencing Learning, Silencing Desire

When a subject is highly controversial – and any question about sex is that – one cannot hope to tell the truth. . . . One can only give one's audience the chance of drawing their own conclusions as they observe the limitations, the prejudices, the idiosyncrasies of the speaker.

– Virginia Woolf, *A Room of One's Own*

The open palm of desire
It wants everything, wants everything
Wants everything

– Paul Simon, *Further to Fly*

Behar is pointed regarding the seamier side of ethnography illuminated by the controversy surrounding the appearance in 1967 of Malinowski's *Diary*: it was, she writes, 'the genre that was *silent* about the privileges of gender, race, class, and nationality, the genre that was *silent* about power, the genre that was *silent about desire*' (Behar, 1999, p. 473; my italics). But Behar's, and indeed Malinowski's, are not the only voices cooking up trouble in the (auto)ethnographic kitchen. Hammersley (1992, pp. 144–5) responds to the commonly held view of practitioner research (grounded in insider knowledge) as more legitimate than that done by an outsider with his assertion that that knowledge and those relationships may not include – and may not be able to include – everything germane to the research in question, partly because 'people can deceive themselves about their intentions, motives etc.'

Silence, desire, self-knowledge, and self-deception preoccupy psychoanalytic thought too. And sometimes they worry education, where desire 'ceaselessly circulates through the *unsaid* of classroom life (manifesting itself in expectations, hopes, visions, and fears)' and 'signals an unconscious want or longing produced and born out of intersubjective contact (both said and unsaid)' (Todd, 1997, p. 239; italics in original).[1] Taken together, Behar's and Hammersley's worries gesture toward the potential of psychoanalysis, with its recognition of the silencing of desires (through repression), the partialness of self-knowledge, and the pervasiveness of self-deception, as a 'thing to think with' (Turkle, 1985, p. 22): an *analytic discourse* that offers to readings of autoethnographic narrative something distinct from socially grounded *discourse analyses*. My aim here is to evoke thinking about the potential for and the limits of what narratives from within education can tell us, as well as about how we might learn to find a balance between pursuing the former and tolerating the latter.

Dropping English: Story/ies as Data

Here is another version of the 'field note' I examined in the previous chapter; this is how I now remember the events surrounding my dropping English. The narrative is divided into three parts; for ease of reference I follow each part with a discussion framed by discourse analysis. After these analyses I will draw the sections together, and offer my psychoanalytic reading of the narrative as a unit.

The Field Notes, Revised, with Feeling, First Part

> It is Grade 11. I'm a shy and awkward adolescent, definitely not one of the popular girls. I get high grades; I wear glasses; I think of myself as overweight; I have no boyfriend and I don't expect ever to have one. I have a small circle of female friends, though, some of whom do have boyfriends, and all of whom have dated. Except me.
>
> A rumour circulates in the school, that a male teacher might be having sexual relations with some girls in grades 11, 12, and 13 who are members of the after-school photography club he supervises. These girls, a group of five or six, are prettier than I, thinner, but no more popular with boys. They don't seem to care about being popular, though, and so are different not only from those like me but also from the girls who have dates every weekend.
>
> It is 1971, and there are two ways to go. While the rest of us experiment with curling irons, short skirts, red nail polish and crash diets, these young women are casual: their hair is perfectly straight, their wardrobes consist of blue jeans, T-shirts and sneakers; their faces are clear and makeup-free. They have been called

tomboys; they seem, to those of us with the curled hair and fishnet stockings, not to care about how they look. And instead of taking up sports or joining the drama club, whose teacher-supervisors are all female, they join the photography club, of which they are the only members, and the supervisor is a male English teacher.

When I hear the gossip, that in the photography clubroom there are nude pictures being taken, that kissing and perhaps more is going on, I believe it, absolutely and utterly without question. It comes from reliable sources, after all: graffiti in the girls' washroom; my friends, and an acquaintance who happens to be a former friend of the girls in question. My friends believe the stories too: 'It figures,' we say: 'Those girls were always weird.' We are disgusted: the male teacher is probably in his 30s or early 40s, to us an old man. The girls, we surmise, are immoral. We stay away from them in the cafeteria, in the halls, on the bus. We decide we hate the teacher too.

I think about their alleged transgressions quite a lot, talk about them with my friends. But where my friends seem to lose interest after a few weeks, I take pains to walk by the room where the photography club meets, its door always closed, on days when I know a meeting is taking place. I contemplate joining, but do not. I watch the group of girls in the cafeteria, eating lunch at 'their' table. I do this for several months. Pretty soon I too start wearing blue jeans to school.

Just now my thinking about this text is informed by two interrelated sets of discourses: the Foucauldian, with its focus on power relations, and the feminist, in particular views of how gender and sexuality are constructed in school settings. Since a method 'anchored in close analyses of texts' (Gouveia, 2005, p. 231) does not seem to mesh fully with my narratives, which are to varying degrees reconstructed versions of revisited events, that precise kind of analysis is not my principal goal the way it would be if, say, the narrative were an actual contemporaneous diary entry. Still, with that disclaimer, I do want to attend to some of the language within the narrative – in particular to certain words and phrases I (remember having) used at the time of the events. For the time being, I consider the circumstances and the events themselves in relation to the discourses that inform and are reflected by them, in order to make connections to the larger question, in education, of what teachers and learners ought to, and can, know of one another (Kaplan, 1993, p. 174; Granger, 2004, p. 119). A little later I will also consider the particular textual form of the narratives, especially the fictionalized counsellor's notes version, in a more explicit exploration of the text qua text.

Several related stories, or storied moments, come together in the narrative: the rumours and my response to them discussed in the first section above, as well as the refusal of learning enacted by my dropping English and the events on graduation night, which are coming up shortly. All of these are told from my perspective (I repeat: as remembered, and with the caveat implicit in that). As well, several discourses seem to be at work informing the situation, the events, and the narrative itself. There are normative and heteronormative discourses of gender, masculinity and femininity, and sexuality, which position identities such as 'female' and 'popular' in specific ways and which, at the time of the events, both grounded my perceptions of myself, the other girls, and the male teacher, and made the rumours believable – made possible, in fact, their very existence *as* rumours. Additionally, discourses of exclusion and marginalization perform the related work of determining who is outside of the normative categories. And various discourses of power – denied and permitted, taken and given – function alongside resistance to them in each of the narrative moments.

Beginning with the first narrated moment – the camera-club rumours – I see that the discursive construction of *popularity*, for instance, stems from a particular concept of femininity that recalls Foucault's notion of 'technology of the body' (1977a, p. 26) as a force that kneads the corporeal into particular shapes. Here, their implicit refusal to perform femininity in expected ways positions the camera-club girls at the edge of recognizability as adolescent females. They do not dress or look like the popular girls; they do not date classmates; they do not seem to care about being popular as other girls do. In this narrative, and in its founding circumstances, of the 'two ways to go' these young women choose the 'wrong' way – a failure to fit in that marks and marginalizes them.

The gossip about the photography club is another site of marginalization made by, and a reinforcement of, then-current understandings of femaleness and femininity. Simply put, in the imaginations of their peers the camera-club girls have no other alternative. Here we see enacted the heteronormative discourse of sexuality as curiously at once both appropriate and inappropriate. My friends and I were disgusted by the rumour that girls our age might be engaging in sexual activity with a teacher. But so pervasive was the presumption of heterosexuality that any other possibility was unthinkable.

Again I emphasize that there was no evidence beyond the gossip that any of the events it alleged ever took place. What is, in hindsight, quite startling to me is that at the time those alleged events could only be imagined (or at least, by myself and my friends they could only be articulated) in one particular way: as a seduction by the male teacher in which the female students cooperated – unsurprisingly for my friends and me because *those girls* were 'always weird.' Well, perhaps not *that* weird: such was the discursive strength of compulsory heterosexuality (Rich, 1986) that the imaginative possibility for what at that time, and in that setting would have been – and indeed may still be (Bay-Cheng, 2003) – deemed utterly transgressive activity, such as sexual expression between or among those female students themselves, simply did not exist.

Here I also observe the curious doubling of discourses that set these 'other' students apart from me yet also connected us. They *weren't* like me, with my nail polish, miniskirts, and curled hair – in fact, in that secondary school in a quite homogeneous 1970s suburb of a Canadian city, even wearing jeans to school, while permitted, was still unusual. And jeans might well have been legible to an adolescent mind of that period, swimming in the heteronormative river of television sit-coms and Seventeen magazine (it is certainly legible to me now in hindsight), as a stereotypical 'sign' of an 'unfeminine' girl (read: Lesbian). At the same time though, those girls *were* (or were presumed to be) like me: however unorthodox and even 'disgusting' their sexual expression (as I imagined it) might have seemed, it was always and only (imaginable as) a *hetero*sexuality.[2] So pervasive was this presumption that, although the gossip presumed the girls to have allowed and participated in their putative seduction, had another version been told – of seduction refused – it could have made sense only with the attribution of a particular version of morality, and not because of a lack of heterosexual interest on the students' part.

As narrator I disclose my own marginal status in the story. By the terms of the discourse that defines and legitimizes a particular kind of adolescent girl I too am an outsider: no boyfriend, studious, myopic. Nor can I be a camera-club girl. External to all cliques, I am homeless, in a double marginalization, self-imposed in the narrative to be sure, but grounded nevertheless in my remembered sense of belonging to neither group. That homelessness persists through this first part of the narrative.

I recognize my own implication in the marginalization that is performed discursively by the narrative itself. I recall Freire's remarks (2005, p. 47) on how 'prescription ... transform[s] the consciousness of the person prescribed to into one that conforms with the prescriber's consciousness,' and wonder whether part of my apparent willingness to accept as given the rumours and gossip about my fellow students might have arisen from my perception of my own marginalized status: that is, whether I took up the position Freire calls 'sub-oppressor' with 'an attitude of "adhesion" ' to the discourses that pushed me to the margins and which, in turn, I called on, though unaware, in order to reinforce the relatively greater marginalization of the girls who were even less typical, less 'normal' than I.

Feel-ed/Felt-notes, Second Part

> When the time comes in May or so to choose the next year's courses, I realize that Grade 12 English will be taught by the reviled teacher. And I make a decision. I, who have always loved reading and books, who had read every book in my elementary school's library by the time I was 10 years old, who spent my summer vacations reading from morning until night, stopping only for trips to the library and periods of experimentation with poetry and short-story writing, decide that I hate English: Shakespeare is stupid, poetry is pointless, fiction in general is irrelevant, short stories are particularly boring, and all creative writing is a waste of time.
>
> Never an assertive daughter, I nonetheless do not ask but rather inform my mother that my chosen course load for grades 12 and 13 will not include English. I know this surprises, worries and angers her. And it worries my guidance counsellor, who advises me that without the English credit I may have trouble getting accepted into university. But I don't care.
>
> And so I have my way. But for the last two years of secondary school I am an anomaly: nearly everyone, except the few boys who take only math and science courses, and those students who take industrial arts if they are male and secretarial courses if they are female, is enrolled in English. Not I. I do not study Romeo and Juliet in Grade 12, or Hamlet in Grade 13. And I do not miss it, not a bit. I am defiant in my resolve; I have taken a stand; I do not want, or need, or like, English. Period.

Chapter 2's Foucauldian and feminist readings of the 'counsellor's notes' argue that the counsellor is dually constructed as knowledgeable and therefore authoritative within the institution but also subject to, or object of, institutional authority and demands. I, the student, am likewise ambiguously positioned.[3] First, I am a child, a body subject to the control that hegemonic institutions such as education require of all child-bodies, and thereby subaltern to the knowledge and authority of the counsellor. At the same time, however, I am a young adult, possessed of the right the institution has bestowed on me to determine my own course of study. This combination of a little power and a lot of control renders me dangerous: to the counsellor's authority, which

I threaten by actually using the decision-making power I have been given; to the institution, grounded as it is in discourses (which I implicitly challenge) of what constitutes a fit and proper body of (and a body for) knowledge; and, it would seem, even to myself and my future – if the counsellor's words about the potential consequences of my decision are to be believed.

In addition, I am positioned by discourses of gender (especially gender-in-education) which, given certain lexical choices in the counsellor's notes, both implicitly and explicitly mark me as transgressive because I do not perform femininity in expected ways. My transgression is itself ambiguous, embodying various forms of resistance to and compliance with the discourses at play. In dropping English I seem to be resisting the hegemonic construction of the good girl student. And yet, as set out in Chapter 2, in waiting until the curriculum allowed the decision, and in having my mother sign the permission form (thereby effecting the transgression in legal ways), I am performing as a body at least somewhat 'docile' and 'disciplined' and 'obedient' (Foucault, 1977a).

Three things stand out in the now larger and more detailed narrative that we might call a statement of (alleged) affairs. First is the affective component, silent in both first and second versions, which arises out of the current variant's movement past the alibi of its earlier iterations – 'I don't like English' – to proffer a context for that claim of dislike. In Foucauldian terms I read that explanation as grounded in the English teacher's and the camera-club members' putative refusal of, or resistance to, their own discursively determined positions, namely as a male educator and adolescent female students. The same affective indicator – my recognition that *I do not want to be a student of that teacher* – might be interpreted in one feminist view as a political act of resistance: a refusal to support or endorse (even implicitly) behaviour that seems (even allegedly) potentially exploitive or otherwise inappropriate.[4]

A second point of resistance paradoxically locates itself in my continued relegation of myself to the margins of the constructed category of girl – or more precisely *good* girl, or *good* student, or *good girl student* – that happens as a result of the choice to discontinue my study of English. As noted in my reading of the first part of the narrative, I am already at the margins of high school life. But in not quite fitting the popular girl category I have nevertheless continued to fit into another: good student. Now that I am not taking English, though, I have subverted that category too: I am doubly Other.

Third, this version of the narrative, in detailing the clash between my historical love of literature and my stated loathing of the subject, tells the reader something is going on here.[5] Both the counsellor and my mother are surprised at my dropping a subject I have always loved and excelled at. Feminist theories might here read dropping English as a self-subordinating act: a use of personal power that has the counterproductive effect of denying a self, or a refusal of the discursively constructed role of *good girl-student* that in fact silences my true interests, the pursuit of which would coincidentally also keep me, so far as grades and discursive expectations are concerned, in my proper place. In refusing learning, the acceptance of which would mark a likewise acceptance of my role as a particular kind of female, I am explicitly (if unconsciously) choosing to make trouble.

That choice is a complicated one, however, because by not fully explaining my reasons for it I capitulate to another construction: the *good-girl student*, the student who does not make trouble. In Foucauldian terms I discipline my own body into a politically strategic yet mundane silence: dropping English, especially without articulating reasons for the decision, makes me, in one way, a bad student – but in another way I am still a good girl.

Felt, and Noted, Third Part

Some two years after dropping English, in the autumn after Grade 13, I am a first-year university student (still not taking English). I am asked to give the valedictory address at the October graduation ceremony. I am pleased, but anxious, as I am about writing essays for my political science and anthropology courses. I wait until the last minute to compose my speech, beginning late in the afternoon on the day of the ceremony, after I have hemmed my dress and had my hair done.

That night, my name called, I walk nervously across the stage to the podium. My mouth is dry; my lips stick to my teeth. Out of the corner of my eye I see the hated English teacher on the far side of the stage. His face is a blur. But somehow it galvanizes me. Forgetting my stage-fright, I begin.

My speech is a great success. I begin with a humorous enumeration of many of our teachers' quirks (not that teacher, though – he gets no mention at all) that has the audience laughing long and hard. I make a typical serious shift to the big open question of the students' futures, move to an extended metaphor, somewhat poetic if also a little trite, that compares the lives of those graduating to a sea voyage, and I exit the stage to sustained applause. It is my most popular moment in all of high school.

Leaving the stage I have to walk past the English teacher. As I pass him, he smiles, and says, 'Really well done. I liked your metaphor at the end.'

I am furious. Don't talk to me about metaphors, I think, don't you talk to me about anything. But I say nothing. I cannot speak, and I certainly cannot thank him for his words. My heart beats, hard and fast. I leave the auditorium and walk quickly to the girls' washroom. There, in a cubicle, I rage and sob silently until I feel calmer.

The ceremony over, I rejoin my friends. At the after-party I drink champagne for the first time. Later, I lose the velvet evening bag my mother has lent me.

This apparent epilogue to the story of my dropping English generally reinforces my feminist and Foucauldian interpretations of the preceding portions. Most of what I see enacted in the events as described here reads as if informed by, and either reproductive of or resistant to (and sometimes both), discourses of power that inhere in the institution of education as a whole, in the graduation ceremony in particular, and in my relationship with both English (as a subject, or object of study) and the English teacher as a subject/object of another kind.

Here again we have the institution as the powerful scene of control. But power and control here are, as ever in Foucault's schema, mutable and fluctuating. I was invited to give a speech – an honour, but not a right. The invitation granted me a legitimacy, both through and for discourse. I was spoken to, and given the power to speak: repositioned as the *good girl student* once more. At the same time I had the right to refuse that honour. I did not, even though I undertook it with anxiety and even trepidation.

Moreover, no one read my speech beforehand, so I might have said anything at all. However, my words were quite conventional, a last-gasp attempt at fitting in, at high-school popularity, at teacher approval, at performing, once more, the *good girl student*. Except, that is, for my deliberate exclusion from it (and thus silencing *in* it) of the English teacher whose course I had refused to take: a deliberate move, as I now read it, that used the power I had been given to speak in a way not unlike my having waited until Grade 11 to fill out the correct forms, thereby making dropping English both possible and legal. That is, once again I followed the rules only to break them in the end.

I broke them in two ways: by speaking, and by silence. I had dropped English, had been warned about the consequences of that choice. And yet, there I was, chosen to speak and speaking, poetically even, using metaphor, being congratulated for that use of metaphor (one construct

I had learned in English before dropping it!) by the teacher I had not mentioned – and, perhaps most significantly, refusing to respond to his words: refusing, to be specific, both his English-teacher words and him as an English teacher. Thus in those two moments, during and after my speech, he was silenced by me – by my silence in relation to him. In that sense my valedictory address was a victory speech.

Of course, the boundaries of discourse are blurry; the idea of perfect closure, perfect victory, is elusive, for after the speech and the applause, after my angry silence in the face of the teacher's congratulatory words, there were also silent tears. There was still silence.

Reading the Field/Feel-ed/Felt Notes

This tripartite version of my memory of dropping English is the fullest and truest so far. It is even narrated in the present tense: not deliberately, I hasten to add – that is simply how it came to me, and how clear the memory now is.[6] And when I read the narrative, I seem to feel the moment again, for the body remembers: my lack of popularity; the scent and gleam of red nail polish; my disgust at the alleged behaviour of the 'weird' girls; the silent hallway outside the closed door of the darkroom; the tight, tense resolve in my decision to drop English. And later, the applause for my speech; my silent rage, and then tears, at being spoken to by that teacher whose course I had rejected; my mother's anger, earlier at my decision to drop English and then later at the loss of her handbag. It is as if it all happened yesterday.

And in a certain sense it did: it happened on the quite recent day when, after more than 30 years, I actually set my memories down in writing. In addition to its visceral *felt*-ness, in the sense in which writing it has made the memory, or at least secured the story of the memory in my consciousness, it is a very immediate experience.

That it is the truest version so far does not mean it is the whole truth. Perhaps part of what Kermode (1995) means when he writes of autobiography and memory as inimical to one another is that memory (in Freudian theory) works, thanks to repression and other mechanisms or processes of defence, as a means of forgetting what we cannot bear to know. What we consciously remember, or 'profess to remember,' is 'so far from the truth that it is precisely what we have devised to protect us from the truth' (Kermode, 1995, p. 42). That is, our conscious memories are actually symptomatic or representative of – or a screen that conceals – those which outside of therapy we cannot normally recall: the events we need

to forget; the material that, for Phillips (1994), repression and other defence mechanisms have allowed us to retain through elimination or
'disowning.' Moreover, what we repress is not just events themselves
(that is, the content of memory or the memories per se) but also, and
more crucially, the desires, or traumas, or aspects of the self that inhere
in those memories, which are 'felt to be incompatible with whatever [we
believe is] ... good or desirable' in ourselves, and which, if really remembered, would come intolerably to light (Phillips, 1994, p. 22).

I grant Kermode this: what I present here is what I *profess to remember*,
not the whole truth. Yet I do not take this to mean (nor is Kermode suggesting) that it holds no truth at all. For many years after I stopped taking English I could not have written the memory of the event as I have
done here. I was consciously aware only of the facts-only version of
Chapter 1. This suggests that there can be a shift, and we can come over
time to a fuller remembering. This can happen through various means,
including, perhaps, the associations of psychoanalysis as well as self-
reflection outside the analytic setting: specifically, for me, through engagement in educational research. And it can be encouraged to happen
by hints, and some of those hints may come in the very process of writing autobiographically.

Kermode's explicit point seems to be that autobiography and the psychoanalytic concept of memory are incompatible: that while the former
aims to reconstruct a life, to make it 'hang together,' the latter, as part of
the psychoanalytic project, invites the analysand to remember his life
'only to forget it as completely as possible' (1995, p. 43). Throughout his
essay he seems implicitly to be inviting that very connection, between
writing one's life and the 'excavation' Freud proposes, in which 'the es-
sentials are preserved' and in fact it is unlikely that 'any psychical structure can really be the victim of total destruction' (Freud, 1937b, p. 260).
Kermode posits autobiography as dependent on 'the action of memory
which may be *memory of memories*' (1995, p. 47; my italics), a claim that
resonates closely with Freud's mystic writing-pad, and even with the
re-visioning of deferred action: the psychoanalytic ideas that conceptualize the self as a perpetually dynamic, constantly recursive, continually
re-written and re-edited series of iterations. Further, he observes two su-
perficially contradictory phenomena: on one hand, the meeting of 'doubles of past and present.' and, on the other hand, the space between the
autobiographer and the life being recorded, as in Wordsworth's lines 'I
cannot paint / What then I was' (cited in Kermode, 1995, pp. 47–9). And
he ends by describing Wordsworth's autobiographical work as a deep,

complex 'making of the past of the present ... recording, combining, and sometimes, alas, evading the truths of the selves that make a self' (p. 50).

The third version of my narrative fills in some of the gaps, for instance by offering an explanation for why the good student turns bad. But there are other silences, other absences: my inability (or refusal) to articulate my reasons for my choice to either the counsellor or my family; the marginalization of the photography club members, and the deeper, if more subtle, silence of individuals and groups whose participation in education is compromised or refused, a silence enforced by discourses that relegate them to the margins. Here Kermode's evaded truths are the silences that paradoxically both escape from and live in narration, that circle outside and haunt a narrative, however many versions we might produce of it and however full or complete or final we might imagine those versions to be. I turn now to my psychoanalytic reading, first of these remembered events, and then of the overlapping questions of chronology and retelling.

Psychoanalysis Reads

My concern, still, is what is silent in the narrative. The second version fills in some of the spaces of the first, and correspondingly, the third version fills in some of the gaps in the second. But even the third version is not final, not complete. Something lurks below the surface.

That lurking thing is what psychoanalytic theory is for. My reading of cultural and institutional discourses of femininity, sexuality, knowledge, power, and their relations to one another considers how those discourses have worked on and through me, as they work on and through all of us, at some times allowing speech and at others demanding silence. A psychoanalytic reading shifts the lens onto the individual, to look at how we perform the work of speaking and keeping silent, positioning and re-positioning identity (Todd, 2003b), finding and making a home and a self in and with the world. Psychoanalytic theory does not forget that the world comes to us with socially informed discursive commands, assertions, and insinuations, but it insists on an ongoing and bidirectional negotiation between the self and the social.

Even theories that assert the primacy of the social in individual development and meaning-making allow for individual-social interaction. From Mead's claim that it is by knowing others' experiences of us and thus becoming 'objects to ourselves' (1934, p. 138) to Ehrman and Dörnyei's contention that '*intra*-personal processes are an important factor in all *inter*-personal processes' (1998, p. 13, italics in original), it seems that to whatever extent the social makes the individual, something exists that undergoes the making: something that is there to be made. Indeed, to take the social constructionist view to its most extreme, even if the human mind were nothing but a blank slate, a blank slate is, after all, something. In Lemke's words:

> Our *personal identity* is constructed by foregrounding certain patterns that we make in our inner dialogue and feelings as we set them against the background of what we are taught to take as "outer" events. Needless to say, what is "inner" and what is "outer," what the repertory of human emotions is taken to be . . . and the nature of "inner dialogues" as activity structures, all differ from culture to culture and . . . even from one biographical individual to another. (1995, p. 89; italics in original)

And so, while I find the theories of discourse analysis I have drawn on to read the narratives very useful and informative, for me they do not quite cover the question of the 'inner dialogue and feelings' that Lemke refers to. Psychoanalysis, with its tender but provocative and sometimes even frightening project of uncovering what lies beneath, invites us to consider what silences might be concealed by the disgusted, angry, and sad responses laid out in the narrative.

At a basic level, one might read in my storied memory envy (of the other girls, both the popular girls and those in the camera club), a wish to belong (to either group), or anger and hurt (expressed in my refusal to take English). Even such a common-sense interpretation, by recognizing in my actions the presence of non-conscious wishes or thoughts or desires, constitutes more than just a reading: it is a *reading into*. A reading that is not a reading into may be possible, if only just, for a stranger to the text, although I would argue, as would psychoanalysis and as might Grumet (1990) or Felman (1993), that it would be unlikely. For me, such a reading is quite impossible.

But a reading *into* is also a reading *from*. We are always using some hermeneutic, even when we think we are using common sense or intuition, for those too, whatever their specific principles or qualities, are interpretive strategies. Still, interpretation is tricky. Having written these narratives long after the events took place, I have, however unwittingly, already performed an interpretation. Too, I write from the nachträglich place of having done some personal and therapeutic working-through of the events, and that has also led to insight. Some of this insight has really snuck up on me, though: it is quite startling how (in my remembering of these events) the sudden shift to hating literature took place, given my previous attachments to it. And that this shift remained unquestioned for so long is itself evidence of a kind of psychical conspiracy with the self – a case of 'know[ing] what is on our minds, but not on the other minds inside us' (Phillips, 1999, p. xx) – for the fact is that in my various post-secondary educational endeavours English literature has taken a fairly prominent place (including courses on Victorian novels – the highlight of a nursing program I never completed – and medieval literature taken purely for interest).

My reading is perhaps a little less tentative than it might otherwise be. But it is still (and in psychoanalysis can only ever be) speculative. I see this as an advantage rather than as a limitation, however, for I want to invite other, more open readings that allow new questions to be asked and new conversations, even speculations, to be had about what troubles education and its participants.

From the slightly altered perspective of psychoanalysis, that is, the (inner) individual as engaged in relating with its (outer) objects, or, put differently, in dialogue with the social, I ask my literature-loving-but-(temporarily)-leaving self – silenced, speaking, and silenced again by a difficulty that seems to be about an indignant anger at some perceived immorality – these questions: What was the nature of its difficulty? That is, what was it that was being silenced, in the moment of refusing the English literature course (or perhaps more properly of refusing the teacher of that course)? What was I using the silence that inaugurated that refusal, and the silence that accompanied it, to do? What, in short, did I think I was doing then – if thinking is even the right word – and what do I think *now* that I was doing back *then*? More broadly, how might such silent moments, and the related yet distinct silences in the *narration of* those moments, serve those who experience and narrate them? How, ultimately, might they speak in the service of some of education's persistent questions about how to do its work in useful and compassionate ways?

I do not have clear answers to these questions. But I do recognize now, long after the events, that the silences had much less to do with hating Shakespeare, or disliking the teacher, or even with disapproval per se of his alleged dalliances with students, than the narratives on their face might suggest. And I have come to this recognition partly through psychoanalytic theory. My story of dropping English, in its several iterations, peeks at a silent moment, or a series of such moments, that speak despite (and at times through) their silences to bring to light, or at least to remove partially from the shadows, some of what Britzman calls 'lost subjects' (1998, p. 19): psychic events in the context of a life in education that the self fears, resists, and may refuse outright, but which keep returning, perhaps many times, perhaps in less intolerable forms, to nettle, disquiet, and demand, and to do so in spite of all our resistance, re-making, re-working, and re-worrying.

Psychoanalysis Reads Resistance

It is important to distinguish between resistance as a political or pedagogical act and resistance as a psychical event. In the educational context, 'resistance' commonly refers either to critical thinking about (or rejection of) hegemonic versions of knowledge, or to a kind of double-negative version of itself: a refusal, by individuals or groups, of efforts arising from that counter-hegemonic thinking that attempt to galvanize them to respond to, and act in and on, the social world – in effect a resistance-to-resistance. In psychoanalysis 'resistance' refers to anything an individual (in a clinical setting the analysand) says or does that impedes access to the unconscious. Freud explains this two ways: earlier, in his 1895 work with Breuer, *Studies on Hysteria* (in Breuer & Freud, 1974), as a phenomenon in which material is held from consciousness by a 'repelling force' originating in the repressed material itself and inhibiting 'the subject's full acceptance' of it (Laplanche & Pontalis, 1973, p. 395); and later as a means by which the ego that performed repression's initial work defends against the emergence of repressed material, in order to 'continue to enjoy its [the ego's] carefully crafted and, in many ways, useful symptoms' (Pitt & Britzman, 2003, p. 769).

Both kinds of resistance can be manifested as silence. The learners who refuse to participate in or appear to ignore anti-racist or anti-sexist curricula; the teacher who cannot speak out in support of a gay student; the analysand who misses sessions, or who dutifully appears but 'has nothing to say ... [and] is silent and declares that nothing occurs to him' (Freud, 1914a, p. 150); the students Pitt observes refusing the 'subject positions that Women's Studies offers as sites of student/teacher recognition' (2003, p. 61); the 'secret selves' of the authors whose narratives I explored in my own earlier work (2004) – all of us are good at our own resistances. We find many ways to be silent. And so perhaps the distinction is not as clear-cut as it seems at first glance.

At the very least perhaps thinking about one kind of resistance can inform thinking about the other, for both have to do with difficulty. In resistance to hegemony, or to counter-hegemonic thinking, there is the problem of dislodging views so deeply held as to seem natural and necessary, while in psychoanalysis the problem is one of allowing entry to consciousness of thoughts that consciousness itself might deem unnatural. There seems to be an almost direct parallel between resistance to the counter-hegemonic ideas presented by critical theory and the Freudian idea of resistance as either a 'repelling force' or an ego defence – in both cases there is a refusal to see differently, think differently, break open old structures, and let in a new light.

Grounding her discussion in the difficulties individuals have with counter-hegemonic education, Pitt (2003, p. 51) asks, 'How do we understand the dynamics of refusing knowledge?' In my own story the learning refused is anything but anti-hegemonic – English was the most entrenched subject area in the curriculum extant at the time of my secondary education (the early 1970s), with Shakespeare and other white male authors infiltrated only minimally, as I recall, by two Canadian women: Margaret Laurence and Susanna Moodie. While on the surface my resistance was to the subject matter, that was of course not the real resistance. Although what Pitt here addresses is resistance to knowledge, mine seems more a resistance to *self*-knowledge – and it seems to locate itself within the psyche, or perhaps between the psyche and the social, in that it constitutes a clumsy and troubled working-through of my own very conflicted morality which, had I been able to articulate it, might have been spoken thus:

'Those' relations between teachers and students are wrong.
So I don't have them.
But because I don't have them, I want them.
But I can't have them, so I won't want them.

But I want them.

I can't have those relations that I want but don't want.
It is wrong – I am wrong – to want them.

This is what my conscious mind cannot tolerate, in Pitt's words, 'a psychoanalytic story [that] locates resistance where the subject meets the otherness of her own unconscious knowledge' (2003, p. 54). The next line of my little monologue might be, *I won't think about that*. And with that refusal it is buried away from my conscious mind, screened by my contrived loathing for the subject.[7] The conflicts and ambivalences, threats and promises that lead to psychical resistances of the kind my narrative hints at cannot be fully located in the relations between me as an individual and the immediate social context to which they seem to be attached. They spring also from my own particularities – of history, personality, psyche – which, granted, may also have been informed by the world that made me and in which I continually make and re-make myself, but which are also constituted out of earlier versions of themselves.

Psychoanalysis Reads Repression

Let us leave behind the first version, the facts-only summary of my narrative, and work with the second and third versions to look at how what is silenced in the counsellor's notes is made a little more audible in the first-person version set out in this chapter. This latter version, a kind of recursive 'symptomatic reading' (Althusser & Balibar, 1972) of its predecessor, reveals what the former keeps hidden: the emotionally laden detail of the events. By filling in some of that predecessor's holes this version speaks to some of its silences, especially in the area of affect. But what it does not address, and what therefore becomes *its* silence, is the source of or impetus for its particular responses to events: it needs its own symptomatic reading, and psychoanalysis is happy to oblige.

Read psychoanalytically, my narrative becomes a story of repression, that subset of defence which for psychoanalysis is the work the self performs of pushing into the unconscious 'representations (thoughts, images, memories) which are bound to an instinct' (Laplanche & Pontalis, 1973, p. 390). Instincts (and their representations) are repressed when to satisfy them would risk other problems – or 'unpleasure' – perhaps at a later time. Such representations are generally taken to refer to thoughts which, if expressed either to the self or to the world outside the self, would bring shame or guilt, or to traumatic events which are defined 'by [their] intensity, by the subject's incapacity to respond adequately to [them]' (p. 465). Certainly, there is a legitimate social and institutional reason why I cannot speak the truth – the truth, that is, as I know it in that narrative moment, namely that there are rumours, that I believe the rumours, and that I want to drop English because I disapprove of the activities the rumours allege. Psychoanalysis reads my emphatic statements about hating English as the voice of my unconscious, speaking evidence of repression. That is, the statement and the emotions it articulates function as a redirecting – for my mother, the counsellor, and me – of something which, in the event, my conscious self cannot quite bear to know or to admit, but which at the same time my unconscious insists on making known, insists on speaking-by-not-speaking.

What might that something be?

If dropping English is a conscious act that hides an unconscious ruse, a way of getting around a difficulty without getting through it – and without articulating it – we might think about the disapproval which functions as a reason for this subterfuge as itself an unconscious feint: specifically, a negation.

Negation is a defensive move that signals the partial rise to consciousness of something that cannot (yet) be tolerated fully by the conscious self: it is a 'lifting of the repression, though not ... an acceptance of what is repressed' (Freud, 1925, p. 236); a hint at something other than itself. We might read my terse expression of loathing for the subject as a negation: 'I hate English' and 'I hate the English teacher' might have meant several things, but what they most definitely did not mean (and as noted earlier there is empirical evidence to support this view) was that I hated either English or the teacher. So dropping English, by giving me a new story to tell, paved the way for a later recognition of the something-below-the-surface that I could not articulate in that moment.

Exactly what was that?

Psychoanalysis Reads Desire

A single clear psychoanalytic definition of desire, or in strict Freudian terms the 'wish,'[8] is impossible to pin down: Laplanche and Pontalis (1973) call it a concept 'too fundamental to be circumscribed' but note that it refers in the main to 'unconscious wishes, bound to indestructible infantile signs.' Lacanian psychoanalysis sees desire as dwelling in the space between need and demand, and attaching to neither (Laplanche & Pontalis, 1973, pp. 481–3), while in the Freudian framework wishes attach to memory-traces as something more than physical needs; their true content is often repressed, but it surfaces in disguised form in dreams and fantasies, or in symptoms such as negations.

Moreover, desire is not just a psychoanalytic term. Here I am considering various desires: for learning and for belonging, and the related yet distinct desires of sexuality. My next question becomes this: precisely what desires are repressed in the narrative of dropping English? There are several layers to this discussion, and precision may not be altogether possible. Still, I will try.

On the face of the narrative we read the desire to belong, to fit in, with one or another group of adolescents. But that straightforward wish does not account for the withdrawal from a once-loved academic subject-as-object, or for the hatred and disgust I felt for the English teacher. Negation, in psychoanalysis, offers a clue to the ways in which claims of hating the teacher and the subject might have meant something other than what their explicit content suggested. Here I propose that part of what *I-hate-English* and *I-hate-the-teacher* was saying-without-speaking can be traced through several negatory moves:

I hate English and I hate the teacher.
I love English *but* I hate the teacher.
I love English *and* I love the teacher, *but* he doesn't love me.

Harper (1997b), in looking at how encounters with new ways of writing may disrupt adolescent girls' previously held ideas about the self, calls on A. Freud's pedagogical question about 'which type of adolescent upheaval is best suited to leading to the most satisfactory type of adult life' (A. Freud, 1971, p. 47). Harper relates adolescence's increasing genital sexual impulses, and the stress they can place on ego defences, to Freud's thinking on the question of the child's movement into 'the major psychic/social project of adolescence, that is, separation from the parents and the search for substitutes' (p. 140) and away from the family of origin and its parental attachments (p. 150). As Harper points out this move bristles with difficulty: first because the adolescent's position is ambiguous, since she is both almost an adult and also still dependent on the parent – and second, because her work is ultimately, in a psychoanalytic sense, futile. This is because the desire for a love-object is not merely a product of hormonal urges, but rather the manifestation of a wish to re-acquire the unity of self and other that was lost in infancy (when the child came to know herself as separate from the world): specifically, the primary separation of inside and outside that Freud called the first judgment, which equates *self* with *good* and *other* with *bad*, and in which 'what is bad, what is alien to the ego

and what is external are . . . identical' (Freud, 1925, p. 237). The impossibility of satisfying this desire can be part of the reason for the adolescent's capriciousness, unpredictability, even explosiveness.

Identification is important here as 'the operation . . . whereby the
human subject is constituted' through a choice of object modeled on
'earlier objects, such as his parents or people around him' (Laplanche &
Pontalis, 1973, p. 206). In the Freudian framework the heterosexual
adolescent identifies with the parent of the same sex, and looks for
opposite-sex love-objects. While I agree with Harper's assessment of
Freud's position (albeit reflective of his time) as overly categorical vis-
à-vis the notion of the primary object of desire as necessarily embodied
by the mother, I do find useful the notion of the importance of finding
an extra-familial substitute for the father-or-equivalent.

Of course, all this work of identification and substitute-searching
happens outside of consciousness. But it seems reasonable to me to
read my rather strong reaction to the rumours of teacher-student relationships as arising from something more than a mere sense of inappropriateness. This is what I mean by the third move – *I love English,
and I love the teacher, but he doesn't love me.*

My conscious (and at the time of these events unmet) desires were
for sexual experiences with boys my own age. But I did not belong
to the popular girls group, which might have brought some of those
satisfactions. Perhaps this side-by-side movement – the psychical shift
away from the family and toward a sexual other, alongside my perception of other girls as having achieved such a connection – can be
viewed as causing a conflation of desires. The teacher became for me
an unattainable object. Triply so, in fact: because he had chosen and
been chosen by the camera-club girls (even if only allegedly); because
I could not imagine myself as a member of that group, and because, if
I had previously imagined teachers as out of bounds to students, the
(newly perceived) fact was that they were off limits only to *me*. And
so, in this model, the disapproval I expressed obliquely by dropping
English was actually a cover for a paradoxical mix of disgust at behaviour I thought wrong, of my own contradictory desire to be that kind of
object and to participate in that wrong behaviour, and of envy because
I could do neither. My claim here is that rather than an identification
with the English teacher it was a kind of *non-* or *anti-*identification that
I perceived unconsciously as having been thrust upon me, and which
became a problem from the point of view of ego – a piece of the work of
moving into adulthood that I was prevented from accomplishing. And

my response to this perceived refusal on the part of the teacher (and by extension his teaching subject) was to refuse him (and it) in return. If he didn't love me, I wouldn't love him – an alternative expression of which might be:

The teacher disgusts me.
I love the teacher.
Therefore, I disgust me.

It seems, then, that what was repressed were not just the rumours, nor the (alleged) reality of their content. Rather, it was a second reality that that first putative one raised in me: my own desires. The rumours forced that repressed content to hint at itself through the negation, before burying it again below consciousness, where it became silent once more. But *I* was not altogether silent. A complete silence would have looked quite different: I could have kept my mouth shut. So what did dropping English do for me? And to me?

Martusewicz tells of her eager childhood self experiencing 'two kinds of love and desire . . . one a strong love of the world, a desire to know it . . . the other a *desire to be loved,* affirmed *because* I want to know this world' (1997, p. 98; italics in original). She further remarks on how 'the violent effects of certain forms of desire turn us away from the conditions necessary for education' (p. 99). One consequence of my unmet desires – or more accurately of their exposure, albeit partial, to consciousness – was my flight from their source (that is, the English-teacher-as-object) and thereby from a particular set of possibilities for learning (English the subject-as-object): my flight, that is, from answers to questions in which, like Martusewicz (p. 101), I sought my self. It seems to me that the moment of deciding to drop English (both teacher/object and subject/object) marked the beginning of a *not-wanting* engendered by my perception of that self as unwanted, even unwant-*able:* I was not wanted, could not be wanted, and so I stopped wanting. Removing myself from English put me out of harm's way, by allowing me to refuse to look at the object-that-could-not-be-mine, but it made me grow silent too: silent on the subject of English, and silent on the subject of my own silence. And most of all, silent *as* the subject of my desires.

Turning to the final section of this version, I notice a comment in Harper (1997b, p. 143) that leads me to the somewhat tangential but not irrelevant question of language as at once a key to gender identity

(Kaplan, 1991, cited in Harper, 1997b, p. 143) and, in Lacanian terms, that which 'turns subjects into human and social beings.' Having looked earlier (2004) at the question of losses and gains that inhere in both psyche and identity in relation to the acquisition of language, I find a curious resonance among three layers: first, the Freudian concept of identification; second, Phillips's claim that acquiring language involves both 'giving things up ... to secure the supposedly more viable satis-factions of maturity' and 'leav[ing] more than one home ... every time [one] speaks' (1999, pp. 39, 42); and third, the fact that it was an English teacher who seems to have figured into my anti-identificatory (if ulti-mately thwarted) leave-taking.

I did not lose a language by dropping high-school English, but I did lose a beloved aspect of that language temporarily, perhaps, for it seems to me that my moment on the valedictory stage marks the start of my return to speaking – a return, in a way, to both the subject and the *sub-ject*. Yet the return was but partial, for while I gave my speech to the audience, I was utterly unable to speak to the teacher.

There is a punch line to this. I confess some hesitation in raising it, partly because it may seem to cross a line between – to poach a little from Winnicott (1963b, p. 63) – being concerned not with developing an argument, or even telling a story, but with psychotherapy, and partly because it raises a stereotype to which I have long objected (the troubled child from a 'broken home'). But I think it is worth mentioning, if only to remind us that even when a stereotype might seem to apply, there is 'always more to the story' (Britzman, 1998, p. 14).

Here it is: by the time the narrated events took place my father had been absent from my life for several years, suggesting that the iden-tification with the father that would normally 'diminish his status as a love object and force the search elsewhere' (Harper, 1997b, p. 151) might not have come to pass, such that my unconscious search might, in some sense, have been about finding a father to separate from. In the Freudian scenario the English teacher's status in my psyche is it-self doubled: he becomes at once both the possible-yet-impossible love-object choice for the daughter moving away from the family dynamic, and a substitute for the father whom that daughter ought to have been moving away *from*.

Oh, one more thing: my father was a teacher too. Of French, not English, but yes, he was a teacher.

Telling and Re-telling: The Same Old Story?

I turn now to consider how I have constructed the three versions of my story. Two questions most interest me in this meta-level reading: Why the earlier versions? Where have those come from, and why do I include them, if it is the third version, with its considerably expanded detail and its affective component, that matters?

The first version of my story conforms most fully to traditional masculinist discourse, in which, observes Bloom (1998, p. 6), any sign of 'fragmentation, conflict, ambiguity, messiness ... and changes in subjectivity' is taken to signal mental instability or weakness, and the lack of 'an enviable, unified (masculine) self.' In this discourse a student who drops a course is merely exercising a right, following up on a decision. But that version only conforms to a discourse of certainty and decisiveness precisely *because of* its brevity: more detail uncovers a messier and more complex subjectivity.

Moreover, such an interpretation is not all Bloom cares about. For both telling and *re*-telling matter: 'a story, as a social construction, can appear to change as if transformed into a different story when the narrator's ... subjectivity shifts, fragments, and becomes refigured' (Bloom 1998, pp. 62–3). The narrating self, a manifestation of the psychosocial whole that embodies both conscious and unconscious elements, is always in flux, making and remaking itself, and in conflict with what is outside – and yes, inside – itself. Bloom's feminist narrative analysis raises the problem of 'master scripts' wherein narratives reproduce hegemonically ordered silences rather than facilitating liberation from them (1998, p. 62). Calling on Sartre's 'progressive-regressive' method (1963), which honours this non-linearity and the back-and-forth re-editioning of a life's events, Bloom shows how narrative, by centralizing conflict and unmasking complexity and ambivalence, emphasizes 'becoming' (p. 65).

The second, counsellor's-notes version of my narrative nudges open the door to complexity. In recognizing the act of dropping English as a resistant, transgressive move, and in articulating that recognition through the counsellor's words, it goes beyond conventional closure, offering a subjectivity that challenges normative understandings of how a good girl student ought to behave. And yet the narrative, in form and content, invokes and privileges the authority of the counsellor. As well, although the decision may be an unconventional one, the apparent decisiveness of the student conforms to traditional expectations of the educational patriarchy of the time, rendering ambiguous the apparent *absence* of ambiguity. On balance, this version comes down on the side of normative discourses of femininity and power in the educational context.

For its part, the third version incorporates the same facts but goes a little further in recognizing my[9] agency and subverting what Bloom (1998) calls the master script's happy ending. Terminating contradictorily – with archetypally feminine tears and the loss of a symbol of femininity – this version fails to satisfy on normative grounds: there is no 'happily ever after' here, either within or outside of patriarchy.

Bloom explores feminist research methodologies through two respondents' narratives. 'Olivia' interests me more, for her telling and retelling of her story parallel my own in significant ways. Olivia relates how she became a role model for other women in the context of workplace sexual harassment. The first telling is utterly positive in tone, grounded in Olivia's acknowledged desire to represent herself as a 'feminist icon' (Bloom, 1998, p. 72). Bloom compares Olivia's first telling with a narrative 'master script' that requires Olivia to position herself as hero (p. 87). Olivia finds this version unsatisfying and incomplete and wants to retell it. That retelling relates not only a more complete story, but also its affective aspects, including her disappointment at a particular turn of events.

I wonder whether Olivia's position as hero in her first version might also be an unconscious attempt to ground her story in a discourse whose guiding principle can be described colloquially as 'making it in a man's world.' While my own narrative is not isomorphic with Olivia's – the conventions that press on me are related to the academic discourses and the procedures and protocols of the institution and the disciplines in which I work – it offers similar grist for the interpretive mill. That is, while I believe my narrative to be a potentially useful interpretive collecting place, a text that might invite ways to think about some interesting and important questions in education, I simultaneously feel a pull to conform to traditional academic form, in large part because of my status:[10] whatever I produce must 'accommodate' to 'constraints of form, of propriety, of proper academic demeanour and scholarly approach' (Miller, 1988, p. 488). My work, and I, must pass muster.

And so, it seems that in the previous chapter I subverted my own voice to write the masculinist (and institutionalist) field notes. In Ehrlich's analysis of the language of sexual assault trials, she remarks on the 'interactional asymmetry' of institutional discourse, in which 'different speaking rights are assigned to participants depending on their institutional role' (2001, p. 105). In the counsellor's notes version of my narrative I have, I now recognize, capitulated to just such an institutional discourse: I speak with someone else's voice. This is something of a paradox, of course. Recalling Remlinger's (2005, p. 116) enumeration of 'linguistic features that restrict speakers ... and limit [their] control of context' I am compelled to note that the restrictions on my voice, my speaking, my control were self-imposed, a deliberate choice on my part. This somehow alters the equation, but the question persists: Why did I do that? How did – and how does – that decision serve me? I believe that I did it partly as a strategic feint, to lend a kind of credibility (ironic, admittedly, given that the credible text is in fact a fictionalized reconstruction) to my own story, for like many new academics I worried about my professional future, and that worry caused a tension: between the belief, nurtured at a point in my life as a graduate student when I had danced all the dances except the final one,[11] that at last this was *my* game, and the awareness that it was (and is) a game I had (and have) to play, to a large extent, by others' rules. Because of course it is their game, their dance, too.

At first my part in this dynamic was unconscious: at the moment of writing my field notes, like Bloom's Olivia I did not quite realize what I was doing, so strong was the pull of the institutional. I am reminded of Fetterley's (1978, p. xxii) insistence that we 'begin the process of exorcizing the male mind that has been implanted in us' and Irigaray's question, 'How can women analyze their own exploitation, inscribe their own demands, within an order prescribed by the masculine?' (1985, p. 81), both of which seem to gesture toward Freud's earlier, 'What does a woman want?'

The implanted mind may be male, but it is also institutional, and at times it is hard to figure out where one ends and the other begins. Foucault (1984a, pp. 48–9) articulates three categories of relation – control over things, action upon others, and relations with the self – which he sees as interwoven. He asks some important questions: 'How are we constituted as subjects of our own knowledge? How are we constituted as subjects who exercise or submit to power relations? How are we constituted as moral subjects of our own actions?' My narrative makes me – I am created as subject by the story I tell – but it also makes me think. The relations of power implicit in both the content and the form of the second version in which I let the counsellor speak for both of us, as well as the third version (more explicitly from my own point of view), both exemplify and illustrate the relations of power in the events recounted. And even as they inform the reader about my participation in and resistance to these power relations, they are informing me too.

Another clue to the reasons behind the delay in coming to my own version of the story – to ownership of it – lies in work that addresses questions of sexuality education for secondary-level students. Bay-Cheng (2003, p. 62) parallels constructions of adolescent sexuality as dangerous (and adolescents as driven exclusively by hormonal impulses) with Foucauldian (1980b) perceptions of the regulation of so-called perversions: both discourses concomitantly construct and meet a presumed 'inevitable and natural [need] for adult intervention and surveillance' over the young.[12] In my own narrative, intervention and surveillance are self-imposed in my use of a fictionalized Other's voice to regulate the discussion of my remembered experience, and particularly the sexual elements of it, at least until I can speak it (for) myself.

Fine (1988) too explores the 'discourse of desire' among adolescent females, finding it silent, even absent, despite an ever-growing concentration on issues of teenage sexuality. Noting the construction of the late-1980s American adolescent female primarily as a 'potential victim of male sexuality' (1988, p. 30), Fine sees sex-oriented discourses as being organized mainly around concerns of violence and victimization, and the degree of subjectivity granted to young women as narrowly circumscribed – an abstinent heterosexuality the only legitimized choice, and desire remaining 'a whisper' (p. 33).[13] Fine is writing in and about the 1980s: as I write this I recall my own formal sex education in the 1960s and 70s, more than a decade earlier, which similarly did not move beyond a 'plumbing and prevention' approach (Lenskyj, 1990).

This chronological placement is significant: things may be a little different now (though for Bay-Cheng, writing 15 years after Fine, little seems to have changed), but those old lessons, and specifically the places where those lessons were silent, die hard. In this vein, and recalling the notion of the recursive presence of and insistence on the past in the present, the adolescent I was, in Fine's language, 'at once taken with the excitement of actual/anticipated sexuality and consumed with anxiety and worry' (p. 35), apparently lives on unexorcized. Even now, it is uncomfortable and difficult to articulate, aloud or on paper or otherwise publicly, the desires I felt as an adolescent: I have had to brace myself, to prepare, to take many pages before getting to the moment where I am able to do so.[14]

It is worth noting that my gradual narrative movement from the facts, through the notes, to the first-person iteration of dropping English is actually representative of the process I have undergone in remembering it. At first, and for many years, the simple fact of having stopped taking English in Grade 12 was all I remembered. Its context and details remained unavailable to my conscious mind notwithstanding the significant contradiction inherent in it – I have always been a lover of literature and of language, despite protests – 'No, I don't *do* English' – that I would make to myself and to anyone else who would listen. Eventually, I remembered the appointment with the guidance counsellor who tried to dissuade me, and ultimately, but fairly recently, I remembered the contextualizing details that appear in the third version of the narrative.

This entire process evolved into a curious but satisfyingly concrete textual exemplar of two Freudian concepts. Each version of the dropping-English story is comprised partly of traces of the version(s) that precede it. Freud would not be surprised: he predicts this process in his mystic writing-pad theory of memory, wherein nothing is truly lost and each writing is also always a rewriting. But if material can be retrieved, it is because it has been buried, however long or deeply. Part of the reason for such an interment is the traumatic nature of the material: even the contents of a mere rumour can provoke a crisis of desire. In turn desire (or more specifically the trauma of disappointed desire) can provoke a crisis in learning that manifests as a refusal of learning. It can also provoke a crisis in memory that may take the form of a necessary and perhaps even happy forgetting. That which cannot be assimilated or dealt with at the time of its occurrence – cannot, in fact, be experienced – remains silent until the conscious mind is able to work through it in the nachträglich time of remembering.

And also, as Britzman points out, in the curious time of learning (1998, p. 117). For if the problem is one of reading, and of writing, it is also a problem of time. Hunsberger (1992, p. 90) points out that 'if the present is structured by the past, it is also pressured by the future.' Part of that future lies with the reader, who always comes to the text after-the-fact but who, in a curious back-and-forth movement, brings to the symptomatic reading her own past, memory, and psyche – all of which, by *reading into* the text another past, in a sense also *write onto* it a future. In this way, we might consider this or any narrative as always both more and less than it seems to be.

Perhaps we can learn from this. Freud asks (1899, p. 322) 'whether we have any memories at all *from* our childhood [or just] ... memories *relating to* our childhood' (italics in original). It is important that for psychoanalysis a memory, rather than a straightforward recollection, may be an image, partial and unconsciously selected or even con-structed well after the fact – effectively a place for collection as well as re-collection. That is, the (re)collected can also be collect*ive:* the reader of a narrative is invited to think not just *about* the details of this re-membering and forgetting, forgetting and almost-remembering, and later remembering more (or differently), but *with* them – by exten-sion to learn not only *about* but *from* them. Here, that learning might be about the partiality (and therefore the partial silence) of a story of learning refused, but it is also about other moments of silence, and the questions we can ask of those silences. And of writing. And through writing.

And *with* writing, particularly women's writing or writing-as-a-woman, which for Cixous is an act of desire that 'is precisely *the very possibility of change,* the space that can serve as a springboard for sub-versive thought' (1983, p. 283; italics in original). In writing-as-myself I come to a place from which I can subvert my own remembered story and thereby, albeit paradoxically, fill in some of its gaps and its silences. But not all of them. We may believe with Harper (1997b, p. 156) that writing 'demands self-consciousness,' but for psychoanalysis full self-consciousness is not possible. Perhaps that is part of what makes the act, the work, of writing so hard: the unconscious is so very difficult to put into words.

Difference, Discourse, Desire. And Moving On

If it is hard to speak one's self, how shall we speak the Other – and speak *to* the Other – when 'working across, through, and with differ-ence means seeing that shifting social articulations ... of [that] differ-ence (along various axes of race, gender, class, ethnicity and sexuality) constitute numerous identity *positions,* rather than a singular, fixed identity' (Todd, 1997, pp. 237–8; italics in original)?

In later work Todd suggests that we take from Levinas the idea of 'attend[ing] to the concrete communicative practices through which responsibility emerges, as opposed to offering prescriptions of what those practices ought to look like' (Todd, 2003b, p. 32). Todd urges us to consider the Levinasian view of communication as inherently ambigu-ous, such that while one's subjectivity is revealed only in relation to an-other's, what is revealed is always incomplete. Ambiguity is less about misunderstanding the significations of communicative encounters than it is about the inherent incapacity of those significations and encounters to offer full knowledge (Todd, 2003b, p. 33).

Riding the bus one day, making notes in the margins of Todd's chapter on 'Rethinking difference, disparity, and desire,' I read incorrectly: where she refers to the *mutability* of difference (1997, p. 239) I read *mutuality*. That slip gives me pause, invites in the thought that if we are all strangers to each other, we are equally strange. Our otherness is not just mutual but equivalent in that mutuality, in other words, and in that there is a kind of balance. This comforts me, somehow, and it seems to shift questions of power to . . . well, to questions. Foucault asks: 'In a specific type of discourse on sex . . . appearing historically and in specific places (around the child's body, apropos of women's sex, in connection with practices restricting births, and so on), what were the most immediate, the most local power relations at work?' (1980b, p. 97).

We might conceive of these 'local power relations' as inhering in the discourses of the institution and its rules (for instance, currently common laws and educational policies that forbid contact between teachers and students that might even remotely be considered erotic), or more locally still in relations between individual participants in that institution. At the same time, we can also consider local power relations concerning sex, and even concerning sex-as-not-quite-sex – in the case of, say, identification or other desires – as circulating within the individual unconscious, where repression of the wish and the wish itself exist side by side, the latter always already there, but in a Foucauldian sense also reduced to silence by its repression (Foucault, 1980b, p. 78). Or, we might view these relations as a kind of combination of the discursive (outer) and the psychical (inner). In the context of my narrative of adolescence that could mean allowing for the possibility that sexual desire, conscious or unconscious, might in fact have lain at the root of things, but that externally originating rules, discourses, and social conventions prohibited my acting on it. Here is a place, then, where Foucauldian, psychoanalytic and feminist ideas, each about desire, can embrace one another in a kind of theoretical ménage.

And here comes another.

Desire and Narrative – Gallop: 'The anecdotal does turn out to be rather insistently sexual . . . Anecdotal theory is theory grappling with its erotics.' (2002, p. 8)

Desire and Difference – Todd: 'Being *like* an Other cannot be easily separated from *wanting* to be like an Other or, perhaps, *wanting* that Other.' (1997, p. 242)

Desire and Education – A. Freud: 'Step by step education aims at the exact opposite of what the child wants, and at each step it regards as desirable the
very opposite of the child's inherent instinctual strivings.' (1974, p. 101)

Education makes children into adults by subverting their desires. But
it cannot eliminate those desires altogether, for they are not easily silenced – one way or another, they make their stubborn way through the
cracks in institutional (and personal) walls.

Todd (1997) suggests that a reading that sits a little away from the
reader might be one means of incorporating discussions into pedagogy
about 'how desire functions in relation to specific articulations of difference' (1997, p. 254). Such a looking-from-a-safe-distance might, she
reckons, make for useful interpretive practices. More precisely, thinking about one story of education, or indeed mis-education, might help
us think about others – and Others – not as mutually isomorphic, but
rather as a set of moving, shifting beings, (id)entities, processes that
might, at some times and in some places, embody in common some history, motivations, and desires, and also some worries and fears.

The idea of stories of education (or mis-education) as themselves potentially educative is relevant to the next part of this study, where I
move to contemplate texts and contexts that are less exclusively my
own. Where this chapter has considered silenced desires of particular,
personal kinds – sexual desire, the wish to be a chosen love-object, and
the desire to make (and concomitant refusal to make) the choice *of* a
particular (love- or learning-) object – in the next chapter I take a look
at a moment when desire, in the form of curiosity, might find a way to
refuse silence.

PART 2

Third Circumnarrative: The Rain

July 2006.
This afternoon, out of nowhere came rain.

The day steaming hot, my little office sticky and sweaty and still even with the window wide open, and suddenly, with one inaugural thunderbolt, the rain comes. Relief, wetter than ever, but cooler. My eyes move from the small bright square of computer screen to the larger illuminated window frame, and through it to the damp-smelling shiny outside, where water falls in great thick streaks, noisy on the shed roof, splashing into bins empty of the garden's weeds that should fill them because it's summer and everything grows, but that don't fill them, that continue to grow, because I am here, inside, trying to grow my [words into my work], trying to fill those theoretical bins with something. Knowledge? Thoughts? Ideas? Something that will pass. Pass muster.

Mustard, wild mustard, grows in the garden.

I have spent this day taking notes from many articles and books – I'm working but also avoiding work. I stop periodically to play solitaire on the computer, to instant-message a friend, to have tea with my daughter who's working on her own essay in the next room.

It's 5 pm. I don't cook much, when I'm writing, but soon I will have to stop and make dinner. First, though, I need to look at the last book on today's pile: Fowler's Curriculum of Difficulty. I have had this book from the university library for many weeks already, but have not opened it. I must do so before it comes due. I don't know anything about it, but it has the word difficulty in the title, and purports to be about narrative research. It may be relevant.

I pick it up, intending to begin at the beginning, but in the table of contents my eye is drawn to an 'internarrative' entitled 'Black oxfords by the quilt: a significant death.' Turning to page 91, I am stunned by the first and third subheadings of this story: 'A factual report' and 'A narrative account of a well-remembered event.' These are so resonant with the structure of my own Part I that reading them becomes urgent.

The narrative is a rich retelling of the last day in the life of Fowler's grandmother. It reaches its climax with the grandmother's 'two great last gasps' and Fowler's sensation of 'a tremendous magnetic force condensing from her [grandmother's] head to her feet, concentrating itself in a shimmering energy about eighteen inches in diameter, just above her chest, and then a whispering of that energy field upwards and away' [p. 95] – the exit from life that the narrative's factual report bluntly names a myocardial infarction [p. 91].

I am undone by this story. It reminds me of the death I was close to. I write nothing for the rest of the week. And for several weeks following, I am unsure: what to do about this interruption, this disruption, to what had been (at least for a time) a somewhat regularized writing process? But eventually I decide to let the interruption be.

And so here it is disrupting, or interrupting, or circum-rupting – breaking, breaking into, breaking around – the story that is my research proper.

4   Curiosity Kills the Silence: On (Not) Representing Sex in Kindergarten[1]

We are the animals for whom something is missing and for whom what is missing is always privileged. . . . Our curiosity depends upon a receding horizon.

          – Adam Phillips, *The Beast in the Nursery*

Underneath your clothes, there's an endless story.
          – Shakira Mebarak & Lester Mendez, *Underneath Your Clothes*

Several winters ago, my partner and I spent about a dozen Tuesday evenings taking Latin dance lessons in a school near our home. That classroom was a lively place. The instructors, a man and woman in their forties, kept the talk flowing and the music playing. The bass was loud: you have to feel the beat, they would say. They encouraged the students to loosen up – feel the music *here, here, here* – and they would point to the head, the feet, the heart. And *somewhere else*, they would insinuate, not saying precisely where, never pointing, but talking in drawn-out murmurs about the *sennsssualllity* of Latin dance. Sometimes, demonstrating a move, they held each other very close, rubbing their thighs against one another's, grinding their hips, almost kissing. Often the woman winked, and purred how *exciting* a particular move was, in what seemed – the instructors were not themselves Latino or Latina – like a caricature of some stereotype of Latin-ness. At times it was embarrassing for some students. Often there was giggling.

One night a student's babysitter cancelled, so she brought her three-year-old daughter to class. At first the child sat watching, her eyes on the feet, legs, and especially the hips of the instructors and the students.

Then she started wriggling. Finally she began dancing herself, sometimes substituting for her mother's partner and sometimes alone, unabashedly bouncing, twirling, and weaving through the room, between the adult students, constantly moving – more spontaneously (and indeed more rhythmically!) than many of us – in time with a mambo or a merengue. At the break she drank a large glass of water, and fell asleep across two chairs placed together for her just beside the dance floor. I noticed that while the child was awake there was less giggling, and the instructors' movements and comments were somewhat more reserved and less suggestive, but once she went to sleep things returned to normal.

Mapping the Body: Pictures, Words, Silence

That room is a dance studio by night and a preschool/kindergarten classroom by day. There are small tables and chairs (pushed to the perimeter for the evening events), low bookshelves, cubbies where the occasional stray mitten, or forgotten pebble, or pine cone resides. The walls are painted bright yellow; the curtains have multicoloured stripes. Children's art is displayed almost everywhere. But that winter, on one bulletin board were posted two large hand-drawn figures, clearly labelled by an adult, representing the front and back of a human body. They looked something like this:

Figure 1: Kindergarten 'map' of body parts

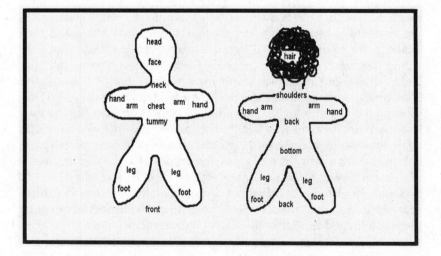

Such diagrams are commonly used in preschools, kindergartens, and primary classrooms to teach young pupils to identify and read the names of parts of the body. Sometimes pupils are given pre-drawn figures to label. Or they may draw their own, lying on large sheets of paper on the floor while a partner traces their outline, which they then cut out, label and paint. And in other classrooms, like the one where I attempted to learn to dance, the teacher draws an outline, has the children name various features, and prints the names.

The figures are stylized rather than representational. They name body parts, but do not really show them: hands are not distinguished from arms; feet are undifferentiated from legs. There are heads but no facial features. It appears that what is being named are not actual parts but rather their relative locations on these body 'maps.' Most striking is the great empty space, front and centre, where the genitalia ought to be, but are not. Like hands, feet, and face, the genitals are not depicted. But unlike the hands and feet and face they are not even named; they are missing, absent, silent. And while other body parts are also absent – noses, kneecaps, navels – nowhere else on the figures is the absence of a feature or a name as conspicuous as in the groin area.

The poster figures remind me of an earlier moment when, as a student teacher in the process of compiling a set of storybooks by children's author Eric Carle for a Grade 2 author study I came upon a copy of his *Draw Me a Star* (1992). This book tells of an artist creating a world one drawing at a time. Among its illustrations is the depiction in collage form of a man and woman, naked. In one of the copies I found in the elementary school library, the penis of the male figure had been rubbed away, leaving a blank translucent space – almost an actual hole – near the centre of the page. The kindergarten diagrams resonate with my memory of this image of two colourful figures standing side by side, and there is a curious symmetry between the literal erasure of the genitalia in the book and their absence from the body-parts diagrams.

We might imagine, looking at the 'maps,' that children either do not yet know or are not yet expected to learn the names for *all* body parts, and that some are therefore left off. But why the genitals? It is not as if there is no space for their names to be printed, as might be argued for fingers and toes, facial features or vertebrae. It is certainly not as if children are unaware of their existence, as they might be of, say, livers or scapulae or Achilles' tendons. It is likely that they already know at least some names for the genitals, though they may not be 'adult' names (Volbert, 2000).[2] And if we consider the Carle book, its representation of a penis almost completely erased, however we might interpret that erasure, we must agree: the blank space was noticed.

Nevertheless, looking at that space – a kind of textual silence – on the body-part diagrams, it is as if the viewer is expected not to notice the genitals. Indeed, it is as if they do not even exist. What might their absence have to tell us? If there is some master list of body parts that young children in schools must be taught to name, are genitalia not on that list? And if not, why not? To recall the dance class, what does it mean that the teachers spoke and moved differently in the presence of a three-year-old? Why did that child's dancing seem so uninhibited to the adults? And what, in the relationship among all these things, hints at what we understand children, and sexuality in children, to be? Might there be, for example, some concern about comfort or discomfort, appropriateness or inappropriateness? And if so, whose?

Granted, it might be argued that to include genitals on such drawings would require the presumption of a binary, mutually exclusive categorization of sexes and/or genders which could potentially be problematic in a world that increasingly acknowledges more (and more subtle) difference and diversity among bodies and identities. One could conclude that their absence is deliberate, an effort either to be sensitive to diversity or to pre-empt difficulty for students who might see *the* bodies on the posters as not representative of *their* bodies. However, in an education system where boys and girls are still expected to self-identify as one or the other and use toilets, play sports, and line up accordingly – and where sexuality education often rarely moves beyond the heteronormative (see Rich, 1986; Fine, 1988; Lenskyj, 1990; Bay-Cheng, 2003), that argument simply fails to pass muster. Something else is going on – or being rendered silent.

In the chapter about 'becoming a little sex researcher' that forms part of her psychoanalytic exploration of the pushes and pulls of learning and teaching, Britzman examines connections between the qualities of sex and the linking of the constructs of 'appropriate sex' and 'age appropriateness' (1998, pp. 66–7), and asks, 'Does education cause sex?' (p. 67). My own consideration of this presumed link begins with the pedagogical texts presented here: the kindergarten posters, the partly erased image of a naked man in Carle's children's book, and the dance class. It continues with thoughts of how social constructions of the child and childhood sexual curiosity, combined with developmentally appropriate practice discourse, reinforce notions of childhood innocence in relation to activities, events, and even body parts whose nature or import adults have constructed as sexual. While education does not altogether disregard young children's sexual curiosity, it frequently conceptualizes it as something best ignored, or at the very least controlled.

Constructing the Child, Constructing Sex

Cannella's (1997) deconstructionist critique of early childhood education posits innocence and neediness as currently privileged signifiers for the child. These are not the only possible signifiers, however. Cannella summarizes several historical constructs, philosophically and culturally determined, which originate in social, religious, artistic, literary, and scientific domains, and range from the preformed homunculus described by Ariès (1962) and Nicholas (1991) to Christian-inspired understandings of children as innocent, vulnerable, and pure, and therefore morally superior to, and consequently in need of protection from, adults. Other constructions include the inherently evil Hobbesian child, Locke's *tabula rasa*, Piaget's 'naturally developing' child, Rousseau's 'innocent,' and Freud's 'unconscious' child (James, Jenks, & Prout, 1998). Crain's survey (2000) adds Gesell's and Montessori's views of the child as governed by intrinsic genetic factors and individual 'sensitive periods' respectively, and the environmentally conditioned or socially created child of Skinner and Bandura.

The fluidity of the category 'child'[3] is implicit in postmodern constructivist perspectives that reject notions of universality and in which, according to Cannella, any concept of the child is subjective. But chronocentric, progressivist notions of current ideas as more complete than earlier ones seem to forget this fluidity: implicit in mainstream Western ideas that 'we have learned what [children] are like' (Cannella, 1997, p. 26) is the view that earlier constructions were inadequate, and that in positioning the child as ignorant and therefore innocent we have finally got it right.

Significantly, this innocent-and-ignorant child is located in opposition to the adult, a construction which Foucault (1980b) argues originated in the classical period and held sway until Freud's 'Three essays on the theory of sexuality' (1905a) and his analysis of 'Little Hans' (1909). A deficiency of 'adult' knowledge on the part of children, alongside a lack of awareness of the need for and ability to handle it, means that adults must determine the need and bestow (or withhold) the knowledge. Implicit in the notion of 'innocence' is the view that childhood sexuality and sexual curiosity are inappropriate, even absent. Mitchell,

Walsh and Larkin (2004, p. 36) contend that constructing children as innocent positions them as 'un-knowledgeable about sexuality, sexual practice and their own bodies.'

Awareness of these constructs and their implications helps us understand why, as Mitchell et al. observe, visual representations of childhood as other than completely innocent are so jarring to many: because they activate tensions 'between the way the community often wishes to see young people – innocent ... as opposed to the way young people actually are ... participating in their own emerging sexuality' (Mitchell et al., 2004, pp. 37–8). Following Higonnet (1998), Mitchell et al. cite, as an example of art that 'can be situated in the very crux between an understanding of innocence and knowing,' photographer Sally Mann's controversial pictures of her own children, which depict them in ways that juxtapose components categorized as both 'adult' (sexual – with cigarettes and 'Lolita heart-glasses' [Higonnet, 1998, p. 204]) and 'child' (non-sexual – with dolls and doll-sized prams), thereby characterizing their bodies as simultaneously knowing and innocent.

Mitchell et al. later draw attention to a booklet produced by two South African organizations, Children in Distress (CINDI) and the Institute of Justice and Reconciliation, as a tool to increase HIV/AIDS awareness (Children in Distress/The Institute of Justice and Reconciliation [CINDI], 2001). While remarking that the content in the booklet consists of 'insightful and engaging' essays written by adolescents aged at least 15, they note that the cover drawing 'looks to have been made by a much younger child' in what, for them, is an odd juxtaposition: 'The implicit notion of the risky site of the sexually active teenaged body is glossed over by the cover image and its message of ... a state of purity that must be rescued and protected' (Mitchell et al., 2004, p. 40).

We are unlikely to expect children in a kindergarten class to know as much as teenagers writing for an HIV/AIDS booklet. Still, the idea of purity, taking the form of a *not*-knowing that is implied or constructed by the blank space in the preschool and kindergarten posters (which, reminiscent of the booklet cover, appear to be drawn by an adult *imitating* a child), seems unrealistic and even excessive: the message (or non-message) of the empty space is of something that apparently does not exist, rendering moot even the notion of rescue, perhaps because, through what that emptiness implies, it has already been completed. The adolescents in the HIV/AIDS awareness booklet are deemed knowing-yet-innocent, but the posters' silence about the genitals locates the kindergarten children as innocent-and-ignorant in some place that, arguably, precedes knowledge, and in some sense lies beyond innocence. If even a little knowledge is a dangerous thing, this story goes, only no knowledge at all can keep us truly safe.

The notion of young children as non- or not-yet-sexual beings contrasts with Johnson's view (2000, p. 70), that 'we know children of all ages understand sexual life.' Also in that camp are teachers such as the one in Milton's study on primary sex education programs in Australia, who, noting individual differences among primary pupils' previously acquired knowledge, commented that 'some kids in [her] class didn't really understand an erection, compared to boys who were asking about oral sex' (Milton, 2003, p. 246). These understandings lean at least somewhat in the direction of the widely accepted idea that the construction of sexual components of identity begins early in life, even at birth (Corbett, 1991; Lively & Lively, 1991; Bredekamp & Copple, 1997; Cahill & Theilheimer, 1999).

Friedrich, Sandfort, Oostveen, and Cohen-Kettenis (2000), investigating differences in sexual behaviours between Dutch and American children from two to six, find that although Dutch children show more of some behaviours defined as sexual (from hugging adult strangers to touching their own and others' genitals to masturbating manually or with objects) than do American children, the behaviours exist to some degree in all groups. Similarly, a German study finds that 'curiosity about other people's genitals is a quite general phenomena [sic] in children who have at least some opportunity for exploration' (Schuhrke, 2000, p. 42). And in their review of research findings from Western European countries, Australia, and the United States on behaviours and feelings 'that can be interpreted as sexual or at least as precursors of adult sexuality,' de Graaf and Rademakers (2006, p. 16) summarize:

> Newborns, unintentionally or when locomotion is sufficiently developed intentionally, touch their genitals. ... [F]rom about 15 to 19 months, some children rub their genitals against furniture or people, masturbate with their hands or – less often – an object. From about 13 months of age, children show their curiosity in other persons [sic] genitals by looking at, touching, or naming these. In children from the age of 3, interpersonal contacts with other children are commonly observed. The sexual behaviors during these experiences are usually kissing, hugging and exposure of genitals. Touching and exploring of each others [sic] genitals is also fairly common, especially in younger children.

But the child is multiply perceived. Tobin's contention (1997a) that sexuality appears to have gone missing from early childhood education, and Theilheimer and Cahill's observation (2001) that sexuality in early childhood education textbooks is limited to mentioning sex roles, sexual abuse, and reproduction, seem to suggest, alongside the kindergarten body-parts posters, that the prevalent perception is of children as non-sexual. And the anxious warning from sex education opponents, to the effect that talking about sex in school 'acts as an unhealthy stimulus to sexual thought and practice' (Irvine, 2002, p. 132) – a warning that I read as one answer to Britzman's question: yes, education *does* cause sex – posits children as both uncritically suggestible and reflexively animalistic in their behaviours.

These multiple views embody other complexities, even contradictions: the child constructed as pure, innocent, and ignorant, uncorrupted by adult knowledge and for whom any reference to sex is paradoxically believed either irrelevant or provocative, is simultaneously understood as amoral and likely to misuse any knowledge she does have, through unacceptable if not malicious behaviour (Silin, 1995, p. 67). She is therefore seen as needing protection *from* such knowledge, and this protection takes the form of control *over* knowledge, and concomitantly over bodies.

Constricting the Child: 'Sitting Up, Shutting Up, and Lining Up' in Kindergarten

Dreyfus and Rabinow's (1983, p. 143) disquisition on Foucault's 'genealogy of the modern individual as a docile and mute body' points out that in *Discipline and Punish* (1977a), rather than isolating the prison as the unique locus for particular kinds or manifestations of power, Foucault uses this 'paradigmatic form of punishment' (Dreyfus & Rabinow, 1983, p. 151) as an exemplar for 'the development of a specific technique of power' (p. 143). Perhaps Foucault chose the prison as the collecting place for his Weltanschauung because the images it rouses are particularly bleak and unsubtle. And perhaps there is some kind of implicit recognition of similarities between the confining qualities of institutions penal and pedagogical that makes some children – who surely have never heard of Foucault – insist that school is 'just like jail.' Whether or not, in both of these institutions it is the body which is targeted in 'the growth of disciplinary technology within the larger historical grid of bio-power' (Dreyfus & Rabinow, 1983, p. 143).

In a Foucauldian framing, technologies of discipline 'colonize' the body through a series of moves that divide it into components which

are given 'precise and calculated training' aimed at 'control and efficiency' along multiple dimensions: 'Control must not be applied spo-
radically or even at regular intervals,' but rather, 'all dimensions of
space, time, and motion must be codified and exercised incessantly'
(Dreyfus & Rabinow, 1983, pp. 153–4). While children's bodies are subjected to varying degrees of adult protection, control, and protection-
through-control from birth onward, in institutions such as child care
centres, preschools, and kindergartens, protecting the child comes to
mean controlling her body for the explicit purpose of 'civilizing' her
into society's behavioural expectations (Foucault, 1980b; Shilling, 1993;
Silin, 1995).

Although it may derive from an assumption that learning is predicated on structure, on a focus on language and socialization, or on a
teacher's personal desire for orderliness (Phelan, 1997b, p. 77), schooling
the body (that is, 'civilizing' the body in school), through the (spoken
or silent) word or the (permitted or prohibited) deed, requires subordi-
nating the individual's desire for personal gratification to a degree that
reflects, contend Leavitt and Power (1997), more concern for classroom
management than for children's well-being. As in the Foucauldian
model, control over individuals and their bodies may be temporal – the
determination of *when* children can use their bodies, which takes the
form of scheduling activities such as playing, eating, and elimination –
or it may be addressed in ways more directly corporeal: Leavitt and
Power enumerate multiple 'body rules' which can be put in place as
policy or 'invented by teachers from moment to moment' and which are
enforced 'through direct instruction, benign manipulation, social comparison, and the promise of rewards and privileges, as well as the threat
of punishment' (Leavitt & Power, 1997, p. 49). The list of rules they provide includes: 'walk, don't run; walk slowly; walk quietly; . . . keep your
hands in your lap/to yourself; raise your hand; use the toilet' (p. 49).

Such rules structure *what* is to be done with bodies, as well as *when*
and *how* it is to be done: how to stand up, sit down, tie shoes, hold cray-
ons, raise hands, move, or stop moving. This is articulated in a letter
published in the *Globe and Mail* newspaper a few years ago, in response
to a report on a study calling for an increase in funding for early childhood education programs. The author of the letter, a teacher of young
children, writes:

> Kids need one-on-one attention, . . . not a one-size-fits-all day of robotic
> group play. The solution is to fund parenting . . . so someone who loves the

preschooler can walk him or her towards the joy of learning. . . . [B]abies
are born ready to learn. You don't teach that. However, a large group setting that urges kids to *sit up, shut up and line up* does not nurture learning.
(Jaremko, 2003; my italics)

Motives for exercising these kinds of control may be logistical: the adult
in charge knows 20 children cannot drink from the same fountain at one
time. Or they may be strategic, as was perhaps the case when my Grade
1 teacher told me to mouth the words rather than sing during the choir
competition. But whatever the motivation, here as elsewhere power is,
at least on the surface, hegemonically vested in the teacher, who has the
authority to penalize those whose bodies do not cooperate. Punishments
can include physical isolation or the prohibition of pleasurable physical
contact with other bodies, of peers or teachers. Such a strategy received
press coverage recently when parents in Shawinigan, Quebec reported
that their son's 'Grade 4 teacher punished [him] by forcing him to sit
at the back of the class, confined in a semi-enclosed pen that separated
the boy from his classmates by a trellis.' The *Globe and Mail* went on to
report that in that jurisdiction 'it was normal practice to place turbulent
children in an isolation area for about an hour throughout the course of
the day . . . [to] rest and calm down' (Séguin, 2007).[4]

Moreover, it may not matter much whether the punishment actually
takes place: for the most part the possibility is enough. I probably did
not really have to drink the apple juice that was provided as part of
the class's snack each day in kindergarten. But my mother had told me
to 'do what the teacher says,' thereby passing the parental mantle of
authority to that teacher. And 'doing what the teacher says' did not,
for me, include either telling my mother that apple juice was the daily
beverage in kindergarten, or advising the teacher that I disliked it – indeed loathed it (a loathing that preceded my entry into school and
persists to the present day) – to a degree that meant a daily fight with
nausea – because following the teacher's direction was not negotiable:
as I understood it, had I not drunk the juice I'd have been in trouble
with the teacher.

The teacher's power can be challenged, even refused, by the learner:
Bailey writes of another kindergarten snack table, at which, right after
she has instructed him on 'how [she thinks] snack should proceed,' a
four-year-old 'stares deeply into [her] eyes and crushes his cracker in
his hand and lets the pieces fall on the floor' in a moment of 'rejecting
the text . . . thorough which power works' (Bailey, 1997, pp. 149–50),

a moment the like of which, however resistant, serves for Foucault (1980a) to confirm and reinforce the existing power structure.

Managing children is an important part of discipline in the Foucauldian scenario, but it is not limited to what they are made to do with their bodies, and how, and when they are made to do it. Curricula and classroom practices, themselves socially constructed and labile, exert control over what, and how, a child *thinks*, about her own and others' bodies. Nowhere is this more apparent than in relation to sexual curiosity. Tobin (1997a), in his introduction to the 1997 volume *Making a Place for Pleasure in Early Childhood Education,* which discusses the disappearance of sexuality, pleasure, and desire from education, lights on the historical period from the late 1800s until the 1970s, when children's sexuality was a significant component of child development and educational discourses (see also Silin, 1995). Tobin puts forward the view that Montessori and Deweyan pedagogies acknowledging mind-body connections, along with psychoanalytically informed approaches recognizing the natural inevitability of sexual interest and the preferability of expression over repression, have in the contemporary scene been replaced by a denial of childhood (and indeed adult) sexuality that has rendered desire and pleasure lost: unspeakable and even at times unthinkable (see also Johnson, 2000).

Tobin supports Fine's well-known contention regarding a 'missing discourse of desire' (1988) and is in turn supported by Allen's claim that sex education ignores dimensions of pleasure and desire, instead focusing almost exclusively on sexual health as involving 'the absence of sexually transmitted infections and the avoidance of unintended pregnancies' (Allen, 2004, p. 151). Tobin attributes this shift to several often contradictory factors, including 'mean-spirited, misinformed, morally panicked public discourses' that yield distorted views of teaching; the active ignoring of and passive inattention to children's needs and curiosity as children themselves perceive them; teachers' own repressed memories; and a widespread fear among educators that talk even remotely related to sexuality will be construed as indicating their prurient sexual desire for children and have severe professional and perhaps legal consequences (1997a, p. 2).

I recall the reaction of my practicum teacher to *Draw Me a Star.* There were two copies of the book, one of which was intact, and it was the intact one that the teacher saw first. She was horrified and angered by my inclusion in an author study display of what she deemed 'filth.' Her panicked response was extreme to be sure, but it was at least partly grounded in a sincere and perhaps even justified worry about the potential implications for her job security if parents found out that such a book had been made available to their children. In a climate in which 'parents have been arrested for taking pictures of their nude children' (Johnson, 2000, p. 28), this is hardly surprising.[5]

A similar moment occurred in a class I was teaching to a group of student teachers, who had just watched an excerpt of the film, *Ma Vie en Rose* (Scotta & Berliner, 1997), which tells the story of Ludovic, a boy who is certain that he is a girl. One student had a particularly strong response: 'That stuff is completely irrelevant, and I don't want to have to look at it,' she announced. 'It's not something I want to deal with, or know how to deal with, or even want to think about. It's nothing to do with me.' As the class discussion continued, it became clear that this student was made uncomfortable not just by the particular story or character, but by any discussion of sexual matters, no matter how general, which she deemed private and personal and something schools and teachers should 'just keep quiet about.'

Much of education's civilizing work is done through prohibitions that amount to silences of various kinds. We do not touch our students or let them touch us; we censor their movements; and there are some things we just don't talk about. But according to Foucault, there is something more going on than the mere cessation of speaking:

> Silence itself – the things one declines to say, or is forbidden to name ... is less the absolute of discourse, the other side from which it is separated by a strict boundary, than an element that functions alongside the things said, with them and in relation to them within over-all strategies. There is no binary division to be made between what one says and what one does not say; we must try to determine the different ways of not saying such things, how those who can and those who cannot speak of them are distributed, which type of discourse is authorized, or which form of discretion is required. ... There is not one but many silences. (Foucault, 1980b, p. 27)

The kindergarten posters provide an archetypal illustration of Foucault's claim. In naming some body parts, but not *those* body parts, the posters both author and authorize the ways a particular knowledge is to be spoken or to remain unspoken; the genitals are not named, and they are not to be named, touched, or touched upon (with words), in what reads much like a linguistic or discursive equivalent of 'keeping those hands away from *there*.'

Early childhood education texts invite similar inferences. In an attempt to find content related to young children's sexuality in the multiply reprinted and commonly used texts which he argues 'clearly have holding power as knowledge sources in early childhood education' (2000, p. 64), Johnson offers a compendium of approaches to childhood sexuality, identifying entries that present normative discourse patterns which position sexuality 'within the grand early childhood narrative(s)' and bury it in chapters about ' "Multiculturalism," "Sexual Abuse," "Social Science," "Special Relationships," . . . "Providing Cross-Cultural, Non-sexist Education," . . . [and] "Science Activities" ' (p. 66). Indeed, he observes, in many texts he 'had to search rather hard [even] to find sexuality in the topical index,' from which he concludes that 'the popular discourse around childhood sexuality is . . . focused not on teaching about sexuality, but on teaching *around* sexuality – a process of erasure' (p. 67; italics in original).

Johnson's observations, and those of Theilheimer and Cahill (2001), are not altogether surprising either. Gammage (1988, p. 192) writes that 'teachers are . . . lacking in confidence about their role as sex educators [and] are very vulnerable to the controversies that flare up from time to time.' Buston, Wight and Scott (2001, p. 357) find that the word 'difficult' crops up frequently when teachers talk about teaching sex education. While it is not quite clear, of the early childhood education texts or the teachers themselves, which constitutes the chicken and which the egg, it does seem that teachers' comfort levels around talking and teaching about sexuality are as varied as those of the general population, including parents, for whom Baldwin and Bauer recommend 'training . . . to be sex educators,' since in the normal course their tendency is to be either 'unwilling or unable to talk with their children about issues of sexuality, intimacy, values, or even basic reproductive processes' (1994, p. 162).[6]

Yet 'even basic reproductive processes,' difficult though they might be to discuss, would seem to lie significantly beyond the naming of body parts on an un-lifelike drawing – perhaps the mildest possible degree of 'talk' about sex or sexuality. Concern about parental disapproval may well be real, but is it really the only thing going on? What else is tying the hands – and the tongue – of the teacher?

Beginning teachers in particular frequently express anxiety about whether touching students is or is not appropriate. Such anxieties are not fully assuaged by texts and discussions which point out the potential for misunderstanding and misinterpretation that may blur clear lines between what is legal and what may be perceived as criminal (MacKay & Sutherland, 2006). Currently the prevalent common-sense view, however unreflective – not to mention contradictory to what educators know is beneficial (Johnson, 2000, pp. 13–14) – seems to be in favour of personal no-touch policies alongside the official ones. If, as McWilliam (1996, p. 3) insists, 'teaching [is] ... an engagement some body has with other bodies,' might we imagine the blank space at the centre of the body-parts diagrams as a way to keep those bodies apart metaphorically – to keep our words, like our hands, to ourselves? What, precisely, is being silenced in the wordless space on the diagrams?

Constructing Appropriateness

Developmentally appropriate practice discourse, already full of tensions (Delpit, 1988; Jones, 1991; Silin, 1995), is one stage on which the contradictory mix of normative constructions – the child as innocent, ignorant, and non-sexual, and bodies as needing to be civilized' and controlled – is enacted. Consider how they play out in two versions of the position statement and guidelines of the National Association for the Education of Young Children (NAEYC) (Bredekamp, 1987; Bredekamp & Copple, 1997). The 1997 version, which 'represents the expertise and experience of literally thousands of early childhood professionals' (Bredekamp & Copple, 1997, p. ix), defines developmentally appropriate practice as including 'what teachers know about how children develop and learn; ... about the individual children in their group; ... and [about] the social and cultural context' (p. vii). Thus, like children's bodies, teachers' perceptions of those bodies, of sexual or other curiosity, and of how and what to teach about such matters are also constructed, managed, and discursively delimited.

Relatedly, Milton's (2003) work on Australian primary school sex education, albeit with pupils somewhat older than those discussed here, is instructive for its suggestion that teachers' decisions on the components of a sex education program are based partly on assumptions about pupils' sexual activity, and partly on judgments about their readiness for information concerning HIV/AIDS. Milton also finds that the implementation of sex education programs varies with teachers' comfort levels, perhaps indicating avoidance of more sensitive topics (2003, p. 252), a finding supportive of both Kehily (2002), whose British ethnography proposes connections between sex educators' biographies and their philosophies and practices, and Corbett (1991, pp. 71–3), whose discussion reminds us that adults' concerns about children's sexuality may be grounded in the adults' own feelings.

Whatley's (1994) examination of textbook and cinematic images of adolescent sexuality similarly raises the issue of teacher (dis)comfort, describing a sex-education textbook photo of an adolescent couple embracing captioned with reference to 'confusion in adolescent sexual behavior' that purportedly results from the fact that 'adolescents in contemporary industrial societies acquire adult status much later than they acquire biological maturity.' To emphasize that it is adults who portray adolescents as awkward, Whatley recasts the caption thus (1994, p. 188): 'Adolescents ... are *awarded* [my italics] adult status much later than they acquire biological maturity. This accounts for some of the *adult* [original italics] confusion and fears about adolescent sexual behaviour.' Although Whatley is exploring adolescent images, her work is instructive for its reflection on the interplay between adult perceptions and concerns and the realities of young people. Moreover, while her writing, like Allen's (2004), addresses adolescents rather than pupils in a preschool setting, it is interesting to speculate on possible relations between early childhood education's silence on body parts deemed sexual and a later dearth of discussion on the pleasurable aspects of using those parts in sexual ways. The difficulty of finding research related to young children's sexuality (however defined) that moves beyond issues of abuse speaks to a widespread silence on the subject (de Graaf & Rademakers, 2006), an observation exemplified by studies such as that by Davies, Glaser and Kossoff (2000), the objective of which was to 'learn about the nature, frequency, and patterns of young children's observed sexual play and behavior in pre-school settings, and staff responses to them' (p. 1329), explicitly in order to examine connections between early childhood educators' reporting of rarely observed behaviours categorized as 'sexualized' and the frequency of child abuse.

Still, as Tobin (1997a, pp. 32–3) has pointed out in relation to the earlier NAEYC document (Bredekamp, 1987), the many worthy objectives articulated in its revision, including explicit efforts to redress some inadequacies within the original document relating to the recognition of individual differences (Bredekamp & Copple, 1997, pp. 35, 40–1), seem to be contradicted to some degree by the text's structure. That is, the numerous lists, charts and tables of activities deemed appropriate and inappropriate tend in general toward the prescriptive and in particular toward a categorization of children by age and/or locomotion: for example, 'infants,' 'toddlers,' 'the primary grades' (Bredekamp, 1987);

and 'crawlers and walkers (8 to 18 months),' 'toddlers and 2-year olds,' and '3- through 5-year olds' (Bredekamp & Copple, 1997). In addition, the document appears to make only passing reference to the importance of physical contact and to be focused primarily on ensuring that such contact is appropriate.

I find but one reference even remotely related to sexual curiosity in either NAEYC document. It appears in the earlier version under the heading, 'Adults facilitate the development of self-esteem by respecting, accepting, and comforting children, regardless of the child's behaviour' (1987, p. 11). This section places 'interest in body parts and genital differences' in the same category as messiness, resistance, aggression, breaking rules, and lying, and calls for responses 'directed toward helping children develop self-control and the ability to make better decisions in the future.' Implicit in this categorization are both a negative view of the listed behaviours and the goal of ending them. That is, while help is here expected to include respect for the individual child, it seems that at bottom there rests a wish to guide that child away from these behaviours, which suggests something about education's worries regarding interest in or curiosity about them. Further, such control-oriented responses seem to recognize neither the importance of curiosity in creating a healthy sexual identity nor the ways in which suppressing it might reveal more about adult discomfort than it accomplishes for child behaviour.

The closest the revised version comes to the topic of sexual curiosity is in several statements requiring teachers to 'hold children accountable to standards of acceptable behaviour' and 'redirect children to more acceptable behavior ... patiently reminding children of rules and their rationale' (Bredekamp & Copple, 1997, p. 19). It is really not a great leap to argue that these directives on responding to behaviours would implicitly apply to so-called sexualized ones, especially since these do not appear to be addressed anywhere else. At the very least, the tone of the text seems to reflect the earlier document's minimal but arguably disapproving mention of sexual curiosity. Its focus on body parts suggests, as does the blank space at the centre of the preschool/kindergarten diagrams, an understanding of childhood sexuality as something to be ignored or avoided. But if children are innocently non-sexual, naming or even talking about their genitalia ought to be no different from naming or talking about any other body part, since in this construction sexual meaning itself is understood as not existing for them. So where does the idea of suggestibility come from? And why keep the genitals off the poster?

Orders and Hints: Reading the Empty Spaces

Tobin's reference to 'the study of children's sexuality [as] also the study of *our own dimly remembered desires*' (1997a, pp. 9–10; my italics) points to the view that adult understandings about children's sexual suggestibility do not arise solely in the social or cultural realm. For the social contexts in which constructions of *child* and *sexuality* come about are always populated by individuals (Burkitt, 1991; Harré, 1993). Simply stated, someone is doing the constructing. Similarly, pedagogy is not made only by curriculum theorists, or classroom guidelines, or teachers or learners in isolation from one another. Rather, it grows out of the intersection of constructs and inner lives: the outside and the inside. I contend, first, that whatever is tipping the pedagogical balance away from acknowledging and naming the sexual involves teachers *in relation with* their students, and second, that psychoanalytic theory invites thinking that can complicate and enrich the explanations and understandings provided by social constructionist theories and Foucauldian analyses.

In the text and context of that kindergarten poster there seems to be more going on than avoidance of a difficult topic and control over potentially unruly bodies. Johnson (2000, p. 70) writes that 'pretend[ing] sexuality is not an important issue, that it doesn't exist for children and for the field of early childhood education . . . keeps [educators] theoretically safe.' But safe from what? What happens when social and educational constructs collide with individuals' inner (and lived) lives – when what is outside the body bumps into the 'endless story' that lies, in Shakira's pop song, underneath the clothes (Mebarak & Mendez, 2001)? With its conceptualization of adult sexuality as a focused, narrowed version of the young child's broader, more polymorphous sexual curiosity, psychoanalysis offers useful ways to reflect on how such collisions may trouble teaching, by pushing open doors in the adult psyche that have long been pulled to.

Psychoanalysis calls these doors repression. They are not quite closed all the way, however, for although polymorphism may be repressed both in the individual and (significantly here) in curricula and classroom practice, it cannot quite be contained. Repression is not absolute; our larger earlier sexuality persists down the years as a kind of ghostly reminder. I move now to listen to these echoes, using, in addition to repression and its return, the psychoanalytic concepts of pleasure and unpleasure and defence against curiosity to suggest that education, through the teacher, might at times sabotage its own repressive efforts, inviting and even insisting upon the curiosity and exploration it manifestly tries to avoid.

Psychoanalytic theory invites diverse readings. For example, Bay-Cheng contends that psychoanalysis, and what she terms other 'drive-reduction discourses,' have been used to construct adolescents as hypersexual, and concomitantly to justify 'a fear-based, crisis intervention approach' (2003, p. 63) to school-based sex education. This contrasts with Tobin's view (1997a) that psychoanalytically informed pedagogies can acknowledge and address the naturalness of sexual curiosity in positive ways. And if, as Bailey claims (1997, p. 152), Freud's theory of sexual stages has been allowed to desexualize children through interpretations that slot them into the latency period, thereby 'remov[ing] from children's lives the entirety of the discourse of desire,' psychoanalysis itself also insists on a story of development that is 'unruly' rather than linear (Britzman, 1998, p. 2), in which repressed early polymorphous sexuality does not end but returns, as a psychical echo, again and again.

Phillips recalls Freud's views on the conflict between children's sexual curiosity and the aims of education: 'Children want to know about sexuality, but the grown-ups tell them they need to know something else – call it culture – to distract them from what they are really interested in' (Phillips, 1998, p. 413). The kindergarten diagrams convey this message succinctly, telling children that the 'something else' they need to know about is language: the names of (some) body parts; and how to read and write those names. But naming, reading, and writing are complex, and the diagrams suggest – and in particular their silent vacancies suggest – a great deal about adults' wishes for and about learning, for children and for themselves.

For psychoanalysis, sexuality is more than genital activity. It is 'a whole range of excitations and activities which may be observed from infancy onwards and which procure a pleasure that cannot be adequately explained in terms of the satisfaction of a basic physiological need' (Laplanche & Pontalis, 1973, p. 418). These excitations and activities are interwoven with curiosity. Indeed, for Phillips the child's sexuality is the 'apotheosis of curiosity ... [It] is almost as though the child is lived by, or lives through, her sexual curiosity [or ...] sexual researches' (1999, p. 10). This view contrasts with the cultural construction of children as innocently devoid of sexual knowledge or curiosity. But whether familiar with psychoanalytic theory or not, adults who live with or teach young children are aware of those children's curiosity about their own (and their peers') genitals as part of a larger curiosity about bodies and everything related to them.

Freud (1905a) proposes that the work of puberty includes the subordination of all other erotogenic zones to the genital. But one's original sexuality, as Britzman emphasizes (1998, p. 68), is 'polymorphously perverse. . . . wanders aimlessly and hence is not organized by object code, true sex, and so on.' Psychoanalysis would thus contend that the physical contact often discouraged or forbidden between young children, peers, and caregivers in educational settings (Weeks, 1993; Silin, 1995; Leavitt & Power, 1997; Tobin, 1997), while not overtly sexual in the sense of genital, is nonetheless related to a child's sexual identity. Conversely, the genitals are implicated, albeit differently, in both the polymorphous sexual curiosity of the child and the adult's focused sexuality, and in their concomitant pleasures. Why then leave their names off the classroom diagram? Are they forgotten? Ignored?

And what is all that giggling in dance class about anyway?

Britzman continues: 'In answering the question of why so many interdictions are stuck to the child's body, Freud attributes the adult's intolerance of children's sexuality to the adult's forgetting of his/her own infantile sexuality' (1998, p. 68). This kind of forgetting – repression – begins with the emergence of the reality principle, which permits the child's psyche to form 'a conception of the real circumstances in the external world' (Freud, 1911, p. 36) and to defend against the 'unpleasure' inherent in the discovery that reality is not, as previously imagined, unified with herself and her desires. Articulated by Foucault as 'an affirmation of non-existence, . . . an admission that there [is] nothing to say about such things, nothing to see, and nothing to know' (1980b, p. 4), repression can be understood as a response to the demand to ignore, and consequently as a defence against curiosity (Britzman, 1998, p. 68). And so if, as psychoanalysis claims, the child's sexual curiosity is predicated on a polymorphous sexuality, we might read the refusal to name the genitals as a *non*-acknowledgment of them, and furthermore as a repression of that curiosity: an unconscious attempt to ignore or deny sexuality.

Whose curiosity is being defended against, and whose sexuality repressed, in the body-parts posters? Is not-naming the genitals really just a defence against children's curiosity? Or, recalling the dance teacher's coy allusions to the *somewhere else* where the music should be felt, might it be that in the diagrams the adult's sexual curiosity as well as the child's is, literally in Tobin's phrasing (1997a, p. 4), 'missing as in uncharted'? In more explicitly Freudian terms, might the defence be against the adult's own unpleasure?

Precisely what is that unpleasure? For the child it is the unconscious realization that her omnipotence is imaginary, her polymorphous desires not fully realizable (Freud, 1911, p. 36). Since the movement of repression is 'dynamic and productive, one of turning and returning' (Britzman, 1998, p. 68), adult unpleasure may translate into a psychical echo of the same realization: the defence is against the rising to consciousness of the recollection of fantasy's failure. Gilbert (2004, p. 110) posits that 'the adolescent, who is seen as having arrived too early to the complications of sexual relations, has the potential to remind adults that they are too late to repair the vulnerability that now attends the risk of sexuality.' Might this imagined potential extend further back, even to the child in kindergarten? Do we imagine that that child's curiosity – which we recognize unconsciously as a first step toward the adolescent's too-late-yet-too-early arrival, and which reminds us of our own vulnerability as human beings – can be deferred if only we avoid giving it a name? For psychoanalysis, writes Gilbert, 'language does not simply stand outside of sexuality, describing and organizing its effects . . . [but it] is also constitutive of sexuality' (2004, p. 110).

Gilbert explores how HIV/AIDS prevention discourses often collapse abstinence and so-called safe sex in an economizing move in which the 'negation of sexuality (no sex is, of course, not sex) erupts into confusion and sexuality returns disguised: abstinence is *sex that doesn't count as sex*' (2004, pp. 115–16; my italics). Her assertion that adolescents construct *sex* and *not-sex* in ways that render moot the question of what 'unsafe' means – they 'aren't having unsafe sex because, according to their logic, they are not having sex' at all (2004, p. 116) – reminds us that while for psychoanalysis sexuality precedes language, sexuality is also constructed – and at times also negated – by language.

The negation of sexuality as an experiential component of the young child's life is enacted symbolically in the negation of the linguistic symbols of that component – the names of sexual organs. This move (itself paradoxical, since the young children from whom those names are being kept are presumed not to know the purpose and potential uses of the organs that the absent names are not-naming) would seem to be insisting on something even beyond an abstinence from sexual curiosity. That is, not only do the posters yield no place for thinking about or playing with sexual curiosity, they offer nothing to think or play *with*.

Or do they?

It seems to me that education desires and requires learning, including learning about sex, but must defend against the sexual curiosity that reminds the adult of both the polymorphous sexuality that preceded language and the loss of that polymorphism to its later, attenuated, genital iteration. Such an ambiguous demand must surely produce ambivalence; perhaps one way of tolerating that ambivalence is to give hints, even if the hints are concealed in orders. Gilbert (2004, p. 113) asks us how language might express and incite sexuality. 'We may,' she writes, 'be able to catch something like a sexuality from language, but sexuality does not always answer in the place where it is summoned.' Nor, I would add, does it always keep quiet when we try to shut it up. The labelled figures – and the empty space – seem to say:

Look. Pay attention. You must be curious about your body, and you must be interested in the names of your body parts. We will tell you what is important about your body, which parts and which names you need to know. But never mind those other parts, the ones that aren't named. Look anywhere but there: name, read, and write anything but that.

But there are hints in that order. Look at the diagrams again: as in the Carle storybook with the penis rubbed out, the eye is drawn to the absence, the empty silent space, the unnamed, unspoken, unspeakable. The 'little sex researcher' whose speculations 'weren't options . . . [but] urgencies' (Phillips 1999, p. 11), sees on entering the classroom the diagrams of himself. He cannot help but focus on what is so obvious: the wordless gap in the middle of a work about words. The pictures, naming many things, but not all – and especially not those which for the child may actually be the most interesting – confirm and even magnify their interest. The little sex researcher takes the hint. *Aha,* he says to himself, *these missing words, these missing things, must be very, very important.*

Eliminating the words does not remove the thing. Well might we imagine a brave little kindergartener – perhaps the one who 'declared war against' Bailey (1997) by challenging her authority at the snack table – querying, at the sight of the space on the poster, or during an activity in which the teacher points to the labels and the pupils read them, 'Where's the vagina?' or 'Why doesn't the boy have a penis?' But that pupil might be asking about more than a missing label, an unspoken word. For the little sex researcher is 'not a crude literalist' and 'won't

settle for a diet of words only. . . . Words are his route back to bodies.'
(Phillips, 1999, pp. 28–9) And on the posters we might see how silence
too – the absence of words – might lead us right back to the body.

Following on Kristeva's (2000) assessment of the Freudian view of
language as allowing us, through 'the primary processes of displacement, condensation and reversal, . . . to bring an otherwise intolerable
sexuality into our everyday lives,' Gilbert (2004, p. 120) writes: 'The
capacity for language is a sublimation: a successful substitution for
engaging in socially and psychically prohibited activities.' If this is
so – if language is one of those acceptable activities to which we turn
in order to manage our forbidden urges or instincts, or if it works
more indirectly as a kind of apparatus *through which* we find for ourselves some degree of gratification, itself attenuated, for those instincts, then how shall we understand the naming of the sex organs?

And how shall we understand *not* naming them? What is language
when it is silence? Can there be a sublimation of the sublimating apparatus? What does it mean to repress an instinct by finding an acceptable
alternative, and then refusing to use it?

Both in the book and on the body map it is the empty, silent space,
from which pictures of – or words about – genitals are missing that
gestures toward the body and its attendant polymorphous pleasures.
Do the teachers who (in not naming those front-and-centre parts) issue
the order to their pupils – to keep not just their hands and their words
but now their *eyes* and their *minds* off those parts – know, albeit unconsciously, that in listening to the order children will take the hint? And
if so, if education needs to defend against sexual curiosity, why invite
it? Why forget in a way that encourages remembering, ignore in a way
that invites attention?

Might we consider that rather than a forgetting of their own early,
wide-ranging sexuality, adults' intolerance for children's sexual curiosity, and the refusal to name and acknowledge its signifiers and signs, is
an indication of a kind of *not-quite*-forgetting, an incomplete repression
that works against itself? If adults retain an unconscious recollection of
the loss of their early polymorphous sexuality, they might also retain
a shadowy trace of the polymorphism itself. But it cannot be recalled
exactly: through maturation sexuality has been subordinated to and
focused on the genital, and the larger signified has faded behind its
more specific signs and signifiers. To adults the genitals have come to
mean both sex and sexual curiosity; it is genital sex, and genitalia, that
now signify both the earlier sexuality and the loss of it. Thus to avoid

naming sex organs is to avoid raising the spectre of the early polymorphous sexuality they have come to represent.

'Education – rather like much developmental theory – offers children a new religion: the religion of substitution,' which sends a contradictory message: 'There is no substitute, but you must find one.' So writes Phillips (1999, pp. 23–4). Perhaps, in the present context, it may also offer a set of rites that, in claiming to ignore, forget, or not notice, actually do the opposite. For in relation to sex, there is a specific, ready-made, obvious substitute for polymorphism: adult, genitally focused sexuality. In the dance class the hint was given more directly – although none of the students ever spoke the word *sex* or named the genitals, our collective failure to do so centred them, in much the same way as do the drawings and the effaced book illustration. And we adults giggled at the suggestion, implicit in the instructor's winks and wiggles, that dance is a kind of sex.

Even the kindergarten pupil accepts the idea that 'some things are too hot to touch,' and creates, from the collision of that warning and her own curiosity, the urgent need to 'handle it because it's too hot to handle' (Phillips, 1999, p. 116).

'Too hot to handle' was a phrase my dance instructors used to refer to moves they believed were too advanced (too sexual?) to teach us just yet. We were, after all, kindergarteners in the school of samba. It was for them to decide when we were ready to learn those moves, just as schools teach sex education when the adults who make curriculum deem that children are ready. In Ontario, for instance, this readiness seems not to arise before Grade 3. To wit, the only reference to bodies in Ontario's current kindergarten curriculum (Ministry of Education [MOE], 2006b, p. 53), apart from distinctions between gross and fine muscle coordination, states that 'young children need to engage in enjoyable and stimulating learning activities that encourage exploration of their world; promote physical skills; enhance neural processing; and develop a general awareness of their bodies' needs, limitations, and capabilities.'

Curiously, this raises the age at which discussion of *any* body part is mandated. In its 1998 iteration the kindergarten Health and Physical Activity curriculum (MOE, 1998, p. 19) states that 'by the end of Kindergarten, children will ... name body parts and talk about their function (e.g., eyes, teeth, ears, nose).' But in the current (2006) version it is not until Grade 1 that children are expected to 'identify the major parts of the body by their proper names,' and not until Grade 2 that they are to 'distinguish the similarities and differences between themselves and others (e.g., in terms of body size or gender), describe parts of the human body, the functions of these parts, and behaviours that contribute to good health.'

Children are expected to demonstrate understanding of 'basic human and animal reproductive processes (e.g., the union of egg and sperm)' in Grade 3, to describe 'secondary physical changes at puberty (e.g., growth of body hair, changes in body shape) [and] ... the processes of menstruation and spermatogenesis' in Grade 5, and to 'identify the methods of transmission and the symptoms of sexually transmitted diseases (STDs), and ways to prevent them' in Grade 7. Curiously, in what might arguably constitute another use of language to sublimate a sublimation, Grade 7 and 8 students respectively are required to 'explain the term *abstinence* as it applies to healthy sexuality' and to 'explain the importance of abstinence as a positive choice for adolescents' (MOE, 2006a; italics in original). *Abstinence* is the only term they are specifically required by this document to explain: *sex* or *sexuality* or *sexual activity* apparently either require no explanation or are considered not yet appropriate, though one might expect that defining *abstinence* might be a good deal easier with some reference to *activity*.

To eliminate the genitals from pedagogical discourses of the body is to delimit the child's polymorphous sexual curiosity. But the empty space this delimiting creates may also hint at a requirement of Phillips's 'gospel of development' (1999, p. 24): the need to 'lose interest in order to find it.' Educators, in declining to name or represent sexuality, may paradoxically be encouraging the re-finding, and perhaps even the augmentation, of that interest.

Naming by not-naming; returning the gaze to what we are trying not to look at: these moves hint at something more than the unspoken, unconscious requirement that children move from polymorphism to adult sexuality. When Britzman speaks of the 'elusive theories of our little sex researchers meet[ing] the elusive theories of our big sex researchers – adults' (1998, p. 77), perhaps she is speaking partly of a contradiction between education's views of children as too young and innocent to know anything, and simultaneously as already knowing too much. This contradiction invokes a conundrum. For the appearance of the reality principle 'implies no deposing of the pleasure principle, but only a safeguarding of it' (Freud, 1911, p. 41). If educators unconsciously recall and even retain something of the pleasure of their own early polymorphism, efforts to help children exit that state might be thwarted by unconscious wishes to safeguard it. And perhaps within those contradictory wishes dwells the hope that the child approaching adult sexuality, like the adult dance student, might not quite forget *all* the pleasure of imagined omnipotence, of polymorphism, indeed of pleasure itself.

In reflecting on these texts, one drawn, another danced, and a child's engagement or non-engagement with them, my questions lean away from the urge to correct and toward Schafer's (1992) 'What have we here?' and Paley's (2004) 'Who are you?' Recalling Felman's distinction between applications and implications of psychoanalysis (1982), and mindful of Tobin's Foucault-inspired urging of a rejection of the 'traps and tropes of the repressive hypothesis' and 'heroic antirepression' (1997a, pp. 11–12), my aim is to invite educators, and others who think about education, to attend to what is left out of these and other texts, reflect on the explanations given for the omissions, and consider whether those explanations truly make sense – or whether the kinds of sense, or meaning, they make might silence other senses and meanings. A psychoanalytic reading of the omissions and the explanations suggests that although the order, founded on cultural constructions of childhood and sexuality and given to teachers by mainstream educational discourses, may be to ignore sexual curiosity, it is carried out in ways that hint at why ignoring is never complete – the partiality of repression and the complexity of sublimation. 'What the speaking being *says*,' writes Kristeva, 'does not subsume sexuality' (2000, p. 32; italics in original). Nor is it subsumed by what that speaking being *does not* say: those little sex researchers pursue their investigations despite aims to thwart them.

I do not know whether the child at my dance class was ever in that kindergarten classroom during the day. But I do know that on one night, her attention was not on the diagrams of bodies pinned to the wall but on the living, moving bodies around her. And while her investigation was clearly her own, it also offered a reflection for the adults, the big sex researchers whose giggles and blushes showed that we knew just what was meant by oblique references to where we should feel the music. The dance class too is a body map, with its own empty space in the middle that, like the gap in the kindergarten drawing, gives both orders and hints. Its orders, however, point precisely and narrowly, directing us to look *at*, not *away from*, a *somewhere else* that is actually *right here*. Conversely its hints, helped along by the little sex researcher, seem to gesture both outward and backward, toward that earlier and larger sexuality that involved the whole body, back when dancing was so much easier.

This chapter has considered some of the dances educators do, moving with and against, and sometimes sidestep or even mis-step, questions of the body and how (or whether) to represent it in teaching and learning. Let us look now at another kind of 'body' that in recent years has become something of a presence in places of – and perhaps in some cases *in place of* – teaching.

5 Another Nice Mess:
Teachers Translated by Technology

Caminante, no hay camino,
se hace camino al andar.
[Wanderer, there is no path,
the path is made by walking.]
— Antonio Machado, *Proverbios y Cantares XXIX* [my translation]

If this episode has taught us anything,
it's that nothing works better than the status quo.
— Principal Skinner, *The Simpsons*

In April of 1997 I used an IBM Selectric typewriter to draft the final paper for the last course of my undergraduate degree. I was not a very good typist, and there were streaks of liquid paper where I had made corrections: the professor told me it looked old-fashioned.

That fall I entered a teacher education program as one of a cohort of 70 student teachers. Some of us had computers at home; many did not. Six of us were recruited for a project called 'Hands On Information Technology' (HOIT), whose aim was to facilitate computer use among novice teachers, practising teachers, and school administrators, and a month or so into the term I drove home with two big boxes containing my first computer. For the whole first term I typed my assignments on my trusty typewriter. Eventually, though, I began using the new machine to type essays. In January I sent my first email. In February I used a chart template for a lesson plan. But that was all.

I recall only one computer instruction session during that year. Near the end of the year the HOIT group met to discuss all the ways in which we had used the computers. Most of what we were asked about – search engines, online conferencing, PowerPoint – was utterly unfamiliar to me. Even though most of my five fellow student teachers were as silent in that meeting as I, I felt sheepish and contrite at my lack of knowledge and at having disappointed the enthusiastic people running the project. Not sorry to pack the computer up and return it, I did not expect to buy another.

I have had several computers since then, and am comfortable using them, though there are still applications I avoid. I still worry that any day now a previously unimagined negative force will make every word I have ever written disappear. At night I save the day's work on a memory stick. Then I email it to myself, at two addresses – when I remember, that is. Sometimes I forget, and I wake in the night afraid it will all be gone by morning. My children, who have used computers since the ages of five and eight, find me amusing, quaint. As do my students: when I teach I have the system administrator set up a desktop conference with access for myself and my students, but I use it mostly for reminders about due dates. I almost never use PowerPoint. The courses I teach are not really amenable to a high degree of technology use, and the overhead projector is just fine. Or so I tell myself.

In 1967, sociologist Waller asked, 'What does teaching do to teachers?' (1967, p. 375) – a curious and crucial question which implicitly recognizes that teachers, like the other participants in education, are in linguistic terms both agent and patient: both 'doing' and 'done to,' interacting with and being acted on by students, colleagues, administrators, politicians, families, and the myriad forces of education as a whole. I recast Waller's question in a technological mould: What does *the computer* do to teachers? Specifically, what does learning to teach with information and communications technologies (ICT) do to the work, the voice, the identity of a teacher?[1]

This chapter grew out of these early uncertain interactions with computers as well as experiences I have had in several research studies involving ICT in education. In early 2000 I interviewed 20 educators for the 'Innovative Models of Learning' project, which aimed to assess innovative ICT use and teachers' responses to it.[2] The following summer I analysed interviews for the Second International Technology in Education Study (SITES 2), a study of innovative pedagogical practices in 28 countries (see Lotherington, Morbey, Granger, & Doan, 2001; Granger, Morbey, Lotherington, Owston, & Wideman, 2002). Over 2001 and 2002, I conducted an assessment of the Academic Services Associates (ASA), a professional development model then in use in the Toronto District School Board (TDSB), and part of the Online Professional-development for Educators Network (OPEN). That project too involved interviewing administrators, teachers, and planners (Granger, 2002).

From my analyses of nearly 100 hours of interviews, patterns of contrast and contradiction emerged. Aims and achievements were measured and defined differently both within and among schools, and enthusiasm for new technologies was coupled with conflict. Even teachers who were outwardly highly motivated toward the use of ICT felt pulled in competing directions. Patterns emerged in the reasons given for the conflicts, relating to material resources, time, technical training and support, and the place of the computer in education. Also present was evidence of ambivalence and resistance. For instance, teachers who expressed appreciation for workshops held during class time later complained that those sessions took them away from their students. Others, concerned about the amount of time the project was taking up outside of working hours, came to divide their engagements with ICT into categories they named work (done at school) and play (outside of school), thereby articulating, in my view, something of a refusal to be controlled by the project and the administrators in charge of it (Granger, 2003).

I wondered whether those patterns might be telling only part of the story, whether in those meetings and projects, and all that talk, there might also be some silent spaces around how we were working with (or against) ICT integration. Several questions arose: How do computers change the work of teaching? How do teachers respond to such changes? Why are some teachers ambivalent about or resistant to ICT implementation? Is something other than technical and pedagogical concerns at stake in implementation demands? How might teachers' identities be affected, even silenced, by these mandates and by the technologies? And how can we engage those worries and those silences in ways that go beyond merely accepting them as simply the way things are or, alternatively, interpreting them as indicating that something is broken and trying to fix it without considering or caring what it might tell us?

The Computer and the Teacher

Conceptions of the computer as rich with potential for innovation and progress converge from many directions. Justifications for its use in education fall into four broad categories: workplace-oriented views of crucial high-tech skills; democratic ideas about ICT as a cure for social inequities; pedagogical convictions that ICT benefits learning and motivation vis-à-vis technical skills and academic content; and, of most interest here, praxis-focused notions of improvements in teaching through increased efficiency and/or productivity and shifts in approach.[3] Following Suppes's prediction (1980 [1967], p. 234) that the computer's speed would let teachers 'deal on an individual basis with a number of students simultaneously' and reduce or eliminate the need to repeat lessons, proponents enthuse over promised benefits regarding test- and worksheet-generation, grading and record-keeping, information searches, and individualized instruction (Hope, 1997; Provenzo, Brett, & McCloskey, 1999), or speak of ICT as offering solutions to issues such as classroom overcrowding and increased teacher workload (Burbules & Callister, 2000).

In contrast are claims to the effect that ICT integration has been slow or otherwise disappointing (Lesgold & Lesgold, 1996; Cuban, 2001; Schwab & Foa, 2001; Bauer & Kenton, 2005; Wang, 2008; Assude, Buteau, & Forgasz, 2010). While there are many reasons for such disappointments, I concur with Sofia's assessment (1996, p. 59) that they are in part grounded in 'technological neophilia' – an uncritical equation of the new and the progressive that understands ICT as a panacea for educational and social problems. They may also be partly due to the unpredictability of technology's consequences. For instance, in some cases relief promised for overcrowded classrooms translates in reality into overcrowded computer labs, as in a school I know where the lab has only enough machines for half a class. The room is too small for students to share terminals, so half the children stay next door in the library, visible by the teacher but not directly supervised, and each student has computer access for only half of the single 40-minute weekly period for which the lab is reserved. In other cases, the promise of ICT to ease time pressures and teachers' workloads may be compromised by increased access to computers, at school and home, which can paradoxically lead to more (and intensified) work (Goss, 1996): 'more routine planning, preparation and one-to-one intervention' according to the Organisation for Economic Co-operation and Development (OECD, 2001, p. 74).

Thus what ICT is presumed to cure it can also complicate; what is good for learners, or for teachers, is not always obvious. Of concern is the flattening tendency to conflate the acquisition of technology with the abandonment of didacticism, in a way that sees ICT as 'a lever that changes basic aspects of instruction ... [and] transform[s] ... curriculum and teaching practice' (Johnson, Schwab, & Foa, 1999, pp. 28–30). Calls for constructivist and learner-centred pedagogies pervade much of the rhetoric on the benefits of computer integration and use, and seem to imply two assumptions: that ICT is essential for constructivist teaching, and that without it the potential for such teaching is very limited. This judgment flies in the face of perceptions teachers may have of themselves as already using constructivist models. And it is potentially even more problematic for those who are not persuaded of the validity of shifting to constructivism, or of a necessary and direct relationship between ICT and that shift, or of the usefulness of technology in general: many researchers concur that despite its promises the actual impact of ICT on teaching varies considerably and in some cases is surprisingly small (Evans-Andris, 1995; Bossert, 1996; Kerr, 1996; Maddux, 1998; de Castell, Bryson, & Jenson, 2001; Ribeiro & vanBarneveld, 2008). Significantly, Cuban (2001, p. 95) finds that even the minority of teachers who claim to have shifted to a student-centred methodology are using primarily didactic instruction 'even in computer-based classes.'

Time is a problem that compounds other obstacles. More specifically, there is never enough of it (Sandholtz, Ringstaff, & Dwyer, 1997, Granger et al., 2002). For example, in the Innovative Models project, just three months were allotted for wiring and hardware installation, teacher training, and curricular integration. Additionally, connectivity issues and hardware breakdowns mean time must be taken to develop non-ICT backup plans for all technology-driven lessons (Cuban, 2001); time spent planning, and on technical matters, means teachers cannot give individual students the attention that ICT promises to free them up to provide (Evans-Andris, 1996): in the OPEN study, teachers found themselves spending many evening and weekend hours, often reluctantly, on improving their computer skills in order to use them in their teaching (Granger, 2002).

The demands ICT places on teachers are part of a larger picture: the similarly mixed and mixed-up, broader and deeper goals of education as a whole. Labaree (1997) and Egan (1997) offer, respectively, sets of 'contradictory' and 'incompatible' ideas – democratic equality versus social efficiency and social mobility (Labaree), and the socialization of children into the status quo versus a Platonic commitment to intellect or a Rousseauian focus on experience (Egan) – which they contend fight for primacy. In tandem with what Cuban (1993b, p. 204) calls 'prized values' of ICT (learner autonomy, independence, and cooperative skills; readiness for work in a high-tech marketplace; efficiency, and productivity in teaching and learning), Egan and Labaree implicitly invite questions around how ICT, along with other perceived instruments for change, works with or against education's aims.

Work in curriculum theory over the past decade (including Noble, 1998; Pinar, Reynolds, Slattery, & Taubman, 2000; Cuban, 2001; Engle, 2001; McNeil, 2002; Kincheloe, 2008; Giroux, 2010) points to a corporate penetration of schools that, according to Giroux (2000, p. 85), aims 'to transform public education ... [so as] to expand the profits of investors, educate students as consumers, and train young people for the low-paying jobs of the new global marketplace.' Nearly a decade on Kincheloe (2008, p. 10) confirms the persistence of this trajectory, asserting that the 'privatization and corporatization of education [has become] a key dimension of the public conversation about schooling and more and more of an actual reality.' Kincheloe goes on to say that post-secondary education in particular has been 'compromised by corporate influences [along with] ... new forms of dependency on corporate and funding as governments back away from fiscal support.'

This incursion follows an institutional shift to the political right in the 1970s and early 1980s, which itself displaced transformative models such as Freire's conscientização (2005).[4] Freirean ideals persist (see, among others, Pinar et al., 2000; Giroux, 2010), in the work of groups from grassroots organizations to faculties of education on discourses and practices of inclusivity, antiracist and antihomophobic education, and, generally, pedagogies directed at social change and democracy – even in the face of varied and contrary ties among governments, industry, and schooling. And yet such transformative discourses, along with those of constructivism, learner autonomy, and student-centred learning, while familiar to most teachers, may be overshadowed by the regulatory language of assessment and accountability (Education Quality and Accountability Office [EQAO], 2006), and by other 'cultures of control' which, asserts Apple (2010, p. 190), continue to be central to education's 'project of conservative modernization,' while 'counterhegemonic practices ... are too often isolated from each other and never get organized into coherent movements and strategies.'

Where are teachers amid the pushes and pulls of these competing ideas? How shall we think about scenarios in which teachers' individual or collective beliefs concerning education's purpose – that is, what is best for learners – remain silent because they fall outside the precepts understood as justifying ICT use and integration? A teacher whose goal is to inspire students to work for social change might see computers as potentially useful for subverting the status quo, or as one of the 'master's tools' (Lorde, 1983) and therefore a capitulation to inequitable commercial and capitalist structures that is by definition counterproductive, or as quite simply irrelevant to her work. Another, valuing meditative reflection and worried by views equating learning with the rapid acquisition of information, might resist or reject technology on that basis alone. We should also recognize that while some teachers may indeed resist ICT, in other cases it is the imposed rush to implementation that is resisted. It makes eminent sense that a teacher might want, need, and even insist on creating an opportunity to decide where she stands – on any change, technological or otherwise – before adopting it. As well, what teachers do with respect to computers tends, like much else, to be externally determined and delimited (see McClintock, 2001), such that even when freedom to choose exists, choices are mediated by numerous factors: professional history, 'personal subjective educational theory' (van den Berg, 2002), and the prevailing perception, summarized by Bryson and de Castell (1998), that the ICT revolution is an inescapable sea change, and that the individual teacher must either swim with the tide or sink like a Ludditic stone.

Foundational (albeit multiple, varied, and sometimes resisted) presumptions exist about teaching and teachers in which contemporary culture is deeply invested, and which shape responses to the question of how the teacher is to carry out her work. I refer here to how the category of teacher is itself conceived: what kind of person a teacher ought to be, or ought *not* to be, and what kind of person ought – or, again, ought *not* – to be a teacher; and how the social and discursive construction of the category informs how individual teachers carry out their responsibilities.

Two areas of interest emerge here, each grounded in discourses of education as both gendered to a significant degree and framed by complex power dynamics. The first area of interest is the ubiquitous and enduring question of whether teaching is, or ought to be, understood as a profession; the second is the consideration of whether notions of love and care are, or ought to be, the principles that inform the teacher's work and her approach to and understanding of that work. Teachers' technological successes often come at a price – both in terms of day-to-day practice and also in ways at once more broadly professional (in terms of disruptions to their autonomy) and more deeply personal, in the sense of profound derangements of their identities as particular kinds of teachers.

The Teacher's Work, the Teacher's Power: Autonomy and Authority

Acker discusses gendered institutional 'opportunity structures' (1989b, p. 9) in which male domination of higher education, and of positions of higher responsibility at elementary and secondary levels, translates into a preponderance of women especially in elementary classrooms. The female-to-male ratio is particularly striking among younger teachers: in 1999, males comprised 39 percent of teachers over 55 years of age but just 22 per cent of those under 30 (Giguère, 1999); by 2006, the percentage of male teachers in Ontario was still only 26 (Jamieson, 2007).

The perception that classroom teaching is women's work is complexly both cause and consequence of the preponderance of female teachers in elementary schools, and the ways *feminine* and *natural* are collapsed is of special interest here.

In her examination of femininity, Walkerdine (1990, p. 20) connects the 'scientific' construction of the child as pedagogical object and the influx of women into teaching (both starting near the end of the nineteenth century) with a shift to 'education according to nature' – the Rousseauian concept of 'a natural path of development' for children, the guiding of which women, believed more intuitive and less intellectual than men, were deemed better suited. Relatedly, Miller (1996, p. 101) reveals the mutually informing constructions of gender, in and out of schools, through which teachers, like mothers, are seen as having a principally pedagogical relationship to their children's development. Miller outlines two polarized understandings of teachers, either as scholars who wander as if by accident into teaching, or as idealized mothers working intuitively. She draws primarily on the latter view to help explain why both 'training ... [and] the paraphernalia of professionalism' (1996, p. 101) are frequently considered unnecessary, even redundant, in common-sense views of teaching as something almost anyone – at least anyone female – can do. To her the apparent contradiction between a traditional Western reliance on women to teach young children and a historical reluctance (until relatively recently) to educate females at all grows less incongruous when looked at in tandem with the notion that the child-rearing and education customarily done by women are natural or instinctual, needing little or no training (1996, p. 1). The work women do is thus collapsed with *women's work*.

Conceptualizing teaching as feminine also has implications for its status as a profession: for Gitlin and Labaree (1996, p. 90), for instance, the socially constructed devaluation of women's pedagogical work, based on general stereotypes of women, creates a systemic barrier to professional status. It does this, Casey and Apple argue (1989, pp. 174–5), by devaluing non-rational, non-intellectual, and affective components of teaching and characterizing it as a 'deviant' profession whose members, in comparison with medical, legal, business, and military professionals, are 'wanting in terms of ... esoteric expertise, autonomy, and so forth.' For Casey and Apple, then, the proletarianization of teaching is unsurprising, since the work women do is seen as 'inferior ... simply because it is women who do it' (1989, p. 179). In this scenario the categories *feminine* and *professional* are, de facto, mutually exclusive: to assert either category is to silence the other.

The proletarianization of teaching is evident historically, in relations between women's growing participation in it and a concomitant increase in external control over it (Apple, 1986). Competing notions of professionalism in educational settings and discourses, as well as in public perception, embody contradictory ideas about whether teachers either possess or lack certain forms of power. In the context of ICT debates, this means that alongside pedagogical and ethical dilemmas, time shortages and logistical problems, non- or limited use of (or resistance to) ICT might for some teachers be related to questions of power (see Apple, 1988; Apple & Jungck, 1998; Kahn & Friedman, 1998). Sarason writes:

> The sense of power is the sense that you have been accorded the respect and given practical responsibility to have *some* voice in determining what and how you will learn and act. To feel powerless is to feel that your ideas, opinions, and interests do not deserve a hearing; you are the object of the discharge of the power of others; your role is to do what you are told, like it or not; your role is to conform, to play the game by the rules of others. (1996, p. 344; italics in original)

Sarason's comment speaks to both the *autonomy*, that 'action that finds its source in the subject' (Todorov, 2002, p. 47), which for teachers means self-direction (Little, 1991) and freedom from control (Benson, 2000), and the *authority*, 'given to professionals in exchange for confidence and trust in their abilities, skills, and ... knowledge about a particular endeavour' (Gitlin & Labaree, 1996, p. 89), the absence of which positions teachers below governments, school boards, and administrators, but above students.

The distinction is somewhat artificial: a teacher's *autonomy* is granted by those in *authority* over her – and both autonomy and authority are limited. This may be especially true in a historical moment when, contends Robertson (1996, p. 29), societal shifts to the political right have resulted in consequences for educators including 'wage roll-backs, ...

larger class sizes, more administration, [and] massive budget cuts.' To this list I add externally imposed curricula, mandated testing, an increasingly multicultural and multilingual student body, ever-growing demands vis-à-vis learner needs generally, and the call to use technology: a 'deskilling' move that disrupts and at least partly silences teacher authority, autonomy, and identity.

Deskilling is bureaucratic control incorporated invisibly into the structure of work (Apple, 1985), which is itself 'broken down into atomistic units, redefined, and then appropriated ... to enhance both efficiency and control of the ... process' (Apple, 1986, p. 209; fn 3). It is particularly significant in the work women do (Apple & Jungk, 1998), of which an archetype is education[5] – where it is manifested as the restructuring of teachers' work toward ever more specialized sets of pedagogical and technical skills that pre-empt involvement with social or moral issues, curricular concerns, 'independent inquiry [and] intellectual critique' (Hargreaves & Goodson, 1996, p. 13). Deskilling is accompanied by intensification, whose implications range from 'being allowed no time at all even to ... have a cup of coffee or relax, to having *a total absence of time to keep up with one's field*' (Apple, 1986, p. 41; my italics). In difficult fiscal times, when demands for ICT integration are juxtaposed with other calls to do more with fewer resources, a teacher who must spend time with basic technical matters may come to feel 'like a mechanic' and to resent ICT (Evans-Andris, 1996). The call to use ICT, and the deskilling and intensification that inhere in its implementation, suggest a truncation of teacher autonomy amounting to a 'deprofessionalization.' In the rush to get it all done (and done quickly), we might ask how much time or inclination is left for teachers to reflect professionally on ICT's potential for them and their students. In circumstances like these, reflection itself might be rendered silent, as the very last thing teachers would be inclined to do – a view supported by the notion that one effect of intensification is an intellectual deskilling (Larson, 1980, cited in Apple, 1986, p. 42). We might also ask if the same could apply to professional interaction among teachers, given claims that ICT is conducive to collaboration and team teaching (Johnson et al., 1999; Lotherington et al., 2001).

I am guided here by Britzman's thinking (1991), that teaching is 'fundamentally a dialogic relation, characterized by mutual dependency, social interaction and engagement,' which grows over-individualized through 'the *supposed autonomy and very real isolation* of the teacher in the current school structure' (1991, pp. 237–8; my italics). It requires no great leap to see that a naturalized cycle of intensified teacher labour, brought about by mandated use of specific technologies and leading to a decrease in time and inclination for collaboration, might both diminish autonomy and increase isolation.

In such a scenario isolation itself becomes naturalized, and resisting it and its implications grows ever more difficult, even unthinkable. But happily, human endeavour is not so easily pressed into the formulaic. Apple (1985, p. 148) notes that attempts at technical control often bump into 'contradictory effects' that subvert them. And my experience in the OPEN project (Granger, 2003) seems to support this view: there, teachers viewed by administrators as overly dependent on their more technologically skilled colleagues may in fact have been subtly resisting both the demand to increase their skills (and concomitantly workloads) as well as the loss of opportunity (or power) to reflect on the value of those skills and on ICT itself. Of course, it might be argued that more skills mean more choices, more power, and more autonomy, such that in a high-tech setting refusing to acquire computer skills is a move not toward, but away from, autonomy. For instance, the OPEN teachers were often delayed by having to wait for support they would not have needed had they known how to reboot their machines or access email. These tasks had to be taught repeatedly to a number of those teachers; what is curious about this is that they are simple operations involving only a few steps. The fact that teachers had considerable difficulty with them suggests that perhaps something more than a lack of ability may have been at play. I read their refusal to jump onto the ICT-skills bandwagon as an astute if unintended way for those teachers to retain a degree of autonomy.

Is ICT a professionalizing or a *de*professionalizing force? Is it a liberatory bump in an otherwise smooth road to external control of education that will allow educators to retain some autonomy? Is it a component of that control? Or is it something more labile, comprising elements of all of these, shifting among them continually to varying degrees and in different contexts? It seems clear that autonomy is curtailed with the imposition of new, incompatible demands. Such working conditions create gaps between what teachers are expected to do with ICT and what they *can* do: gaps grounded in distinct and often contradictory views of what education as a whole ought to be doing.

It seems that a technology presumed to liberate and empower is beset from the start by constraints and limitations, such that educators might well be suspicious of calls for a wholesale commitment to ICT integration. Teachers are professionals, not superheroes. Obliged to undertake a set of tasks that are mutually incompatible in circumstances that facilitate neither implementation nor success, and to do so with little support, they are bound to perceive their autonomy as threatened. Deprofessionalization is more than deskilling; and deskilling is more than the dumbing-down of work. Both threaten autonomy, and both have an impact on identity.

A teacher's professional identity is affected by multiple and conflicting demands. At issue is how she will meet all those demands. And if she cannot, how will she determine which have priority? What will happen to the others? Must they be pushed out of the way, effectively silenced? But alongside this conundrum, her personal sense of herself as a teacher is also affected. What kind of teaching is she supposed to do? And what kind of teacher is she supposed to *be*? For one's work as a teacher is implicated in one's being-as-a-teacher; 'the problem of authority is a problem of identity' (Pagano, 1988, p. 525).

A Problem of Identity: The Teacher Relocated

In postmodern discourse identity is usually understood as socially and historically informed, and also continually in flux. A teacher's identity is grounded partly in her personal history as learner and teacher, and partly in historic, institutional, and societal views of the role. Egan's tripartite categorization of how that role is perceived (1997, p. 239) – the model who guides learners to 'approximate the ideal of adult citizenship'; the Platonic authority who brings students to mastery of important knowledge; and the solicitous Rousseauian facilitator who encourages individual development – illustrates the idea that identity is a matter of perspective. But some perceptions of the category of teacher have persisted for centuries: one of these is the notion of the teacher as master.

That word means many things. Teachers are never entirely in control of every aspect of their work – even if they had unfettered freedom to determine curriculum and pedagogy, the determination would be informed by their social and professional milieu. Equally, given the vicissitudes of daily life, the classroom is never predictable. Still, teachers have traditionally been understood to be the masters of at least the classroom domain, not only charged with teaching their students, but also in charge of those students. This authority is understood and largely unquestioned even by teachers themselves. Teachers are also viewed (and view themselves) as masters of their knowledge and skills: academic content and pedagogical knowledge, personal practical knowledge (Clandinin & Connelly, 1995), and skills such as classroom management, goal-setting and 'community building' (Apple & Jungk, 1998, p. 134). Here, the teacher-student dynamic approximates that of master and apprentice. Educators hold the knowledge, dispensing it to learners as appropriate; in what Freire famously named the 'banking model' (2005, p. 72) they make 'deposits which the students patiently receive, memorize, and repeat.' They also hold the knowledge needed to determine that appropriateness, to know precisely when and how 'deposits' should be made.

A third version of teacher-as-master blends the first two, positioning the teacher as the focal point of the student's gaze: the pedagogical, relational, and even geographical (Bourdieu & Passeron, 1990) centre of her classroom. The principal in Rice's 1892 study, who, on being asked if students in his school were allowed to turn around in their seats, replied, 'Why should they look behind them when the teacher is in front of them?' (Rice, 1969; cited in Cuban, 1993a, p. 28), embodies Freire's view of the teacher as 'narrating Subject' and pupils as 'patient, listening objects' (Freire, 2005, p. 71). That principal's view might be articulated less baldly today, but it does persist, particularly where cries for accountability complicate calls for constructivist teaching and self-directed learning.

These entrenched classroom structures, along with externally originating, time-draining curricula that teachers have trouble getting through even without the addition of technological integration, have important implications for both thinking about and using technology. My own teacher-education students report that in many of their practicum classrooms time at the computer centre, located off in a corner, is still used almost exclusively as a reward for students whose 'real work' is done. And while there are certainly many teachers enthusiastically using computers in their teaching who are quite untroubled by its demands (see, for example, Barrell, 2001; PyllikZillig, Bodvarsson, & Bruning, 2005; Sigafoos & Green, 2007; Lever-Duffy & McDonald, 2008), some research suggests that educators often remain ambivalent, uncertain, or unprepared for computer use (Barrell, 2001; di Petta, Woloshyn, & Novak, 2008; Warren, 2008). Even when technology is taken up it is often done in didactic, teacher-centred ways (Evans-Andris, 1996; Cuban, 2001; de Castell et al., 2001; Smeets & Mooij, 2001), such that while enactments of the teacher-as-master metaphor vary in degree, and flexible pedagogical approaches can and do shift the focus away from the teacher now and then (Scardamalia & Bereiter, 1996), the teacher is still at the centre even of a relatively democratic classroom.

This may not be deliberate, but it is no less true: ICT acts on both conscious and unconscious structures of teaching, and with the drive to implement it come challenges to the trope of teacher-as-master. Among these are the related questions of skills acquisition and the assessment of ICT for curricular relevance, usefulness, and appropriateness. Teachers come to technology with very different degrees of interest in or expertise with both ICT and its use in education (McClintock, 2001; Granger et al., 2002). At least some have not yet mastered the computer, especially as a pedagogical tool, and whether deferring to experts in these matters, or using professional development time to acquire relevant knowledge, in relation to ICT the teacher is no longer master or teacher. She is a learner.

While at times 'students teaching teachers can re-orient power relationships within classrooms, giving students a more equitable voice in relation to the authority figure of the teacher' (Lotherington et al., 2001, p. 144), this may not always be what a teacher wants or can tolerate. For Lawson and Comber, shifting relations can be uncomfortable 'precisely because the blurring of the boundaries cuts across ... traditional perceptions [and] ... teachers can experience a loss of certainty in their own roles and status' (2000, p. 426). The new constructions – *teacher-as-student-as-learner* on one hand, and *teacher's-student-as-teacher* on the other – may also be at odds with the expectation that teachers' learning should be grounded in their teaching, thus challenging the notion that teacher development ought to arise out of earlier mastery. Additionally, there may be a sinister implication, in teachers knowing less than their students, that something which ought to be known is not. Here is where the naturalized discursive notion of teacher-as-master can break down, in a subtle devaluation of what they have always done and been.

Pervasive in ICT discourse is the idea that to *do* what needs to be done with technology, and to *be* good teachers-using-technology, educators must change both their teaching and their thinking *about* teaching. The claim of computer promoters (see Papert, 1993; Hativa & Lesgold, 1996; Bromley, 1998; Jonassen, 2000, Engle, 2001) is often that ICT integration can and should provoke a movement in the teacher from didacticism to constructivism – from 'sage on the stage' to 'guide on the side' – and ultimately a related shift in the student, to autonomous and self-directed learning. But it may be tricky for a teacher to make that move, in effect to translate her way of being-as-a-teacher from master to facilitator.

The challenges may be further magnified if a teacher's authority is destabilized by her undeveloped technical skills and ambivalence or uncertainty as to the computer's pedagogical usefulness. Simon's (1992) claim that new ideas can threaten established worldviews supports the possibility that teachers might infer, in the demand to adopt ICT, a judgment that *non*-ICT constructivism lacks a crucial feature that only computers can provide.

Another rupture is implied in the teacher's relocation from *master* to *facilitator.* More specifically, that relocation, coupled with the tendency in some pro-ICT rhetoric to equate the computer with infinite information, and that information with knowledge (OECD, 2001), underlines the fact that the teacher no longer has all the answers. Not only may she know, and be seen to know, less about the computer (and its use) than her students, but in addition, what knowledge she does have is vastly outdistanced by the computer itself in terms of content qua information. And so, while she retains the authority to guide internet access and limit computer use, she does so from the side rather than the centre.

The mix of potential dilemmas and destabilizing implications tosses a big wrench into the machinery of the teacher's work. Indeed, wrench may be the operative word, as the teacher is yanked from her location as master of the classroom domain and thrown into a new position where, given all her other duties, she may have little capacity even to consider these concerns. How then is she to think about all this? For although a teacher may theoretically support a constructivist view, of teaching and learning in general and/or ICT in particular, to enact that view is no small matter, especially in view of the centuries-old discourse that positions her in the centre to begin with, and current mandates that seem to shift away from teachers' (and by extension students') self-determination and toward standardized processes, objectives, and results.

A teacher may even imagine being wrenched from the profession altogether. Papert's (1984, p. 38) perhaps ironic prediction that 'the computer will blow up the school' hints at a fear some teachers may have in relation to ICT. Hannafin and Savenye report teachers feeling 'suddenly dispensable' in the face of ICT (1993, p. 26), while the OECD's report on ICT in education acknowledges the possibility of replacing teachers, 'at least in part – for the development of a course unit,' though it discounts the possibility of their total replacement (2001, pp. 25, 73). Concern for professional self-preservation is understandable – what teacher would willingly jump through the hoops that ICT places in front of her if as a consequence of doing so she might compute herself right out of a job? At the same time, however, it is also a concern for the preservation of the *self as teacher*, for if the school is blown up metaphorically in the kind of reconfiguration some claim ICT has the power to do, what happens to the teacher then? Indeed silence, as a strategy, might just make sense.

Lest we interpret this scenario as exaggerated, let us look to Levine's (2000) prediction, in relation to university education, that in a rapidly expanding online environment, 'faculty members will become increasingly independent of colleges and universities ... [and the] most renowned faculty members, those able to attract tens of thousands of students in an international marketplace, will become like rock stars.' I contend that the computer and demands for its use have the potential to interfere profoundly with both autonomy and authority; the former by disrupting professional discourses and practices, and the latter by displacing the teacher as locus of knowledge and power and redefining her in relation to her students. This 'existential concern,' write Worthington and Zhao (1999, p. 301), arises from 'a challenge to [a teacher's] world view ... [that] forces her to revisit and attempt to rejustify her beliefs and assumptions about the world.' Interwoven with these worries are personal responses rooted not in the *doing* of teaching but in the *being* of the teacher – her self. And I locate them in the notion of translation.

What does the computer do that can disrupt a teacher's *being*, silence part of her self, force a translation? First, in what may be the most usual sense of the word – the movement from one language to another – the traditional didactic approach to teaching is for most teachers the pedagogical mother-tongue. It is the model in which they were taught and which they have most often observed – even if it is not the model they were taught to use as teachers. Further, research suggests that it is still the predominant model in relation to teaching with ICT (Bowers, 1988; Evans-Andris, 1996; Kahn & Friedman, 1998; Smeets & Mooij, 2001), even when non-ICT teaching is less didactic (Cuban, 2001). Second, the perpetual negotiation a teacher must do, while juggling ICT with the many other requirements of her work, can be seen as a continual translation, an ongoing demand to reposition herself. And third, when these translations are themselves interrupted in ways that require the teacher, poised to let learning happen the new way, to shift suddenly into a non-technological backup plan, they are effectively a kind of simultaneous translation. The teacher must be two teachers, in the same moment.

But while these are interesting ways to conceive of the movement into ICT use (and accompanying pedagogical changes) as one kind of translation, the word can also refer to a transformation, alteration, change, or adaptation, or, as in physics, to a 'transference of a body, or form of energy, from one point of space to another.'[6] I want to consider these meanings in relation to the work and the being of the teacher, as altered by computers, even if the displacement they hint at seems more metaphorical than physical.

In the idealized constructivist scenario to which many educators and much ICT discourse aspire, the teacher moves aside and the pupil takes centre stage for learning. But with the teacher's metaphorical translation in the ICT context, it is the computer that is repositioned as the classroom's cynosure of information and knowledge. The figurative translation of the teacher into a new position relative to the computer and the students, in which she is still a teacher and yet *not* a teacher in quite the same way, changes the metaphorical angle from which she and her students perceive one another. This translation is more than a relocation. It is a crucial *dis*location, and, I contend, more than metaphorical; I turn now to consider the impact on the teacher of the computer as physical – and psychical – artefact.

Self, Love, Work: The Unconscious (in) Teaching

Language is tricky. To place *being* and *doing* in opposition is to imply that one is static, the other active, and the two quite separate. I suggest that identity is not always only one thing and that being and doing are entwined. There may be aspects of being a teacher – aspects of how one's *ways of being as a teacher* (Heidegger, 1996) are informed and constructed – that lie beneath the manifest level of teaching as practice. These aspects both inform and are informed by practice (and of course a multitude of other influences) but are not isomorphic with it.

Turkle (1985, 1997) links computers with psychoanalytic theory's bungled actions (parapraxes). Both are 'objects-to-think-with,' tools for an intellectual bricolage (Lévi-Strauss, 1968, cited in Turkle, 1985): the first compatible with postmodern epistemologies, and the second an 'appropriable theory ... with which people can become actively involved' (Turkle, 1997, p. 47–8). Taking her cue, I think *with* one object, psychoanalysis, *about* the other – the computer: specifically about the impact of that object on the teacher's psyche. My claim is that, alongside logistical, pedagogical, power-related, and professional reasons why the shift to ICT is sometimes difficult, there may also be, for some teachers, a vested psychical interest in the educational status quo.

That this thinking is speculative is key: I follow Felman (1982) in considering implication rather than undertaking application, for I concur with her and with Markham (1999, p. 63) that it would be inappropriate and incorrect to try to map a psychoanalytic encounter precisely onto a pedagogical one. Indeed, psychoanalytic theory itself asks that, rather than 'propagate the letter of our doctrines ... [we] rethink ... [them] constantly, in relation to a new object' (Lacan, 1950, p. 13, cited in Markham, 1999, p. 63). In that vein, my interest is in taking up the hints that psychoanalysis offers about computers, students, and teachers in relation to each other. My questions in this work are grounded in psychoanalytic theory's conviction that there is much going on in the psyche of which the conscious mind is unaware.

What is it about computers that interferes with unconscious aspects of the being-of-the-teacher? Viewed through a psychoanalytic prism, these questions hint at the idea that teaching – and *being* a teacher – meets particular intrapersonal needs and that it does so, as traditionally structured, in particular ways. Disrupting these structures, and the prevalent ways of thinking about them, has implications for education as a whole and for the ways teaching and learning are enacted. But such disruptions can also interfere with the meeting of those needs in ways that may have profoundly destabilizing implications for the teacher's internal world, even if she is not consciously aware of disruption or implication.

For Phillips (1999, p. xxii), 'lives are livable only if they give pleasure.'[7] And pleasure is crucial: for Freud (1911, p. 36), the 'pleasure-unpleasure principle' is the earliest of the drives that govern humans. This impulse, which aims to maximize pleasure and minimize its opposite, persists throughout life in increasingly attenuated form as the unconscious, in coming to know reality, gradually learns that the urge for immediate gratification can be deferred for longer-term gains through sublimation into socially acceptable, differently pleasurable, intellectual and/or creative activities – of which learning, with its attendant pleasures and other benefits, can be one. There are psychical pleasures we cannot articulate, which cannot really be said to be experienced consciously. And just as not all pleasures are consciously understood, nor are all reasons for choosing teaching as a profession.

This is not to say, however, that pleasure is not consciously experienced by teachers. Indeed it is one of the most frequently cited reasons for taking up the profession. Lortie's seminal sociological study (1975) suggests that the pleasures gained through interaction with, and influence on, students are key to teacher satisfaction. He also finds that the choice of teaching as a profession is rooted, for many, either in a family history of teaching or in positive childhood experiences with individual teachers (1975, pp. 43–8). My own experience as a student of education and as a teacher educator bears out these findings.

Working from a feminist perspective C. Luke (1996, p. 289) writes, of the pleasure of teaching, 'As authorized and authoritative signifier of knowledge, the teacher embodies both engendered power and authority, and a substantial amount of pleasure is invested in that position and embodiment of knowledge.' It seems to me that Luke is referring specifically to the *pleasure* the teacher experiences *by dint of* the power in her position; what is crucial here is the idea that power is valued because it gives pleasure, though the connection may not be consciously recognized and the educator may herself be unlikely to name power as either an impetus for the decision to teach or an informing component of the pleasure gained from teaching. Perhaps this is so partly because much educational discourse has, in recent decades, tended to privilege the Freirean idea of teachers as potential agents of liberation, a tendency manifested in what Walkerdine has termed, in part, 'a denial of power' by teachers who 'believed [they] could be friends with children, be partners in learning – no power, no hierarchy, called by [their] first names' (1990, p. 23). But perhaps it is also partly because teaching is categorized normatively as women's work in ways that implicitly frame power as masculine and therefore inappropriate for the woman teacher.

Here I return briefly to my earlier discussion of the perceived suitability of teaching as women's work, a set of perceptions reflected (as in Lortie, 1975) in educators' expression of their reasons for taking up teaching which tend to articulate their work as less an occupation than a calling guided by the desire and capacity to serve others (Miller, 1996). This commonplace view sees mothers as the crucially important 'first teachers of children' presumed to possess an innate pedagogical instinct (p. 1), and teachers as loving, caring (and for the most part passive) facilitators of children's natural development (Walkerdine, 1990). These discursive connotations of the categories of mother, teacher, and woman, grounded in historical, pre-feminist notions, persist in informing contemporary conversations even though it is well understood that not all teachers are women, and not all parents are mothers.

Indeed, the interweaving of the concepts of woman, teacher, and mother (see Dreeben, 1970; Acker, 1989a; Oram, 1989; Walkerdine, 1990; Miller, 1996) is crucial to understanding the inverse relation between the ages of school children and the preponderance of women as their teachers, as well as the value placed upon those teachers' work: here conceptualizations of personal qualities, beliefs, and practices are gendered. Noddings's ethic of care (1992), for example, informed and accompanied by beliefs in the primacy of relationships that turn on dynamics of caring for (and meeting the needs of) others, belongs to women no more inherently or exclusively than cognition does to men, but thus has it been understood. And this ethic of caring is simultaneously one of the chief commitments motivating teaching as a career and also one of the reasons it is devalued as a profession.

It is not, however, the only defining quality of teachers or teaching. Walkerdine (1990) argues that although higher education ultimately became available to aspiring female teachers, its initial purpose in training them to facilitate the 'natural development' of their pupils was to enhance their presumed innate ability to give children a 'a quasi-maternal nurturance' in a 'natural education' context that displaced overt discipline with 'covert surveillance ... enshrined in a word – "love" ' (1990, p. 21). This view has persisted:

> The position of women as teachers ... is vital to the notion of freeing and liberation implied in [progressive] pedagogy. It is love which will win the day, and it is the benevolent gaze of the teacher which will secure freedom from a cruel authority (in the family as well as the school). Through the figure of the maternal teacher the harsh power of the authoritarian father will be converted into the soft benevolence of the bourgeois mother. (Walkerdine, 1990, p. 19)

Miller (1996) echoes Walkerdine (1990) in citing love as an impulse informing both the desire to teach and the practice of teaching, describing the perception of the archetypal teacher as an 'idealised and indefatigably loving mother [who] watches over "her" children in order to bring out their latent talents.' She goes on to articulate the presumed reciprocity between teaching and mothering, pointing out that 'the teacher of young children has been thought of as "the mother made conscious" ... engaged in the ostensibly contradictory business of fostering nature while also intervening to improve on nature. ... [M]others are encouraged to believe that they have a primarily pedagogic relation to their children' (Miller, 1996, pp. 100–1).

Miller's articulation of the teacher as 'the mother made conscious' (p. 101) invites a psychoanalytic reading of the tropes of teacher-as-mother and mother-as-teacher. So too does Walkerdine's summary of the fantasy of education as transforming authority into motherly love – a fantasy articulated in explicitly psychoanalytic terms by A. Freud (1974, p. 120), for whom the teacher 'assumes for each of the children under his control the role of superego, and in this way acquires the right to their submission.' Here the claim is for something more and other than a parental role for the teacher of a child in the latency period, because the child too is both more and other than in earlier stages, having an inner voice or superego that mediates the more instinctual ego drives of infancy. The 'compulsory obedience' of the younger child has shifted to encompass a 'voluntary submission' to the internalized ideal that superego, in the form of the teacher and his or her authority, represents.

This new relation between (submitting) child and (submitted-to) teacher suggests a differently nuanced reworking of the earlier child-parent dynamic, which for psychoanalysis persists as an unconscious shadow. There is in this reworking or translation a suggestion of the Freudian concept of the mind as mystic writing-pad, unconsciously retaining shadowy yet influential traces of past psychical events (1924, p. 433) in a kind of translated version of an old script. And it is not just the learner's but also the teacher's relational script that is translated and which persists, as a shadowy form that *in*forms later relations with students, other teachers, and her unconscious self.

Narcissism and Transference: The Teacher in the (Lacanian) Mirror

A satisfying life, psychoanalytic theory tells us, requires that we be able to work and to love. And in listening to teachers talk about their work, it is hard not to think of love. The two are easily intertwined: a veteran primary teacher I know tells me, 'I've never given birth but I have hundreds of children. Teaching is a labour of love.' But love and work – and love *for* and *in* and *as* work – are complicated matters. I contend that alongside concerns about social and institutional constructions of the teacher's autonomy and authority, beliefs about the work of teaching are rooted in individual psychical histories, and social constructs, that enmesh the maternal and the pedagogical, care, and love.

We reveal much about our unconscious selves through language. Accidents of speech can be telling, as can metaphors; when a teacher refers to students as 'my children' a parental element shows itself. Given the evidence that the choice to teach is grounded in positive early experiences (Lortie, 1975), it is no great leap to suggest that teachers' feelings of caring and compassion for their students, while genuine, might arise to an extent from their own psychical needs, in part from a wish for power manifested in what might be read as the kind of love for the self that psychoanalysis calls a narcissistic object-choice (Freud, 1914c). In this architecture, parental love may embody elements of a parent's narcissism reborn – one's childhood self reflected in the off-spring who was once literally part of (especially) the mother.

So varied is the use of the terms 'primary narcissism' and 'second-ary narcissism' in psychoanalytic literature that a comprehensive and precise definition is 'impossible' (Laplanche & Pontalis, 1973, p. 377). While this variability enriches psychoanalytic theory, it also compli-cates it. Given that I am using psychoanalytic concepts as a thinking-object and not a diagnostic tool, a comprehensive disquisition on narcissism and the narcissistic object-choice would be excessive here: it is sufficient to note that for my purposes here, narcissism can be understood as a 'stage in the development [between] anarchic, auto-erotic functioning ... [and] object-choice,' a kind of peculiar double moment that accompanies the inception of the ego, but also involves the ego as the love-object of the narcissistic self (Laplanche & Pontalis, 1973, p. 338).

This moment coincides with what Lacan (1968, p. 72) calls the 'mirror stage' of human development, in which the child, joyful to discover her own reflection, engages playfully with it. It marks the 'transformation which takes place in the subject when he assumes an image' which it-self is 'the *I* ... precipitated in a primordial form, before it is objectified in the dialectic of identification with the other.' That is, the infant takes on his own image as a kind of symbolic prototype of his existence sepa-rate from other beings, in a process or moment occurring before the establishment, in the psyche, of the reality of that separateness, which can come about only with 'real' others. The mirror stage gives rise to a process 'in which the subject experiences herself through the "double" of the ego' (Piper, 1997, p. 60). This is an 'illusion of unity, in which a human being is always looking forward to self-mastery [and which] en-tails a constant danger of sliding back again into the chaos from which he started' (Lacan, 1953; cited in Markham, 1999, p. 64).

Of course, as a developmental 'moment' the mirror stage ends, and the individual comes to live fully in the world populated by others. But the dynamics of this the mirror stage, foundational to the negotiation of all future social relationships, echo through life; since it is a structural stage rather than a point on a developmental line, the individual can and does return to it, repeatedly, when the self-image (that is, the image the self creates *of* itself) fails to live up to its promise to represent that self (Markham, 1999, pp. 64–5). As in the idea of a psychical shift co-inciding with superego development, from a child's obedience to her parents to her submission to a teacher, there is here something analo-gous to the notion that impressions of past conflicts – and psychical responses to them – never quite disappear (Freud, 1924).

Lortie (1975) suggests a similar idea in the identificatory reflection of a child-become-a-teacher whose parents are teachers or who has had positive experiences with teachers. My view is that for some individuals teaching as a career choice may in part embody an unconscious narcis-sistic desire to re-experience an early positive encounter with a teacher, or to relive the self as reflected by, and similar to, an earlier version of itself. For if, as Cozzarelli and Silin (1989, p. 812) remark, teachers, 'like parents ... represent idealized figures' for students, perhaps it is also the case that students represent idealized figures for teachers.

This sketch of the psychoanalytic concepts of narcissism and the Lacanian mirror stage evokes an image of the classroom as itself a kind of mirror, reflecting multiple images: not one but 20 or 30 faces gazing up at the teacher, metaphorically reflecting her face as it once was (or as she idealizes it), and as it once reflected another teacher or a parent. Thus might a teacher unconsciously choose, as a kind of pedagogical love object, a reflection (or even more than one) of 'what she herself was,' a choice rendered easier and less conflicted by the 'voluntary submission' of the child now possessing a superego that tends, like the teacher's influence, to rein in the unresolved childhood conflicts (A. Freud, 1974, pp. 118–20) which could otherwise distort the idealized reflection.

Insofar as the student/object in this scenario resembles the teacher/subject who chooses, we might understand part of the resemblance as reflected in that student/object's choice of the teacher as *her* object: those students-as-objects whom I choose because they resemble and reflect me may mirror my choice, choosing me for my resemblance to them. Or I may imagine that they do. Usually a teacher does not consciously choose her students; they are assigned to her. But we can speculate on a kind of projection of an idealized fantasy that effectively makes those objects – her students – by imagining (*imaging*) them loving her as she loves them, and choosing her as their own pedagogical love-object.[8] We can read a kind of transferential reflection in the gaze of the teacher-subject toward all those student-objects.

In Freudian theory a 'disturbance' known as transference takes place in the therapeutic relationship when 'the patient has transferred on to the doctor intense feelings of affection . ... justified neither by the doctor's behaviour nor by the situation that has developed during the treatment' (Freud, 1917b, pp. 440–1).[9] While the transference can raise difficulties it is also an effective tool for opening a window into the analysand's unconscious. In fact, it 'creates an intermediate region between illness and real life' (Freud, 1914a, p. 154), 'by creating in the patient's relation to the doctor ... new editions of the old conflicts' (1917c, p. 454).

But transferential relating does not take place only in the therapeutic context: it 'operates throughout life and influences all human relations' (Klein, 1952a, p. 48). In Freud's important essay on 'Remembering, repeating, and working through' he makes a crucial connection between the transference and the 'compulsion to repeat' or re-enact dynamics and associations from earlier life that are not consciously recalled: the transference is 'itself only a piece of repetition' (1914a, p. 151). And repetition is a fundamental part of the process of making and re-making relationships with other people and with oneself, developed early in life and persisting through it:

> Even during the first six years of childhood the little human being has established the manner and affective tone of his relationships ... The people upon whom he fixates in this way are his parents and siblings. *All the people he meets later on become substitutes for those first emotional objects* ... [and] must thus bear a kind of emotional inheritance, they encounter sympathies and antipathies to the acquisition of which they themselves have contributed very little; all later choices in terms of friendship and love take place on the basis of memory traces that those first models have left behind. (Freud, 1914b, p. 356; my italics)

Here the fantasy, embodied in that reflected gaze, is that for those objects, who themselves are the subjects of their own experience, the teacher is a love-object, as she was (or as she imagined herself to be) for either her parents or her own early teachers. In this sense the students can be understood as reflecting back to their teacher her own love of the object that is like herself (in part because, in turn, it loves her as *its* object).

Taubman elucidates this complex dynamic in his discussion of the psychoanalytic transference in the beginning teacher. At first, he explains, the new teacher with his or her fragile identity is still in the realm of the imaginary and transfers onto the students the unconscious relationships that constitute that identity. . . . It is in the eyes of the students that such a teacher looks for affirmation. Or, conversely, it is in the eyes of the students that the teacher looks for a reflection of himself or herself as the original other in whose gaze that teacher came into being. It is not unusual at this level for new teachers to talk about being friends with their students, about taking care of them, or about saving them in some vague way. Boundaries between teacher and student are diffuse. (Taubman, 1992, p. 219)

Given what psychoanalytic theory has to say about repetition – the mirror stage; the mystic writing-pad; Freud's own description of transference itself as the re-editioning of early conflicts (1917c) – this dynamic is not restricted to new teachers. The classroom constantly 'invites transferential relations because . . . it is such a familiar place, one that seems to welcome reenactments of childhood memories' (Britzman & Pitt, 1996, p. 117). It is also constantly changing, and to speculate even briefly on transference as peculiarly characteristic of places of beginning is to allude to its implications in a setting that is in flux, say, because of a new technology. What happens to idealizations, to fantasies, to the transference, when the reflecting gaze of the students shifts away from the teacher, or when something comes between them, blocking the view?

Along comes the computer. And if boundaries between teachers and students are blurred, as Taubman (1992) and Lawson and Comber (2000) claim, the same might be true of computers and persons – be they teachers or students – as subjects and objects in relation to each other, in ways that remind Turkle of a kind of 'transitional object' (1997, pp. 30; 273 fn 1). Later I have a few words to say about this Winnicottian concept.

But first, here is a little reflection on the computer screen.

Translating and Reflecting: Computer Screen as Pixellated Mirror

'The looking glass,' writes Ferneding (2002, p. 54), 'is a technology of reflection and surface which signifies simulacra, creation of appearance as objective abstraction and . . . the voyeur's gaze – Narcissus's seduction by the calm and steady surface of pure reification.'

The monitor is a bit like a mirror. When I type I do not see my whole reflection, but I can see the shadow of it, my head silhouetted on the screen. My thoughts, deposited there in black and white words, are reflected too: onto my silhouette

I can impose, propose, suppose, superimpose ideas – placing on the outside what usually remains within. If I do not like the ideas, with the push of a button I can depose them.

And when the screen is blank and the light through the window just right, I can see my features. They are not quite as clear as they would be if I were bending over a pool of still water. But the reflection is there.

. . .

Picture for a moment a typical computer lab in a school. The computers are arranged around the perimeter of the room or in back-to-back rows. Each student is seated at a monitor. The teacher stands in the centre or at the front, and they turn in their chairs to face her. The teacher goes over the lesson, and gives the instructions. The students turn to face their monitors.

I wonder how it would seem to Rice's nineteenth century principal today, in a school computer lab, when students' gaze does shift and their attention focuses on something other (and perhaps more compelling) than the teacher. One response to this question, to this curiosity about what happens when what is supposed to happen in a classroom does not happen, is suggested by teachers in Hargreaves's study of professionalism in education, who express fear at losing contact with their students and at 'the loss of their psychic rewards' (1994, p. 68). What can it mean for the teacher when her students' eyes are no longer focused on her but on the computer monitors, when what is reflected, what she sees, is not their faces but the backs of their heads? And what can it mean when it is the teacher herself who is compelled to direct their gaze away from her?

A psychoanalytic reading of this scenario speculates on the computer, this new object of the learner's gaze, as an interruption of what may be understood in part as a mutually narcissistic, Lacanian mirroring relation between teacher and students – that is, as a 'self-image' that embodies both *self* and *image* (as students and teacher might imagine them). If refocusing the gaze on the computer screen ruptures the relational link between learner and teacher, even briefly, might something similar also happen when the teacher has to translate herself, relocate to the sidelines, become not the 'object reflected' but the facilitator of the learner's own reflection in the monitor? Might we think of the computer as thus displacing the teacher at the centre of the pedagogical dynamic? Such a displacement (or translation), which she herself has caused and which severs her from her students-as-pedagogical-objects and also severs her *as* an (imagined) object from them, might, I suggest, effectively silence an important part of the teacher's self-concept, thereby occasioning for her a grave psychical disappointment.

With the computer at the centre the teacher-learner pair now translates to a trio. In Freirean terms (2005, p. 71), students remain 'mere objects' but the computer can be understood to become a second 'Subject' of the process of learning. This can be a problem, for teachers do not always welcome alterations in the relational dynamics of their classrooms. Echoed in Lawson and Comber's (2000) recognition of the discomfort implicit in the loss of certainty regarding roles and status that may accompany relational shifts between teachers and learners is Sarason's more focused observation (1996, pp. 193–4) that teacher aides are often viewed as 'far from an unmixed blessing' for a number of reasons, including teachers' unwillingness to 'work with another adult in the room . . . [because they think] it would be distracting both to them and the children.'[10] Notwithstanding the common view of computers as useful *because* they hold children's attention, Sarason's observation is helpful if we consider the presence of the computer, endorsed at least nominally by the teacher and embodying its own pedagogical authority as collecting place of information, as another being in the room.

In recognizing concerns articulated by de Castell, Bryson and Jenson (2001) regarding a frequent focus on achieving teacher comfort around computers, perhaps a psychoanalytic examination of these dynamics might offer hints about teacher discomfort related not just to practical considerations of technology but to the teacher's professional purpose and her concept of herself as a teacher. All this shifting and decentring, this relocation and translation alter the relational focus in the classroom. Teachers have a heavy investment in relationality, and I wonder what happens to that investment when they are compelled to move aside to make way for technology.

Walker's (1998) paper is a written version of a talk in which he decided, at the last moment, not to use the PowerPoint presentation he had prepared. Here is the explanation he gave his audience:

> Like me, you may feel that the purpose of teaching should be to reduce the dependence of the student on the teacher and to focus the gaze of the student on the text. I agree that our aim should be to foster intellectual autonomy but I have come to believe that this can only be achieved through a *developing* relationship between teacher and student. The apparent

> objectification that takes place when we move what we want to say to a set of slides, a web page or a CDROM (or a book) is often in fact a diversion from our need to attend to a relationship within which our purpose is the intellectual development of the student. (italics in original)

Walker is acknowledging the intersubjectivity at the heart of pedagogy, and the importance of maintaining a balance between different kinds of relations. While his claim views the participants in such relations as somewhat more equal, and the dynamic as more democratic, than they might in reality be, it is nevertheless significant for its recognition of the importance of their locations relative to one another. To realign the locations and translate the dynamic in ways as significant as computer technology can do must surely have complex consequences. We might thus approach the question of comfort as located less in the technology itself than in the implications of the translation that the technology demands: in the ways the computer creates, for teachers, 'unfamiliar situations and relations ... [and] a loss of certainty' (Lawson & Comber, 2000, p. 426) – alongside, once more, a silencing of the teacher's knowledge of what a teacher is, and therefore of what, and who, she herself is. If it is this loss of certainty that teachers are resisting, in a fundamental, existential way as well as at the level of classroom practice, seeking comfort might at times just be the best they can do.

Of course for some the computer itself offers comfort. Although my primary focus is on how technology can trouble teaching, I also want to consider the ways in which philic views of ICT might manifest some of these ideas of reflection. For if the computer screen can serve as a mirror for the students then perhaps at times it can also reflect the teacher. Whether it does or not might have something to do with the technophile's interest in the machine in the classroom. That is, in addition to status, respect, and other benefits believed to accrue from its use, what might the computer do for the teacher? Might it function as a reflective device, not just for images but also for ideas?

Through all these multiple relocations of teacher, student and computer, the teacher is expected to translate herself over and over: from novice computer user to expert, and from didactic holder of knowledge and provider of instructions to constructivist facilitator – remaining on the sidelines as students engage with computers, glancing up at times for help and then looking back at the screen where their work is. These multiple and repeated translations are no simple matter, given that they involve the demand to silence at least some of what grounds the teacher's sense of herself – her *being* as a teacher. Moreover, the teacher's silence may be enacted in even more concrete terms, for if teaching is already viewed as a solitary profession (Britzman, 1991; Goss, 1996; Sarason, 1996) in which the educator in her classroom has little contact throughout the day with other adults, how much more lonely might life be, how much more unspoken the worries and dilemmas, when the students too are occupied elsewhere? It is not only the computer in the classroom that has the student's attention, it is the whole culture of the world outside as well. And so, in the sense in which the computer is a 'children's machine' culturally (Papert, 1993), might the teacher's engagement with it offer something in terms of status vis-à-vis the student, perhaps yet another kind of reflection, or even another connection with the outside world?

Clearly computers can interrupt praxis in multiple ways – positive, negative, often both at once. While I neither claim to be exhaustive nor wish to be accusatory, it is worth reiterating that the matters I am considering are outside consciousness; we would not expect teachers to self-identify as narcissistically involved with either their students or their computers. Nor do I forget that whatever might be unconsciously at play in the complex dynamics of teaching and technology, there are other things of which educators are indeed conscious, sometimes with pleasure, at other times painfully. One of these is a frequent lack of sufficient support in terms of technical assistance as well as time for learning or reflection.

While these concerns are extremely important to recognize and address, I suggest that such outward issues are only part of the picture, and that a kind of psychical support may also be relevant. Just as an individual moving from one language to another is engaged in a kind of translation of the linguistic self, a process that can involve moments of being caught, or lost, between languages (see Granger, 2004), so might a teacher find herself caught in the multiple self-translations she must make between pedagogical methods, between positions of authority and facilitator, expert and novice, knower and learner, and, perhaps most significantly, between the centre and the margins of her own practice. Here silence imposed from the outside may threaten the teacher's understanding of herself, but resistance to technology, or perhaps a refusal to engage with it, forms a kind of silence which might protect that understanding.

Who or what will support the teacher through these various silences and relocations, these translations of her work as a teacher, these disruptions to her beliefs about what it means to be a teacher? Who or what will give her comfort in the midst of anxiety? Once more I turn to psychoanalysis for hints at what support might mean for teachers whose authority, autonomy, and identity are compromised and even silenced in the push to implement new technologies.

For Winnicott (1963b), central to human development is the attainment of 'the stage of I AM' (p. 56; emphasis in original), comprising 'a continuity of existence ... [and] a sense of self, and eventually result[ing] in autonomy' (p. 28), which is achieved by means of a healthy 'environmental provision of the holding variety' (p. 119). It is similar to the successful movement through and beyond the Lacanian mirror stage, subsequent to which the individual exists as a self in a world of other selves.

This 'holding' begins with the physical contact of the mother-infant nursing relationship, but eventually comes to be the work of the family, and ultimately of society (Winnicott, 1963b, p. 107). My work on second language learning examines this concept of holding in relation to the shift between first and second languages, suggesting that a fundamental shift in environment might ultimately threaten autonomy, leaving an individual caught between languages in a state I call linguistic homelessness (Granger, 2004, p. 7). I find it useful here to consider the possibility that for some teachers the demand for a pedagogical and psychical translation, into technology use and constructivist pedagogy simultaneously, might similarly strain both professional and personal identity – another kind of homelessness, either literal or figurative, that is pedagogical, professional, and psychical.

Truly adequate support from the professional environment, a holding perhaps of a Winnicottian kind, must leave open a space for teachers' existential concerns – however unconscious – about the nature of their work and about their being-as-teachers. To be useful, such holding must neither presume uncritical technophilia nor bury concerns in discourses that reductively conflate machines with pedagogies. For a significant number of teachers in the present day, and especially in terms of actual use and integration, both the fact and the discourse of technology are still new. This presents a double difficulty: on one hand reconciling the apparently contradictory fact that many teachers may not quite be ready for the computer despite its ubiquity; and on the other hand squaring the insistence on technological integration with education's other demands, including the call for translation from didactic to constructivist and other learner-centred pedagogies. Education at present may be described as being at a kind of mid-point in relation both to such pedagogies generally and to ICT adoption in particular.

Turkle makes a link between the computer and Winnicott's 'transitional object' (Winnicott, 1971), locating both 'on the border between
self and not-self' (Turkle, 1997, p. 30; p. 273 fn. 1). Were Winnicott writing today, might he theorize a transitional stage in the move toward
full computer integration? Indeed, to offer a different take on Turkle's
object to think with, if he could be persuaded of the value of new technologies as tools for learner-centred education, might Winnicott even
understand the computer itself, used as it is by many teachers in limited ways, as an *object to mediate with* in at least two spaces: between
the didactic and the constructivist teacher-as-subject, and between the
teacher's being and her work?

My aim in this chapter has been to invite mindful concern regarding
the potential impact of the call to transform and translate the teacher's
work, and her identity as teacher, in order to arrive at a considered wisdom that tolerates the complexity, and the surprise, and the difficulty
of those demands and translations. And so, in the spirit of surprise, and
of translation, as a last word I return to the first word, to the fragment of
Machado's poem (1963 [1913]) quoted at the beginning of this chapter.
In the original Spanish it reads:

Caminante, no hay camino,
se hace camino al andar.

Here is my own translation:

Wanderer, there is no path,
the path is made by walking.

There are numerous other translations; but the one I like best is the version generated by Google. It is unexpectedly poetic, fluid, charming.
Without conscious intent it comes closest to the original in meaning,
reminding us that movement is made by moving, that change comes to
be through change:

Traveller is no way,
way when walking becomes.

Although in this case the software has its own fluency, and the translation is surprisingly complete, Google's note about the translation, which
tells us it 'was produced automatically by state-of-the-art technology,'

goes on to say: 'Unfortunately, today's most sophisticated software doesn't approach the fluency of a native speaker or possess the skill of a professional translator. Automatic translation is very difficult' (Google Translate, 2007).

And indeed it is – as we have seen.

Let us leave the computer lab now, and head to a different room in the school of education: the space where the student teacher learns to teach.

PART 3

Fourth Circumnarrative: The Snow

I always kept a journal. From the small, thick diaries of childhood, their covers red 'leatherette' and their pages edged in 'gold' that matched the tiny keys I locked them with (and often subsequently lost), to spiral-bound notebooks of a more utilitarian sort, to (still later) more elegant versions made from handmade paper and covered in moleskin or linen, I recorded thoughts, observations, secret pleasures and private furies. Some I have discarded; one or two I tore to shreds; a few I have still.

A little over nine years ago, in January of 1998, I stopped. It was nearly two years before I started again. My first entry in a cinnamon-coloured, leatherbound notebook is dated January 27, 2000, during the period when I was writing my master's thesis. It reads:

> *Cold outside. Cold inside too, frustrating. Trying to work, but no ideas. Taking (looking for?) any excuse for an interruption. And there are so many pulls. Could clean the house. Could do laundry. Probably won't do either. Would rather read a mystery, something bloody and mindless.*

> *Alice [my advisor] wants chapters but Alberto [my spouse] wants to talk. He says I spend too much time working, 'doing stuff for Alice.' She once said that I 'sure do a lot of travelling.' Implying that I spend too much time with him, I thought. Sometimes even not working seems like work.*

> *A&A. Alice. Alberto. Both giving me a C? These days I'm not a great student, not much of a girlfriend either. Feeling pulled between two As.*

> *Meanwhile, the snow needs shovelling and the kids just want dinner. Whatever I do, there's always more to do, someone else wanting something else.*

> *Sometimes I want to leave all of them.*

6 Neither Here Nor There: Difficult Moments in Teacher Education

> I think the trouble with writers writing about writing (or speaking about it) is the trouble anyone has discussing his or her own profession. . . . [W]riting strikes me as a many-layered process, only the top three or four of which have anything directly to do with words.
>
> – Samuel R. Delany, *About Writing*

> We can't return
> we can only look behind from where we came
> and go round and round and round
> in the circle game.
>
> – Joni Mitchell, *The Circle Game*

I begin writing this section of my study on a bright day in early February, several years after the journal entry that precedes it, in what was until a few days ago an unusually mild and snowless winter. Today is bitterly cold. It stormed all last night and this morning, and outside all is muffled by snow except the scraping of the neighbour's shovel as he clears his driveway. I have had to turn on the electric heater in my chilly little upstairs office, and I've lit candles and made tea, and I sit at my desk with a woollen blanket over my lap. The radio is tuned to a folk music station. Joni Mitchell's *The Circle Game* is playing. I know it well, this tender song about growing older, and growing up, and the cycles of memory and dreams. It was first sung to me on a snowy mountainside in northern Italy in February of 1977.

My mind wanders. I grow curious about the song's origins. An internet search (Ruhlman, 1995) tells me Mitchell wrote it in 1966 in response to Neil Young's nostalgic (1964) coming-of-age song, *Sugar Mountain*. And I marvel at the resonance of things, for tacked to my office bulletin board is a photograph I took in the summer of (I think) 1980, at a bus stop near where I lived at that time. The snapshot shows a red mailbox on which someone has scribbled in chalk, 'Oh to Live on Sugar Mountain.'

I begin next to think about what Delany (2005) has written, about writing, about how hard it is to write about one's own work, about the layered-ness of writing. I have some idea about this – already I expect this chapter to be difficult to write.

And it may take some time to get to the point.

That it will take a little time, and that this process, a big part of which for Delany is not 'directly' about words, will nevertheless involve a significant number of them, does not really surprise me. Equally, I have anticipated that this chapter will be difficult to write: perhaps that is why I have waited to write it. I expect this difficulty because I must write about, speak of, a particularly difficult and, until now, largely silent time in my educational history: my time as a student teacher. Somehow – and not just because of today's weather – I need to be comforted, to treat myself kindly, something I have not felt to anything like the same degree about the sections already written. The candles, the music, the blanket over my knees, the warmth of the room, are all necessary, because thinking about those months leaves me cold. Literally. It makes me shiver.

I reread the previous paragraph. The phrase 'must write about' is a curious one, for the fact is that I am *choosing* to write about this experience. And given that I have been excited of late to arrive at a point in my academic life at which I can make choices about the work I do, it seems odd, even to me, that I have elected to write about a particularly difficult and troubling time. I am referring to the months I spent as a student teacher,[1] more particularly to the five-and-a-half months in which I was placed, for the second practicum portion of my preservice teacher education program, in a classroom of Grade 2 pupils and their teacher. Wait – another correction – in which I placed myself: I also chose to enter that classroom. Here is what happened.

After a successful first-term practice-teaching placement, I was asked by the practicum course director to take a position in a different class in the same school, with a host teacher who was reputed to be inflexible in her practice and inexorable in her relationships with student teachers. This was not the usual procedure at the time, but the student teacher who had been in this particular host teacher's class the previous term had found it an exceedingly frustrating experience, and the practicum director, kind of heart and good of intention, believed that, as an older and perhaps more assertive student, I would be better able to engage with this individual. Feeling quite brave – here I am not being flippant, for I had worked in the school for a term already and knew well my colleague who had already experienced this host teacher – I accepted, flattered to be thought of as 'someone who can stand up to her.' As things turned out, I could not.

So why not simply forget the experience? Well, I've tried. But there seems to be something more (or other) to this than simple choice.

As I say, I'll get to that. In a moment.[2]

It isn't just me: the moment or the process I am writing about (or at this precise point not-quite-writing about) is difficult for many of those who undertake it. What could it be, then, that makes teacher education – learning to teach – so difficult?

This part of my study is a speculation on difficulty, and difficult moments, in the time of learning to teach. It is about relationships within that process, between knowing and knowers, theory and practice, teachers and learners, student teachers, practicum host teachers, and teacher educators. It is about the privileging of some aspects of these relationships, and silences of, and in, others. And it is about calls to speak from one part of the self that at once inaugurate and are symptomatic of the silencing of other parts.

Coming to Theory: Assumptions and Beliefs about Teaching and Learning

For over 10 years I have worked in the same Faculty of Education in which I completed my own Bachelor of Education degree, as well as in two others. During those years, as student teacher, graduate student, teaching assistant, lecturer, and course director, I have come to know hundreds of Education students and dozens of faculty members. The one observation that persists is that things in education – more precisely, in teacher education – are not simple: the path is neither smooth nor straight, however much we might wish or expect it to be.

Education – and this includes teacher education – is not a transparent enterprise. It is 'an enormously difficult job that looks easy' (Labaree, 2000, p. 228). It is difficult because it can be isolating and because of the many masters that must be served (curriculum, administrators, parents, and of course students), and because some of our students might rather be elsewhere – as indeed might some of us teachers.

But it does look easy. In the public's eyes it looks easy because of what seem to be short working hours and long vacations. It looks easy because the knowledge and skills it imparts are neither elite nor esoteric, but rather the generic accomplishments of the adult population (Labaree, 2000). It looks easy because on some level it is ubiquitous: a friend teaches a friend to play a new riff on the guitar; a parent teaches a child to ride a bicycle, swing a hammer, or bake a cake; a child teaches a parent to play a video game. In fact, teaching is a thing almost anyone can do. Or so goes the story – a story born from the emergence, in the nineteenth and twentieth centuries, of the notion that teaching is a 'natural,' instinctive extension of parenting, particularly mothering (Bolin, 1990; Feiman-Nemser & Remillard, 1996; Miller, 1996; Wideen, Mayer-Smith, & Moon, 1998). By such a definition it should scarcely require any formal preparation at all. Alongside understandings of the classroom as a home, the class as a family, and the teacher as a mother, persists a related assumption: that performing the motions of teaching (as in some grownup version of playing school) makes one a teacher. In this 'happy family' conception, difference is flattened and dealing fairly with students means treating them the same – rendering teaching easier on one level but obliterating recognition of the impact of multiple inequities on pupils' lives and learning.

Teaching also looks easy to student teachers (Labaree, 2000), many of whom, armed with Lortie's 'apprenticeship of observation' – all those years spent watching teachers teach – believe that knowing what teachers *do* is all one needs to *be* a teacher. This view, however, lacks an analytic component, for student teachers 'are not privy to the teacher's private intentions and personal reflections' (Lortie, 1990, p. 62), such that while they may know something of the *what*, the *why* is missing:

> Teaching from this observational and nonanalytical perspective appears to be simple action, guided either by custom (this is the way teaching is done) or by nature (this is the kind of person I am). . . . What students don't see is the thinking that preceded the teacher's action, the alternatives she considered, the strategic plan within which she located the action, or the aims she sought to accomplish by means of that action. (Labaree, 2000, p. 232)

'What students don't see' may also be what student teachers don't see, or, given the delimiting function of the observational apprenticeship, what they *cannot* see.

Other assumptions with which student teachers enter preservice programs include the idea that learning is a passive exercise in which knowledge is a 'fixed collection of facts, concepts and skills' (Feiman-Nemser & Remillard, 1996, p. 70) straightforwardly given by the teacher and absorbed, unmediated, by the learner (Cuban, 1993a). A later version of this presumption is Korthagen and Kessels' 'transfer problem' (1999, p. 5): a shift in the new teacher toward local school culture and away from the scientific insights of her preservice education courses, predicated in part on her presumption that her pupils can and will learn in the same ways she herself learns, if only she teaches as she herself was taught. And another misconception, again related to the metaphor of school-as-home and teacher-as-mother, is the ubiquitous thinking that experience is the best – indeed the only – way to learn: to learn anything, really, but especially to learn how to teach (Britzman, 1991; Richardson, 1996).

These assumptions form, and interact with, student teachers' 'biographically embedded private theories' (Bullough Jr. & Gitlin, 1994, p. 78). Without intervention, the 'existing conceptions and beliefs of student teachers will remain unchallenged' (Tillema, 1998, pp. 217–8). In particular, Holt-Reynolds finds that student teachers' 'lay theories' (1992, p. 326) may lead to their resisting the constructivism taught in their preservice programs – because the latter contradicts the former.

The student teacher may be unaware that her understanding constitutes a theory; to her it may just be the way things are. But even if she does recognize it as a particularly organized set of beliefs rather than a collection of objective truths, it cannot easily be proven wrong, or even incomplete (Holt-Reynolds, 1992, p. 327; see also Bolin, 1990; Stofflett & Stoddart, 1992), for there she stands, with (in many or most cases) the successful record that brought her to teacher education, as fleshly evidence of its validity. For example, in York University's Faculty of Education, many students come to the preservice program with teaching experience in various areas, including classroom work as volunteers, teachers' aides, and in some cases even full-time teaching in private schools or adult education – indeed it is that very experience that gets them accepted into the program. Beliefs grounded in such experience, and often articulated as hard evidence for universal truths, affect how teachers (new and experienced) organize their classroom priorities, resist or accept or otherwise judge theory, and do or do not work with colleagues (Tillema, 1998; Korthagen & Kessels, 1999).

It follows that student teachers' views on teaching and learning affect how they see the process of learning to teach (Bolin, 1990; Stofflett &

Stoddart, 1992; O'Brien & Schillaci, 2002). Goodlad's comparison of a 'generalized intellectual orientation' within teacher education and the practical goals of novice teachers 'oriented to filling a large handbag with discrete bits and pieces of know-how' (Goodlad, 1990, pp. 114–15) resonates with my own experience. Student teachers worry about course readings seen as 'too abstract,' ask for exercises involving packaged scenarios (in which student teachers find or are given strategies to solve or deal with specified classroom problems or incidents), and make comments such as, 'All I really want to do is get into the classroom' or, more bluntly, 'There's too much theory in this program.' Similar observations are made by Wideen, Mayer-Smith, and Moon (1998; following Bolin, 1990, and Richardson, 1996), to the effect that 'students coming into teacher education with craft knowledge ... believe they know how to teach, and that all they require are a few strategies to get them started' (Wideen et al., 1998, p. 142), and similarly by Feiman-Nemser and Remillard (1996, p. 69), that student teachers often believe that 'teacher education ha[s] little to teach them.'

Tied to the trope of experience-as-the-best-teacher is the idea that practice-teaching components of teacher education programs are the most (or the only) important or relevant ones. In a survey by Book, Byers, and Freeman (1983), student teachers early in their programs (of whom, incidentally, about 90 percent rated themselves as at least moderately confident, and 24 percent as 'highly or completely confident,' in their ability to teach immediately) ranked practice-teaching in classrooms as the most important source of professional knowledge, followed by educational psychology courses and their own experience as students. Educational foundations courses came dead last (Book, Byers, & Freeman, 1983, pp. 10–11). Britzman's doctoral work (1985, cited in Britzman, 1986) uncovers comparable expectations of pedagogical knowledge as an object to be 'acquired, possessed, and immediately applied.' The student teachers in her study understood the theory offered in their courses as speculative, idealistic, and on the whole 'a waste of time' (Britzman, 1986, p. 447). Duquette (1997) similarly observes the prevalent perception that it is in the practicum classroom that the most authentic, most useful, truest learning happens.[3]

But while it seems clear that the exaltation of practice-teaching, as the apotheosis of teacher education, contributes to the hierarchization of practice over theory, it is not the only contributing factor. Pragmatics enters the mix also, in the practice-teaching experience students often describe as a 'year-long job interview.' This aspect cannot be ignored:

while success in teacher education programs depends on both course-work and practicum components, it is understood to be determined primarily by practicum evaluations and recommendations from host teachers, overseeing principals, and adjunct professors in the schools. This perception may help explain why, when faced with choosing be-tween pedagogical approaches favoured by methods and/or founda-tions classes and those practised by a host teacher in whose classroom she finds herself, the student teacher may tend to veer in the latter di-rection. More generally, as Smagorinsky, Cook, Moore, Jackson, and Fry (2004, p. 10) point out, student teachers are apprentices in their practi-cum classrooms, where their aim may simply be to be found competent in terms of the school's local culture. Writes Martinez (1998, p. 103): 'If the supervising teacher is assessing their teaching, then the supervising teacher's knowledge of teaching is definitely *the* way, the truth and the light' (italics in original).

This eventuality meshes with mentor teachers' tendency to privilege a 'mimetic mentoring approach' (Smagorinsky et al., 2004, p. 17), fo-cused on the same role-modelling and observation they experienced in their own preservice education (Korthagen & Kessels, 1999; O'Connor, 2003), such that a student teacher's arrival might challenge or threaten established patterns and structures. Host teachers have their theories too after all, and in some quarters it appears that the 'way and the truth' of good teaching fall under just one 'light' – classroom manage-ment – for host teachers and student teachers alike (Feiman-Nemser & Remillard 1996; Phelan, 1996). This is not new: Taubman (2006, p. 20) reports that teachers often cite loss of control as their worst fear about teaching, and it has long been a commonplace of education that teach-ers are judged on their 'ability to orchestrate classroom control rather than to articulate pedagogical theory' (Britzman, 1986, p. 447, citing Descombe, 1982). A recent focus on programs such as 'Tribes' (Gibbs, 2001) and 'Tools for Teaching' (Jones & Jones, 2000) further reinforces the view that class management is 'the most important – and the most difficult – skill a new teacher has to master' (EducationWorld, 2004; see Stewart-Wells, 2000; Smagorinsky et al., 2004).

The privileging of control, be it an overarching philosophy of peda-gogy or a response to a specific teacher's wish for classroom order, can be useful for the beginner to adopt. Perhaps already uncertain, on en-tering practicum, about either her grasp of theory or her ability to ma-noeuvre between competing theories and practices, she may find her learning, and her uncertainty, superseded by the need for just-in-time solutions to problems, especially in a classroom where the prevailing pedagogy is grounded in the 'presentism ... of ... short-range goals and an identification with the immediacy of the classroom life' (Phelan, 1996, p. 341). But Martinez (1998, p. 101) calls for a reconsideration of the uncertainties in the student teacher's position. Drawing on her own observations of a preservice program, she remarks on the confusion of student teachers in relation to their education. 'General discipline studies,' she writes, tend to offer 'a wide range of varying views on the construction of knowledge, usually operating at an implicit and assumed level. In turn, students frequently take from those subjects an understanding about learning and teaching which may or may not match that expounded by their curriculum methods lecturers.'

The situation is complex.

To gain certification the student teacher must succeed in all portions of the program, including those that are theoretically based. Most are quite accustomed to intellectual and theoretical work: they have completed or are in the process of completing a university degree. Clearly, pragmatics alone cannot account for the privileging of practice and practice-teaching.

Such privileging may be rooted in the notions of teaching as a non-intellectual, quasi-instinctive, natural and ultimately feminine activity – women's work – as outlined in Chapter 5 and evinced by one of my recent teaching assignments, in which just six of 68 class members were male. These ideas are so deeply entrenched that not just the perception but the conditions of teachers' work have been informed by the notion that women work with children 'out of "natural" inclinations and needs, of a kind men are unlikely to share' (Miller, 1996, p. 99). The child-centred model is often conflated with ideas of learning and development as individually paced, and of knowledge as defined in ways that reproduce a view of the 'normal woman' (mother or teacher) as a passive facilitator, 'invested with a nurturance which ... amounts to a capacity for facilitating and enabling the development of children' (Walkerdine, 1990, p. 37).[4]

Rooted thus in notions of naturalness, womanliness, maternity, and 'feminine' experience and activity, and similarly to the ways in which the structures of education as a whole influence its function – from building architecture and classroom organization to curriculum design and evaluation (Foucault, 1977a; Bourdieu & Passeron, 1990) – teacher education program design influences perceptions of its work. Currently in Canada it is organized around two major elements: academic courses, including methods and theory courses, and a classroom practicum.

Some institutions (McGill University, 2006; University of British Columbia [UBC], n/d; University of New Brunswick [UNB], n/d) follow the traditional progression of coursework followed by a culminating practice-teaching term, reflecting the presumption that 'academic study offers the most important preparation for teaching' (Feiman-Nemser & Remillard, 1996, p. 64). But that model is not universal. For example, the website of York University's Faculty of Education (2006a) states that its 'strong emphasis on practicum is a vital connection in linking theory and practice.' Here, in the one-year consecutive preservice program (for students possessing an undergraduate degree), the practicum consists of one or two days weekly for nine months, as well as longer practice-teaching sessions, including a final three-week block. In the concurrent program, students work simultaneously on two degrees (in education and in another discipline), beginning a 'field-related experience' in the first year, and a 'year-long [part-time] placement' in the second. This configuration reflects a move in many jurisdictions from a university-based to a more school-based approach (Duquette, 1997; Korthagen & Kessels, 1999), which shifts the theory/practice balance in favour of the latter. An example of how such a shift is articulated comes from the University of Texas at El Paso (n/d): 'We have become more clinical and field-based, working closely with our colleagues at local schools. Teachers are now prepared more like doctors and nurses, and less like philosophers and historians. Our teacher candidates spend more time in the classroom, and they are there earlier in their college careers.'

Similar shifts are evident at the level of policy. Phelan's (1996) analysis of an Alberta Ministry of Education document (Alberta Education, 1995) that moves teacher education from 'qualification-based' to 'competency-based' reveals a reorganization of beliefs: 'Competence is directed toward control, efficiency, and certainty of desired student learning outcomes (as per provincial programs of study)' and the document lacks any 'mention of teachers as intelligent, inquiring, perceptive, and informed professionals' – rather, it understands policy as something 'to be accepted and followed not to be understood and rethought' (Phelan, 1996, pp. 336–7). This kind of shift Phelan describes, as do Duquette (1997) and Korthagen and Kessels (1999), would seem to appeal to many student teachers, whose devaluing of academic courses provokes, for Book, Byers, and Freeman (1983, p. 11), 'serious questions as to . . . preservice teachers' view of teaching as a profession.'

True, not all the research is in agreement on this point. In her study of a 'field intensive' teacher education program at an (unnamed) Ontario university, Duquette (1997, p. 266) reports that some student teachers (and, significantly, first-year practising teachers) whose teacher preparation had emphasized practicum teaching[5] 'expressed a need for more theory ... [and] more program hours devoted to course work, particularly in the foundational areas.' But notwithstanding these findings, more than 20 years after Book, Byers, and Freeman (1983) and Britzman (1985) I frequently hear those same sentiments – 'a waste of time,' 'too much theory' – expressed in the corridors of the faculties of education where I work. I have also repeatedly witnessed a significant privileging, in concrete terms, of the practicum (submitting methods course assignments late in order to finish lesson plans, or skipping foundations classes to prepare handouts, coach sports, or attend staff meetings in placement schools).

My claim here is that both practical concerns and the structures of teacher education programs reinforce those 'personal theories' (Tillema 1998, p. 218) of student teachers (and others) that privilege practice (and practice-teaching). Ironically, some of these personal theories manifest as *anti*-theory – especially those that view experience as a self-explanatory, self-revealing consensus omnium. But there is no consensus. The image Britzman identifies as the 'the natural teacher' (1986, p. 451) serves two masters, one illustrated by a participant in Bolin's study of student teachers' beliefs (1990, p. 16): 'Teachers aren't made, they're born,' and the second by a platitude ubiquitous in teacher education: that practice makes perfect. This construction of the teacher as simultaneously 'born to teach' and 'self-made' embodies a 'diminish[ed] recognition of the importance of social forces and institutional contexts in the teacher's process of growth' (Britzman, 1986, p. 451). Helped along by preconceived ideas, program structures, and practical worries, it also embodies, at least in part, the 'anti-intellectualism' that for Britzman prevails in teacher education, and which finds a home in the practicum setting, where 'university theory counts for little' (1986, p. 447).

Resisting Theory: Changing Minds and Making Trouble

The fact that students enter teacher education with preconceived ideas does not mean that those ideas cannot or will not change (see McNulty, 2000; Stuart & Thurlow, 2000; Lloyd, 2005; as well as literature reviews including Wideen et al., 1998; Zeichner, 1999). Efforts do not guarantee results, however, either in the direction attitudinal change takes, or in the translation of such changes into practice. Holt-Reynolds's (1992) review of studies conducted in mathematics pedagogy courses (Ball, 1988; McDiarmid, 1989) found that those emphasizing constructivist and investigative approaches led to changes in student teachers' ideas about the amount of content knowledge required to teach effectively, but not in their 'well established, tenacious, and powerful' belief in traditional didactic methods as the most effective (Holt-Reynolds, 1992, pp. 343–4; see also Stofflett & Stoddart, 1992; Ashton, 1996). Similarly, while Tillema (1998) credits the intermingling of theory and practice in a preservice program with facilitating changes in thinking, he notes that these changes were not always in the desired direction.

Why the emphasis on changing previously held ideas? It is, of course, necessary to adjust patently incorrect understandings, but it would be worrying to presume that all the understandings a student teacher holds on entering a preservice program need changing. Yet the oft-spoken wish among student teachers to 'make a difference' in the lives of those they teach (see, among others, Bullough & Gitlin, 1994) reflects the assumption that those lives *need* to be changed.

Perhaps these seemingly parallel ideas concerning the importance of change stem from the idea, central to education's entire project, that the world can be better than it is, and that good educators are just the thing to help it become better. This view might seem surprising, given how difficult it seems to be to actually effect change, or if, as Greene does, (1995, p. 66), we look at the history of education and understand schools as 'agents of normalization, oriented to the reproduction of an inequitable, consumerist, stratified culture.' But Greene acknowledges that hegemony is not absolute, in education or elsewhere, and points to the belief among at least some teachers and teacher educators that education has the potential to provoke growth, critical thinking, and participation in the democratic project (see also Stuart & Thurlow, 2000). And if social change is one of education's aims, one way to achieve that aim ought to be through remedying some of the misconceptions that prevail in education.

One such misconception is the theory which, by extolling practice, paradoxically refuses theory. The split between theory and practice, perceived and enacted through a complex combination of the structuring of teacher education programs, evaluation policies and practices, and the personal theories of its participants, is at bottom a split between two prominent orientations within teacher education, which

I tentatively name a *theory of practicum* and a *theory of theory*. In this formulation, the theory of practicum might perhaps have as a slightly ambiguous slogan, 'experience makes the best teachers.'

Of course, we must be careful not to be seduced by slogans. For the theory of theory, understood on the most basic level as aimed at changing minds, must not be seen as a naïve or single-minded call. Similarly, this discussion should not be read as implying that there is no relationship between theory and practice. Teacher education programs involve both components, and we would be hard pressed to find one that had no overlap. My aim is to think about how, despite the distinction between these two orientations, they are very much bound together.

In its demand that we think about and make relationships with new and perhaps difficult ideas, theory sometimes makes trouble.[6] Old ideas do not cease to exist when new ones are adopted – they keep demanding to be heard. Coursework/practicum rifts may prevail even where a student teacher adopts the theory put forward in her courses. For example, in the preservice program examined by Bullough and Gitlin (1994, p. 71), 'methods courses were disconnected from curriculum courses; and both were disconnected from practice-teaching. Similarly, foundations courses, and their concern for the aims of education, were unrelated to methods courses, and their emphasis on means.' With such gaps between elements of a teacher education program, and the more practical reasons (enumerated above) for placing practice and practicum ahead of theory, it is not surprising that a student teacher seeking a professional home might lean to the familiar. For theory might not only confuse us, it can scare us too. Simon's (1992) work on the 'fear of theory' invites us to think about the displacement of 'official' theory[7] in teacher education by the ostensibly more practical concerns of classroom management, curriculum implementation, and (on the student teacher's part especially) making a success of the practicum.

Simon begins his exploration by observing that educational encounters are a 'volatile mix' of fear and hope (p. 79), despite the fact that both learners and teachers, especially at a university level, may be reluctant to admit to fear. Taking care to note that fear can indicate a imminent breakthrough in learning or understanding – a moment 'in which old investments are about to be questioned, modified, or possibly displaced' (p. 81) – and might thus be a container for hope, Simon nevertheless worries that it might also, less helpfully, inhibit learning, thinking, and hope itself in pedagogical relations.

One possible manifestation of such fear, suggests Simon, is anger. A student might express anger in 'an attack on what is posited as deliberately marginalizing obscurantist "jargon" and [on] those responsible for propagating it' (Simon, 1992, p. 83)[8] or on the text, the author of the text, even the teacher who selected the text for the course. It may be just this anger that I have witnessed in teacher education classes in which some students have vociferously rejected various texts or authors as being either 'too hard' or 'stupid' (Cooper, 1991; Silin, 2006); obsessed with sex (Freud's [1924] 'A note upon the "mystic writing-pad"'); too expensive to buy (a memoir of childhood that raises the question of gender ambiguity: Pendleton Jiménez's [2000] *Are You a Boy or a Girl?*); irrelevant (Scotta & Berliner's 1997 film *Ma Vie en Rose*); or 'a load of crap you need a dictionary to decipher' – Winnicott's '*Sum*, I am' (1963b), on links between a sense of self and the mathematical concept of unit.

In his look at fear-as-anger Simon quotes from Williams's discussion of jargon as implicitly adversarial 'in branches of knowledge which bear on matters which already have a common general vocabulary' (Williams, 1983, p. 175, cited in Simon, 1992, p. 83). In the educational context, Simon writes,

> students both fear and resent the potential humiliation of being excluded from a discourse that is supposed to have some relevance to everyday lives. ... On the other hand, Williams is also pointing to the disruptive character of theoretical language; the fact that it may call into question the adequacy of ... taken-for-granted ways of communicating about daily realities. (Simon, 1992, pp. 83–4)

Jargon can be understood here as a particular subset of what Bourdieu and Passeron (1990) identify as 'cultural capital': a symbolic 'good' coveted in the educational setting because its possession marks status and power. But its use is also implicitly, albeit inadvertently, a symptom of the exercise of that status and power. It is the text, its perhaps familiar ideas spoken in esoteric language, that positions the student teacher as uninformed, ignorant, inferior – a potentially serious challenge, in particular if she believes (Feiman-Nemser & Remillard, 1996; Duquette, 1997; Wideen et al., 1998) that she already *is* a teacher and is in a preservice program as a mere formality or to pick up some strategies. And so jargon (and the theory it articulates) may be resisted, refused, even despised.

Anger as a symptom may also be grounded in a particular aspect of the theory or knowledge at hand, which it acquires from its very newness or strangeness, or because its content is simply too difficult or uncomfortable: to wit, the student mentioned in Chapter 4 whose response to *Ma Vie en Rose* was a distinctly antagonistic – albeit paradoxical – articulation of the refusal to respond, in one fell swoop taking up and rejecting the text in question: 'I don't even want to think about it, it's nothing to do with me.'

That student's response was the most vocal in her class of 35. I cannot know if her views were shared by anyone else in the group, but they might well have been, since silence is another way of demonstrating a fear of new ideas or a new theory. For Simon it may be the most pervasive (1992, p. 82) – though I note that to make such a determination is tricky, in that a silent response is hard to spot or to calibrate. Further, I am mindful, as is Simon, of the trope of reductionism: while the insistence on a particular theoretical approach may actively silence learners, the reverse is not universally true – not all silences are imposed. This is important, because certainly there are many possible reasons for a silence, and it would be as wrong to assume that silence is *always* born of fear as to claim that it *never* is. Silence could, for example, be a disguise for anger, which in turn might or might not be a symptom of fear. For Simon, though, silence hints at the twin worries of being ridiculed by one's peers or one's teacher, and being exposed as 'even more unworthy than one already [thinks one] is' (1992, p. 82).

Unworthiness nips at the heels of the question of who and what we perceive ourselves to be. Even a student teacher who thinks the program in which she is enrolled has little to teach her may grow uncertain in the face of new and strange and difficult ideas. Referring to the Foucauldian 'power/knowledge' nexus (Foucault, 1980a), Simon articulates the disruption caused by education's demand that students 'take the theory we offer seriously' as 'the potential negation of aspects of . . . personal and professional identity and the corresponding investments one has in retaining those identity positions' (1992, p. 86). In a Foucauldian view (1980a), the institution regulates and controls the student's self-perception by insisting that she remake her subjectivity to fit with the theory at hand, thereby becoming both subject to and object of that theory.

For Foucault, though, 'theory does not [merely] express, translate, or serve to apply practice: it *is* practice' (1977b, p. 208; my italics). So the theorist, the practitioner (here the teacher educator) by whom the theory is applied *to* and *onto* the student teacher, is as invested in her theory-practice as the student teachers are in theirs – be they lay theory-practices or theories-of-practicum. This creates a complicated arrangement – even within a dialogic pedagogy and most certainly in a didactic one – in which 'both student and teacher [or student teacher and teacher educator, or host teacher and student teacher] are doubly ignorant, not only of their structured resistances but as well of the knowledge of what it is that resists in the other' (Simon, 1992, p. 97).

It is useful to read Foucault's (1977b) remarks on France's 1968 student and worker uprisings as relevant to the *theory-of-theory* issue in teacher education:

> The masses no longer need [the intellectual] to gain knowledge: they *know* perfectly well, without illusion ... and they are certainly capable of expressing themselves. But there exists a system of power which blocks, prohibits, and invalidates this discourse and this knowledge ... [and which] profoundly and subtly penetrates an entire societal network. Intellectuals are themselves agents of this system of power – the idea of their responsibility for 'consciousness' and discourse forms part of the system. (Foucault, 1977b, p. 207)

I read this passage not as implying that student teachers always already know everything that can be known about how to teach, for to impute that would be as incorrect as to say that theorists know everything they need to know about theory. But everyone *knows* – and everyone theorizes: has, and makes, theory. In a Foucauldian sense the issue is that relations and structures of power/knowledge, as well as discourse in general and language in particular, work to position the theorist/academic as hierarch and, by default, the theorist/practitioner as subordinate. True, the teacher educator is a practitioner too, so the relationship is not straightforward. These confounding relations weave in multiple directions, in all configurations involving teacher educators, student teachers, host teachers, adjunct professors, classroom pupils, and beyond: families, administrators, school board hiring committees, deans in faculties of education, and so on.

If the directionality of the relationship is complex, so is the dynamic of power. For although it seems at first glance that all power rests abstractly in the intellectual/academic/theorist category (and more concretely in the body of the teacher educator, which holds the power to pass or fail her students), the ostensibly subaltern student teacher is not utterly powerless. This is partly because in any context silence can be a very powerful response. I mean that in its most literal sense: silence is *full of power:* 'if a teacher asks for comments on an assigned reading and receives complete silence as a response, the ordered character of a particular classroom process is both disrupted and revealed' (Simon, 1992, p. 88). That is, Simon's hypothetical students (and my actual one), by refusing to discuss and thereby refusing the reading (or the film) itself, subvert the 'natural' order of things in which, as good students, they do as they are told; at the same time, in the act of resisting what is naturalized they both confirm its power *as* naturalized (we do not resist for resistance's sake – something is always *being* resisted) and (re)create that power. This multidirectional flow of power is emblematic of a framework in which there is no 'massive and primal condition of domination, a binary structure with "dominators" on one side and "dominated" on the other, but rather a multiform production of relations of domination' (Foucault, 1980a, p. 142).

Yet the balance is imperfect. Silence is not always powerful, and the regulatory structures of education's institutional processes may prevail in the end, despite resistance. Simon (1992, p. 99; fn 20) identifies the 'self-policing nature' of these boundaries in the student who 'finds herself at two in the morning unable to grasp just what it is that Foucault is saying [and] decides that perhaps graduate school is beyond her abilities' (p. 88). If that student withdraws from her program – if in missing the idea of power as multi-directional she also misses the fact of her own power – it might seem that hegemonic discourses and structures have succeeded. Absent, she cannot challenge or change them: their entrenchment is confirmed and further secured. Equally, if a student teacher leaves before completing the program, and never enters a classroom again, we might assume that the buttresses of the institution have held.

Conversely, it would be easy to infer that a student teacher's overt consent to a theory endorsed by her program marked a genuine shift. But resistance takes many forms. Such a conjecture might prove incorrect if, say, in her own classroom that individual were to practise the same previously valued pedagogy she had ostensibly rejected in a course, not in order 'to "live through" the course in a position of subordination' (Simon, 1992, p. 93), but tactically, to *get* through it and into that classroom-of-her-own. Indeed, pedagogy is 'never innocent' (p. 56). Likewise, 'the language of the classroom is never innocent, but structured by the social grammar not only of schooling but as well, the societal forms through which a public culture is expressed' (p. 89).

I suggest that theory is never innocent either, for in the injunction to think new thoughts, and/or to express thoughts in new language, it has the potential to interrupt identities, in ways ranging from the merely inconvenient to the downright shattering. Simon refers to two kinds of identity position imposed theory might threaten (p. 85): one's professional identity and accompanying practices; and one's location in relations of gender, class, and ethnicity, which are implicated in theory's demand to relinquish 'knowledges and commitments that people have grown up with and which constitute important resources for coping with everyday life' (pp. 86–7).

Perhaps, too, part of the difficulty of Simon's invitation to consider a 'pedagogy of possibility' as a counter-discourse to hegemony (p. 60) is that the commitment histories of some student teachers may embody a nostalgia not easily abandoned for the cause of social justice, worthwhile though that cause might be. But we continue to hope: once, after interviewing applicants to York University's preservice program, I shared with a faculty member my frustration at what seemed a common wish to repeat early idyllic school experiences, expressed in terms of love – 'I just love children'; 'I loved school and I want to share that love'; even, on one memorable occasion, 'I get all the love I need from children' – which I saw as flattening larger concerns such as social and economic inequities. He responded, 'Ah, all that love-stuff is what gets them here. And then we help them see there's more to it.'

What I wish to do now is take Simon's thinking on 'identity positions' and on silence as symptomatic of a fear of theory, into the realm of psychical affect, to consider some of the silences that constitute responses to the perceived imposition of theory as a demand to make over in a new theoretical skin not only 'one's practice' and 'one's thoughts and feelings' (pp. 93–4), but also one's very self.

Before I do so, however, a word on 'self' is relevant. The concept is different in Foucauldian theory than in psychoanalysis. At the simplest level, for Foucault self is a surface that reflects the images we create of ourselves, while for Freud it is a storehouse of experience. But what the two systems share in common is the idea of dynamism: in Foucault's philosophy, the self 'is not a substance . . . [but] a form, and this form is not primarily or always identical to itself' (1997, p. 290); for psychoanalysis the perpetual ebb and flow of conscious and unconscious mean that it is 'fundamentally dialectic in nature' (Ogden, 1994b, p. 7). And while I do not want to ignore postmodern views on the importance of the social, and particularly language and discourse, in the making of self (Burkitt, 1991; Harré, 1993), I do wish to reassert my own position (fairly close to Harré's): that although it is very often in social contexts that meaning, and selves, are made, unmade, and remade, at the heart of things there is an 'I' who does the making. Mitchell (1993, p. 107) speaks of this 'I' as having both 'changeable content' and 'a sense of self that is independent of shifts over time.' Like Mitchell, even on a day when 'I am not myself,' I 'do not, even for a moment, consider the possibility that I actually have awakened as someone or (Kafka notwithstanding) something else.'

Let us press on.

Troubling Theory: A Psychoanalytic Reading

The implicit calling-into-question of previously acquired and deeply cherished knowledge and/or beliefs can be occasioned in other ways, and other contexts, than learning to teach. My work on second language acquisition posits, following Ehrman and Dörnyei (1998, p. 185), that individuals may resist the acquisition of a second language because the relationship with the self of the first language is shattered by the call to remake that self in (and through) the second language (Granger, 2004, p. 54). Insofar as we might consider a new philosophy, or discourse, or theory, or any new idea at all, as a kind of new language for thinking, they might be perceived – perhaps not consciously – as tacitly critical and potentially disruptive of the pre-existing philosophy, discourse, idea, or theory. We are attached to our theories, even if we do not give them that name. And when we are asked to give up a long-held theory and take up a new one, we suffer a loss. We suffer a loss even if what we gain (an exciting new set of ideas; an 'A' on an essay; a teaching certificate and a job) is what we have long desired.

Losses must be mourned.

In his essay on 'Mourning and melancholia' (1917a) Freud outlines these two interrelated psychical processes which result from the disappointment by, or loss of, a love-object. Briefly, mourning is 'the reaction to the loss of a loved person, *or to the loss of some abstraction* which has taken the place of one, *such as* one's country, liberty, *an ideal*, and so on' (Freud, 1917a, p. 243; my italics). Specifically, it is the process of working through loss that becomes necessary when a beloved object ceases to exist. In such a moment, the individual subject's libidinal energy or psychical attention must let go of its investment in that object. But letting go is difficult: for the libidinal attachment to come to an end the subject must accept the demand of reality-testing[9] to acknowledge fully that its object is permanently gone. Until this necessary libidinal withdrawal comes to pass and the mourning process is completed, the object's existence is 'psychically prolonged' (Freud, 1917a, p. 245) by the subject.

Melancholia is related to mourning in that it too can begin as a response to the loss of a beloved object (or abstraction). But the nature of the loss differs. Freud writes:

> The object has not perhaps actually died, but has been lost as an object of love . . . [The analyst] feels justified in maintaining the belief that a loss of this kind has occurred, but . . . cannot see clearly what it is that has been lost, and it is all the more reasonable to suppose that the patient cannot consciously perceive what he has lost either. This, indeed, might be so even if the patient is aware of the loss which has given rise to his melancholia, but only in the sense that he knows *whom* he has lost but not *what* he has lost in him. (1917a, p. 245; italics in original)[10]

The allusion to the analyst in Freud's elaboration should not be inferred as suggesting that any part of the process of learning (or resisting) theory is disordered or unhealthy. I view the mourning of abstract losses as a natural component of the learning process, and potentially productive. Further, though Freud conceptualizes melancholia variously as pathological (1917a, p. 244), an ailment (p. 257), and even dangerous (p. 252), I use the concept here as a thing-to-think-with and not a categorical absolute: a process may embody melancholic elements without altogether *being* melancholia. My work here is to read psychoanalytically the hints silence – literal, metaphorical, or disguised – offers, in ways that allow a consideration of what lies beside or beneath the more socio-political manifestations and identity positions Simon (1992) examines. If, for instance, we can imagine silence as hinting that, in psychical terms, the process of learning theory is also at times a problem, we may be able both to begin understanding its complexities without flattening them, and to work with rather than against them: that is, to work through our own fear of (the fear of) theory. And if we in teacher education can find ways to do this, it might just be that education as a whole can begin to do it. For of course faculties of education are not the only place where new theories invite, insist on, and precipitate worried and consequently worrying responses.

In melancholia the object-loss is 'withdrawn from consciousness' in a devolving departure from mourning, in which 'there is nothing about the loss that is unconscious' (Freud, 1917a, p. 245). Briefly, what happens is that although a person suffers a shattering of the relationship with an object (pp. 248–9), in melancholia this shattering fails to result in a progression toward replacement with a new object-relationship. The libidinal energy that would have been directed at the new object is taken up by the ego, which develops an identification with the lost object that blurs the boundary between ego and object, and the loss of or disappointment by the object may become an impoverishment of ego. For Freud (1917a, p. 246), 'In mourning it is the world which has become poor and empty; in melancholia it is the ego itself.'

There are two lost or disappointing objects in my iteration of this model: the old theory framework in which the individual is invested, and that part of the individual's theorized (*theory*-ed?) other-than-conscious self, made by and through the theory, that is lost in the transformation/ translation from the original theoretical framework to the next. In light of this, might the demand to learn theory, and the psychical activity of that learning, invoke a process similar to mourning? And if the old theory-object does not disappear permanently, but still exists – perhaps concretely in the practicum classroom – could the process even approach melancholia? Might learning that provokes a transformation thus be a potentially shattering force? Without directly mapping the categorization 'melancholic' onto the student teacher in the process of learning theory, I find it helpful for speculating on some of the reasons for the deep attachment of some student teachers (or host teachers or teacher educators, or for that matter anyone) to the beliefs, attitudes, and values that make up a personal theory.

Specifically, there seems to be a reverberation between Freud's idea of ego impoverishment on one hand, and the problem of theory for teacher education on the other. The psychoanalytic idea that a child gives something up in learning to speak (Phillips, 1999), a loss which I have argued is re-enacted in the learning of a second language, is instructive here too. Briefly, the child acquiring language, while clearly achieving a very important social gain – entry into the world of language and communication with others – is at the same time 'giv[ing] up what she can never in fact relinquish, her inarticulate self, the self before language' (Phillips, 1999, p. 42). That pre-language self embodies a kind of unconsciously perceived or remembered (fantastical) omnipotence, grounded in the infant's primal sense of unity with its world and the consequent non-necessity of communication that inhere in its very condition as a being whose needs, although unspoken, are met. True, the self is remade as a user of language, but for psychoanalysis what is repressed is never truly forgotten and may be re-awakened, remembered, or even re-experienced, over and over (Freud, 1915a). So the unspeaking, pre-language self never quite goes away, but persists as a psychical echo.

The individual acquiring a second language undergoes a qualitatively different shift, not from silence to speech but from one speaking self to another. Of course, the persistence of the first-language self is more readily observable than the pre-language self, because the first language is not completely lost in the process of learning the second. Still, I argue (2004), this later process parallels first-language acquisition in its demand that the self be remade in a new language, and through that parallel, and the accompanying disappointment at the loss (albeit in a sense more partial) of the former self, the recollection of the earlier loss is awakened.

In the present discussion I understand theory as a kind of language. But more than just a new lexicon (though that too is significant), a theory (or theory-in-practice) also embodies the ways of thinking, acting, and making meaning that its language opens up but also delimits and defines. A theory is told and understood *in* a particular kind of language, but it also *is* a language, a hermeneutic for interpreting, reflecting, acting, being, and making relations in the world. And so the demand to learn (and apply) a new theory is, like the demand to learn a new language, also a call to remake the self *in* that new theory, which implicitly involves at least partially abandoning the former self.

In the context of teacher education, I suggest, the learner of a new theory more closely resembles the second- than the first-language learner. She has come to the encounter with an existing theory-self (her personal beliefs about teaching and learning, and maybe too some official ones, acquired along the way), so that the explicit or implicit demand to abandon old theory extends only to aspects incompatible with the new one. In this way, as a theorized self, a holder of theory, she is not quite comparable to the pre-language individual. And yet, her relationship to a familiar theory, whose concepts she wears like a skin and uses, with its language, to speak and to act, shares qualities with her relationship to language proper.

For we are our theories, and our theories are us. Thus does the loss of this in-vestment – this state of being *dressed* or *wrapped in* a theory[11] – resemble the ego-loss (or the ego-prior-to-loss) of the melancholic, and thus might it reinforce the view that in psychical terms there are losses as well as gains implicated in learning, be it a new language or, in the present discussion, a new theory.

A part of the self is lost in the move that learning demands. But for psychoanalysis, recalling Freud's mystic writing-pad (1924), those aspects of the self that *were* there *are* there, albeit attenuated to psychical echoes or memory traces, whether the forgetting has been an unconscious repression of trauma or the deliberate rejection of an idea. And in the world external to the self, the loss is likewise never complete or absolute, so that a formerly privileged didactic pedagogy, replaced in thinking and intent by a new constructivist one, may still be in use in a practicum classroom and thus never far away. New and old theories, practices, and selves coexist, ebbing and flowing in tension with one another. Or they split off from each other. As Simon (1992, p. 86) recognizes, an attenuated version of the demand to abandon social and intellectual commitments might be to 'compartmentalize' them.

We might, then, understand the student teacher as a self compartmentalized by external demands to be a student in her classes and a teacher in her practicum; a theorist and a practitioner; a thinker one moment and a doer the next. She is split between the rock of theory and practice's hard place – between new and old ideas, between a theory classroom and a practicum placement, and more generally between her past and present of, and in, teaching and learning. This is not altogether surprising, for the nexus in which such splits come about is itself made from disagreements, contradictions, and different perspectives. And the splits are not absolute. Theory in general, and theoretical class discussions in particular, are often explicitly *about* practice. The idea that the past informs the present is a view as widely accepted (though rooted in somewhat different soil) in education research as in psychoanalysis. And of course, one theory may embody aspects of another. This notion of the student teacher as a self divided resonates with Foucault's thinking on the 'objectivizing of the subject' through 'dividing practices' that result in a subject 'either divided inside himself or divided from others' (Foucault, 1983, p. 208), and with the psychoanalytic notion of splitting.

Splitting (through) Theory: The Self Divided

Psychoanalytic thought helps us understand the self as non-unitary. Laplanche and Pontalis (1973, pp. 427–8) assess work done in the 1890s by Breuer and Freud (1974), on 'splitting of the mind' in patients suffering from hysteria or who had undergone hypnosis, as contributing to Freud's hypothesis of the conscious and unconscious minds as separated from each other through repression. Predicated in part on this, Mitchell's (1993) writing on self as at once multiple *and* singular, integral *and* discontinuous, speaks to another kind of split, the 'splitting of the ego,' consisting for Freud in 'two attitudes persist[ing] side by side throughout their lives without influencing each other' (1940, p. 203), and differing from Klein's version, in which it exists as a necessary accompaniment to the very basic, and very early, defence[12] against anxiety that Kleinians term the 'splitting of the object' (1946).

Felman's important (1982) caution concerning the distinction between applying psychoanalysis to pedagogy on one hand and reading, and thinking, psychoanalytically on the other seems germane in relation to Klein, whose understanding of early life as a place of hate and envy as well as love (1957, p. 205), of 'sadistic impulses . . . in the earliest stages of development' (1946, p. 27), and of 'positions' she named 'paranoid-schizoid' and 'depressive' (1946, p. 34), have marked her in popular perception as a harsher critic of the human condition than even Freud. Before continuing, I stress that my use of these concepts is meant to consider these difficult moments not as examples of pathology but as embodying aspects of a *process* that may, for some individuals in some circumstances, be a little bit like those the psychoanalytic terms describe.

Kleinian object-splitting, one of the 'typical defences of the early ego' (Klein, 1946, p. 2), arises out of the infant's fantasy of 'omnipotent control of the internal and external object,' in turn grounded in an extreme form of denial that 'amounts to an annihilation of any frustrating object or situation, and is thus bound up with the strong feeling of omnipotence which obtains in the early stages of life' (Klein, 1952b, p. 65). In this formulation the infant experiences the first object – the breast – as gratifying but also frustrating (because it does not always gratify) and, again in fantasy, separates the breast-as-object into an idealized 'good' and a hated 'bad' object (Klein, 1946, p. 2).[13] This split is 'accompanied by a parallel splitting of the ego into a "good" ego and a "bad" one, the ego being constituted for Kleinians essentially through the introjection of objects' (Laplanche & Pontalis, 1973, p. 430). Introjection and projection, a metaphorical ingesting and expelling, are thus implicated in the splitting of objects and, I argue, of ideas-as-objects or theory-as-object.

From here it is a small step to recognizing introjection as a precursor to identification. For we are not only partial to or fond of our 'good-object' theories. I repeat: we are attached to our theories. We *are* our theories, and *our theories are us*. Indeed, Laplanche and Pontalis describe introjection and projection as prototypes of identification in which 'the mental process is experienced . . . as a bodily one' (1973, p. 207). And although the link between introjection and 'oral incorporation' is more literally readable in the context of language acquisition (Granger, 2004), it is a significant symbolic interpretation in the context of learning in general, and learning (or refusing to learn) theory in particular:

> Expressed in the language of the oldest – the oral – instinctual impulses, the judgement is: 'I should like to eat this,' or 'I should like to spit it out'; and, put more generally: 'I should like to take this into myself and to keep that out.' That is to say: 'It shall be inside me' or 'It shall be outside me. . . . ' [The] original pleasure-ego wants to introject into itself everything that is good and to eject from itself everything that is bad. What is bad, what is alien to the ego and what is external are, to begin with, identical. (Freud, 1925, p. 237)

Transposing this inside-good/outside-bad distinction into the discussion of old-versus-new theory, or theory-versus-practice, I read in the student teacher who resists or refuses a new theory, or who rejects theory altogether and insists that the only legitimate learning comes from the 'experience' of practice-teaching, a kind of splitting symptomatic of multi-level conflict: first, between the theories or approaches on offer, and second, at a deeper intra-personal level, between the *inside* theory – the 'personal theory' that she brings with her – and the new, *outside* theory that the program presents. In this configuration, old theory is 'good' and new theory, outside the self and by insinuation at least partly counter to the old, equates to 'bad.' In addition, 'idealization is bound up with the splitting of the object, for the good aspects of the [object] are exaggerated as a safeguard against the fear of the persecuting [object]' (Klein, 1946, p. 7). In other words, good becomes better, bad becomes even worse.

But there are complications here. First, psychoanalytically speaking, if our good theories are part of us, so are our bad theories, which persist despite our rejection of them. Britzman (2003, p. 130) clarifies: 'All of these bad injuring objects that terrify the inside are banished to the outside. Yet because these also are the "bits" of the infant, identification follows on the heels of expulsion. Then this projected content threatens to return to have its revenge.' Might we understand, in the student teacher's worry about theory, an implicit recognition of the vengeful-ness of a rejected set of ideas? Second, as Britzman (2003, p. 141) points out, the terms 'good' and 'bad' are themselves 'unstable and subject to confusion.' And so, thereby, is the organization of so-called good and bad objects. If the individual's ego deems the old inside theory good and the newly imposed outside theory bad, at the same time the teacher education program, as an aspect of that outside by which she stands to be judged, introduces a categorizational dilemma.

It is this. Most student teachers come to teacher education with a history of success in schools. In psychoanalytic terms education itself is, for them, a 'good' object. Moreover, they are a 'hardworking and serious' bunch, who, having 'grown up in a school system that rewards passivity and obedience ... have learned to see teachers and texts as authoritative sources of knowledge' (Feiman-Nemser & Remillard, 1996, p. 68) and not to challenge the status quo (Goodlad, 1990). If indi-viduals come to teaching with the tacit understanding that the teacher and the system hold the knowledge that matters, they also understand, equally implicitly, that what they have already learned about teaching and learning is correct, precisely because they have learned it in and from that system and those teachers. And so those 'preordained,' 'natu-ral and self-evident' meanings (Britzman, 1991, p. 7), such as the notion that human development and learning are linear and always progres-sive, may have for them a nice round satisfaction.

And then along comes teacher education, with its (sometimes) eman-cipatory projects, and its insistence (in some cases) on recognizing he-gemonic structures, and its deliberate challenges to those internalized precepts. Ideas of development as messy, circuitous and unpredictable may intrude, contradicting already acquired, institutionally authorized understandings. For the student teacher, then, those new ideas *cannot be true.* Yet they originate in another branch of the same authoritative institution: the teacher education program, or course director, or text. So in the conceptual realm that accepts that institution and its repre-sentatives as authoritative, they *must be true,* because the teacher – the 'expert,' the 'bearer of power,' and 'product of experience' (Britzman, 1991, p. 8) vaster than that of the student teacher (or perceived that way) – says so.

Ideas that cannot be true yet must be true? A new status quo that one is reluctant to challenge, but which challenges or even contradicts outright an earlier version of itself? Is it surprising then that the stu-dent teacher feels worried? That a new theory might be troubling? That student teachers – like the students of whom Ellsworth writes, who 'are not talking in their authentic voices, or . . . are declining/refusing to talk at all' (1989, p. 313), or are talking from 'within communities of resistance . . . [as] a condition of survival' (p. 310) – might not feel empowered by new theories or discourses, but rather ambivalent, oppressed, even silenced? Might silence be, in part, a non-response (which is really a response) not only to threats to gender and other identity positions (Ellsworth, 1989; Simon, 1992) but also to threats to the intrapersonal attachments, investments, and self-concept that live beneath consciousness?

Here we might consider another silence as a response, itself split, to the demand *to* split. This is the silence of whichever part of the individual cannot, for whatever reason, make itself known in a given moment: either the old idealized 'good' theory-object that one does not speak in class because it does not mesh with the official theory-object, or the new theory-object, simultaneously good and bad, that may not quite be reconcilable with the old. Either one of those may find no place in a host teacher's classroom in which still other theories prevail.

Mourning and splitting, then, are psychical responses to conflicts within, and disruptions of, self that come about when new theory threatens to usurp old. Such threats might be felt particularly strongly by student teachers who understand themselves as teachers already, and believe that there is little teacher education can teach them that they do not already know – little, that is, that they can change without fundamentally changing who they are. And so the desire to 'make a difference' in the world through teaching stands in conflict with the fear of change; the same knowledge (or theory) that is powerful, important, and good has the potential to destroy: in a psychoanalytic sense we must, posits Britzman (2003, p. 128), destroy it first. Our desire for knowledge is thus equalled or surpassed by our desire *not* to know, a passion for ignorance (Silin, 1995; Britzman, 2003) or wish to ignore which Simon (1992, p. 95, following Lacan, 1975, and Felman, 1982) summarizes as an 'active refusal [that excludes] from consciousness . . . whatever it does not want to know' (Simon, 1992, p. 95).

Which seems to be plenty. The picture I have painted looks like nothing but trouble: resisting, refusing, mourning, splitting. Falling apart. But the news is not all bad. One consolation prize for object-splitting is the protection it offers against the total shattering of the ego, which in early life does not possess the cohesion it will ultimately acquire (Klein, 1957, p. 191). Through splitting, 'the good part of the ego and the good object are in some measure protected' (Klein, 1963, p. 300). Perhaps something similar can be said for the student teacher, whose teaching-ego/self is not quite developed and whose desire to make things better leaves her vulnerable to the disappointment of finding out that *her* theory is not quite *the* theory, and that perhaps she is not quite, not yet, a teacher. Simon's reminder that fear can sometimes signal a 'significant moment of learning' or an expansion of possibility toward a pedagogy of hope (Simon, 1992, pp. 81–2) is likewise encouraging.

These are tender processes. The task of teacher educators is a difficult one. But I agree with Phelan (1997a, p. 176) that part of that task is helping beginning teachers to 'understand how their practice has been [discursively] framed.' Without framing *them;* without nailing them down. Perhaps the trick is in not insisting too hard on making significant moments happen, but rather letting them happen, or in acknowledging the fact of uncertainty by being, ourselves, a little more tentative about our own theoretical investments and positions.

We might even consider letting a little bit of destruction happen first. On this point Britzman is reassuring: 'If, in the first instance, we must destroy knowledge before it destroys us, then we also are able to make second thoughts and so allow our thinking to be a resource for its own repair' (Britzman, 2003, p. 128).

'Destruction' need not mean annihilation, but a kind of normalization of the expectation of the uncertain, the worrying, even the contradictory might be helpful. For example, a 'teacher candidate practicum evaluation protocol' recently developed by Murphy and Gaymes San Vicente of York University's Faculty of Education moves in that direction, by including some of the language of uncertainty and doubt in its questions. The mentor teacher is asked, 'If you were teaching this lesson for the first time what would be your *concern(s)*?' and, 'Knowing that there are *differences* in your teaching style and your [student teacher's] teaching style . . . what advice would you give for *thinking about handling these differences*?' Questions for the student teacher include: 'What *worries* you the most about the lesson?' and 'How did you work with the *contradictions* . . . in materials/resources and advice you received about the planning of the lesson?' (Murphy & Gaymes San Vicente, 2007, pp. 2–3; my italics). These questions invite both awareness and acceptance of, and thoughtful responses to, some of teacher education's complexities.

Yes, the rough road of teacher education exhibits all manner of forks, bumps, and sharp turns. As a course director I have listened to student teachers' stories of frustration, exhaustion, and overwork, negotiated and re-negotiated their assignment deadlines, occasionally dried their tears. As a teaching assistant I have fielded complaints about the type and length of required readings and discussed the perceived uselessness of essay-writing. And dried some tears there too.

And I have been a student teacher.

Oh, have I ever.

In Chapter 5 I dealt with the psychoanalytic question of the mother-child relation, and some of its implications for pedagogical relations. The next chapter turns again to look at that dynamic in a continuation of this exploration of difficult moments and silences in learning to teach. Specifically, I look at the (re)enactment of that primary relationship in a primary classroom, and in a very specific circumstance: my own.

But now, it is time to end this chapter, before I get ahead of myself. Or before I get *to* myself. I'll explain what I mean. In a moment.

7 Ghosts That Haunt Us: 'Forbidden Narratives' of Learning to Teach

Where I am, I don't know, I'll never know,
in the silence you don't know,
you must go on, I can't go on, I'll go on.
> – Samuel Beckett, *The Unnamable.*

Remembering begins in the body, in vague feelings, in the sensuous before it claims its story. Memory is made from traces, fragments, and images, from what cannot be let go, from what insists on a psychic place.... I tell my tales ... with a sense of injustice, of cynicism, and, despite what my mother might think, I think with a sense of dark humor.
> – Ronald J. Pelias, *A Methodology of the Heart*

Thinking Theory: From Splitting to Insight

The Kleinian concept of splitting of the object, and concomitantly the ego, marks the origin in psychoanalytic thought of object relations theory. Developed by Fairbairn (1952), Winnicott (1990) and others, it posits (in a moment of almost-meeting with pure social construction-ism) that the human psyche is made, and makes itself, in relation to the social world. This making is inaugurated when the infant begins to perceive its separateness from its mother[1] in a process in which ego is the force that mediates between inside and outside. In the classic Freudian view (1948), the infant prior to this awakening has no sense of itself as separate from the outside world, indeed no sense at all of the world *as* a world, or of itself *as* a self. This first separation, physical and psychical, marks the beginning of identity, as 'the infant separates out objects and then the environment from the self,' becoming a unit that permits 'a complex interchange between what is inside and what is outside . . . [which] constitutes the main relationship of the individual to the world' (Winnicott, 1963a, p. 72).

Winnicott posits that breaches in these relationships can disrupt the newly individuating self. For instance, when the intervals grow longer between the sensation of hunger and the crying that informs the caregiver of the infant's need, and between the crying and the feeding that satisfies, the child loses the sense of immediate connection between need and gratification. But the intellect finds clues (a soothing voice; the smell of milk) that help it to tolerate the delay by recognizing that nourishment is on the way. While this is fortunate, Winnicott goes on, in that it allows the mother to free herself somewhat from the baby, and the baby to grow toward an integrated independence in which its environment and relationships can be trusted, in some instances 'the baby and the mother may collude in exploitation of the intellect which becomes split off – split off, that is from the psyche of psychosomatic existence and living.' The child starts to exist less in affect and more in intellect: it 'begins to develop a false self in terms of a life in the split-off mind, the true self being . . . hidden and perhaps lost' (Winnicott, 1963b, p. 59). The breast (or other food) is the prototypical object that meets the hungry infant's need and makes all things right. In the case of the split-off intellect, that need (and others) persists unmet despite all rationalizations; eventually both the world outside the self and the individual's feelings in relation to it come to be perceived as unsafe or unreliable, and she comes to 'live in' and value mind over body, thinking above affect. The non-intellectual self grows silent.

Well, guess what. The paragraphs you have just read began as part of the previous chapter. I intended to make a case, as in my second language acquisition work (Granger, 2004, p. 95), for an inversion of Winnicott's split-off intellect into a split-off affect – a condition of hyper-affect in which the student teacher's attachment to personal theories of teaching and learning might cause her to defend them by refusing an encounter with new ones and privileging practice. But there has been a change of plan.

Why then do I include that segment at all? I could have quietly deleted it and no one would be the wiser. But here is what happened: as I typed those sentences, reworked, and reworded, and edited, and otherwise fussed with them, spending far more time on them than was necessary, it dawned on me that in terms of both content and the act of writing I was doing two things. First, I was delaying coming to my own story. This seems to be a habit of mine – demonstrated by the first three chapters of this study, in which I worked through several successive, and successively more complete, versions of the 'data.' Additionally, along the way my work has shifted a bit in structure, away from an earlier intent to use my narratives to launch a theoretical discussion, to a less linear, more meandering exploration of moments small and large, personal and theoretical, and of the processes of narrating and remembering.

Second, and more importantly, I was writing my own symptom. Winnicott's words on the split-off intellect are so close to my own story that he could have been writing them about me. What is more, it is plain, from clues in present-day family dynamics, hints in family legends, my history as a learner, and my personal work in psychoanalysis, that the concept of the split-off intellect is relevant to more than my early life. Here is another clue: immediately following his discussion of the phenomenon Winnicott mentions one of his patients, who sought treatment for it, writing that she was 'over fifty when she got free in the course of her analysis' (1963b, p. 59).

Why does it take so long to 'get free' – or even to begin to imagine that there is some place called 'free' that we might want to get to? Why does it take so long to arrive somewhere? While I do not take up those questions in great detail in this work, I have noticed, not just here and not just now, moments in writing when I realize, all at once, that *that* – whatever that might be in a particular circumstance – is what I have been trying to say all along, or what I have been saying without knowing I was saying it. Pitt (2006) notices this too. Writing of the 'symbolic act' (or in psychoanalytic theory the fantasy) of matricide with which 'the need of the infant to become a speaking, symbolizing being is tied up' (p. 89), she turns partway through her piece to reminisce about her own experience reading (and coming to know something about herself through) Grumet's *Bitter Milk* (1988). She describes, years after first reading that text, a discovery that marks a moment of seeing what has previously been overlooked: '[Grumet's] perspective seemed somehow to have been lurking all along in the margins of my own work, unrecognized and unclaimed' (p. 101). Part of what Pitt learns as a result of that bi-directional encounter with herself in another's work, and with that Other in her own work, is that her earlier dismissive reading of Grumet was 'trapped within the confines of object relating masquerading as critical thought' (p. 102).

My own trap wears a different mask: object relating disguised as what object relations theory names 'object use.' The distinction is that in the latter the subject perceives the object as truly external to the self and outside its control (Winnicott, 1971). What this means here is that I have studiously avoided my own implication as a subject while reading the object relations theory-as-object into and onto other subjects, and I have attempted to use the split-off intellect as a thing to think with – about anyone except myself. In effect I have split myself off from splitting-off, in a kind of self-similar conceptualization, a reverse 'Droste effect' that yields in the discussion a manifestation of what is being discussed, which paradoxically keeps alive what is abstracted but silences much of the story.[2]

The splitting-off of the intellect inaugurates and maintains a silence of affect. The individual is divided between thinking and feeling, or more accurately, between thinking and *not*-feeling – for when the split is effective there is not much feeling at all. In my case, the split is between the part of my story that *thinks about* itself, and the part that *feels* itself but which I do not want, or am not able, to feel. This split has, I think, been necessary as a protection against shattering (Klein, 1946): recalling Winnicott's secret self, both wanting and fearing to be found (1963c), like Schaafsma and some of the students whose personal writing he examines, albeit in a different context (1996, p. 110), 'I know some stories I cannot tell you.'

I confess that I have worries, in addition to those I articulated earlier, about saying too much, and about whether it might be better to say nothing; about veering so close to an analogy with pathology that my interpretation (or the material of my own which I am interpreting) might itself read as pathological. In the course of this study I have read enough about autoethnographic work to concur with Miller's observation (1992, p. 505) that it is at times 'dismissed as "soft," "idiosyncratic," "undertheorized," "individualistic," even "narcissistic",' and that those who do it may be accused of self-indulgence or a lack of academic rigour (Coffey, 1999; Sparkes, 2000; Spigelman, 2001; Holt, 2003). I will not restage my earlier discussions on this topic, but I will join Pinar (1981, p. 184) in the view that 'our life histories are not liabilities to be exorcised but are the very preconditions for knowing. It is our individual and collective stories in which present projects are situated, and it is awareness of these stories which is the lamp illuminating the dark spots, the rough edges.' Moreover, I will keep to my position on the value of speculation:

that one moment, or experience, or story can help us to theorize others. And so, like Beckett's *unnamable* – the unnamed self that cannot find its own story (1959) – I will go on.

I first read Winnicott's paper on the split-off intellect as an assigned reading in one of the theory courses in my preservice teacher education program. The piece is called '*Sum*, I am,' its title at once a play on the Latin *sum* (meaning 'I am') and the English word 'sum' (total), and it links the sense of self, as an individual being separate from other individual beings, with the mathematical concept of one. Though it helped awaken my interest in psychoanalytic theory, I did not notice then how relevant, how resonant, the piece was with my personal story.

But of course I didn't – for while I could engage with and learn about it *as theory*, I could not yet learn *from* it (Freud, 1919; Britzman, 1998; Phillips, 1998): the split-off intellect can 'function brilliantly without much reference to the human being' (Winnicott, 1963b, p. 60). Although I could not see it then, I now believe that that little chapter, in a book called *Home is Where We Start From* (another hint), may have been the beginning of a shift in my academic trajectory, away from a wish to teach children and toward the interests in educational discourse, the multiplicity of text, and psychoanalytic theory as a hermeneutic that have brought me to this moment.

In her exploration of the relationship between narrative and psychoanalytic theory's Nachträglichkeit or deferred (re)vision, King (2000) explains that autobiographical narratives highlight events that are understood retroactively as significant. As well, a split text can be 'a narrative reconstruction of [a] split . . . between the "child who knew" and the conscious self who had no knowledge' (p. 65). King's reference is to Fraser's (1987) chronicle of sexual abuse, but the observation is suggestive for me too. For remembering, and writing what we remember, can identify splits and even help mend them: looking at links in Freudian and Foucauldian thinking between identity formation and coherence (whether perceived or imposed) in life events, King makes the further point that in psychoanalysis or in writing, using story to connect past and present may be both 'necessary and therapeutic' (2000, p. 24). But while in both social science research and the psychoanalytic relationship there is an effort to consider how various silences of resistance, contradiction, and forgetting allow 'the illusion of narrative coherence to be maintained,' for psychoanalysis (and for a psychoanalytic reading of narrative and other texts) 'these forgettings, contradictions, and refusals implicate the unconscious of the individual psyche rather than the hegemonic traces of dominant ideology' (Pitt, 1998, p. 543).

Writing abstractly about the split-off intellect functioned as a delaying tactic that postponed arriving at the details of my student teaching experience and also laid the groundwork for an important insight into that experience.[3] That is, the shifting of that passage to this chapter marks my recognition of my intellect/affect split, different in temporality from Fraser's but similar in formation – between my present self, the 'author who knows' and my earlier self, my student-teacher conscious self of a decade ago, who had no knowledge of that split. Paradoxically, then, writing about the split-off intellect has both kept me from, and brought me to, my own story, my own self. So too has my writing, also in that chapter, about another split: between theory and practice. Here I mean both the act of writing and what is written, namely these two very similar passages:

We are attached to our theories, even if we do not give them that name.

And

For we are not only partial to or fond of our 'good-object' theories. I repeat: we are attached to our theories. We are our theories, and our theories are us.

These variations on a theme reverberate with a passage in Britzman's adventure (2003, pp. 125–6) in 'theory kindergarten,' where 'the ego is not yet prepared to encounter its own thoughts.' A little door opens onto my insight, through Britzman's:

We do know what holds theory back from its own precocious curiosity. One trouble is resistance, not in the sociological sense of escaping power but in the psychological sense of refusing to know, of leaving psychical significance without thought.... Resistance, too, is a sticky affair: deny it and it is proved; accuse someone of it, and you may be characterizing yourself. (p. 126)

In juxtaposing my own two iterations, each alluding to our attachments to knowing what we think we know, and thinking what we know we think, with Britzman's sharp compendium on how a psychical resistance that saves us from knowing what we cannot tolerate can also wall us off from our own meanings, as well as with the mental calisthenics in my now-quashed plan to massage the intellect/affect split, I arrive at my own split between theory and practice – actually, between theory and practic*um*. Unlike most of the student teachers I have known, worked with, and read about, I chose theory.

So it happens again – learning as a vicissitude of writing; writing as a vicissitude of learning. I began with no intention of talking about a theory/practice split in my own educational life. For a time I wondered if the notion belonged in the study at all, so distant did it seem from anything I might say in an autoethnography. But of course: my discussion of that kind of split was grounded in my thinking, with Simon (1992), about a 'fear of theory' that was patently not my own. For I *love* theory; as a student teacher I looked forward to the foundations courses, thrilled at the readings, stayed up late to write essays rather than to perfect practicum lesson plans.

But here is the punch line: what I truly fear is the *absence* of theory, the silence of theory departed. I fear no theory, but I fear *no*-theory, the anti-intellectualism of which Britzman speaks (1986). As an almost archetypal example of a split-off intellect, I hold theory as my *good* object. Thinking is what I do best.[4]

Some research suggests that student teachers may seek a larger theoretical component in their programs than is typically present (Duquette, 1997). I would not be shocked to learn that some of my preservice education classmates felt as I did, but we did not speak of such things. The prevailing culture valued common-sense notions of experience as the best teacher, and practicum as the best experience. Still, I make no claim of uniqueness here, any more than I would claim that everyone who prefers theory over practice has the same reasons for doing so. Rather, I offer these speculations hypothetically, as openings rather than conclusions.

Affect 'threatens the omnipotence to which theory in silence aspires,' asserts Britzman (2003, p. 132). Theory is its own answer for everything, its imaginary omnipotence a startling echo of the undifferentiated, omnipotent (albeit also imaginary) state of early infancy in which instincts imply their own gratification and wishes their own fulfilment. But the promise of theory is a partly empty one: the adult, as a being in and of the world rather than the other way around, knows too much to follow that echo back home, because one of the things she knows is that that home never really existed.

Theory is a rich place in which to live: it can do many things, help us think many thoughts. And theory and affect are not mutually exclusive; I remember still the *frisson* I felt when a professor asked me, 'Have you ever fallen in love with an idea?' Still, finding or making a balance between intellect and affect is a tricky recipe, a bit like making meringue: beat the egg whites too little and they won't stand up; beat them too much and they'll separate. And then you'll get weeping.

Just as privileging practice can keep theory away, and old theories can keep new ones away, theory (new or old) can (maybe for a while; maybe longer) keep insight away, perhaps – to call up once more the ability of bad objects to shatter the self – until that self is ready to bear the weight of the insight. But it is time now to deliberately move a little away from the purely abstract, to consider the implications of these theoretical worries in the differently textured milieu of the practicum classroom. The arguably prevalent expectation (discussed in Chapter 6) is that practice-teaching will be the place or the moment to apply the theory that has been learned in coursework. But to do this is not necessarily straightforward. For even if the student's and the host teacher's theoretical orientations are similar, there remains the question of working together in a territory where, formally or by hegemonic custom, one is designated master and the other apprentice (Lortie, 1975). In this regard Martinez (1998, p. 97) calls for a consideration of 'affective, ethical and interpersonal' aspects of all components of teacher education, but particularly of practice-teaching, while Labaree (2000) narrows it even further: education is difficult because of the 'irreducible complexity' that inheres in the 'vast array of intervening variables that mediate between a teacher's action and a student's response' (2000, p. 231). My own contention, hardly revolutionary, is that since teacher education too is a relationship or a set of relations between those who teach and those who learn, it follows that the *teaching* of teaching and the *learning* of teaching are likewise complex.

Let us move forward; it is time now to tell the tale that instantiates my personal acquaintance with the larger question: Why is teacher education so difficult?

Practising Practicum: Coming to the Data

Well, it is *almost* time to tell the tale – did we imagine it would happen so suddenly, after all this? It is a strange thing, to know something so well and yet be unable to speak it. My practicum experience was difficult to live; remembering it is equally so. Indeed that is likely another reason why I 'chose' theory: practice – practicum – was not working.[5]

I had concerns coming to the data. How to write about experiences that were mine but that involved other people: could I avoid identifying them sufficiently to protect their privacy, and could I interpret those experiences without importing to those others meaning and intent that

I cannot verify? The former is easy to solve by changing non-crucial details and using pseudonyms. The latter is a more complex, but still reconcilable: my interpretation speaks first to institutional (and institutionalized) structures and power relations and second to my own psychical processes and experiences – no one else's. There were other concerns too, relating to the question of what constitutes 'legitimate' data, the problem of representing personal experience, the validity of that personal experience as a starting point for theorizing, and, always, the problem of silence. Earlier I located my response to the first three in meta- discourses about ethnographic research and 'the personal,' and to the fourth in psychoanalytic theory.

I soon found, however, that a further problem lay in determining how to write or otherwise record difficulty. Convictions about the richness of silence aside, what is spoken that surrounds those silences also matters, and while it is one thing to remember an event it can be quite another thing to translate it onto a page. Partly it is that difficulty is, well, difficult. But in addition, memories are made from what Casey (2000) categorizes as bodily recollections, sensory echoes, place and time, as well as language, while a study of this kind condenses it all into language – specific kinds of language that cannot fully retain or transmit the flavours and textures of the events themselves.

An interview was suggested as a way to turn memories into concrete narrative 'data.' Having been on both sides of the microphone in earlier researches (Lotherington et al., 2001; Granger et al., 2002; Morbey & Granger, 2002; Pitt & Britzman, 2003) I knew well its potential, even in more typical circumstances, for complications, including (mis)representation due to shifting interviewer/respondent boundaries and roles (Fontana, 2002, p. 162), leading questions, exploitation, partiality, the myth of the detached interviewer, and in general, gaps between what people think and what they tell about their thinking (Hammersley, 1992; Hollway & Jefferson, 2000; Gubrium & Holstein, 2002). This situation added another layer: How does one interview oneself? Even if one designates someone else to take on the role of interviewer, is it possible to devise questions that are truly open enough not to predict their own answers? Does that even matter?

It matters in some ways, of course. It would be of little use to be interviewed by someone who had no idea about my project – fascinating though my analysis of pork-belly futures or World Cup soccer or *The Canterbury Tales* might be – and so to that extent at least I would have to be involved in establishing any questions or other protocols. Where it might matter less, though, is in an 'openly ideological research' context

(Lather, 1986), such as this one, in which neutrality and objectivity are not merely unsought, nor even recognized as impossible, but also, frankly, pointless, since my goal is to push thinking in useful directions rather than to prove some fact.

There are also issues, in any research, about what is done with the data. Or with what is silent in, even absent from, the data. Mazzei (2003, p. 367) opines that while 'listening to the silence' allows a researcher to 'probe the silences for the latent meanings and understandings found therein[, a] real danger . . . is our forcing the silences to say what we want to hear. It is essential that we listen for the meanings that are present (and absent) and the motivations and sources of those meanings – that we let the silence speak.'

I do not believe it is so easy to distinguish the meaning in any text from the meaning we make of it. But perhaps part of my work in this research is to look into and work through the meanings we do make in an effort to find their (and our) 'motivations and sources.' Hollway and Jefferson (2000) propose an interview method which, by eliciting stories whose significance surpasses 'the teller's intentions – [as does] the psychoanalytic method of free associations' (p. 35), makes space for understanding the research subject as 'one whose inner world is not simply a reflection of the outer world, nor a cognitively driven rational accommodation to it.' That is, it allows the teller's unconscious mind to intrude into the story.

That was what I wanted, with my Foucauldian and psychoanalytic investments. For 'experience is made or fashioned; it is not encountered, discovered, or observed, except upon secondary reflection,' and even conscious 'introspection does not encounter ready-made material' (Schafer, 1992, p. 23). Thus I turned to the conceptual framework set out in Pitt and Britzman's project on 'difficult knowledge' (2003), with its series of 'prompts' designed to enable respondents to 'set their emotions and intellect side by side as they considered experiences of difficulty in knowledge' (p. 762).

There are definite differences between that work and this. First, the specific strangeness of my project, in which the researcher's self is the deliberate site of research, is largely absent from the Pitt-Britzman collaboration. Second, my work uses personal traumas to work with and through social (and institutional) concerns while theirs focuses on how social traumas can inaugurate personal worries. Nevertheless, the problem I had finding ways to articulate my difficulties drew me to their question: 'What is it to represent and narrate "difficult knowledge"?' – a question that 'foregrounds issues of encountering the self through the otherness of knowledge' (Pitt & Britzman, 2003, p. 755).

My colleague Lorin Schwarz had agreed to conduct the interview, and he suggested that I provide him with my questions in advance. I tried to imagine an interview protocol that would depend, like Pitt and Britzman's, on the precept that 'conflict provokes learning' (2003, p. 762), and that would invite representations of silent and difficult moments that embodied, again like theirs, 'an odd combination of new editions of old conflicts, of relations and fights with new and old forms of authority, as ambivalent and partial, and as charged by tonalities of love and hate' (p. 762) as those earlier conflicts, relations, and fights. Reading through their series of prompts I noticed that the ones that tugged hardest at me were those embodying notions of conflict, loneliness, isolation, betrayal, abandonment – themes that seemed at the time to close off possibilities for the interview. I thus decided to devise more specific questions.

In that process I noticed something else: as I asked myself hypothetical questions, in a curious double rush to application I seemed already to be anticipating my responses, and changing the questions, albeit subtly, if my hypothetical answers did not mesh with what I imagined myself to be looking for. In the back-and-forth, push-and-pull of question and answer it did not seem possible either to select key words or prompts, or to devise specific questions, that were not in some sense anticipatory or leading.

I had begun to lose sight of what I really wanted: to find a way to articulate some experiences I had not, theretofore, been able to speak. I wanted to end, to begin to end, a silence. Fundamentally, my question to myself was simple: 'What happened during practicum?' And so that is where we began. The interview became a conversation that was open enough to be a collecting place for the most significant events of my student-teaching experience, and on which I could base my theorization.

Curiously (if unsurprisingly), in the event a series of missteps – in psychoanalysis the parapraxes that signal an unconscious trying to make itself heard (Laplanche & Pontalis, 1973, p. 300) or, in this case, *not* heard – resulted in only about half the conversation being recorded. This was not catastrophic, though, as my aim was not to perform a detailed lexical analysis of a huge corpus of data, but to theorize a relationship based on my perceptions of it. Moreover, speaking the stories aloud articulated their shape in memory; thus I have selected two excerpts from the extant part of the taped conversation, and have added four other anecdotes, told in the interview and transcribed from my memory of their telling. Together these six narratives reflect the tone and atmosphere of the practicum setting and relationship, and provide a sufficient and useful archive for this work.[6] Below is a summary of the circumstances of the placement, which expands on Chapter 6's bare-facts version. This is followed in turn by the interview excerpts and the anecdotes, in the order in which the events occurred.

Telling the Tale: The Data

My preservice program consisted of one-week practice-teaching sessions interspersed with weeks on the university campus. During the five months of the practicum assignment I am exploring here, the second of two that year, there were also longer teaching blocks of two and three weeks. I knew before entering Ms K's classroom for the first time that it was likely to be a challenge, for several reasons. First, the methods and foundations portions of York's preservice program were oriented toward constructivism, cooperative, and child-centred learning, Gardner's theory of multiple intelligences (1993), and teaching approaches that valued interaction, inquiry, and reflection. This corresponded with my personal philosophy of teaching, honed through the period of my own children's education in an alternative school (with mixed-grade groupings, cooperative learning, and substantial parental involvement, and without report cards or rows of desks) in which I had participated for a number of years.

Second, I had been placed in this particular classroom specifically as someone the program director thought would be 'strong enough to handle' the 'difficult' host teacher. The classmate who had been there the previous term had briefed me on how this teacher liked things done, and I was aware that I was entering a vastly different world from that of my first placement where, despite differences between my host's pedagogy and my own, I had nevertheless been given considerable latitude to 'fly and fall' in my teaching.

Room 27 reminded me of a version of my own Grade 2 classroom, 35 years earlier: the walls were covered with word lists printed on large sheets of chart paper; the desks were neatly arranged; the smell was of chalk dust. The teacher's desk, beneath the window at the back, was immaculate, imposing; a chart on the blackboard showed the pupils' names, with stars in some of the little boxes. Ms K's approach was for the most part traditional too. After the daily opening exercises the class assembled on the carpet in front of a huge calendar on the wall.

Ms K would ask questions about the day, date, month, season, and weather, and choose the day's monitor. There would be a rhyme to memorize or recite, in unison, and the students would be dismissed to their desks.

Ms K's overarching view was that too much stimulation and too much freedom were not good for Grade 2 pupils; structure and routines were what they needed most of all. Those structures and routines were well established by the time I entered her class in January. All was very ordered, from morning procedures to washroom rules, to lining up to leave and re-enter, to the way shoes had to be placed outside the door, to afternoon dismissal. The pupils knew this: on the very rare occasion when I was alone with them and did something even slightly differently, they swiftly reminded me that 'that's not how Ms K does it.' And when she was there, she reminded me herself.[7]

All this made a strong impression on me. Many of Ms K's pupils loved her and frequently said so. She did not kiss or hug or touch them, but they often wanted her to. They brought her special things: cookies from home; photographs from a Saturday dance recital; flowers. They almost always cooperated in doing assigned work, and competed eagerly to be singled out for special jobs. Ms K's room was always tidy, and mostly quiet. And she made it very clear from the first moment that it was *her* room. I recall shaking her hand that first morning, and saying with a confidence I only partly felt, 'I'm looking forward to working together.' She replied, 'I'm sure you'll be a great help.'

Excerpt 1: The Author Study
In the missing portion from the taped conversation I describe the week-long author study focusing on books by Carle that I was to plan and teach.[8] Ms K instructed me to devise language and literacy lessons and activities. Here is where the tape picks up.

Colette: And she told me to go to the library in the school and the public library and collect as many of his books as I could, in multiple copies if possible, to have on display in the room and to use for free reading time. So I did. I was really proud because I managed to find two copies of most of his books – it was a lot of books. But there was one that turned out to be a problem.[9] It's kind of a creation story, where an artist draws a star, and then trees and mountains and people. And there was, there were two copies of it in the school library. I took them both, and I admit I hesitated about one of them, but I took it anyway. Because, you know, she wanted me to get two. On one page it had a picture of a man and a woman, a collage, not photographs, right, but they were naked. And one of the copies, the, someone had rubbed with an eraser or a finger or something so there was a worn spot where the man's penis was. . . .

Anyway, there was almost a hole. You could see right through the page. And I did think she might be upset because someone had ruined the book, but I took it out anyway and brought it to class. And I could not have predicted her reaction. And I was all set for her to say something, you know, about the hole, and I was planning to say, oh for goodness sake, I'd just looked at the other [undamaged] one. I'd thought this through. Well. She came to me and said, Missssssssss Granger. I need to see you right now at my desk, and . . . I could tell she was angry, and I mean at that moment I didn't even know it was about the book. It could have been anything. . . .

She said, who do you think you are, bringing this filth into my class? And I said, what do you mean? She said, these filthy – I'm not kidding – these *filthy* books.

Lorin: She used that word?

c: Yeah. I mean they [the illustrations] were collages, so there were, it wasn't photographs, right? And even if it had been, if it had been my class, well, but – I said, these are Eric Carle books. You told me to get the Eric Carle books. What's the problem with them? I, I, mean, I was, you know, by this point of course I knew what she was talking about. Not just the hole. But I wasn't going to give, I wasn't going to say, oh yeah, there's nudity in that one and I think nudity is great. No way. And she, I mean, there was a big, she lectured me for, I swear, half an hour. The kids got extra reading time that day. . . .

And you know I felt like if she'd taken out a strap and started hitting me, or put me in the cubicle,[10] or sent me to the principal, I wouldn't have been surprised. And there was a whole bunch of comments about, I can't believe your judgement is so poor, and I'm gonna, you know – if any parents complain I'm gonna have to deal with it, and you know, I had responses to all of these things ready

l: Did you say anything?

c: I do remember saying, you know, I'm happy to take the responsibility for the choice of books if a parent should complain, but she wasn't hearing it. It was venomous. Spit was coming out of her mouth.

l: Do you think she was mad about the content, or do you think she was more scared she was going to get in trouble, or do you just think it was a control thing?

c: Well I think it was all of those things, and probably some other ones too. Yeah, I think definitely, although – it's hard for me to rationalize how a parent could get upset, sorry, how a teacher could get upset thinking that parents might object to something in a book which was after all in the school library. It wasn't like I'd gone and got copies of – what are some sex magazines? . . . You know, they were in the library, in the primary section – someone thought they were okay.

L: The librarian.

c: Yeah, and she [Ms K]'d asked me to get them. And then when I got them, she was angry.

Excerpt 2: The Word Chart
[This was a lesson I was teaching to half the students in the library while the other half were in the school's computer lab next door with Ms K.]

c: We were doing vowel sounds, and we were working on different sounds the vowel U could make. And I said, what are some words with different sounds for U? and one girl ['Kate'] said, how about puke? And – this was after the penis incident – I panicked because I just knew I couldn't write the word. And I said you know, we have to think of another word with that sound, because I knew that if we used that word we'd get in trouble, even though the student had suggested it

L: Didn't you want to so much?

c: Oh so much. So that I could then say, well, *Kate said it* – me as a six-year-old in Grade 2 – I said, you know, I don't think Ms K would be happy if we used that word, and she kinda smirked at me, because well, it was almost like she knew, she was a little girl in frilly dresses every day, but . . . [laughing] 'How about puke?' I loved her. I could have hugged her. And she was my little ally – we had this secret.

Anecdote 1: Days of the Week
During daily calendar time the class sat, audience style, on the floor facing toward the wall on which Ms K's large calendar was affixed, along with the numerals and the assorted stickers (suns, clouds, umbrellas, mittens) that the children would attach to the appropriate square to indicate the weather and the date for the day. After this Ms K would point to the calendar and the class would recite the days of the week. One boy ['Bert'], newly arrived in Canada from Jamaica, pronounced the initial /th/ in Thursday as /t/. When this happened Ms K would have the class wait while he repeated the word until, in her words, he 'got it right.'

The first Thursday I was placed in charge of calendar time, I did not do this. Ms K interrupted the recitation from the back of the room to say, 'Someone, and I think I know who, isn't speaking properly.' I pretended not to hear. Later, Ms K reminded me that it was 'important for the kids to speak correctly.' The next day she told me to 'watch and learn' and did calendar time herself.

Anecdote 2: The Cardboard Screen

['Annie'] acted out quite frequently. She spoke out of turn, made faces when Ms K wasn't looking, pulled hair, and once, when angry, kicked the children's neatly placed boots all over the hall. One day Ms K brought a large, three-sided cardboard screen to class, and when Annie misbehaved placed it around her desk, telling her that it would be removed when she 'calmed down.' From where I was standing I could see Annie stick out her tongue at Ms K from behind the screen. I caught her eye and winked. On another difficult day when Annie was again behind the screen, Ms K was teaching the class and I was at the back. I saw Annie, nearly crying, looking at her book but unable to join in with the class. I went over, patted her head. Right away Ms K called me, 'Miss Granger, I need you to stand at the front please.'

Anecdote 3: The Worksheet

Ms K told me several times that she understood that teacher education 'doesn't like you to use blacklines'[11] but that 'they are a time-saver, and anyway, some children like them.' She used them sometimes, for arithmetic practice or for book reports or spelling exercises: in the latter two instances they generally had cloze exercises where the students would fill in missing words. They were not a favourite teaching tool of mine, but I knew she liked them so I decided to develop one for the unit on 'The Farm' that I was teaching near the end of term. On the top half of the page I typed sentences with blank spaces for the children to fill in, but as a compromise I drew a rectangle in the bottom half that was large enough for the children to print a sentence or some words of their own and draw a picture of their favourite farm animal. By this point in the term my relationship with Ms K had deteriorated to the point where I was not confident that that I could satisfy her, so I asked her if she wanted to see the worksheets before I photocopied them. She replied, 'No, I should be able to trust you with those.' After I had made the copies, she saw the empty rectangle at the bottom of the page, told me they were a waste of paper and that I couldn't use them, and threw them away.

Anecdote 4: The Barn
For the unit on 'The Farm' Ms K allowed me to decorate the classroom thematically, but I had to clear my ideas with her first. She told me, 'I don't want you to change my whole classroom' but she did let me display books about farm activities on the shelves, set the children's containers of germinating bean seeds on the window ledge along with samples of various grains, and post pictures of produce and a Canada's Food Guide poster on one bulletin board. I also covered another bulletin board in green paper to resemble a field which I edged with a paper fence to display farm-animal paintings. I asked her if I could 'do something' on the walls just outside the classroom and she agreed. So, for my pièce de résistance, I attached a large paper barn mural I had painted to the hall walls surrounding the classroom door, which I covered with paper also painted to look like a barn door. I was pleased with the way it looked and when other teachers passing in the hall praised my idea I felt relieved, sure that Ms K would approve too. Her comment was, 'Interesting, but it's going to get in the way. I'm glad it's in the hall and not in my class-room.' Although I was not sure how a flat paper mural taped to the wall, in or out of the room itself, could be 'in the way,' I said nothing.

* * *

As indicated, these events took place over the course of the approxi-mately five months I spent, alternating more-or-less weekly between the practicum and my foundations and methods courses. The practi-cum culminated in a three-week teaching block during which, accord-ing to the program's mandate, I ought to have had 'responsibility for all aspects of the class for the full academic day' (York University, 2006b). In recognition of this requirement, which Ms K's and my deteriorating relationship had made unattainable, I met with the practicum direc-tor, who knew of my difficulties but not their extent. She offered to find me another placement, but given the short time remaining and my concerns about how a transfer would read in my final program assess-ment, I turned down her offer. Ultimately it was decided that, during the three-week block, Ms K's class would combine with another Grade 2 class for part of the day, and the other student teacher and I would plan and teach the Farm unit together.

Power and Resistance: Reading Stories with Foucault

In the Foucauldian story of how institutions discipline and pun-ish human bodies and their inner and outer workings (1977a), the technology of the body-that-must-be-controlled comprises 'a "knowledge" of the body that is not exactly the science of its functioning, and a mastery of its forces that is more than the ability to conquer them' (p. 26). Together knowledge and mastery, which operate at all levels from the individual or cellular to the group or organismic, in factory, army, or school, and which allow precise observation and comparison (p. 145), constitute the discipline that works to render bodies docile. But this power, a strategy rather than a property, is not owned exclusively by dominant social groups. Rather, it is enacted in complex ways and multiple directions:

> [It] is not exercised simply as an obligation or a prohibition on those who "do not have it": it invests them, is transmitted by them and through them; it exerts pressure upon them, just as they themselves, in their struggle against it, resist the grip it has on them. This means that these relations . . . are not localized in the relations between the state and its citizens or on the frontier between classes and that they do not merely reproduce . . . the general form of the law or government; that, although there is continuity . . . there is neither analogy nor homology, but a specificity of mechanism and modality. Lastly, they are not univocal; they define innumerable points of confrontation, focuses of instability, each of which has its own risks of conflict, of struggles, and of an at least temporary inversion of the power relations. (Foucault, 1977a, p. 27)

It is through this multidirectional lens that I peer into my practicum stories.

Given the importance to student teachers of the practicum experience it stands to reason that they hope to relate well to the host teacher, with whom they spend substantial time and who may, in addition, participate in the evaluation of their performance (either directly, or indirectly through hiring recommendations). Of course 'good' can be differently defined; some may want direct input and clear instruction, others a chance to experiment with ideas and techniques. I was of the latter sort. My previous term's practicum, in which I had worked in a regular classroom but also, part of the time, with a Special Education teacher, had leaned very much in that direction, and I had begun to feel my feet as part of a teaching team. Entering Ms K's room changed that. It was clear immediately that I was expected to conform utterly to her approach.

It is important to recognize that host teachers, in helping student teachers become independent practitioners, may risk 'diminish[ing] their own status and power in order to enhance the capacity and independence of their student [teachers]' (Labaree, 2000, p. 233). Similarly, MacDonald, Baker, and Stewart (1995) find hosting a student teacher to be a mixed blessing that brings new energy, ideas, and methods but also, perhaps, disruptions to established routines, possible personality conflicts and a potential loss of authority (pp. 83–4). Said one teacher in that study, 'My position in my classroom is really all I have in terms of status as a teacher' (p. 85).

On an obvious level, then, it makes sense that Ms K saw the classroom as 'hers.' Still, the collegiality and collaboration I had experienced in my previous placement were palpably absent, to the point that I often wondered why she had agreed to host a student teacher at all. Questions and statements she made – 'Who do you think you are, bringing this filth into *my* class?' about the storybook, and (over four months into the term) 'I'm glad it's in the hall and not in *my* classroom' about the barn mural – maintained this division.

Throughout the narratives it is apparent that I conformed to a substantial degree: I placed the barn mural outside rather than inside the classroom, and designed worksheets quite similar to Ms K's. She pre-approved the displays I created for the farm unit, and the lessons I taught (calendar time, vowel sounds) were closely modelled on hers (and very different from those I would have designed given the freedom to do so). The anecdotes are also instructive at the levels of lexicon and syntax: I was *instructed* to plan and teach a unit, and *really proud* when I thought I had carried out instructions correctly. Ms K *told me* to go to the library and *told me* to get two copies of each book, *allowed me* (to a degree) to decorate the room for the farm unit, *lectured* me for my *poor judgment*. I worried about *getting in trouble*, and over time I came to be *not confident that I could satisfy her.*

This continued throughout the term. I still *had to clear my ideas* with her; work I had done was dismissed, even discarded. Throwing away the worksheets I had created (themselves a compromise) and leaving me without a resource for my lesson was both a rejection of my attempt to address multiple learning styles – as my methods courses had taught me to do – and an undermining of my effort to do so from within Ms K's paradigm. It left me at a more practical loss too, needing to fill an empty chunk of time I had not planned for, and diminished my authority as even a quasi-teacher, since the seatwork the students were used to doing was not forthcoming. Lecturing me about books in the presence of the students did likewise, as did 'allowing' me to decorate the classroom but requiring me to have every idea approved.

Not only did I feel I lacked authority, but the anecdotes suggest that at times I actually felt like a child – reflective of our difference in status but curious in that Ms K and I were about the same age. This feeling, reflected in the interview transcript nearly 10 years on, can be inferred at various moments, such as with my apparent need to defer almost petulantly to another authority in relation to the controversial children's storybooks: 'they were in the library, in the primary section' and *someone* had 'thought they were okay.' And elsewhere it is articulated even more concretely: first, in the story of the author study, when 'if she'd taken out a strap and started hitting me, or put me in the cubicle, or sent me to the principal, I wouldn't have been surprised,' and second, in my recollection of the word-chart lesson when 'Kate' suggested using the word 'puke':

> I panicked because I just knew I couldn't write the word. And I said you know, we have to think of another word with that sound, because I knew that if we used that word we'd get in trouble . . .
> So that I could then say, well, *Kate said it* – me as a six-year-old in Grade 2 . . . And she was my little ally – we had this secret.

It is one thing for a student teacher to feel like a student – that is, after all, part of what she is – but one does not usually expect to find, in a relationship of adults, the suggestion of such a large power differential that emerges from one of those adults locating herself with the other six-year olds in the class.[12]

It is important at this juncture to remember that the narratives are not verbatim records – for 'in all remembering, there is [also] forgetting' (Miller, 2005, p. 27) – but a partial set of my recollections, chosen because for me they are emblematic of the relationship in that classroom. They demonstrate that the prevailing dynamic was one in which I was not seen as an equal, or even as an adult. But here is something I neither would nor could have predicted before reading the author-study and word-chart portions of the data. I confess that it is more than a little disconcerting for me, as a principled adult, to notice from a Foucauldian standpoint my duplicity in a relation of power which, at the time, seemed like a unidirectional oppression. Yet there it is. At the relatively manifest level of lexicon and syntax, the anecdotes reflect not only Ms K's perception of me as an inexperienced, ignorant subordinate, but also my contribution to that perception and to the construction of her as the holder of (near) absolute power in the classroom; my articulation of events in language that relegates me to the position of approval-seeking subaltern comes as a surprise.

My self-positioning as the object of Ms K's directives suggests that my silencing by Ms K was just part of the equation. The other part was self-imposed, achieved by my participation in creating and maintaining the dynamic in which she *did*, and I was *done to:* a dynamic we made together.[13] This joint construction is further evident in the calendar time narrative. I left out one of Ms K's usual procedures – making the Jamaican-born 'Bert' repeat the word *Thursday* until he could more closely approximate the local, southern Ontario accent – because, first, I believed it was potentially detrimental to a child's self-esteem to be centred out in this way, particularly for such a reason, and second, I understood the notion of correctness in pronunciation as largely false (even elitist), and moreover that in time, pronunciation adjusts to the local variety. Later, when Ms K told me to 'watch and learn,' I chose not to respond with this information, thus maintaining my position as lacking both knowledge and authority.

Still, if a reading of the anecdotes demonstrates the co-construction of power and authority in our relationship, it also highlights at least a few 'points of confrontation' (Foucault, 1977a, p. 27) between us, small moments of resistance which for Foucault contribute to the construction no less than moments of acquiescence. Such moments are articulated or implied in the narrative from the beginning of my tenure in that classroom: for instance, the fact that the pupils reminded me that 'that's not the way Ms K does it' suggests that I did try to stake out some pedagogical territory of my own. A second point of confrontation, indirect yet resistant and even insubordinate, occurred when I patted Annie's head as she sat unhappily behind the cardboard screen. Ms K's goal was to isolate Annie, who she thought was too easily distracted. I undermined that goal by initiating contact with her.

With my prior knowledge of Ms K's reputation, it might seem that the least impolitic approach would have been simply to do things her way rather than attempting to put my own stamp on them.[14] Sometimes I had pedagogical reasons for my choice, such as my partial change to the worksheet (designed to allow even students who had trouble printing to express themselves). At other times, such as when I hung the barn mural in the hall, my pride was at play: I had been 'chosen' for this placement because the practicum director thought I could 'stand up to' Ms K, and I wanted and needed to meet that expectation. Maybe the mural was a signpost of resistance – an effort to make my presence *in*side the room known *out*side it.

I find resistance most plainly readable in the author-study and word-chart narratives. Here was a moment when I undertook to use the 'master's tools' to 'dismantle the master's house' (Lorde, 1983). The copy of *Draw Me a Star* with a damaged page was one issue, but the reasons I give for including it read like a petulant child's whining litany of justification: *she had told me* to get as many Eric Carle books as possible, and this was an Eric Carle book; *she had told me* to get more than one copy, and so I got two; *she had told me* to get books from the school library, and this book was in the school library. In the narrative I position myself as blameless, just doing as I was told. But combined with the admission I make in the narrative about having an explanation prepared in case of a challenge – 'I was all set for her to say something . . . and I was planning to say, oh for goodness sake, I'd just looked at the other [copy]. I'd thought this through' – the suggestion that I had no idea at all that she might object to the picture itself seems not quite innocent.

Another moment of resistance was my refusal to correct Bert's non-standard pronunciation. My reasons for this were pedagogical and ethical. My resistance, though, was partial and passive, and my decision to keep silent on the issue (and likewise on Annie's isolation behind the cardboard screen) weighs on me to this day. Perhaps these partial-but-partially-silent moves denote a variation on the strategic self-interest which, following Simon (1992), I describe in the previous chapter as never innocent, where the student teacher complies with a less-valued pedagogy in order to arrive at a moment when she can practise a preferred one: in my version I passively refused to support what I believed was wrong, but in the interest of getting through practicum I did not confront Ms K.

Here the notion of resistance gets tricky. There was the question of immediate good (the choice, as I saw it, not to participate in humiliating a student). At the same time there was also the larger question of whether or not to take on the work of persuading an experienced teacher, whose pedagogy was unlike my own but who stood in a position to influence my career prospects and by extension the opportunities I would have to effect change as a teacher. Perhaps a similar concern, rooted in the wish not to be perceived as a student *needing* to change placement (which I believed would negatively affect my employability), played into my refusal to accept the practicum director's eventual offer of a last-minute placement change, and to stay in Ms K's classroom. At the same time, that refusal constituted an inadvertent act of resistance. This resistance became quite conscious when, later in the practicum some of my planning and teaching were combined with that of another student teacher, and I took a perverse pleasure in noticing how much more positively Ms K seemed to judge ideas that she thought came from the other student teacher, but which in fact were mine.

A more general sense of being watched and judged – and of worrying about that judgment – pervades my memory of the entire practicum. The narratives imply that worry in several places: when Ms K called me away from the screened-off Annie; her interjections when I diverged from her usual practice during the calendar exercise; my panicked response to Kate's word choice. That feeling of constantly being under surveillance is reminiscent of Foucault's *panopticon* (1977a). Drawing on British philosopher Bentham's late eighteenth-century design for a prison (that would, through particular arrangements of space which prevented prisoners from knowing for certain that they *were* under observation, ensure that they knew that at any moment they *might* be), Foucault's version is a metaphor for a gaze of power that even in its absence disciplines both body and mind, by 'inducing in the inmate a state of objectivity, a permanent visibility' (Dreyfus & Rabinow, 1983, p. 189) that ultimately leads to self-policing. When Ms K sat at her desk, ostensibly doing paperwork, her interruptions reminded me that she was omnipresent and at any moment her eyes were likely to be on me.

The examination is a related form of discipline that 'combines the techniques of an observing hierarchy and those of a normalizing judgement ... mak[ing] it possible to qualify, to classify and to punish' (Foucault, 1977a, p. 184). In the practice-teaching context, the examination takes the form of classroom observations of the student teacher and a culminating course director's report.

And here, another detour, into another of the surprising vicissitudes of this project. While searching for a quotation to use in writing this chapter I located, quite by accident, my own final report. I was surprised that I had kept it, but even more surprised to read in it that my lessons 'excite, motivate and enrich students,' that my planning is 'clear, detailed and related to previous learning,' and that I am viewed by the practicum director as 'creative, well prepared, ... enthusiastic and dedicated.' The report summarizes my performance as 'highly successful.'

It is a positive report. But it interrupts the story I have just been telling.

In some way mentioning it here mitigates the sense of failure I have had about that part of my educational history, and the sense of regret

I continue to have about failing to challenge (and thus by default colluding with) Ms K, especially on pedagogical grounds. In addition, however, although it is a little odd to consider an evaluative document like the practicum report as subversive or counter-hegemonic, both because it testifies to the student's ability to fit into the status quo, and also because in the teacher education hierarchy the practicum director who writes the report has higher status than the host teacher, its inclusion might also be read as resisting the local status quo of Ms K's classroom; by presenting a contrary view of myself and my abilities I am, however belatedly, challenging my earlier depiction of our co-construction.

The reading I am giving to text (the narratives) or context (the practicum as embodied in the report) is not the only possible or reasonable one. For example, although a Freirean view of oppression might apply more to the student teacher who is, as yet, unremunerated for her work and thus more at the mercy of the institution, it could also position both Ms K and me as individuals oppressed by education's standards and structures and 'inhibited from waging the struggle for freedom so long as [we felt] incapable of running the risks it requires' (Freire, 2005, p. 47). Such a view might also argue that the inclusion of the report here constitutes a capitulation to that larger institutional status quo.

I am reminded here of Freud's proviso in her lectures to parents and teachers (1974, p. 121): 'We must not demand too much from one another.' Perhaps we should not demand too much of ourselves either. Finding the report has made me question my perception of the practicum experience and recognize concretely what I knew in the abstract: that as with any experience and its representation, not only are the two not isomorphic (Brodkey, 1987), but *my* experience is not *the* experience – my perception is not the whole. The anecdotes are remembered impressions, not verbatim testimony. The report, its contrary contents the only concrete and official statement I have about that period, is not the whole story either. Nor is the supporting evidence, in the form of the practicum director's and the previous student teacher's awareness of the potential for difficulty in Ms K's classroom.

When we speak we are also silent; whatever we say, there is something else that we are leaving unsaid. 'The speaking subject is not innocent,' writes Kristeva (1994), because it has the 'capacity to disorganize meaning, structure, and teleonomy' (p. 155). The very large question of how meaning can become disorganized is explored metonymically in the next section, through a psychoanalytic look at the narratives that also asks why it is the events they recount, and not the report, that I remembered.

The Ghost and the Host (Teacher): Reading Stories with Psychoanalysis

This chapter's title, which draws on Church's (1995) similarly named exploration of the psychiatric survivor movement, speaks to my sense of this part of my work as opening up the messy cupboard of teacher education. It is the cupboard in which my worries about learning to teach are stacked, stuffed, and spilling over, and whose door, once opened, is not easy to shut. There is no shortage of writing about issues and problems in teacher education. But there is a tendency to keep silent about one's own difficulties: mine is a self-initiated 'forbidding.' And of course we hear nothing at all from those who have left teacher education altogether.

An overarching theme in Church's work is 'unsettlement.' She examines 'ways in which the knowledge/power relations of community mental health are significantly disrupted by processes which bring forward survivor knowledge repertoires' (p. xiii). Unsettlement – disorganization – splitting – these seem to have become motifs in my work too. And I like the word *survivor*, though in using it to describe my situation I may risk accusations of exaggeration. For teacher education wasn't cancer. It wasn't a war.

It wasn't, was it? Wasn't it?

It seems I am writing about surviving teacher education. It may be that much writing about education is about survival, particularly in the sense A. Freud (1974) defined it, as a limiting of what is natural and desired by the learner. But there is something different about this chapter. While ethnographic research generally, and autoethnography and work on 'the personal' more specifically, have made it more common to write the personal into academic work (Church, 1995, p. 3), it is a little trickier to write, or speak, of one's defeats: to make the admission that one has not been successful in the field in which one has tried to make a home.

Perhaps that is one definition of surviving.

Perhaps another, relevant particularly to the educator, is acknowledging that there are defeats – that education sometimes defeats its own purposes – and that even if a defeat is only partial or temporary, the happy stories of learning to teach are equally so. Here I return to Olivia, the respondent in Bloom's (1998) examination of feminist research methods, whom I first discussed in Chapter 3. Olivia's first narration of a sexual harassment incident at work positioned her as a role model and, by her own acknowledgment, a 'feminist icon' (p. 72), a

positioning that in Bloom's analysis met the demand for a kind of hero-
ism imposed by a narrative 'master script.' But this version of her story
was unsatisfying to Olivia, who later chose to retell it more fully, in
terms that included its conflicted and ambivalent 'less satisfying side'
(Bloom, 1998, p. 72). Pitt (2003, pp. 89–90) describes Olivia's double tale
as 'an exemplary demonstration of the movement between fantasy and
reality' that can mark personal narrative and, in addition, that can perhaps be worked through to an arrival at a 'more complex social reality
[that allows the narrator] to contemplate her own complicity and relative vulnerability in the maintenance of unequal power relations.'

Here is where Olivia and I are similar: unwilling (or unable) to maintain the silence of the partial telling, we each require of ourselves as full
a story as we are capable of. For me in the first part of my study, as for
Olivia, that meant a multiple telling of the same set of events. In this
part it has meant including the documentary evidence of the practicum
report, even though it counters my narrated subjective experience. As
mentioned above, this inclusion might constitute the embodiment of
elements of a personal sense of failure, or a resistance to a practicum
dynamic in which I felt powerless, or a capitulation to the hegemony
of that document qua documentation. However, although like Olivia
I initially believed that my recollection was in fact *the* story, where she
and I part company is that in my own recollection it is the 'less satisfying' parts – the *bad* story of me as a *bad* student teacher – with which
I began.

Who Do I Think I Am? The Return of the Repressed

My student teaching story is no longer the straightforward tale of mis-
ery it used to be. Looking at the narratives now, with my course director's report at hand, I see fairly mild anecdotes of two people, with
distinct pedagogical orientations, who did not get along.

So why, then, does my stomach tell me something else? When I reread the narratives it is as if I have swallowed a lead ball, or a piece of
bad meat. I had the same sensation while I was narrating them to my
colleague, and I had it while transcribing the tape of that conversation.
I had it every morning driving to practicum, and I have it now, nearly
10 years later, whenever I pass that exit on the highway. I also had it
much, much earlier still, when as a child I hadn't finished my homework, or when I heard my parents arguing, or when I had broken a rule
or told a lie, and knew my mother would be angry. It is a sensation that
has come to be known in my internal lexicon as 'the feeling.'

Casey (2000, pp. 154–7) describes 'traumatic body memory' as a particularized kind of remembering that happens when a sensation at a precise point in the body brings to mind a specific traumatic episode and the events surrounding it. Conversely, King (2000, p. 16) considers Fraser's (1987) 'detective work of memory' in which remembering abuse leads to the body re-experiencing it. Though informed by experiences quite distinct from Casey's example, and not comparable to Fraser's ordeal, 'the feeling' is similar to yet distinct from them both. It is a particular sensation, felt in a precise bodily location, but it neither conjures nor remakes one specific trauma. Rather, it is evoked by an experience (or the memory of an experience), and in turn it evokes its own previous incarnations. That is, the practicum stories give me the feeling, and the feeling reminds me of feeling-the-feeling during the practicum, and of other prior occasions on which the feeling was occasioned by other events. Perhaps this process is not so different from what Casey, King, and Fraser each describe. Might it be that there is just an extra layer, that beneath or behind the feeling-evoked-by-the-feeling dwells the trauma, or a trauma-like occurrence?

Wait. A *trauma-like occurrence*? Can we see the resistance here, how one does not want to think of one's life as traumatic? Correction: how *I* do not want to think of *my* teacher education experience as traumatic?

Along the trail that winds back through the feeling to the events it evokes, and through those events to other moments of feeling-the-feeling and their connected events, I start to connect the events-that-remind-me-of-the-feeling, not just to the feeling-that-reminds-me-of-other-events, but to the other events too. Remembering has taken a long time, has become something of a pain in – well, in the belly.

The feeling is very *familiar*.

It reminds me.

At least, something is certainly reminding me, of something. What is being remembered, re-minded? What hints does this remembering re-member, this reminding re-mind? And what clues get covered up? What is silent here? To ask the same questions in a more psychoanalytic way – and yes, here I do need psychoanalytic thinking – why is (or was) the 'good' part of the story repressed?

Repression is the name psychoanalysis gives to the unconscious process of tucking away traumatic events that cannot be tolerated when they occur (Freud, 1915a). That material is the psychical ghost of the past that haunts the present: in an inversion of the timeworn cliché, it is forgotten, but not gone. Something about a repressed memory turns it into a secret (King, 2000, p. 15) that may be screened from the self who has forgotten but for whom the memory still exists, somewhere 'in there,' anywhere but here, any-*when* but now. And when the ghost-memory slips through the screen and lands again in the here-and-now, it is re-experienced, perhaps bodily.

In Freudian theory screen memories embody 'not only *some* but *all* of what is essential from childhood' (Freud, 1914a, p. 148; italics in original). The screen memory, as both phenomenon and process, counterbalances 'the forgetting of impressions, scenes, experiences' that is really a matter of 'shutting them off' (p. 148). Here is how a screen memory forms, when two psychical forces – one seeking to remember an event because it seems important and the other resisting that preference – collide and compromise:

> The compromise is this. What is recorded as a mnemic image is not the relevant experience itself – in this respect the resistance gets its way; what is recorded is another psychical element closely associated with the objectionable one.... The result of the conflict is therefore that, instead of the mnemic image which would have been justified by the original event, another is produced which has been to some degree associatively *displaced* from the former one. And since the elements of the experience which aroused objection were precisely the important ones, the substituted memory will necessarily lack those important elements and will in consequence most probably strike us as trivial. (Freud, 1899, p. 307; italics in original)

Might there be such a thing as a fleshly version of a screen memory – a *physical sensation* that corresponds to the *psychical element* 'closely associated with the objectionable one,' and which is recorded in place of (that is, in displacement from) the image of the original significant (but 'objectionable' or objected-to) event? A physical memory-image that substitutes for the memory of the original event and which, like the psychical image, seems trivial because it lacks the important aspects of that event?

Can a sore psyche become a bellyache? Perhaps we can think of 'the feeling' as a *physio-mnemic image* that works in two directions: as a *later* (imperfect) screen over memories of earlier events, and as a remembered *earlier* screen that blocks the full memory – in my case, the 'good parts' – of the later event (the practicum).

The feeling is very *familial*.

Doing a little digging of her own in a discussion of 'memory as archaeological excavation,' King (2000, pp. 12–16) finds metaphors for memory as a process and an activity. One of these, after Benjamin (1932), is the idea that while images might be what an excavation uncovers, their reconstruction is only possible 'within the language that is always inevitably a translation or interpretation' (King, 2000, p. 14). Interpretation is inevitable in a psychotherapeutic relation (and in an autoethnography), at the very least because the individual now remembering is no longer quite the same individual who underwent the experience being remembered. Perhaps too there is a kind of back-and-forth movement in the process of remembering: a retroactive – or nachträglich – translation of the *earlier event* by the *later self* that in (re)turn (re-)translates the later event, mapping the one onto the other in what is always already an interpretation, stirring up and stirring in meaning and affect from both now and then.

Here is what I mean: the question, *Who do you think you are?* spoken by Ms K in a moment of anger, awoke in me 'the feeling' and in so doing roused the long-forgotten memory of my mother, angry, using precisely those same words, dozens or perhaps hundreds of times. And that memory in turn put its affective imprint on Ms K.

This is, of course, the transference.

And poor Ms K didn't have a chance.

Who Do I Think You Are? Transference in the Practicum

In Freud's reflection 'On the psychology of the grammar-school boy' (1914b), he contemplates the forward and backward psychical movement between present and past through which the pupil unconsciously transfers onto the teacher any number and kind of qualities, 'imagined sympathies or antipathies' (1914b, p. 355), before even knowing that individual. Writing about a time and place when boys' teachers were predominantly male, Freud centres the latter part of his discussion on the connection between, on one hand, the child's break with the father, and on the other hand those teachers who 'were not even all fathers themselves [but] became father-substitutes' (p. 357). Taking into account the concrete historical shift of women into teaching (Walkerdine, 1990) and the attendant shift in common-sense thinking toward the idea of teaching as women's work, and supported by Pitt's (2006, p. 89) discussion (to which I turn shortly) on destruction (in fantasy) of the mother and the concomitant search for substitute objects, it is almost too easy to recast Freud's sentence to read, 'These *women* . . . became *mother* substitutes.'

What holds for education in general regarding transferential relations holds similarly in teacher education, particularly in the intimate dynamic of practicum. This is so first because the host teacher-student teacher relationship is at bottom a relation between teacher and student, and second because, as noted, the transferential substitution of later 'emotional objects' for earlier ones is a perpetual dynamic that does not cease when childhood ends. For Pitt and Britzman, writing about the difficulty of representing knowledge, 'school memories do not just invoke relations with authority but also repeat one's own *childhood helplessness, dependency, and desire to please*. This strange combination means that reflecting on one's learning seems necessarily to pass through these unbidden repetitions of love, hate, and ambivalence that make the transference, reminding us of the very earliest scenes of education' (2003, p. 760; my italics).

Keeping this contention in mind, let us look again at the anecdotes for other hints of transference.[15] For while Ms K's question, 'Who do you think you are?' is for me a metonymic, nachträglich crystallization of the transferential aspect of our relationship as well as of the precise moment when I see that *that* was what was going on the whole time (or at least a central aspect of it), the transference was inaugurated much earlier, and is reinforced by the written narratives in multiple ways.

As I remarked in my earlier Foucauldian analysis, I position myself in the narratives as subordinate to Ms K, to a greater degree than might be expected in the context of our relationship as host teacher and student teacher. While we might expect that the host teacher would be more likely to give direction and the student teacher more likely to take it, it is perhaps a little surprising that my articulation of this dynamic is as clear as it is, particularly as this is, after all, my story. Granted, content determines structure to some extent, but in my nachträglich reading the stories seem to place Ms K at their centre, and me, 'helpless' and 'dependent' on her wishes, on the periphery: the narratives are largely framed around things she wants, or customarily does, or tells me to do, and my responses to the wanting, doing, and telling. I consistently articulate a dynamic in which Ms K gives the orders and I follow them. Indeed, only once do I use the word 'decide' to refer to my own action, and that is in an attempt to do something 'I knew she liked.'

This desire to please is a key element of the transference evident throughout the anecdotes. The phrasings that I read as illustrating (in the narratives) my perception of myself (in the practicum) as lacking authority and wanting to satisfy Ms K invite a slightly different interpretation psychoanalytically. To reiterate some of these: I *hesitated* over choosing books, thought she *might be upset*; made a worksheet because

I knew she liked them; worried about *getting in trouble* over the vowel lesson; *didn't think* Ms K *would be happy* if *we* wrote 'puke' on the vowel chart. These statements not only speak generally to efforts to please the one in authority, they also invite the question of why I assumed that specific ways of pleasing would be the right ways: to the question, in other words, of what 'pleasing' meant in that context.

What I know, and what the reader who might have guessed is about to have confirmed, is that my efforts to please Ms K were precisely the same kinds of effort that characterized my childhood. In truth I had no idea at all whether Ms K would object to the word 'puke,' but I knew, profoundly and for certain, that my mother would.

Who Do I Think I'm Kidding?

As an adult reading, and reading into, my own history, I plumb my memory and vocabulary for a way to summarize the dynamics of the family in which I grew up. It is of course no easy task to condense the myriad interactions of multiple individuals living lives that are separate even as they are joined together. And families are complex; I recognize this, and do not mean here to paint a monochromatic picture. But it does seem fair to say that the grounding principles, the prized attributes, in my family of origin were strength for adults and obedience for children, and that a prevalent operating dynamic was aggression, expressed verbally (and often loudly) by adults, and passively – or not at all – by children. In that environment, parents got frequently, unpredictably, angry, and children learned very early not to upset those parents; to be protective of their feelings; not to speak. One small example: my mother spanked me once for tearing a button off the blouse of a neighbourhood friend. The back-story, the motivation for the fight that resulted in that damage, was that the friend had insulted my mother. But I could not tell my mother that: it would have hurt her feelings. So I silently accepted the punishment.

Curiously, just now as I remember the torn-blouse incident, I am reminded of a practicum moment that resonates with it. It is another blackline master story. This time I got the format 'right' and there were plenty of blanks to fill in, but somewhere on the page appeared the word *children's* (the correct plural, possessive form). Ms K read over the sheet, told me that I had misplaced that apostrophe, and that I could not use a sheet 'with that error on it.' I did not change the worksheet but, in a way somehow similar to that earlier scenario with my mother, I kept quiet, protecting Ms K from her own mistake by choosing not to insist that that apostrophe was right where it ought to be. I remade the sheet, minus the offending word.

The narratives too speak to my perception of the importance of protecting the 'adult' that originated in my family relationships and was repeated in the practicum. First, the author study anecdote details how I worried not only about upsetting Ms K but also about being unable to predict her reaction (and so had an explanation planned, just in case). And when I did realize the reason for her anger, I neither capitulated nor defended: I simply remained silent.[16]

Indeed, my various silences in and around both the events told by the narratives and the narratives themselves, whether absolute and explicitly noted or oblique, similarly suggest a re-enactment of childhood dynamics that implies the presence of transferential elements. But more than this, even, the narratives seem to suggest a re-enactment of childhood itself. Specifically, there are multiple moments in the narratives (and the events they render) in which I position (and positioned) myself with the pupils in that Grade 2 class. In the author study anecdote, my comment, 'I felt like if she'd taken out a strap and started hitting me, or put me in the cubicle, or sent me to the principal, I wouldn't have been surprised,' speaks to precisely that same construction, of myself as a child in a Grade 2 class. So do later statements about the vowel lesson: first, my recollection of the feeling (in the event) that little Kate 'was my ally' with whom I shared a 'secret,' and second (appearing at the meta-level in the narrative), on being asked in the interview whether I had perhaps wanted, deep down, to include the word 'puke,' my response to the effect that (like a six-year-old) I (might have) wanted to include the word to bait Ms K but would have blamed a(n *other*?) pupil for saying it. Finally, an element of the same kind of positioning is suggested by my conspiratorial wink at Annie. (In a different moment I took the role of an insubordinate adult or a rebellious child by patting her head and implicitly 'taking her side.')

I acknowledge at this point that it is important to leave room to question who is interpreting what, given my discussion in Part 1 about the different versions of self that experience, remember, and narrate. Would another individual reading these narratives from a psychoanalytic perspective theorize them in the same way? Am I simply finding what I want to find in the text and context of the events and the narratives? Do I come to my particular reading because I need an interpretation that proves what I already believe? I suspect that the answer to all of these questions might be a qualified yes: clearly other readings are possible, and equally obviously my own is not exhaustive. But the question persists as to why I believe this story and not another, enough to look for support for it (if that is what I am doing). And the plain fact (or as plain a fact as I can muster) is that the similarities between my relationship with Ms K and my early familial relationships in an unpredictable, authoritarian home, especially with my mother, are just too strong to ignore.

In her autobiographical rendering of a protracted textual encounter that invoked, for her, feminist and psychoanalytic reflections on the question of matricide, Pitt (2006) reflects: 'It is not a coincidence that, for this reader, the text that gave so much trouble and turns out to have such a powerful influence on me was about women and teaching.'

I almost forgot to mention – my mother was a teacher too.

And so I take the liberty of recasting Pitt's insight thus: It is not a coincidence that, for this *student teacher*, the *context* that gave so much trouble and turns out to have such a powerful influence on me was about *a woman, teaching*.

It's my transference, and I'm sticking to it.

Who Do I Think I'm Killing? Matricide and the Practicum

And so, psychoanalytically speaking, the similarities between those two relationships are there because I put them there.

But why? To consider this question, I pick up some of the threads of object relations theory and head back to the time early in life when the infant begins to become a self separate from other selves. Pitt's discussion of matricide (2006) is helpful here, as it returns us to the early moment when, in beginning to acquire language, we re-experience the terrible loss, foreshadowed at birth, of our primal sense of unity with the world (Freud, 1948). Coming to language requires that we give up the 'inarticulate self' (Phillips, 1999, p. 42), which (in its fantasy) did not need language because its needs were met by objects that it did not understand as existing outside of itself. The loss of the omnipotent, inarticulate self (or *pre*-self state, for prior to separation there is no sense of any self), fiercely felt but not representable in language for as yet there is no language, embodies the tacit recognition of the mother as other to the self. With language comes the shock of separateness.

Pitt summarizes the Kleinian concept of matricide as the fantasy (inaugurated by the destructive drives that in fantasy split first the breast

and then the mother into 'good' and 'bad' objects) that 'one's destruc-
tiveness has effected a murder, and that this agony can be mitigated
by representing the loss' (Pitt, 2006, p. 99). In Winnicottian terms the
phenomenon of representation evolves, and in time, shifts from object
relating (when the fantasy of the object as the baby's creation is maintained) to object usage, 'when the infant can tolerate the reality of the
object's existence as outside of her control.' The catch, Pitt tells us, is that
when the individual recognizes the object's separateness 'it is, from the
vantage of having been created by the subject, destroyed' (Pitt, 2006,
p. 99).

This destruction-in-fantasy leads to the ability to form relations, and
it ultimately 'founds the human subject' (p. 100). But it is no less a loss
for that. And, as Pitt sets out earlier in the same chapter (p. 89), it gener-
ates, together with the infant's need to move into the world of language,
a kind of 'suffering . . . [that] brings the search for objects that substitute
for the mother and so the possibility of living a life.' The force of the language in this assertion seems a little different from Freud's reference to
teachers for whom their students 'were equally disposed to love and
to hatred, to criticism and to worship' (Freud, 1914b, p. 355), and who
'became father-substitutes' (p. 357), in which there can be read a suggestion of the transference as accidental, even passive. But although it
may be unconscious, passive it is not. To read it as such would be to say,
for instance, that I met Ms K and she reminded me of my mother, and
that is only part of the story. A fuller version, that I think captures better
the unconscious-but-deliberate movement that is the transference, goes
more like this:

I went searching for a mother substitute, and I found Ms K.

Still, I am left with the question of why the transference is so selective:
specifically, why the practicum director's report and the practicum's
other positive aspects were forgotten. To consider this question it is
useful to recall Klein's notion of object-splitting, in which the idealized
'good' object is introjected, taken into the self, while the 'bad' object
gets rejected.

It is also important, though, that the notions of *good* and *bad* that inhere in the psychical object-split are *imagos* – metaphorical fantasy images of objects distorted by a metonymic move that turns, for example,
gratification *by* an object into goodness as a quality *of* the object – rather
than evaluations of concrete characteristics. I suggest that the object,

split in fantasy, might become enmeshed with and a party to the transference, because, as Klein emphasizes, what undergoes the transference
is not the object as such, but rather the object as the splitting process
fantasizes it: the *good*ness-imago or the *bad*ness-imago. Laplanche (1992,
p. 222) summarizes Nachträglichkeit as involving an 'enigmatic message'
that moves both 'from the past to the future, and . . . from the adult to
the baby.' The transference takes that message, and other remembered
(and repressed) material, in a similar backward and forward movement
through time, in which traces of past relationships that inform the making of new ones also give rise to a repetition of the 'omnipotent denial
of the existence of the bad object' (Klein, 1946, p. 7).

   The constituent component of the transference is the object not as it
is (or was) but as we imagine(d) it to be. Or, put differently, the object's
essence, its '*is*-ness,' is the one the subject has imagined, or *imago*-ed. In
such a scenario, what *good* and *bad* mean relates to how gratifying or
disappointing the object is *as an imago*: to how well it conforms to the
individual's fantasy of it as gratifying or disappointing.

   In this speculative scenario, what conforms to the fantasy is 'good,'
and what contradicts it is 'bad.' If what informs the transference is the
bad-object-imago, then in order for it to remain gratifying through and
beyond the transference, the *good*-object-imago (aspects of the transferred imago that contradict its *bad*-object qualities), which does not fit
with the expectation the transference holds, cannot be admitted. If the
self makes new relations in recognition (a psychical re-cognition) of old
relations, there is a kind of wish to duplicate – an impulse to repeat.
And if what is being repeated is or was disappointing, it is nevertheless
paradoxically satisfying in that disappointment. Here 'bad' is confirm-
ing of the fantasy, and therefore good; 'good,' as that which contradicts
the fantasy, is bad.

   A transference can have positive or negative (or mixed) results. We
might imagine that a new relationship cast using the transferential
mould from earlier ones would do just fine, provided either that the
old relationships were positive – or that we use in the transference
mostly their positive aspects. But that is not always what happens. My
own early relationships with those 'first emotional objects,' from whose
memory traces subsequent relationships 'bear a kind of emotional in-
heritance' (Freud, 1914b, p. 356), were of course more complex than I
have said here. But for whatever reason, which might even have included a coincidental, inaugural resonance between *some* characteristics
of my mother, as relegated in the fantasy split to the positive-but-*bad*

(because it contradicts the fantasy) imago, and *some* characteristics of Ms K, the transference was fixed in a particular direction. And so just as I did not (and do not) easily associate my mother's expert tailoring skills or wide smile with Ms K's sophisticated wardrobe or adroit joke-telling, until the director's report is lying on the desk in front of me I do not connect the positive parts of my practicum experience, concretized in that report, with my mother's occasional heartfelt praise. The report fails to mesh with the fantasized mother-object, of which the bestowing of praise is not a characteristic, so there is no place for it in the formulation of host teacher as object-resembling-the-mother. The *good-imago* object cannot be imbued with aspects of the contradictory *bad-imago* object, so the psyche leaves them out of its story.

Remembering and Repeating, Objects and Stories: What Comes Next?

The psyche 'makes' its objects, and its relations with those objects, partly in the world and partly through fantasy. The stories we tell ourselves, including stories about why we want to teach, embody those objects and relations. And so the story of wanting-to-teach-and-then-teaching is perhaps a little oversimplified; so too is the story of teacher education whose plot lines are drawn as the easy, linear learning of theory followed by its application, in a smooth, uncomplicated progression from novice (student) to expert (teacher). For learning to teach involves making relations with knowledge and with other people, all of whom have their own histories, their own relations with institutional structures and hierarchies, their own transferential inclinations. Remembering is implicated in these (and all other) relations, which for psychoanalysis also involve repeating the earlier relationships that made us who we are (Freud, 1914a) and, more importantly, that make us into who we imagine ourselves to be.

The question, *Who do you think you are?* has become very important. In addition to the 'devious routes' and 'secondary formations' (Laplanche & Pontalis 1973, p. 398) by which repressed material can rise to consciousness, narrative itself might inaugurate such a return. That seems to be part of what has happened here – in what has come to be my psychoanalytically guided version of the autobiographical method that Pinar and Grumet (1976), themselves informed by the Sartrean (1963) method of interweaving backward- and forward-looking reflection, call *currere*. For me telling-through-writing has become the third component of Freud's conceptual triptych: the working-through of a difficult and heretofore silent moment. It has taken ten years to arrive at this story.

There is undoubtedly more that could be said about this investigation of a particular experience of learning to teach. Writing about the relation between field notes and ethnography, Coffey (1999, p. 121) describes personal 'sharing' as 'both managed and partial' and the ethnographer's self as 'remain[ing] hidden and distinct from the texts that are consumed and read by others.' Psychoanalytic theory would not altogether disagree. The work of the unconscious, of analysis, and of self-theorizing have at times been described as 'retranscription' and '(re)translation' (Freud, 1937b; Laplanche, 1990; Benjamin, 1992). In his lecture on 'Psychoanalysis, time and translation' Laplanche identifies interpretation, which takes place in analysis but also in mourning, fantasy, and deferral (1990, p. 167), as the work of dismantling a current translation in order to 'rediscover' what existed prior to it and translate it again, only 'better' (p. 172). A better translation, perhaps, but never a perfect one, for even when we think we are telling all, there is more that we could not tell even if we wanted to, because we do not have conscious access to it. And what we do know, and do tell, is edited. There is really no other choice: even trying not to edit is editing. So whatever we do, we must proceed from that realization.

Still, something is revealed, if not everything, and there is a cost implicated in the catharsis of a sharing of self. Pitt (2003, p. 86) reminds us of the 'paradoxical desires of hiding and being discovered' that characterize the Winnicottian 'secret self' for whom revealing the personal is at once both pleasurable and catastrophic (Winnicott, 1953c). And it is not quite enough to say that by being subjected to an interpretation the narrated personal becomes more than a mere telling since, especially when the narrator is also the interpreter, an interpretation too is a telling, however imperfect.

But so what? What is all this transcribing and translating and interpreting useful for? What are the larger issues that reading psychoanalytically can help us to think about? And how can reading about someone else's transference help us with our own?

First, with Church (1995, p. 5), I take the view that it is 'possible to learn about the general from the particular.' Stories about difficulty are not always happy, but they may sometimes prove more useful than happy stories by inviting or nudging readers toward new and relevant insights. One such insight might be recognition of the very fact of difficulty. For if we start from the presumption that the life we make as a teacher will be precise, and transparent, and changeless, a perfectly unambiguous translation of the life we (think we) remember having as a pupil, or of the life (we imagine) our once-beloved teacher had, we are likely to be disappointed. Taubman reckons that student teachers' (and teachers') fantasies of teaching centred around 'loving and sacrificing for the students' serve to defend against 'very powerful aggressive impulses' (2006, p. 30), and need to be worked through if educators are 'to overcome our own distorted perception' (p. 31) – and, I would add, to mitigate the psychical shock of finding out that sometimes, in fact, we hate our students. Or our teachers.

This is perhaps where psychoanalysis can be of help. Its hindsight and insight let us not only uncover meaningful past events, but also make meaning retroactively, out of events in the past whose very remarkableness arises from their resonance with later ones. Hutton (1988, p. 137) posits that in a Freudian view the self is shaped irrevocably by past experience while, for Foucault, 'we continually reshape our past creations to conform to our present creative needs.' I see it a little differently: for me, while there is a continual interplay between past and present, creation and interpretation, there is also a self, however mutable and shifting, that undergoes the reshaping.

To claim it exists is not, however, to assert that we can ever know it fully, in ourselves or in others. Appel (1996, p. 2) contends that 'psychoanalytic theory may change the tradition in educational theory of viewing society and the self as a dualism.' A reworking of his proposition in the context of teacher education might read: 'Psychoanalytic theory may change the tradition in *teacher education* of viewing the *host teacher* and *the student teacher* as a dualism.' I do not think Appel is suggesting here that one-plus-one equals one. Neither am I: indeed, I lean to the Levinasian view, set out in Todd (2003a), of difference between self and Other as ultimately 'absolute' and the Other as ultimately unknowable, a view articulated slightly differently by Pitt (2006, p. 100) as the 'radical impossibility of ever fully accounting for either cultural or personal history or of subsuming the narratives of one to those of the other.'

While I did not (and do not) know precisely what historical, cultural, psychical, and transferential elements informed Ms K's way of relating to me, it is crucial that I remain aware that *something* was going on – for her as well as for me – because something is always going on. Transference is ubiquitous and, as Cohler and Galatzer-Levy (2006,

p. 254) contend, failing to recognize its presence and import can result in teachers 'repeating rather than dealing with central emotional issues in the classroom – either putting unconscious fantasies into action or distorting their relationships to students in an unconscious effort to avoid such actions.' When two sets of psychical goings-on are going on in the same space, many things are possible.

And so in the present context of learning to teach (and by extension learning to teach those who are learning-to-teach), perhaps this consideration of one individual's silence, or difficulty, or transference can invite insight into the complex and sometimes contradictory dynamics of host teacher/student teacher (and other pedagogical) relationships more generally. For Pitt (2006, p. 100), considering social and psychical orientations to matricide is a way to engage with 'what we think we know, how we have come to know it, and what we use our knowledge to do.' And, I would add, with who we think we are, and who we think the Other might be, and what we use that Other to do.

I am mindful of Winnicott's charge to educators, that 'teachers of all kinds do need to know when they are concerned *not with teaching their subject*, but with psychotherapy – that is, completing uncompleted tasks that represent parental failure or relative failure' (1963b, p. 63: italics in original). Pedagogical relations involve not only the bodies in the room but also their histories, as well as the ghosts of their past learning, unlearning, and relearning. And along with what each participant *brings to* the encounter, those relations involve what they *make*, together, *in* it and *of* it, even in moments that in the living or the remembering might seem mis-educative: these are the 'second thoughts' which Britzman (2003, p. 128) argues can permit us to repair our thinking.

Following on Winnicott's notion that 'there is no such thing as an infant' without its mother's care (and therefore its mother) (1960, p. 39, fn), Pitt describes the 'strange mathematics' of the space between child and parent in which 'two becomes three' as questions of learning are 'observed, delayed, engaged, and so on' (Pitt, 2003, p. 119). Similarly, I am drawn to Ogden's (1994a) conceptualization of intersubjectivity in the analytic setting. The 'analytic third' 'represents an elaboration and extension of Winnicott's proposition': that is, 'there is no such thing as an *analysand* apart from the relationship with the *analyst*' or vice-versa (Ogden, 1994a, p. 463; my italics). It is 'a third subject' co-created by the analyst and the analysand which develops 'in dialectical tension with [their] separate, living subjectivities . . . [and] has a powerful structuring influence on the analytic relationship' (p. 487). I find this idea potentially useful. All our individual sets of goings-on are, always, on-going. Perhaps, if we can begin to take into account those goings-on in the Other that we do not know, and those goings-on in ourselves that we cannot know, we can imagine a kind of *pedagogical third,* made out of that very unknowability, that contributes to the structure and the movement of an educational encounter.

Fifth Circumnarrative: The Spring

> ... [H]is body was invaded by the kind of joy that leaks
> around the edges of music or from
> certain kinds of scenery,
> the singular and untellable sense of arrival.
>
> – Carol Shields, *Happenstance*

March 21, 2007
In my mind I wander back to the frozen day when I began writing what has be-
come Chapter 6. The bitter winds of winter have gone, and though it is still cool
outside most of the snow has melted, and the calendar says it is the first day
of spring. I remember, that other day, the radio playing Joni Mitchell's 'Circle
Game.' I do not think that Mitchell's thinking was deliberately psychoanalyti-
cal when she wrote 'We can't return, we can only look behind from where we
came.' But looking back, it seems to me, is a kind of returning, that gives, if not
a completely clear picture, perhaps a slightly clearer one, of how we came to be
where, and who, we are.

My intellectual interest in teacher education as one of many potentially diffi-
cult aspects of education is very real, as is my interest in the other areas I have
explored. But in addition, on a deeply personal level I have felt compelled to
write the chapters of Part 3 as part of the working-through of my own version
of this particular 'difficult silence.' Because of that personal immediacy, I feel
similarly compelled to write about *the* writing of *these chapters, as part of*
working through *the* working-through.

Do we see what can happen? For an assignment during my preservice program
I wrote about Scott's [1992] piece on 'Experience.' I worried in that short essay
about her worry, about the necessity of historicizing experience-in-quotation-
marks in ways that refuse what is presumed to be foundational and contest
rather than reproduce assumptions of meaning as transparent and identity as
immutable. My concern was that as important as it is to analyse the discursive
events that have created my own identity and knowledge, such an analysis
involves recognizing that discourse is itself constituted through the experi-
ence of others, whose experience was born of other discourses born of other
experiences, and so on down the line, in a layering of historical consciousness,
about which I asked: 'Does it have a centre, an origin? If it does, must such a
beginning point not be, by definition, foundational? And if there is no point

of origin, can such a consciousness go on indefinitely, even infinitely?' That same worry can be inverted: I could write now about writing about the writing about my working-through of the mourning of the loss in this or that moment, and on and on, in a potentially interminable process that would end only when ink, or interest, or time ran out.

Yet this much seems to have been worthwhile.

And soon, the cherry tree in my garden will bloom.

(In)Conclusion

In the end, I do not know if the stories I tell about going there, being there, and living in its aftermath are tales of recovery or tales of symptoms. I do not know if the wound continues to live in the scar . . . I do know that in the telling I become my stories.

— Ronald J. Pelias, *A Methodology of the Heart*

With all this new knowledge, what exactly did I know?

— Nancy Miller, *But Enough about Me*

We have to rely on reflections.

— Stephen Mitchell, *Hope and Dread in Psychoanalysis*

On a summer evening in the early months of developing this study, I went for the first time to the home of a new friend. Located in a sleek high-rise in a recently rebuilt part of the city, his little apartment was a cluttered labyrinth – the small hallway made even narrower and more cramped by stacks of books, magazines, record albums, and all the detritus of a life in which things get put down but never put away. The walls were dark too, covered with photographs in frames, paintings, and yellowed architectural drawings. I turned a corner into the living room and could almost feel my pupils contract from the light pouring in through the wide window with its glorious view of the boats on the lake.

In the centre of the room was an enormous dining table, dark gleaming wood, echoing and reflecting the lake's bright, smooth surface and clearly the centre of all activity in the room: a good surface on which to rest a life. It is where my friend sits with others who come to share food; it is where he sits alone, reading a book before he puts it, down but not away, on one of the stacks in the hall. It is where we two sat, with wine and music, telling each other our stories.

Conversation

In conversation, stories are told: in dialogue between two friends sitting at a table, or in the much larger conversation that is education, or in any of the myriad smaller conversations within and about education, of which I hope this autoethnographic study is one. But the *each* and the *other* (or Other) must do something more than just tell stories. A conversation is probably not quite a conversation at all if this *something more* does not happen. For while articulating stories of educational experience (whether educative or mis-educative) can empower the powerless and critique institutional mechanisms of oppression (Simon, 1992), or function as a useful starting place for thinking and theorizing (Brodkey, 1987; Pitt, 2003), stories do not in themselves explain experience easily or ground knowledge straightforwardly (Pitt & Britzman, 2003). And so, writes Simon (1992, p. 61), the teacher who invites (or in my own case the researcher who undertakes) the telling of stories is 'confronted with the difficult question of what to do after [those] personal stories are told.'

Some other things we might do 'after stories are told' include agreeing or disagreeing, reflecting, refuting, resisting, ignoring, analogizing, extrapolating, synthesizing. And if all goes well, insight, meaning, and ideas may be made. If a story in itself is not a conversation, it can nevertheless lay the groundwork for one. And that is what I have tried to do here. I have offered up narratives of some difficult moments in education: my own and others' variously configured personal silences, brought into language and (at least partially) spoken throughout these chapters. In addition, I have used these stories of experience, and silence, and experience-as-silence, and silence-as-experience, to bring several discourses – social constructionist, feminist, psychoanalytic – into a theoretical conversation with one another and with some larger and varied pedagogical questions: worry about sexual curiosity and desire; ambivalent responses to the impact of new technologies; and the contradictions and ambiguities of learning to teach. But the crucial conversation, it seems to me, is the one that might come into being between the text and the reader – between you, the reader, and me, the writer.

My decision to frame the reader/author relation as a metaphorical conversation arises to a degree out of a wish for the pedagogical: that the experience of reading these chapters might be at least a little educative. But that wish is imprecise. For you and I are not sitting at the same table overlooking boats on a lake, nor physically together in place or time. Still, despite the asymmetry of the conversation and our participation in it, there is nevertheless an element of relating that happens between the personal and the theoretical parts of the stories which I set out on these pages with you in mind, and you read, bringing me, or my story, into *your* mind. It is not merely that the text teaches and the reader learns, though that may in some cases be part of what happens. Rather, it is that despite space and time you and I make something, separately but together, through and in and with and from the text.

In Chapter 7 I wondered if we might imagine, in educational encounters or relations, a co-constructed pedagogical third, a kind of subjectivity both more and other than a single participant, which arises from what those persons do not and cannot know of one another. Here I suggest that the text itself may constitute a third participant in our asynchronous conversation – a *narrative third*: perhaps not quite a subjectivity in itself, but an intersubjective *something* that we construct mutually out of and between our learned and invented theories, our personal stories, and even our silences.

In this way the autoethnographic aspect of my work, at once a place for *collecting* remembered experiences and for *connecting* them with some larger questions of education, might also offer potential connecting spaces for you, the reader. This is not to imply that our stories are the same: I have been clear throughout, I hope, that that is not my intention. Rather, it is to suggest that by engaging as readers with narratives we may come, in various ways, to new or altered modes of narrating, or thinking, or making meaning from the narrated, as we experience how our own stories and those we read – be they factual accounts of events, or fictions, or the stories that theories themselves make as they interpret or speculate on other stories – weave through one another. Thus does a writing (or written) self converse with a reading self, and thus is a story about one of us also a story about the other: a notion that extends to anthropology writ large as evinced in Cole's assessment of one of the goals of hermeneutic anthropology as 'the comprehension of the Self through the detour of the Other' (1992, p. 114).

Reflection

As a young girl I sometimes went with my father to the Eglinton Theatre in Toronto. There, in the women's room foyer, two of the walls were mirrored, the dim light of the room and the watery green of the glass together creating a kind of reflective corridor. I stayed there gazing at my reflection until the last possible moment, when the opening music of *My Fair Lady* (Warner & Cukor, 1964) or *Mary Poppins* (Disney & Stevenson, 1964) or *2001: A Space Odyssey* (Kubrick, 1968) or some other blockbuster would come filtering in. And even then I stood, leaning left and right, shifting first to this side and then to that, watching my reflection, trying to see past the image of my face to that of my back, reflected from the mirror behind me, and the multiple *re*-reflections, both front and back, created by the two mirrored walls – a kind of visual-spatial mise-en-abyme or Droste-effect form, structured like a fractal, whose corresponding narrative cousin is the scenario in which a character in a story writes a story in which she is a character who writes a story about a character writing a story about . . . and on and on, potentially infinitely.

Although in this kind of 'hall of mirrors' the reflected images appear in front of and behind the self who is reflected, they breathe and move contemporaneously with – literally *in time with* – that 'real' self: that theatre anteroom is horizontally or geographically articulated. Contrasting with that breathing and those movements, the narrative that relates them – or the memory of them – is their historically inflected, vertically drawn counterpoint. And in its historicity it is like all memory, all autobiography: it reads and interprets events from a past-oriented moment in their future. In so doing it recalls the psychoanalytic notions of deferred revision and the mystic writing-pad, which illuminate both the psychical capacity and the unconscious desire (or more: the urge, or even the compulsion) to return to, rework, retell, and relive the early self, with the wholeness, unity, and integration we once imagined it embodied but which was lost at the moment of coming to know that self as separate.

To relive old events, by (re)telling or (re)writing them with new (re)interpretations and making from them (re)new(ed) meaning, is in a sense to (re)run the same narrative course – a second time, or a third time, or more. Here *currere* (Pinar & Grumet, 1976) becomes *re*-currere. And while *currere* 'is not the course to be run, or the artefacts employed in the running of the course [but rather . . .] the running of the course' (Pinar, 1976, p. 18), in this re-running the anchoring artefact – the story – *recurs*, becoming, again, current: *a* current, running in more than one direction. My moments with the theatre mirrors are a past geography that forms a layer of my history: a history that includes my experience of my reflection in those mirrors, the memory of that experience, the meaning I make from that experience and that memory, and the telling of all of these, itself part of the larger layered history containing all the narratives that contribute to this study. For Schafer (1983, p. 219), 'the self is a telling' – I tell myself; I account for myself; I identify myself. I tell *my self*, to me and to the Other. As Ricoeur writes (1985, p. 214), 'It is in telling our stories that we give ourselves an identity.'

But this giving, or making, of identity is not a one-way street, the writing of autobiography not a solipsistic enterprise. In Chapter 2 I considered some of the ways recursive qualities of memory and narrative (Grumet, 1992; Chambers, 1998: King, 2000) involve not only the one remembering and the one narrating but also the one who reads and responds. As the story of one can come to inform another's, that Other, in hearing, reading, and interpreting the story, contributes to the teller's story, and identity, too. The current runs, flows, between us.

Instructive here is Arendt's writing on *The Human Condition* (1958), particularly her claim that in acting and in speaking people 'reveal actively their unique personal identities and thus make their appearance in the human world' (p. 179). Arendt does not maintain that identity is fixed and lies waiting to be revealed when a narrative curtain is pulled aside. Rather, she stresses, acting, and speaking as that part of action which 'identifies . . . the actor, announcing what he does, has done, and intends to do' (1958, p. 179), are intersubjective undertakings that require an Other: speech and action reveal the self *to that self*, and to other selves, 'when people are *with* others . . . in sheer human togetherness' (p. 180; italics in original). The self's agency is disclosed through its story into a pre-existing nexus of human relationships and their stories, and a new story affects and is affected by each pre-existing story in the nexus. That is, the teller of the tale is doubly its subject: at once the performer and the focus of the action (p. 184).

This concept is important for understanding Cavarero's (2000) view that while each person's story matters to that person, more crucial to identity than the content of those stories is the fundamental and profound desire that they *be narrated*, the 'uncontrollable narrative impulse of memory that produces the text' and which coincides with the self that Cavarero calls 'narratable' (2000, p. 35). As *narratable* rather than simply *narrated*, this self is 'at once the transcendental subject and the elusive object of all the autobiographical exercises of memory' (p. 34). The narrative impulse exists always; the narratable self is both separate from and mixed in with its story. 'I know that I have a story and that I consist in this story – even when I do not pause to recount it,' writes Cavarero (p. 35). Narratability, and the concomitant desire to hear the self *'personally* narrated by an Other' (p. 33; italics in original), are uniquely human attributes that recognize and insist on the particularity of each of us – self and other – as lived *in* and *through* our own stories (by *being* and by *telling*, we might say). What we want to hear narrated is our uniqueness, the 'life-story that is this and not another' (p. 34), about the self, the *I*, which is this and not another.

Perhaps our perception of this uniqueness, in another but particularly in the self, consoles us for the psychical losses (of imagined unification and its concomitant if also imaginary omnipotence) that inhere in the self's coming to know itself as a separate being: the bad news is that I am separate, forever disconnected, but so is everyone else, and the good news is that none of those others is quite like me. And perhaps the desire to have the self's uniqueness told or read by another is a kind of double confirmation, of the uniqueness itself and of the Other's recognition of it. For, recalling Grumet's (1992) twin contentions, that *reading* one's narratives about one's own self enacts a kind of doubling of that self, and that *writing* about oneself is an act both personal and public, we might extrapolate the possibility that, even done by another, *a reading is also a telling*, a 'way of demonstrating the reciprocity of objectivity and subjectivity and their interdependence [that] extends to the reader/researcher the artist's awareness that subjectivity transforms any objectivity it seeks to describe' (Grumet, 1992, p. 37). The narrative of the theatre's mirrored anteroom, like all other narratives, happens in more than one time and place: both inside and outside the events, and inside and outside the moments of remembering, of writing, and of reading.

Still, if being read or narrated by another confirms the existence and the uniqueness of one's story and one's self, the story can never be quite complete. I cannot be certain, but I think now that my gazing and shifting in that theatre mirror were really an effort to see behind and beneath the topmost reflection to a single essence – to a whole, 'real' self. Those attempts were in vain. I never saw all of me.

Silence

In the lobby of the theatre there was a small niche, mirrored on top, bottom, and three sides, that always reflected from several angles the vase of flowers it held. I might have been able to see more of myself had I been in the multiply mirrored niche than I could in the women's room with just two mirrored walls. Yet I still could not have seen myself the way I saw the flowers, nor the way another person could have seen me. There were views of the flower arrangement not available to the flowers themselves, and views of myself not available to me.

The quasi-conversational encounter between reader and text, or between reader and writer-through-text, may offer a differently angled and possibly fuller view. But even so, neither the making nor the reading of the self through narrative can do everything, just as the mirror cannot show all sides (and especially not the inside) of the thing it is reflecting. Parts of our stories remain hidden, to the self and to the Other. These are the silences within our stories that we leave out of the telling. And if, as Cavarero contends, 'each one of us *lives him or herself* as his/her own story, without being able to distinguish the *I* who narrates it from the *self* who is narrated' (2000, p. 34; italics in original), it is also true, I posit, that we 'live ourselves' at least as much *as*, and *in*, what is absent from or left out of those stories. Silence itself, some of the time at least, is not quite silent. This is true not only in the psychoanalytic encounter where, writes Pitt, 'even though the analysand cannot speak about her unconscious knowledge, the unconscious nevertheless speaks' (2003, p. 542), but in the empty spaces in the stories we tell, and in the stories we hint at but do not tell aloud, and in the stories we delay telling, and in the stories we do not tell, ever.

What do we use silence to do? I have shown here that silence can resist, refuse, postpone, divide, connect, conceal, and protect. It can offer ways to resist knowledge or refuse demands perceived as troublesome or threatening, thereby preserving an individual's self or self-concept, as in the case of teachers' sometimes ambivalent responses to new technologies. It can permit us to avoid addressing or even naming what might be uncomfortable or difficult, such as the vacant spaces at the centre of diagrams of the human body, while at the same time pointing our attention toward it. And it can buy us time, hold in abeyance what we cannot yet speak, until we are willing and able to tell it.

Silence works on at least three levels. There are conscious silences within events, such as the decisions I made not to challenge my host teacher. There are unconscious silences, or silences of the unconscious: my lack of awareness, at the time of the events, of the aspects of desire inhering in the events recounted in Parts 1 and 3. And finally, there are the silences in some of the narratives qua narratives, specifically those in Part 1, which arrived only gradually at anything even remotely close to a full telling.

Each of my silences has served a fairly specific purpose here. Contemplated more generally, however, these kinds of psychical silence can work in two important ways. First, they can allow for a period of waiting and working through – a space of time between the 'difficult moment' or troubling event itself and the later moment(s) in which the processing of those difficulties becomes possible. Second, and somewhat paradoxically, a silence can itself constitute a working-through.

To be even more precise, narrative – with the silences it embodies, recognizes, and ultimately speaks – can be a working-through. This happens partly in what we might consider as another multiply articulated conversation: between the narrative and its silences; between the self that narrates and the self that is silent; between the nachträglich time of remembering and narrating and the time and events remembered or narrated. And, always, between events and the psychical processes that those events inaugurate, recall, and cause to be remade and re-experienced.

The personal silences I have explored in my discussions about difficult moments in my experience of learning to teach, as well as in those about refusing knowledge and its relationship with desire, endured nearly 10 and over 30 years respectively. These, as well as the silences examined in the chapters on representing body parts and on new technologies, are silences that in one way or another have required working through. 'Working through' is a process, but a paradoxically partial one, a conceptual mise-en-abyme, a recursive silence-within-a-silence, one part of a whole that is itself never more than partial. That is, part of what never quite gets worked through is the difficult fact that not everything gets worked through. For every story can be read in many ways. The circumnarratives are an example of this: not only can they be read in multiple ways, but there are other narratives that could, in theory, surround them too as the first of a potentially infinite layering of *circum*-circumtexts.

Silence can keep us psychically safe and it can hold our tongue until we are ready and able to speak. But although telling our stories may eventually bring an end to that silence, the telling is never complete: narrative embodies its own silences.

Secrets

Our narratives and our silences are unique; so are the ways we come to them, and the ways they come to us. We might co-opt the famous declaration of *Twelfth Night*'s Malvolio, recasting it to say that 'some are born *silent*, some achieve *silence*, and some have *silence* thrust upon them' (Shakespeare, 1635): silence can be given, or chosen, or both at once. My chapters illustrate some moments where an individual is silenced by institutional discourses, or inequitable power structures, or fear, and other moments in which silence is consciously chosen for pragmatic, or philosophical, or personal reasons, and still other moments when the choice is made (consciously, unconsciously, or both) to acquiesce to an imposed silence as a combination of *given* and *chosen:* for instance, my decision as a student not to interfere with the hierarchical status quo in the school by revealing my 'real' reasons for dropping English.

The given and the chosen, as components that inform our autonomous actions (Todorov, 2002) and, presumably, our quiescence, manifest themselves in both narrative and silence. Obviously I have made conscious choices about stories to include and stories to leave out of this project: I am quite sure that you, my reader, would not want to know *all* my stories, and I am certain that I do not want you to know them all. Even so, it is not always clear, even to me, even so close to the end of this process, why I have included these narratives and not others. What is clear is that there are some stories only one's analyst is permitted to hear, and some that remain unspoken, perhaps forever, because they cannot be told in even that most deliberately revelatory setting.

It may be because the self is made and remade in relation to other selves, and interpreted and understood *by* those other selves, that our 'need to communicate … is countered by the equally pressing need to defend against communication' (Pitt, 2003, p. 83) held by the 'secret self' that wants both to be, and not to be, discovered (Winnicott, 1963c). Arendt conceives of something similar when she posits that 'although nobody knows whom he reveals when he discloses himself in deed or word, he must be willing to *risk the disclosure'* (1958, p. 180; my italics) – a risk Simon (1992, p. 62) elaborates in slightly different terms as the 'challenge to go beyond one's existing knowledge and identities [which] constitutes no small degree of risk; risk of failure, loss of coherence, rupture of existing relations with family and friends [and] social ridicule.'

As humans we cannot be faulted for being unable to take – or for choosing not to take – a particular risk in a specific moment or context.

But in my view it is not a question of fault quite so much as it is one of fault-*lines*: the intersubjective, always-already otherness of each of us that persists, however close we might approach, however hard we might bump into, and however much we might move with or against, one another in our big and little dances. If, as Cavarero maintains, we know at the outset that 'the *I* is ... the *self* of her own narrating memory,' and that 'the other [is] the *self* of her own story' (2000, p. 34; italics in original), we might also know, or at least suspect, that like the 'I' the Other has stories she cannot (yet) tell, or chooses not to tell (yet): secrets she is keeping to herself.

Ethics

And here lie some ethical dilemmas, for teaching and learning especially, that are not easy – and that may even be impossible – to resolve. At numerous points throughout this text, I have alluded to or spoken outright about the dynamics of power that attach to and inform relations within education. In Chapter 5 especially, I have addressed some of the ways these dynamics contribute to the teacher's perception of herself as teacher: how ideas about what it means *to be a teacher* are bound up with assumptions that position the teacher as the centre of the classroom; the holder of authority, autonomy, and knowledge in terms of both subject matter and pedagogy. And so, put bluntly, while there are things about which teachers can be certain at least some of the time and in at least some circumstances, in the ICT scenario new technologies invite (or command, directly or indirectly) the teacher to translate herself from the position of an expert knower to that of a learner who, in some cases, must learn from her students. It is a call to relinquish certainty.

Right at the centre of the preface to their inaugural work on *currere* (1976: viii) Pinar and Grumet place these words, still astonishing more than three decades later: '*We must lie in waiting for ourselves*. Throughout our lives. Abandoning the pretence that we know' (my italics).

With these words they ask us to accept that we do not know who we are, and that finding out is a lifelong and possibly interminable enterprise. But read psychoanalytically the first part of this little passage is particularly rich. The phrase 'lie in waiting' evokes for me the image of a wild animal, hungry and hunting, poised still and silent in long grass with its teeth and claws at the ready, waiting for its prey to emerge from its nest and be devoured. For we *do* wait for our selves to come to us, in the form of another who we imagine will know us, and be like us, and think and feel and love the way we think and feel and love. And we make that Other, transferentially and through projection and introjection, into our own image or into the image of what we think we know about who we imagine we are. But because the Other *is* other, those selves for whom we lie in waiting do not, cannot, come. And so as we abandon 'the pretence that we know' ourselves we must also, eventually, let go of what we think or imagine we know about those Others, and ultimately of the notion that we can know much at all about them.

This demand is deeper and potentially more dislocating than that made by curricula, or new technologies, or the ambiguous position of the student teacher. Understanding one's students (or indeed one's teachers) as other to oneself arises from, and embodies, the radical call to recognize that those students' (or teachers') inner worlds are not merely unknown to us but actually *unknowable*. Pinar and Grumet go on to express their thesis thus: 'I don't know, and I must study, and search. I must be open to my experience, open to others, and be willing to abandon what I think in the face of what I see' (p. viii). But we must also be aware that there is more than what we see; and the unseen, the unheard, the silent, is the greater part.

Still, we do have something in common. For if I do not know the Other, the Other does not know me: what we share is our mutual unknowability, which if all goes well we make together into that *something* I have referred to as a 'pedagogical third' – or alternatively, a 'narrative third.' This paradoxical notion, that all we share is our mutual otherness (or at least the notion that otherness is all that we can be certain of sharing) offers an equally contradictory insight: we are at once alone and not alone.

Phelan (1997a, pp. 175–6) calls for a 'pedagogy of conversation' that refuses simple, single answers to complex problems, recognizes relations between self and other, and focuses on a kind of responsibility of individuals toward one another that consists in a Levinasian recognition of both another's 'fundamental strangeness' and the importance of learning *from* – rather than simply about – that strangeness. I think this is a fine idea. But it is a complicated one. For if silence is, as I have argued, a part – and a significant part – of our stories, a pedagogy of conversation must find the space for those silences and the will to tolerate them, to 'let them be.' And this is no small thing, for even when we try to let silence be we have a difficult time doing so.

In her examination of 'the culture of classroom silence' Bosacki (2005) looks at cultural meanings and spiritual and pragmatic causes and functions of silence among adolescents. Arguing that silence ought not to be feared (p. 38), and that it can strengthen self-awareness, deepen relations with others, and serve as a strategy of power, self-expression, self-preservation, or for coping (pp. 65, 87–8), she offers 'educational strategies that aim to promote the benefits of silence' (pp. 122–3), and calls for a conceptualization of education that 'balances the inter, intra, and extrapersonal' (p. 168) partly through the 'schooling' of silence. True, Bosacki is working from a developmental psychology perspective on ways to address silences grounded in gender, ethnicity, ability, and the like. Still, much of her focus, and her longest chapter, seem to be on thinking about ending silence: through dialogue, openness, participation, reflection (for students and teachers), journalling and drama activities (p. 129), and 'conversation about silence and the self' (p. 157). While these ideas do not lack usefulness, they seem to hint at the assumption that silence per se is something not-quite-desirable, and that the goal of education and educators ought to be to end it.

For my part, I am not convinced of this. And yet I too have difficulty, even in my own work, even here. Like Bosacki, who 'knew . . . that [she] could not – and did not plan to – provide answers' (p. 172), I did not enter this study imagining that I would end it with a specific plan of action for addressing silence. Yet now, as I get close to its end, despite my strong belief in silence as a presence rather than a lack and as a methodology rather than a pathology, and despite my more general view of the impossibility of a 'one-size-fits-all' approach to the question of silence in education. I feel the pull to provide answers. I am an educator, after all, and educators are trained, not only in the months or years we spend in faculties of education but in our decades-long observational apprenticeship, to want answers: to refuse silence.

These are just some of the tricky aspects of making relations with silence. Granted, there are many kinds of silence, and they do not all look the same. Silences born of (or imposed by) fear, or discrimination, or oppressive power structures may not be those we wish to encourage (though there is no single way to address even these). But I do think it is important to reiterate (as Bosacki herself intimates), that in addition to being 'given' silence may be, at least partly, chosen. Perhaps leaving silence *un*schooled, some of the time, could paradoxically be part of 'schooling' it – or, more accurately, part of schooling education to tolerate, to coexist with, to listen to silence.

Listening

Rosen 1998 (p. 5) asks us to recognize that life events are 'an essential base' for learning, and to consider that classrooms ought to be places where students talk to each other. I do not disagree. But of course, if we are to think of education as a conversation, we must also listen. We might also, sometimes, be silent together, and listen to that too, for we each need time to develop, and hear, and explore, our own thoughts.

But it is hard to know which silences to listen to, and how to listen to them. Schwartz (1998) divides silence into two sub-categories which she names after Harpocrates and Larunda, the Roman god and goddess of silence. In her formulation, 'Harpocratic silence depicts the notion of emptiness . . . [and] is the empty silence of reflection and meditation; Larundic silence is the full . . . silence of communication' (pp. 185–6). Schwartz contends that although silence communicates its meaning in often obscure and 'slippery' ways, a kind of listening that involves considering and accounting for the silence's context, the listener's prejudices, external forces of tradition and history, and factors such as relevance and consistency can result in helpful interpretations. Still, even this may not always be enough. Schwartz herself points out that an interpretation that is not 'radical, lazy [or] opportunistic' may be 'difficult to achieve' and that multiple interpretations of a silence may need to be 'played with until an interpretation is reached which can be agreed upon' (1998, pp. 190–1).

This work of trying to know when and how and which silence matters is no simple undertaking. Recent years have brought a spate of widely publicized incidents of violence in schools, among them the story of a young man who, in April of 2007, shot and killed 32 students and teachers at the Virginia Polytechnic Institute before taking his own life. A headline in the *New York Times* a few days later read: 'Before deadly rage, a lifetime consumed by a troubling silence.' The accompanying article elaborated that the student was withdrawn, 'unresponsive and taciturn in class,' that 'a classmate once offered him $10 just to say hello but got nothing,' and that his mother 'just wanted him to talk' (Kleinfield, 2007). This tragic story is, however, quite incomplete, for we can never know whether things would have turned out less terribly for this young person and his victims had he somehow been 'made' to communicate. Nevertheless, the headline and story in the *Times* seem to imply assumptions of silence as a cause of violence, and even to convey a sense that things could have been different, if only this young man had been more vocal.

Education, like parenting, can be thought of as an experiment with no control group. It is simply not possible to know *what might have been.* This is a very hard thing for educators: not only to do it but also to recognize its limitations. There is only so much education can do, and we do not always know how much that is. Can thinking psychoanalytically help? Might psychoanalytic theory's particular ways of listening to both self and Other, that recognize interaction and *intra*-action as both significant in the making of lives and of a world, help us to engage with those who are other to us? I have offered some reasons to use psychoanalysis as a hermeneutic for thinking about narratives of education and their silences. But it is worth taking a moment to consider another question: why psychoanalysis-and-education at all? After all, there are many discourses we can use to read, interpret, and make conclusions about the events articulated in these narratives and others like them.

To help with this question I turn to Bettelheim's 'Psychoanalysis and education,' written in 1969 and still carrying considerable force. Bettelheim laments what he sees as education's failure to recognize that the fundamental goal of psychoanalysis – 'where id was, there ego shall be' (Freud, 1933, p. 80) – might 'humanize and enrich' pedagogical practice. Bettelheim's position is that education must initially involve some element of fear, because reason, slow to develop in the human being, is at first 'easily drowned out by the noisy clamor of the emotions' (1969, p. 78). He argues that while fear may be necessary at first, it must ultimately be replaced with the 'rational purpose' (p. 79) that will take the child through to adulthood. This has to happen in a context where id and superego must be not privileged but rather put to use in developing ego: that is, where instinct and conscience are each subordinated to the reality principle that 'life in our society is worthwhile, ... that things are essentially all right, though sometimes difficult and in need of improvement' (p. 83).

Of course it is not only the child who experiences fear. Fear exists in teachers too, and in education as a whole. And one of the things most feared seems to be uncertainty. We so seldom know if what we are doing is 'the right thing,' or even if there *is* a right thing. But while the work of education might indeed help in some way to smooth out some of our deep fissures in the ways humans engage with each other, it alone cannot save us unless we can find ways – individually and collectively – to listen: to others, and to ourselves.

I acknowledge that it is idealistic to imagine that educators can (or will want to) find ways of understanding their personal psychical processes in order to facilitate their work with children in ways that that avoid both 'repressive molding' and 'an acting out ... of old fears and resentments' (Bettelheim, 1969, p. 74). But in present-day education, at times apparently ruled by pressures of curricula and testing and a presumed 'real world' that brooks little individuality, it may be that a little idealistic listening wouldn't hurt. Perhaps too it might move us into a realism, a reality, that attends to and takes account of, without always accounting for, the Other.

On the cover of Bosacki's book is a blurred photograph of a facial profile, in which only the ear is in focus: a visual metaphor for listening. What might happen if education took up listening as a way to culture – that is, to cultivate, to grow – a 'culture of silence' despite, or even because of, our discomfort with it? Bosacki argues that 'silence builds no bridges' (2005, p. 90). But maybe – and here I recall once more the Winnicottian notion of the secret self – there are times when we do not want to build bridges; times, even, when a bridge would be more a thing to leap from than a means for getting across to somewhere, or something, or someone else. These difficulties, these struggles against rushing to answer questions that we are just beginning to ask, are felt not only in conceptual writing but also in the classroom where, as I have suggested, the theoretical sometimes has a hard go making itself known at all.

I may not understand why you are silent; you may not understand my silences either. But if you are my teacher and I am your student it may not be easy, for either of us, to accept this particular aspect of what Todd (2003a) calls our mutual strangeness and nonreciprocity, because the institution within which we interact demands of us something more and other than silence: something that does not always include the luxury of choice. In addition to concerns about when to invite or insist on conversation and when not to, education's worry about silence is particularly evident in a setting whose prevailing discourses are of accountability, test results, and 'excellence.'

How is a teacher to know whether or not learning is taking place? Such a question is transparently problematic in second language education, where it is patently difficult, if not impossible, to assess whether or not a language is being learned if the learner does not speak (Granger, 2004). The difficulty is equally present, if less conspicuous, in other areas of curriculum. This is because a significant component of the structure of contemporary education is participation, and participation tends to mean very particular things; among others, speaking in class, entering discussions, answering questions, reflecting in journals and essays, and sharing those reflections.

Caring, Loving, Hoping

'Letting silence be' is not the same as letting go of connection or of the wish for connection. It is emphatically *not* not-caring. Maybe part of what it is is a kind of love. Love is complicated – as I have posited throughout these chapters it informs and forms teacher/learner relations in many formulations – but we must take care not to let love get too mixed-up with something else. And one trick of caring, as of loving, is not to do it too much. It is important for educators to recognize that the Other's otherness extends to how much, and how, we care for him or her: the aim is to avoid, as much as possible, trying to make the Other into an image of ourselves. Once I, as a teacher, come to understand that my interpretation of what students need is at least somewhat founded on what *I* need (or what I imagine those students-as-projected-or-transferential-reflections-of-myself need) I may be able to co-exist with their taking up the autonomy to determine their own needs and find ways to meet them.

Letting silence be is not an easy way out, for it demands rigorous attention to our own ways of being as educators and learners, and particularly to our ways of being together and what we make from that togetherness. It is delicate, this thing we make between us, fragile in a sense similar to the 'fine risk' (Todd, 2003a, p. 68) we take in 'seek[ing] a radical openness toward the Other, susceptible to being moved by the approach of the Other.' This kind of risk, in a Levinasian sense, incorporates and expresses something of the idea of sacrifice: 'the self offers itself for the Other' (Todd, 2003a, p. 69), responding to difference without being erased or subsumed by it (pp. 69–73). For Todd such risky relations embody components of a kind of love that 'gives itself over to the other in a gesture of communicative openness' which, sometimes, 'erupts into an ethical interaction' (p. 85) – a concept not unlike that of Cavarero (2000, p. 111), who maintains that 'the joy of love lies indeed in the nakedness of a shared appearance . . . that does not tolerate qualifications but simply exposes two uniquenesses to each other.'

Todd and Cavarero seem to be conversing with one another in important ways. Todd understands love to be an offering of '[one's] own uniqueness as a response to the absolute limit the Other imposes' which concomitantly 'sustains a mode of relationality where the self comes into being through the Other' (Todd, 2003a, p. 73, 89). And for her part Cavarero comments that although it is 'possible that the lovers will *remember* the twofold movement of the relation with the mother, at once passive and active: the originary impulse toward self-exposure' (2000, p. 111; italics in original), the belief that love occasions a 'fusing into the one-all' that echoes and attempts to re-inaugurate the infant's unification with the mother is a mythical one, because the truest wish of lovers is not to be incorporated into one another but rather to experience 'the full splendor of the finite according to [their] reciprocal uniqueness' (p. 111).

What might this mean for education, this notion of a shared ground made somehow out of the silence of a mutual not-knowing that might just incorporate some of the love that teachers are so prone to talk about? I think it might mean hope. For Simon hope is 'the acknowledgment of more openness in a situation than the situation easily reveals; openness above all to possibilities for human attachments, expressions, and assertions' (1992, p. 3), and it is what allows him to envision a 'pedagogy of possibility' (1992). This phrasing calls to mind both the optimism and the partialness inherent in thinking about what is possible in and for pedagogy. First, to suggest that *anything* is possible is not to say that *everything* is possible; and second, what is possible is by no means certain. A pedagogy of possibility acknowledges that there may be *im*possibility too.

Perhaps this need not be so terrible a surprise. Recognizing that education, like psychoanalysis and government, is for Freud an 'impossible profession' (1937a, p. 248), Appel (1996, p. 11) holds onto the conviction that 'impossibility ... should not lead to despair,' particularly if education can open itself once more to 'the notion of unconscious desire' (p. 12).

Even the pedagogical 'impossible' may not be altogether hopeless. Recognizing that behind all speech is silence, and that beneath what we know about ourselves and one another there is much more that we do not know – and noticing that despite this we nevertheless find and make ways to live together – opens us to thinking of education as a mutually (and potentially even democratically) constructed conversation in which we not only invite one another to choose whether to speak or be silent but also let some of those silences (and thereby one another) *be*. I wonder if doing this might allow us, eventually, to form attachments, pedagogical and otherwise, that are grounded less in what we think we know than in what we believe we think. And feel. And hope.

Epilogue

Curtis, age 7:   [singing] One is the loneliest number . . .
                            [speaking] No, that's wrong. Zero is the loneliest number.
                            Because it's nothing.

Paul, age 5:   I think minus-one is the loneliest.
                            Because you had one, and it went away.

                                                 – personal communication

He thinks, too, about all the longing there was inside her . . .
Where does it all go to, he wonders, when the person you long for dies?

                                       – Anita Shreve, *Eden Close*

Sixth Circumnarrative: Around and after Words

This work has been a long time coming. At the point when I had imagined I would be beginning to write, my partner, Alberto, was diagnosed with cancer. At the point when I had imagined I would be adding the final touches to the finished piece, he died. I had no choice but to wait until after his death to begin writing, yet for a long time his death made writing impossible. And if it was impossible after he died it was even more emphatically so while he was alive but sick: for reasons practical, logistic, and otherwise the last two years of his life consumed all my energy, all my intellect, all my passion.

There is no language for the visceral fatigue of that time. In fact 'visceral' doesn't even begin to get at it. Exhaustion permeated skin, ligament, muscle, its debilitating toxicity like mercury or lead, echoing in my bones the tumours that grew and multiplied in his. I was skeletally tired.

The tiredness came, of course, from far too little sleep, and such sleep as there was careful, tense in order not to disturb the one whose rest was enormously more precarious. But it came even more intensely and exquisitely from the unrelenting sadness, the despair, the weight not only of the pain, physical and psychical, that Alberto's increasingly fragile muscles and bones and organs, and his never-fragile mind, despite its strength, despite its failure to fail, could not bear and which had to be borne for him, but also of my own pain, in no way comparable to his, but real nonetheless: of a profound loss anticipated, of a planned-for but now impossible future, and of the day-by-day, minute-by-minute, helpless beholding of the strength leaking out of a once-strong body, the witnessing of a man returning – and seeing and feeling himself return – to a state of need and dependence the shame and humiliation of which no amount of love and care could soften. This was the weight that, as it grew, could never be spoken but only felt, carried, shared, silently, as if to speak it would cause it to leak out and onto the others, the family and friends, mostly the children, who, he insisted, must not be asked to share it.

In his last days he came to what a more religious person would have called a state of grace. A few days before his death he told me quietly, 'It's happening now. The life is sliding out of me.' He said it quietly, with weariness but also with a kind of relief. And then he said, 'I think I'm ready.'

Perhaps this is the best any of us can hope for: to be ready.

There's a small photograph of him on my desk, taken the night before the morning of his death because a publicity picture was needed for an award he was to be given. My memory of the preparation for taking this photo is one of the most tender I have of his last days. That afternoon I had trimmed his hair and beard, one of the last small caring acts I could perform for him. He sat in his chair in the kitchen, a warm summer breeze drifting in. Halfway through he felt cold, needed the window closed. Sitting up was difficult for him, so I had to work quickly, and my work, never quite expert, was imperfect. He looked out the window at the garden, green in the summer light, noticed a squirrel, two robins, asked about the tomatoes I had planted two weeks earlier: when would they be ready to eat? When we were done he had to lie down and rest.

Early in the evening he awoke, unusually cheerful. Our children were home for dinner; his mother was there too. We ate, a family meal. There was laughter, chatter. He was quiet, but bright and very present, and enjoying his family. He told a joke; I don't remember it now. It was, though we did not know it then, a fine last meal. Afterwards we prepared for the photos. He wanted to wear a dress shirt, and I helped his arms into the sleeves, and did up the buttons. No tie; he refused that. He had become thin, the shirt was too big. He lamented this, and insisted that it be tucked in behind him as he sat on the sofa, to look as if it fit properly. He fussed about the books on the shelf behind him, and about whether the lamp should be on or off. He worried about what to do with his hands.

Astonishingly, the photographs do not disclose a dying man. Buoyed by his happiness at achieving this honour, pleased by the presence of his family, and summoning what I now know to have been some of the last remnants of life in him, in the pictures he has lifted himself up to a place of dignified pride. He wants to be remembered in these particular ways, as professorial, wise.

And in all but one of the photos he succeeds. The last one shows a raised eyebrow and an ironic smile. Patiently he has let me snap away with the camera, but now he is tired. And he is, I know, beginning to get annoyed: the needed pictures have been taken, and he wants the camera gone. Yet his look is so mild, tender, fond. Forbearing, even amused. He knows what I am trying to do, what I deeply need to do; he knows this will be the last photo. It is one of his last caring acts.

The next morning he has slipped into semi-consciousness. I call an ambulance and we go to the hospital, where I am told he will not survive to another day. He waits, though, until his mother and our children can gather beside him. He does not speak, but he turns his head toward them when they speak to him. Then they leave the room, while a nurse tends to him. Apart from her silent presence we are alone. And his gasping stops, his breathing slows, he holds my hands with a strength that stuns and shakes me. And then his hands relax, and without letting go he slides away, softly, soundlessly. A life, so quietly ended.

Leaving the hospital a few hours later I walk down the corridor arm-in-arm with his mother. We hear a high, thin, urgent cry. We look at each other, and at precisely the same moment we say, each in her own language, a baby's been born; nació un bebé.

Bochner [1997, p. 429] writes:
   This is the work of self-narration: to make a life that seems to be falling apart come together again, by retelling and 'restorying' the events of one's life. At

certain junctures in life, this narrative challenge can be a terrible struggle, and we do not always succeed.

I cannot think, just now, about success, only that some things have to be done. Metaphors about phoenixes rising from the ashes make me cringe. Anyway, the phoenix isn't real.
But this is:

The Rose of Jericho (Selaginella lepidophylla) . . . is a desert plant growing in the sands of Egypt, Arabia, Syria and Mexico. For long periods, these 'roses' live in desert regions, growing and reproducing . . . until the environment no longer supports an adequate existence. When this time has come, the flowers and leaves are dead and fallen, they lose moisture and the drying branches curl inwards, forming a round ball. They retract their roots from the soil and allow the desert winds to carry them across the desert, until one day they arrive in a damp place where they can continue to grow and spread. . . . You could say they feel their way through this process, as they don't necessarily remain in the first place they stop, but feel into the nature of the place to see if it is adequate to enhance growth. There they may stay, and grow, or indeed they may move again many times. (Azarius, 2007)

And so, we begin, again.

Notes

Introduction

1 According to Harper, whose work addresses political, social, and historical questions related to gender and race in educational contexts, the post-
World War II position of minimizing difference that understood individual
identity as transcending aspects such as femininity, masculinity, sexual
orientation or ethnicity to focus on 'individual ability, energy, and motivation' (1997a, p. 197) was not seriously challenged in Canada generally, and
in Ontario in particular, until policies of multiculturalism were developed
in the early 1970s.

2 Michaels (1997, p. 138).

3 Although I would argue, if pressed, that any confusion caused by a
multiple layering of narratives (and names for narratives) is worth it if it
helps us think in new and useful ways about old questions, I am mindful
of the potential for such confusion. Thus I hesitate to name these passages *meta-meta*-narratives. That name might make sense given that
many of the chapters in this study offer writing about the work of writing, and thinking about thinking processes, and delays that are about
delaying, but I prefer *circumnarrative* as a descriptor for narratives that
wrap metaphorically around the entire thinking/writing/delaying process. I find the word *circumnarrative* in only one other place: an art installation in Hobart, Tasmania. That work, with its 'parallel lines of 10cm
high plywood [that] curve around the timber floor forming the likeness
of a walled road or some other passageway,' is a 'structure which evolves
as you walk around it and consider the shape of the whole and the journey within' and as offering 'a unique understanding of Tasmanian [sic]
as "an *other* place" ' (Hawthorne, 2007; my italics).

1. Thinking about Facts

1 Denzin's use of the plural 'voices' here is curious. I wonder whether it is simply a typographical error unnoticed by both author and editor. Whether or not, I read it as an (obviously inadvertent) anticipation of the turn I take in this study, to psychoanalytic discourse, with its insistence on the self as multipartite, and the implicit understanding of such multiplicity as perhaps the only consistent feature in the identities of all authors, all ethnographers – and indeed, everyone else.

2 In principle, given this definition, what ought to distinguish autoethnography from any other writing about the self (*auto-graphy*) is the connections it makes between that self (those selves? those voices? – see note 1, supra) and a culture or institution. But as I argue later, following Winnicott (1990) among others, it is difficult to conceive of either a self-without-culture or a culture-without-self: inside and outside are necessary to each other.

3 I include in the category *text* not just 'any instance of written and spoken language that has coherence and coded meanings' as well as the 'visual, audiovisual [and] gestural' (A. Luke, 1996, p. 13), but also relational texts such as classroom structures and institutional hierarchies within education as a whole.

4 As discussed in Chapter 2 it can also help connect the *auto* to the *ethno* more explicitly.

2. Thinking about Stories

1 See also Lakoff (1975), Spender (1980), Hollway (1984) and Tannen (1991).

2 Here I also consider Talbot's consideration of the 'intertextuality of victimhood and choice' (2005, p. 168) that connects, in ways she finds tenuous at best, discourses of women as victims on one hand and as 'good' citizens on the other. The advertising materials from which she quotes invoke phrasing straight from feminist discourse – the 'right to choose' and 'violence against women' (pp. 173–4). Thus they appear on the surface to correspond with liberal and even radical feminist aims of women resisting victimhood. But that phrasing is being used to support a weapons-rights project grounded in right-wing doctrines which typically oppose the very reproductive rights to which those phrases customarily attach. There is something of a parallel between this kind of intertextuality and my own approach to this story of dropping English.

3 Attribution of the phrase 'the personal is political' is not definitively settled. See, for example, comments on the Academic Women's Studies Listserve (among others, Korenman, 1998).

4 The one-paragraph story, 'On exactitude in science' (in Spanish 'Del rigor en la ciencia'), was developed as a 'quotation' from a fictitious seventeenth-century author, one 'Suarez Miranda.' It ends: 'In the Deserts of the West, still today, there are Tattered Ruins of that Map, inhabited by Animals and Beggars; in all the Land there is no other Relic of the Disciplines of Geography' (Borges & Casares, 1999, p. 325).

5 Indeed, given that in a Derridean formulation, which refutes the phenomenological view of language as deriving from preconceptual experience and posits that language and history occur in the gap created by the deferral of experience – Derrida's *différance* (Pinar et al., 2000, p. 49) – 'reading must not be content with doubling the text [and] . . . cannot legitimately transgress the text toward something other than it, toward a referent . . . or toward a signified outside the text . . .' (Derrida, 1976, p. 158), we might even propose that all *reality* is a matter of remembering.

6 This layering of event, story, telling, and re-telling of a story is similar to my daughter's 'memory' of an event in her early childhood which is in fact a memory of the *story* our family reminds her of, at every birthday, about the-time-she-stuck-a-bean-in-her-nose. I refer to Freud's (1899, p. 322) discussion on this point in the next chapter. While in other contexts this might well be a concern (if I were a witness in a legal proceeding, for example), as noted earlier in this chapter and following Ellis (1993), it matters less in the present instance where my aim is to use my recollections of the events as collecting places for thinking about the questions they raise about silence and difficulty rather than their specific details.

7 In mathematics, the terms 'recursion' and 'recursive' refer to a class of objects defined in terms of previously defined object in the same class. Similarly, in the linguistic sub-discipline of transformational grammar a recursive rule is one that can be reapplied repeatedly to its own output: the recursive power of a grammar is its ability to generate an infinity of sentences. (OED online, s.v. 'recursive'). I am considering recursion here as the perpetual interaction (with consequences) of phenomena on one another: an event is understood in terms of one's knowledge, theory, socialization, and so on – and the revised event then informs the knowledge, theory, etc. These keep working back and forth together such that each act or moment of revision, and each version of the event, embodies all the previous revisions and versions. I visualize this as two entities: the self

and the world (the *me* and the *not-me*) each simultaneously revolving and moving in a vertical direction, up and around in a kind of spiral, and also overlapping with each other at intervals, each changed by those moments of connection/confrontation but at the same time retaining something of its former condition. This is an imperfect metaphor, both because the contact is continual rather than intermittent and, following from this, because the boundaries between self and world are less definite than the image might suggest, but it does give an idea of the interweaving of the two.

8 In that first topography a third level, the *pre*-conscious, is located between consciousness and the unconscious. In a given moment most of what we call conscious knowledge, memory, affect, and so on is in fact 'psychically *un*conscious' – temporarily latent – since the conscious mind cannot hold all its contents simultaneously. What we are *not* conscious of in a particular moment has retreated into the preconscious: sitting at my desk I am not conscious of the fact that a cake is baking in the oven downstairs, though I put it there myself 30 minutes ago; it is only when I smell it burning that I am again aware of its existence.

9 Freud's 'second topography' – dating from 1923 – divides the mind somewhat differently than does the first, into *id, ego,* and *superego.* While a full elaboration of these concepts is beyond my task here, I note that though it is the id that acts as the primary collecting place for repressed instincts, psychoanalysis situates unconscious elements in all three regions of the psyche. Repressed content located in the id 'can communicate with the ego through the id' (Freud, 1923, p. 24), but is no longer *known* in the sense of being actually, or even potentially, conscious.

10 I am I, but I am also not I. But what does it mean to analyse one's own story from long ago? The subject is not quite the object – because the reader and the one experiencing the events (i.e., the one being read about) are not the same, and neither is the writer of the story the same as the one who experienced those events.

11 The mystic writing-pad Freud describes is completely erasable: no trace remains of what was written on the celluloid once it is lifted. But in fact, this is rarely the case. For instance, if one presses with a pen on the top sheet of a pad of paper, the sheet below retains traces of the pressure. Similarly, in a twenty-first-century conception, 'traces' of deleted material or typographical errors remain on computer hard drives.

12 The interpretation is ongoing, in psychoanalysis anyway. And of course it can be ongoing here. Things can always be fleshed out more fully – that there is always more to the story is a part of every story.

3. Field Notes, Felt-notes, Felt and Noted

1 For similar articulations see also Fine (1987, 1988); Garrison (1997); Bartlett (1998); Petress (2001); Hull (2002); Granger (2004).

2 Having become somewhat accustomed to reading psychoanalytically, I have trouble with this statement immediately on typing it. Of course, I can speak only for myself – I do not really know what my peers did or did not imagine at the time. But even in relation to my own thinking, I confess to a bit of scepticism, particularly on noticing the emphatic tone in the denial that reads almost like a Freudian *negation* (about which I have more to say later) as to whether the thought of same-sex activity was utterly impossible. At this point, suffice to say, I do not remember thinking it.

3 As I write this I notice that I am referring to myself in first person, which I did not do in the second version of the dropping-English story. This is a significant point, suggesting from both psychoanalytic and discourse analysis perspectives the beginning of self-acknowledgment: with this syntactic shift the story begins to be *my* story.

4 Keeping in mind, of course, that these events took place years before the advent of now-common formalized policies on either sexual harassment specifically or more general personal contact between teachers and students, I acknowledge, following McWilliam (1996), the complex dynamics of sexual power and relations, and make no judgment here about propriety or appropriateness.

5 Of course the details of this narrative have been intentionally placed. Recalling Brodkey's (1996) self-observation, which appears as an epigraph to Chapter 2 – 'This memory of myself is carefully staged' – I acknowledge that there was a goal in constructing the narrative as I have: I want the reader to see the gap between my hidden, but real, interest in literature and my refusal of it, and to recognize that my dropping English was no accident, no fulfilment of a prophecy, but something more like its opposite.

6 See Pitt (1998) for a discussion of the use of past tense in journal writing, as implicative of 'tensions just below the surface' that complicate what seem to be transparent relations with particular kinds of knowledge.

7 In Kaplan's memoir, *French Lessons*, she connects her obsession with learning French to the loss of her father and the subsequent need for the 'quiet mastery of a subject' (1993, p. 203). This beautifully ambiguous phrase echoes here, as I note the far less graceful ambiguity of *my* use of 'subject' – another unintentional but telling double-entendre.

8 *Wunsch* in the original German is translated in Spanish as *deseo* and in French as *désir*. I follow Laplanche & Pontalis (1973) and use 'desire' to refer to an unconscious wish.

9 In addition to the shift into first-person narration in the third (and fullest) version of the narrative, I note that in *discussing* versions 1 and 2 I have also referred to 'the student' and 'she' rather than to 'I' and 'me,' which I seem to have reserved (quite unwittingly) for version 3: more evidence that this third version is most authentically 'mine.' That is, even though I am the creator of all three, it seems that only with version 3 do I feel able to articulate explicitly that I am speaking both as and about myself.

10 At the initial time of writing, I was a doctoral candidate.

11 Again, at the original time of writing, the dissertation defence.

12 Bay-Cheng's reading of Freud is, I suggest, a blunted one that simplifies somewhat his views on the power of sexuality. Nevertheless, her point that society (and in particular education) has picked up and run with a 'drive reduction model' (2003, p. 62) that frames adolescence as an explosive period does seem to be reflected in the models of school-based sexuality education her paper examines.

13 For a UK perspective, see Gammage's finding of, among other things, a 'backlash against any kind of sex education at all . . . [alongside decisions to] include AIDS education' (1988, p. 189).

14 And even when I do 'get to the moment' I don't quite get there – my discussion of my own desires is filtered through Freud's (and others') discussion of desire writ large. But perhaps that is the academic imperative.

4. Curiosity Kills the Silence

1 An earlier and shorter version of this chapter was published in February 2007, in the Taylor & Francis journal *Sex Education: Sexuality, Society and Learning* 7 (1), under the title, 'On (not) representing sex in preschool and kindergarten: a psychoanalytic reflection on orders and hints.'

2 Volbert cites various studies that, interestingly, have demonstrated that girls have more genital knowledge than boys, but that their knowledge is not always about themselves. For example, Bem (1989) found that 'female subjects had as much genital knowledge at age 3 as males had by age 5' (cited in Volbert, 2000, p. 7). And Fraley, Nelson, Wolf, and Lozoff (1991) found that girls between one and four years of age were 'less likely than boys to receive a label for their own genitalia [from] their mothers, [but] more likely than boys to receive a term for the genitalia of the opposite sex.' It would be interesting to speculate on possible reasons for this

apparent discrepancy: might there be a marked/unmarked distinction at work – i.e., 'Your brother has a penis, and you don't' – that contradicts the more usual male-as-unmarked model? Indeed, the fact of the erasure of the male but not the female genital region in Carle's book suggests something similar: the penis as *something* (to be erased) and the female genitalia as *nothing*.

3 The category may be labile, but to use it is to risk reification. 'The child' has often been conceptualized as an abstraction or generalized representation. That this is not my intention should become clearer in my discussion of how individuals make relations with constructions of 'the child' and 'the body.' Still, where practicable, I try to refer to 'children' rather than 'the child'; 'teachers' rather than 'the teacher,' and 'bodies' rather than 'the body.'

4 A variation on this approach is described in Chapter 7.

5 The other copy of the book, with the effaced penis? I whisked that away before she saw it. This incident is discussed further in Chapter 7. Incidentally, some six years after it took place, at least three school districts in the U.S. (two in Texas, one in Washington) banned *Draw Me a Star*. See University of California at Los Angeles [UCLA] (2006), Micek (2007); and Mountains & Plains Booksellers (n/d).

6 In the introduction to her *Once Upon a Potty* toilet-training children's books, by now exploded into an entire line of children's merchandise including videotapes, DVDs, and dolls, Frankel (1979) remarks that although 'potty talk has long been considered taboo in conversation – even between parent and child . . . this attitude is changing.' Curiously, however, the books seem to defer to this taboo, since (in the boy's version) little Joshua has 'a pee-pee for making Wee-Wee . . . [and] a bottom for sitting [with] a little hole for making Poo-Poo.' It seems, then, that there is difficulty in talking not only about sexuality and reproduction, but also about basic eliminative processes – though it is not clear whether it is in parents or the publisher (or the publisher's perception of parents) that the reluctance lies. In any event, millions of these little books have been sold.

5. Another Nice Mess

1 A note on terminology: While 'new technologies' and 'information and communication technology' (ICT) can be used to refer to computers, and also to streaming video and electronic learning, my main focus is on the technology of the computer. This is because, as a new technology ubiquitous in Western society as a whole and the first to be encountered

by learners and teachers in and out of schools, it serves as both a pivotal archetype and the focus of much research and theoretical literature. And so, I use ICT or *technology* or *the computer* interchangeably, though when I am speaking of a particular machine, I say so. The same is true for *teachers* and *the teacher* – individual experiences with ICT vary widely as individuals themselves, and my intent in using these words and phrases is not to over-categorize them.

2 Innovative Models was sponsored by the Ontario Knowledge Network for Learning (OKNL), a 'provincial initiative to improve the use of information and communication technologies in the Ontario education system[, whose] purpose is to harness technology to . . . improve student achievement; enhance teaching; involve parents more in their children's education; and give students the educational opportunities they need to succeed in the twenty-first century economy' (TDSB, n/d).

3 See, among others, Dwyer, Ringstaff, and Sandholtz (1991); Johnson, Schwab, and Foa (1999); Gardner (1999); Lotherington et al. (2001); Brown (2004).

4 See Pinar et al. (2000).

5 Traditionally, teachers are female; administrators male. While of late more women are becoming administrators, divisions persist: in Ontario for example, teachers, but not principals, are union members.

6 Oxford English Dictionary, 2nd edition. s.v. 'translation.'

7 Elsewhere (Granger, 2003) I suggest, taking a hint from Phillips, that perhaps *work* is only *workable* if it gives pleasure, and that the teachers such as those in the Innovative Models project may have found ways, through the use of 'play' as a metaphor for their engagements with computers, to find or make pleasure for themselves.

8 It may not be just the teacher's imagination; young children frequently express love for their teachers. My point here is that, actual affection notwithstanding, the teacher's particular love for her students may be considered psychoanalytically as rooted in an idealization.

9 Here affection means not only positive regard but any and all feelings that originate in and relate to relationships outside the psychoanalytic dyad onto which they are transferred.

10 Student teachers can cause similar worries, as I discuss in Part 3.

6. Neither Here Nor There

1 York University's Faculty of Education, where I completed my teaching degree, uses the term *teacher candidate* most frequently, though *preservice*

teacher is also sometimes used. But I prefer *student teacher,* which better captures the contradiction and ambiguity of the category, and the (at least) dual position of the individual living it. Similarly, institutions have various terms for the practising teacher in whose classroom the student teacher works during the practicum portion of the program. York's current custom is to use 'mentor teacher,' but I have settled on 'host teacher,' which was in use during my time in the program.

2 As it happens, I don't actually get to it until the next chapter. It seems I was right. The chapter I thought I was beginning, when I wrote that I expected it to be difficult to write, was indeed difficult – so much so that for a time I could not write it at all. Eventually I did, but I had to write this one first. That difficult, even 'forbidden' chapter follows this one. Precisely how that happened – along with the reasons for keeping intact my prediction about things taking time – is part of what I discuss there.

3 Additionally, it seems that the valuing of practice over theory holds not just among student teachers. An Ontario Institute for Studies in Education survey finds that 59 per cent of the general public and parents and 48 per cent of teachers believe more preservice practice-teaching would improve education, but that while 49 and 52 per cent of the public and parents respectively think longer preservice programs as a whole would be beneficial, only 19 per cent of teachers agree (Livingstone, Hart, & Davie, 2001, p. 25).

4 Relatedly, teaching-as-women's-work has been adjudged as being of lesser quality and importance than that performed by men: Noddings (1992) and Gilligan (1996) have both recognized the importance of a morality founded on the notion of care, as one of 'the very traits that traditionally have defined the "goodness" of women, their care for and sensitivity to the needs of others, [but that have nonetheless marked] them as deficient in moral development . . . [as] derived from the study of men's lives,' particularly among educators (Gilligan, 1996, p. 18). But in a curious twist, if the notion of a de facto 'moral deficiency' has been attributed to women teachers, it has also been exploited as a pseudo-rationalization for how those men who have chosen for themselves the 'lesser' profession of teaching, especially at the primary level, have often been regarded – namely with discomfort, anxiety, and even the suspicion that sexual predation may be at the root of a career choice deemed so 'unnatural' for them (Tobin, 1997). Naturalized notions of teaching, what it is, how it is done, who does it, and who ought properly to do it – what Britzman calls 'well-worn and commonsensical images of the teacher's work' that presume to know 'what a teacher is and does' (1991, p. 3) – evolve and persist through the almost

universal experience of being a pupil. Put a little differently, the women teachers Miller calls 'figures of ... impossible familiarity' (1996, p. xii) are also familiar because they are *possible;* male teachers are in some sense im-*possible* because they are in a sense im*plausible.*

5 In the program Duquette examined, students spent 'approximately two-thirds of their time in the schools and the remaining portion on course work' (1997, p. 264).

6 Practice (in the form of the practicum teaching experience) can certainly make trouble of its own, as the following chapter shows.

7 By 'official theory' I mean the theory/ies that is or are introduced and discussed within teacher education courses – especially as contrasted with the 'unofficial' theories (which may be composed, as discussed, largely out of supposition, opinion, even stereotype) that many student teachers bring to the encounter.

8 Circulating on the internet and in the online 'jokes' conference in York University's Faculty of Education is a set of tongue-in-cheek rules for a game that purports to help teachers 'stay awake during inservices.' The player creates a chart of 25 blocks, writing in each a current educational catch-phrase such as *result-driven assessment* or *core competencies* or *action plan* or *No Child Left Behind* (it is an American joke: in Ontario we could add 'rubrics' or 'accounting formula' or 'accountability'). Players then mark each box when its phrase is uttered during a staff meeting or inservice. When a player marks five boxes in a row, s/he stands up and shouts, 'Bullshit!' The game is called 'Bullshit Bingo.' I do not know who devised it, but I think it speaks, in a Freudian sense as a 'hostile joke (serving the purpose of aggressiveness, satire, or defence)' (Freud, 1905b, p. 97), to the anger at jargon that Simon addresses. See Pinkman (n/d).

9 Reality-testing is the psychical process that lets us distinguish 'stimuli originating in the outside world from internal ones' and prevents confusion between the truly perceived and the merely imagined (Laplanche & Pontalis, 1973, p. 382). In mourning it is what allows (or compels) the bereaved to 'modify his personal world, his projects and his wishes in accordance with [his] real loss' (p. 385).

10 In translation the last portion of this passage is ambiguous: 'he knows whom he has lost but not what he has lost in him.' Does he 'fail' to understand what (he himself) has lost in (losing) the object – or what he has lost *in himself* along with losing the object? Berman (2007) confirms that the German original 'unambiguously relates the loss to the lost object, not to the subject.'

11 'Invest' is rooted in the Latin preposition *in* and the verb *vestire:* to dress or clothe (OED, s.v. 'invest').

12 For Klein this defence comes earlier than repression and is therefore contrasted with it, though their roles are similar (Klein, 1946, p. 7).

13 *Good* and *bad* here are judgments made in fantasy (Laplanche & Pontalis,
1973, p. 188): objects – or more accurately the 'imago' or 'phantastically
distorted picture of the real objects on which they are based' (Klein, 1935,
p. 282, cited in Laplanche & Pontalis, 1973, p. 188) – are felt as good (or
bad) not because of their inherent qualities but because they are perceived
by the individual as satisfying (or frustrating) and have therefore been
introjected (or ejected).

7. Ghosts That Haunt Us

1   As discussed in Chapter 5, the moment or process of individuation in
Lacanian pychoanalysis is not quite isomorphic, temporally or in terms
of actual dynamics, with those set out by the Kleinians or the Freudians,
but the three branches resonate with one another in that they each include
such a moment.

2 The Droste effect, describing a recursive visual image, is named after a
Dutch brand of cocoa, whose tins picture a woman carrying a tray on
which is a tin of the same cocoa, with the same picture of a woman carrying
a tray on which is . . . and so on, theoretically infinitely (although of course
the resolution of the picture does not permit that).

3 I suppose this section too functions as a delaying tactic, for I have not yet
arrived at the details I have promised (to myself and the reader). The difference is that I have some awareness of this function, which may, if I am a
little bit economical with words, mean that I come to those details in fairly
short order.

4 I am frequently pleased by little coincidences of language or technology.
It is my habit when writing to use acronyms, for efficiency's sake, to stand
for concepts or phrases that come up frequently. Here, I have abbreviated
'split-off intellect' to *SOI*: the computer easily allows the change to the full
form at the editing stage. But *soi* in French means 'self' – and I concoct an
image of my own movement, from SOI to *soi*, from the split-off intellect to
a 'true self' (Winnicott, 1990). (That I have long used *PA* as an abbreviation
for *psychoanalysis* is an observation better left for another discussion.)

5 Reading what I have just typed, I see that again there is something to say
before I get to the story proper. I wonder if I will ever get there. Still, it
has taken years: what's another page or two? I think of these small stuck
moments as involving splits (this one between telling the story and *coming to tell* the story) that read as another self-similarity of the whole and
its parts. My writing process keeps subdividing into smaller parts that

maintain the structure of the whole, in a version (albeit less poetic) of Catalan artist Ramon Dachs's 'fractal writing' (2007): 'conceived as echo, reflection and shadow, splitting and unfolding . . . [through which] one specific realisation of writing takes physical form and comes into being.'

6　Another textual artefact, of which I was unaware at this point in the writing process, arrives on the scene a little later.

7　My purpose here is not to criticize or otherwise evaluate Ms K's pedagogy, just to describe it to the extent necessary to give a flavour of life in her classroom.

8　Carle's books offer verse and/or prose that in general reinforce early literacy and other skills through repetition and the use of familiar vocabulary. For example, *The Hungry Caterpillar* (1969), which teaches the days of the week and counting, is constructed with holes in the pages. The reader follows the caterpillar as grows into a butterfly, eating its way through the days of the week. *The Mixed-Up Chameleon* (1984) teaches colours and enumerates salient features of animals (a turtle's shell, an elephant's strength). *From Head to Toe* (1997) involves the child in naming body parts and making simple movements. Carle illustrates his books using tissue-paper collages.

9　*Draw Me a Star* (1992), in which an unseen 'artist' is asked to draw first a star, then a sun, then a tree, and so on until a whole universe is drawn. The fourth request, 'Draw me a woman and a man,' is the one that caused all the trouble. (See also Chapter 4, supra.)

10　The 'cubicle' is how I referred to the cardboard 'screen' described in anecdote no. 2.

11　Blackline masters are worksheets available for virtually all subjects that teachers photocopy for pupil use.

12　In fact, by the second half of the year almost all Grade 2 pupils are not six, but seven, years old.

13　That self-imposed silence was both pedagogical and affective. I realize now, in the clearer light of 'afterwards,' that my hiatus from personal journal writing was closely connected with my practicum experience. I do wish I had diaries from those months. At least I think that is what I wish. I am suspicious, though, since I am not at all sure that if I had them I would want to read them.

14　Curiously, as I wrote that sentence I suddenly recalled a moment (one of many) when I did take that pragmatic approach. Dismissing the class for recess one morning, rather than use one of my own strategies to quiet them I chose Ms K's version of rhythmic hand-clapping. Her suggestion on seeing this was that I 'try to find a more original way of getting their attention.'

15 The hints the narratives offer are not the first that resonate with transferential elements in my remembering of these events. As discussed earlier, the interview prompts in Pitt and Britzman (2003) that seemed most relevant were those related to abandonment, isolation, and/or conflict – a resonance that seems much less surprising now.

16 And when I did speak up, asserting that I accepted responsibility for my choice of books, 'she wasn't hearing it. It was venomous. Spit was coming out of her mouth.' It is beyond my scope here to deal at length with the kinds of symbolism suggested by this passage and, relatedly, by my earlier rendition of Ms K calling me to her desk in a hissing voice: 'Missssssssss Granger . . . ' But in a paper on 'Snakes and us,' psychoanalyst Abse (2004, p. 210) observes that in addition to their more typical interpretation as phalli, snakes have also served as female symbols, often of the malevolent mother.

References

Abse, D. W. (2004). Snakes and us. In S. Akhtar & V. Volkan (Eds.), *Mental zoo: Animals in the human mind and its pathology* (pp. 201–36). Madison, CT: International Universities Press.

Acker, S. (1989a). Introduction. In S. Acker (Ed.), *Teachers, gender and careers* (pp. 1–3). Barcombe, UK: Falmer Press.

Acker, S. (1989b). Rethinking teachers' careers. In S. Acker (Ed.), *Teachers, gender and careers* (pp. 7–20). Barcombe, UK: Falmer Press.

Adler, P. A., & Adler, P. (1999). The ethnographers' ball (revisited): Reflections on ethnography at the turn of the century. *Journal of Contemporary Ethnography, 28*, 442–50.

Agar, M. H. (1986). *Speaking of ethnography.* Beverly Hills: Sage.

Alberta Education (1995). *Quality teaching: Quality education for Alberta students.* Edmonton, AB: Alberta Government.

Allen, L. (2004). Beyond the birds and the bees: Constituting a discourse of erotics in sexuality education. *Gender and Education, 16*(2), 151–67.

Althusser, L., & Balibar, É. (1972). *Reading 'Capital'* (B. Brewster, Trans.). London: New Left Books.

Appel, S. (1996). *Positioning subjects: Psychoanalysis and critical educational studies.* Westport, CT; London: Bergin and Garvey.

Apple, M. W. (1985). *Education and power.* Boston: Ark Paperbacks.

Apple, M. W. (1986). *Teachers and texts: A political economy of class and gender relations in education.* New York: Routledge & Kegan Paul.

Apple, M. W. (1988). Teaching and technology: The hidden effects of computers on teachers and students. In L. E. Beyer & M. W. Apple (Eds.), *The curriculum: Problems, politics, and possibilities* (pp. 289–311). Albany, NY: State University of New York Press.

Apple, M. W. (1996). *Cultural politics and education*. New York, London: Teachers College Press.

Apple, M. W. (2010). The measure of success: Education, markets, and an audit culture. In T. Monahan & R. D. Torres (Eds.), *Schools under surveillance: Cultures of control in public education* (pp. 175–93). New Brunswick, NJ: Rutgers University Press.

Apple, M. W., & Jungk, S. (1998). 'You don't have to be a teacher to teach this unit': Teaching, technology, and control in the classroom. In H. Bromley & M. W. Apple (Eds.), *Education/technology/power: Educational computing as a social practice* (pp. 133–54). Albany: State University of New York Press.

Arendt, H. (1958). *The human condition*. Chicago: University of Chicago Press.

Ariès, P. (1962). *Centuries of childhood: A social history of family life* (R. Baldick, Trans.). New York: Knopf.

Aronowitz, S., & Giroux, H. (1993). *Education still under siege*. Toronto: Ontario Institute for Studies in Education Press.

Ashton, P. T. (1996). Improving the preparation of teachers. *Educational Researcher, 25*(9), 21–2, 35.

Assude, T., Buteau, B., & Forgasz, H. (2010). Factors influencing implementation of technology-rich mathematics curriculum and pratices. In C. Hoyles & J-B. Lagrange (Eds.), *Mathematics education and technology – Rethinking the terrain: The 17th ICMI study* (pp. 405–19). New York: Springer.

Austin, J. L. (1962). *How to do things with words*. New York: Oxford University Press.

Azarius (2007). Rose of Jericho. Retrieved April 23, 2007, from http://azarius.net/productinfo.php?productmain=295&tabID=1&category=5

Bailey, C. (1997). A place from which to speak: Stories of memory, crisis, and struggle from the preschool classroom. In J. Jipson & N. Paley (Eds.), *Daredevil research: Re-creating analytic practice* (pp. 135–60). New York: Peter Lang.

Baldwin, C., & Bauer, K. E. (1994). Teaching sexuality: Schools supporting families as primary sex educators. *Journal of Humanistic Education and Development, 32*(4), 162–71.

Ball, D. L. (1988). Unlearning to teach mathematics (Issue Paper #88-1). East Lansing, MI: National Center for Research on Teacher Education. Cited in D. Holt-Reynolds (1992), Personal history-based beliefs as relevant prior knowledge in course work. *American Educational Research Journal, 29*(2), 325–49.

Banks, S. P., & Banks, A. (2000). Reading 'The critical life': Autoethnography as pedagogy. *Communication Education, 49*(3), 233–8.

Barrell, B. (Ed.). (2001). *Technology, teaching and learning: Issues in the integration of technology*. Calgary: Detselig.

Bartlett, A. (1998). A passionate subject: Representations of desire in feminist pedagogy. *Gender and Education, 10*(1), 85–92.

Bauer, J., & Kenton, J. (2005). Toward technology integration in the schools: Why it isn't happening. *Journal of Technology and Teacher Education, 13*(4), 519–46.

Bay-Cheng, L. Y. (2003). The trouble of teen sex: The construction of adolescent sexuality through school-based sexuality education. *Sex Education: Sexuality, Society and Learning, 3*(1), 61–74.

Beckett, S. A. (1959). The unnamable. In *Molloy, Malone dies and The unnamable: Three novels* (pp. 293–418). New York: Grove Press.

Behar, R. (1996). *The vulnerable observer: Anthropology that breaks your heart.* Boston: Beacon Press.

Behar, R. (1999). Ethnography: Cherishing our second-fiddle genre. *Journal of Contemporary Ethnography, 28*(5), 472–84.

Bem, S. L. (1989). Genital knowledge and gender constancy in preschool children. *Child Development 60,* 649–62. Cited in R. Volbert (2000), Sexual knowledge of preschool children. *Journal of Psychology and Human Sexuality, 12* (1/2), 5–26.

Benjamin, A. (1992). The unconscious: Structuring as a translation. In J. Fletcher & M. Stanton (Eds.), *Jean Laplanche: Seduction, translation and the drives, a dossier* (pp. 137–57). London: Institute of Contemporary Arts.

Benjamin, W. (1932). A Berlin chronicle (E. Jephcott & K. Shorter, Trans.). In *One way street and other writings* (1979) (pp. 293–346). London: New Left Books.

Benson, P. (2000). Autonomy as a learners' and teachers' right, in B. Sinclair, I. McGrath, & T. Lamb (Eds.), *Learner autonomy, teacher autonomy: Future directions* (pp. 111–17). London: Longman. Cited in R.C. Smith (2001), Teacher education for teacher-learner autonomy, in *Proceedings of 'Autonomy in language teacher education' II (The 9th IALS Symposium for Language Teacher Educators)* (H. Trappes-Lomax, Ed.). Edinburgh: University of Edinburgh. [CD-ROM.] Retrieved April 5, 2007, from http://www.warwick.ac.uk/~elsdr/Teacher_autonomy.pdf

Berman, E. (2007). Review of *This art of psychoanalysis: Dreaming undreamt dreams and interrupted cries. International Journal of Psychoanalysis, 88*(1). Retrieved March 3, 2007, from http://www.ijpa.org/bookreview2001.htm#2001

Bettelheim, B. (1969). Psychoanalysis and education. *The School Review, 77*(2), 73–86.

Bevir, M. (1999). Foucault and critique: Deploying agency against autonomy. *Political Theory, 27*(1), 65–84.

Bhabha, H. (1994). *The location of culture.* London: Routledge.

Bloom, L. (1998). *Under the sign of hope: Feminist methodology and narrative interpretation.* Albany: State University of New York Press.

Bochner, A. P. (1997). It's about time: Narrative and the divided self. *Qualitative Inquiry, 3*(4), 418–38.

Bochner, A. P., & Ellis, C. S. (1999). Which way to turn? *Journal of Contemporary Ethnography, 28*(5), 485–99.

Bolin, F. S. (1990). Helping student teachers think about teaching: Another look at Lou. *Journal of Teacher Education, 41*(1), 10–19.

Book, C. L., Byers, J., & Freeman, D. J. (1983). Student expectations and teacher education traditions with which we can and cannot live. *Journal of Teacher Education, 34*(1), 9–13.

Borges, J. L., & Casares, A. B. (1999). On exactitude in science [orig. pub. 1967] (A. Hurley, Trans.). In J. L. Borges (Ed.), *Collected fictions* (p. 325). New York: Penguin.

Bosacki, S. L. (2005). *The culture of classroom silence.* New York: Peter Lang.

Bossert, P. J. (1996). Understanding the technologies of our learning environments. *NASSP* [National Association of Secondary School Principals] *Bulletin, 80*(582), 11–20.

Bourdieu, P. (1982) *Ce que parler veut dire: L'économie des échanges linguistiques.* Paris: Fayard. Cited in A. Esterhammer & D. Robinson (2005), Speech acts, in M. Groden, M. Kreiswirth, & I. Szeman (Eds.), *The Johns Hopkins guide to literary theory and criticism* (2nd ed.). Baltimore: Johns Hopkins University Press. Retrieved June 12, 2007, from http://litguide.press.jhu.edu.ezproxy.library.yorku.ca/cgi-in/view.cgi?section_id=1815

Bourdieu, P., & Passeron, J.-C. (1990). *Reproduction in education, society, and culture* (2nd ed.) (R. Nice, Trans.). London: Sage.

Bowers, C. A. (1988). Teaching a nineteenth-century mode of thinking through a twentieth-century machine. *Educational Theory, 38*(1), 41–6.

Bredekamp, S. (1987). *Developmentally appropriate practice in early childhood programs serving children from birth through age 8.* Washington, DC: National Association for the Education of Young Children.

Bredekamp, S., & Copple, C. (Eds.). (1997). *Developmentally appropriate practice in early childhood programs* (revised ed.). Washington DC: National Association for the Education of Young Children.

Breuer, J., & Freud, S. (1974). *The Pelican Freud library, Volume 3: Studies on hysteria* [orig. pub. 1895] (A. Richards, Ed.; J. Strachey & A. Strachey, Trans.). Harmondsworth, UK: Penguin.

Britzman, D. P. (1985). Reality and ritual: An ethnographic study of student teachers. Doctoral dissertation, University of Massachusetts, Amherst. Cited in D. P. Britzman (1986), Cultural myths in the making of a teacher: Biography and social structure in teacher education. *Harvard Educational Review, 56*(4), 442–56.

Britzman, D. P. (1986). Cultural myths in the making of a teacher: Biography and social structure in teacher education. *Harvard Educational Review, 56*(4), 442–56.

Britzman, D. P. (1991). *Practice makes practice: A critical study of learning to teach.* Albany, NY: State University of New York Press.

Britzman, D. P. (1998). *Lost subjects, contested objects: Toward a psychoanalytic inquiry of learning.* Albany: State University of New York Press.

Britzman, D. P. (2003). *After-education: Anna Freud, Melanie Klein, and psychoanalytic histories of learning.* Albany: State University of New York Press.

Britzman, D. P., & Pitt, A. J. (1996). Pedagogy and transference: Casting the past of learning into the presence of teaching. *Theory into Practice, 35*(2), 117–23.

Brodkey, L. (1987). *Academic writing as social practice.* Philadelphia: Temple University Press.

Brodkey, L. (1996). *Writing permitted in designated areas only.* Minneapolis: University of Minnesota Press.

Bromley, H. (1998). Data-driven democracy? Social assessment of educational computing. In H. Bromley & M. W. Apple (Eds.), *Education/technology/ power: Educational computing as a social practice* (pp. 1–25). Albany: State University of New York Press.

Brooks, J. L., Groening, M., Long, T., & Simon, S. (Producers). (Nov. 17, 2002). Bart vs. Lisa vs. the third grade [*The Simpsons,* episode 294]. Los Angeles: Fox Broadcasting.

Brown, E. L. (2004). Overcoming the challenges of stand-alone multicultural courses: The possibilities of technology integration. *Journal of Technology and Teacher Education. 12*(4), 535–59.

Bryson, M., & de Castell, S. (1998). New technologies and the cultural ecology of primary schooling: Imagining teachers as Luddites in/deed. *Educational Policy, 12*(5), 542–67.

Bullough, R. V. Jr., & Gitlin, A. D. (1994). Challenging teacher education as training: Four propositions. *Journal of Education for Teaching, 20*(1), 67–81.

Burbules, N. C., & Callister, T. A., Jr. (2000). *Watch IT: The risks and promises of information technologies for education.* Boulder, CO: Westview.

Burkitt, I. (1991). *Social selves: Theories of the social formation of personality.* London: Sage.

Buston, K., Wight, D., & Scott, S. (2001). Difficulty and diversity: The context and practice of sex education. *British Journal of the Sociology of Education 22,* 353–68.

Butler, J. P. (1990). *Gender trouble: Feminism and the subversion of identity.* New York: Routledge.

Cahill, B. J., & Theilheimer, R. (1999). 'Can Tommy and Sam get married?' Questions about gender, sexuality, and young children. *Young Children,* 54(1), 27–31.

Cannella, G. S. (1997). *Deconstructing early childhood education: Social justice and revolution.* New York: Peter Lang.

Carle, E. (1969). *The very hungry caterpillar.* New York: Penguin.

Carle, E. (1984). *The mixed-up chameleon.* New York: Penguin.

Carle, E. (1992). *Draw me a star.* New York: Penguin.

Carle, E. (1997). *From head to toe.* New York: Penguin.

Carter, K., & Doyle, W. (1996). Personal narrative and life history in learning to teach. In J. Sikula, T. J. Buttery, & E. Guyton (Eds.), *Handbook of research on teacher education* (2nd ed.) (pp. 120–42). New York: Macmillan.

Casey, E. S. (2000). *Remembering: A phenomenological study.* Bloomington, IN: Indiana University Press.

Casey, K., & Apple, M. W. (1989). Gender and the conditions of teachers' work: The development of understanding in America. In S. Acker (Ed.), *Teachers, gender and careers* (pp. 171–86). Barcombe, UK: Falmer Press.

Cavarero, A. (2000). *Relating narratives: Storytelling and selfhood.* London: Routledge.

Chambers, C. (1998). On taking my own (love) medicine: Memory work in writing and pedagogy. *Journal of Curriculum Theorizing,* 14(4), 14–20.

Church, K. (1995). *Forbidden narratives: Critical autobiography as social science.* London: Gordon & Breach.

Children in Distress/The Institute of Justice and Reconciliation (CINDI) (2001). *How AIDS affects me – Children speak.* Pietermaritzburg, South Africa. Cited in C. Mitchell, S. Walsh, & J. Larkin, J. (2004), Visualizing the politics of innocence in the age of AIDS. *Sex Education: Sexuality, Society and Learning,* 4(1), 35–47.

Cixous, H. (1983). The laugh of the Medusa (K. Cohen & P. Cohen, Trans.). In E. Abel & E. K. Abel (Eds.), *The signs reader* (pp. 279–99). Chicago: University of Chicago Press.

Clandinin, D. J., & Connelly, F. M. (1995). *Teachers' professional knowledge landscapes.* New York: Teachers College Press.

Clifford, J., & Marcus, G. E. (1986). *Writing culture: The poetics and politics of ethnography.* Berkeley: University of California Press.

Coffey, A. (1999). *The ethnographic self: Fieldwork and the representation of identity.* London: Sage.

Cohen, L. (1992). Anthem. On *The future* [Audio recording: compact disc]. Sony Music.

Cohler, B. J., & Cole, T. R. (1996). Studying older lives: Reciprocal acts of telling and listening. In J. E. Birren, G. M. Kenyon, J.-E. Ruth, J. J. F. Schroots, & T. Svensson (Eds.), *Aging and biography: Explorations in adult development* (pp. 61–76). New York: Springer.

Cohler, B. J., & Galatzer-Levy, R. M. (2006). Love in the classroom: Desire and transference in learning and teaching. In G. M. Boldt & P. M. Salvio (Eds.), *Love's return: Psychoanalytic essays on childhood, teaching, and learning* (pp. 243–65). New York: Routledge.

Cole, S. (1992). Anthropological lives: The reflexive tradition in a social science. In M. Kadar (Ed.), *Essays on life writing* (pp. 113–27). Toronto: University of Toronto Press.

Cooper, A. (1991). The search for Mary Bibb, black woman teacher in nineteenth-century Canada West. *Ontario History, 83*(1), 39–54.

Corbett, S. M. (1991). Children and sexuality. *Young Children, 46*(2), 71–7.

Coulthard, M. (1985). *An introduction to discourse analysis.* London: Longman.

Cozzarelli, L.A., & Silin, M. (1989). The effects of narcissistic transferences on the teaching-learning process. In K. Field, B. J. Cohler, & G. Wool (Eds.), *Learning and education: Psychoanalytic perspectives (Emotions and behavior Monograph 6)* (pp. 809–23). Madison, CT: International Universities Press.

Crain, W. (2000). *Theories of development: Concepts and applications* (4th ed.). Upper Saddle River, NJ: Prentice Hall.

Crawford, J., Kippax, S., Onyx, J., Gault, U., & Benton, P. (1990). Women theorizing their experiences of anger: A study using memory-work. *Australian Psychologist, 25*(3), 333–50.

Crawford, L. (1996). Personal ethnography. *Communication Monographs, 63*(2), 158–70.

Cuban, L. (1986). *Teachers and machines: The classroom use of technology since 1920.* New York: Teachers College Press.

Cuban, L. (1993a). *How teachers taught: Constancy and change in American classrooms, 1880–1990.* New York: Teachers College Press.

Cuban, L. (1993b). Computers meet classroom: classroom wins. *Teachers College Record, 95*(2), 185–210.

Cuban, L. (2001). *Oversold and underused: Computers in classrooms, 1980–2000.* Cambridge, MA: Harvard University Press.

Dachs, R. (2007). *Geometric writing, fractal writing: Institut Valencià d'Art Modern, Valencia, Spain.* Retrieved March 22, 2007, from http://www.ivam.es/asp/ficha.asp?idpag=1999&tipo=exposicion&id=125&idioma=i

Davies, S. L., Glaser, D., & Kossoff, R. (2000). Children's sexual play and behavior in pre-school settings: Staff's perceptions, reports, and responses. *Child Abuse and Neglect, 24,* 1329–43.

de Castell, S., Bryson, M., & Jenson, J. (2001). Object lessons: Critical visions of educational technology. In B. Barrell (Ed.), *Technology, teaching and learning: Issues in the integration of technology* (pp. 113–27). Calgary: Detselig.

de Graaf, H., & Rademakers, J. (2006). Sexual development of prepubertal children. *Journal of Psychology and Human Sexuality, 18*(1), 1–21.

de Saussure, F. (1983). *Course in general linguistics* [orig. pub. 1907]. (R. Harris, Trans. and Ed.). London: Duckworth.

Delany, S. R. (2005). *About writing: Seven essays, four letters, and five interviews.* Middletown, CT: Wesleyan University Press.

Delpit, L. D. (1988). The silenced dialogue: Power and pedagogy in educating other people's children. *Harvard Educational Review, 58,* 280–98.

Denzin, N. K. (1997). *Interpretive ethnography: Ethnographic practices for the 21st century.* Thousand Oaks, CA: Sage.

Derrida, J. (1976). *Of grammatology.* Baltimore, MD: Johns Hopkins University Press.

Derrida, J. (1978). Freud and the scene of writing. In A. Bass (Ed.), *Writing and difference* (pp. 246–91). Chicago: University of Chicago Press.

Derrida, J. (1979). Living on: Border lines (J. Hulbert, Trans.). In H. Bloom, P. de Man, J. Derrida, G. H. Hartman, & J. H. Miller, *Deconstruction and criticism* (pp. 75–175). New York: Continuum.

Derrida, J. (1982). Differance (A. Bass, Trans.). In *Margins of philosophy* (pp. 1–27). Chicago: University of Chicago Press.

Descombe, M. (1982). The hidden pedagogy and its implications for teacher training. *British Journal of Sociology of Education, 3,* 249–65. Cited in Britzman, D. P. (1986), Cultural myths in the making of a teacher: Biography and social structure in teacher education. *Harvard Educational Review, 56*(4), 442–56.

Dillon, G. L. (2005). Discourse theory. In M. Groden, M. Kreiswirth, & I. Szeman (Eds.), *The Johns Hopkins guide to literary theory and criticism* (2nd ed.). Baltimore: Johns Hopkins University Press. Retrieved June 12, 2007, from http://litguide.press.jhu.edu.ezproxy.library.yorku.ca/cgi-bin/search.cgi

Di Petta, T., Woloshyn, V., & Novak, J.M. (2008). Touching the interface of technology. In T. Di Petta (Ed.), *The Emperor's New Computer: ICT, teachers and teaching* (pp. 125–39). Rotterdam: Sense.

Disney, W. (Producer), & Stevenson, R. (Director). (1964). *Mary Poppins* [Motion picture]. Buena Vista Pictures.

Doll, W., Jr. (1993). *A postmodern perspective on curriculum.* New York: Teachers College Press.

Dreeben, R. (1970). *The nature of teaching: Schools and the work of teachers.* Glenview, IL: Scott, Foresman and Company. Cited in K. Casey & M. W. Apple (1989), Gender and the conditions of teachers' work: The development of understanding in America. In S. Acker (Ed.), *Teachers, gender and careers* (pp. 171–86). Barcombe, UK: Falmer Press.

Dreyfus, H. L., & Rabinow, P. (Eds.). (1983). *Michel Foucault: Beyond structuralism and hermeneutics* (2nd ed.) (L. Sawyer, Trans.). Chicago: University of Chicago Press.

Duquette, C. (1997). Conflicting perceptions of participants in field-based teacher education programs. *McGill Journal of Education, 32*(3), 263–72.

Dwyer, D. C., Ringstaff, C., & Sandholtz, J. H. (1991). Changes in teachers' beliefs and practices in technology-rich classrooms. *Educational Leadership, 48*(8), 45–52.

Education Quality and Accountability Office (EQAO) (2006). With learning in mind. Retrieved April 1, 2007 from http://www.eqao.com/categories/home. aspx?Lang=E

EducationWorld: (2004). Classroom management. Retrieved March 3, 2007 from http://www.education-world.com/a_curr/strategy/strategy 047.shtml

Egan, K. (1997). *The educated mind: How cognitive tools shape our understanding.* Chicago: University of Chicago Press.

Ehrensal, P. A. L. (2003). Constructing children in schools: Policies and the lessons they teach. *Journal of Curriculum Theorizing, 19*(2), 117–34.

Ehrlich, S. (2001). *Representing rape: Language and sexual consent.* London; New York: Routledge.

Ehrman, M. E., & Dörnyei, Z. (1998). *Interpersonal dynamics in second language Education: The visible and invisible classroom.* Thousand Oaks, CA: Sage.

Elliott, J. (2005). *Using narrative in social research: Qualitative and quantitative approaches.* London, Thousand Oaks, New Delhi: Sage.

Ellis, C. (1993). "There are survivors": Telling a story of sudden death. *Sociolgical Quarterly, 34*(4), 711–30.

Ellis, C. S., & Bochner, A. P. (2000). Autoethnography, personal narrative, reflexivity: Researcher as subject. In Y. S. Lincoln (Ed.), *The handbook of qualitative research* (2nd ed.) (pp. 733–67). Thousand Oaks, CA: Sage.

Ellsworth, E. (1989). Why doesn't this feel empowering? Working through the repressive myths of critical pedagogy. *Harvard Educational Review, 59*(3), 297–324.

Engle, R. K. (2001). The neo sophists: Intellectual integrity in the information age. *First Monday 6*(8). Retrieved April 2, 2007, from http://firstmonday.org/issues/issue6_8/engle/index.html

Esterhammer, A., & Robinson, D. (2005). Speech acts. In M. Groden,
M. Kreiswirth, & I. Szeman (Eds.), *The Johns Hopkins guide to literary theory and criticism* (2nd ed.). Baltimore: Johns Hopkins University Press.
Retrieved June 12, 2007, from http://litguide.press.jhu.edu.ezproxy.library.
yorku.ca/cgi-bin/view.cgi? section_id=1815

Evans-Andris, M. (1995). Barriers to computer integration: Microinteraction among computer coordinators and classroom teachers in elementary schools. *Journal of Research on Computing in Education, 28*(1), 29–45.

Evans-Andris, M. (1996). *An Apple for the teacher: Computers and work in elementary schools.* Thousand Oaks, CA: Corwin Press.

Fairbairn, W. R. D. (1952). *An object-relations theory of the personality.* New York: Basic Books.

Fairclough, N. (1989). *Language and power.* London, New York: Longman.

Fairclough, N. (1995). *Critical discourse analysis: Papers in the critical study of language.* London, New York: Longman.

Fairclough, N. (2003). *Analysing discourse: Textual analysis for social research.* Abingdon, UK: Routledge.

Fairclough, N., & Wodak, R. (1997). Critical discourse analysis. In T. A. van Dijk (Ed.), *Discourse as social interaction* (pp. 258–84). London: Sage.

Feiman-Nemser, S., & Remillard, J. (1996). Perspectives on learning to teach. In F. B. Murray (Ed.), *The teacher educator's handbook: Building a knowledge base for the preparation of teachers* (pp. 63–91). San Francisco: Jossey-Bass.

Felman, S. (1982). Psychoanalysis and education: Teaching terminable and interminable. *Yale French Studies, 63,* 21–44.

Felman, S. (1987). *Jacques Lacan and the adventure of insight: Psychoanalysis in contemporary culture.* Cambridge, MA: Harvard University Press.

Felman, S. (1993). *What does a woman want? Reading and sexual difference.* Baltimore, London: Johns Hopkins University Press.

Ferneding, K. (2002). Stepping through the looking glass: Education within the space between modernity and postmodernity – The lifeworld, the body, and technology. *Journal of Curriculum Theorizing, 18*(3), 53–64.

Fetterley, J. (1978). *The resisting reader: A feminist approach to American fiction.* Bloomington, IN: Indiana University Press.

Fine, M. (1988). Sexuality, schooling and adolescent females: The missing discourse of desire. *Harvard Educational Review, 58,* 29–51.

Fink, B. (1995). *The Lacanian subject: Between language and jouissance.* Princeton: Princeton University Press.

Fischer, M. M. J. (1986). Ethnicity and the post-modern arts of memory. In J. Clifford & G. E. Marcus (Eds.), *Writing culture* (pp. 195–233). Berkeley, Los Angeles: University of California Press.

Fontana, A. (2002). Postmodern trends in interviewing. In J. F. Gubrium & J. A. Holstein (Eds.), *Handbook of interview research: Context and method* (pp. 161–72). Thousand Oaks, CA: Sage.

Foucault, M. (1977a). *Discipline and punish: The birth of the prison* (2nd ed.) (A. Sheridan, Trans.). New York: Vintage.

Foucault, M. (1977b). *Language, counter-memory, practice: Selected essays and interviews* (D.F. Bouchard, Ed.) (D. F. Bouchard & S. Simon, Trans.). Ithaca, NY: Cornell University Press.

Foucault, M. (1980a). *Power/knowledge: Selected interviews and other writings* (C. Gordon, Ed.) (C. Gordon, L. Marshall, N. Mepham, & K. Soper, Trans.). London: Harvester Wheatsheaf.

Foucault, M. (1980b). *The history of sexuality: Vol. 1. An introduction* (R. Howard, Trans.). New York: Vintage.

Foucault, M. (1983). The subject and power (L. Sawyer, Trans.). In H. L. Dreyfus & P. Rabinow (Eds.), *Michel Foucault: Beyond structuralism and hermeneutics* (2nd ed.) (pp. 208–25). Chicago: University of Chicago Press.

Foucault, M. (1984a). What is enlightenment? (C. Porter, Trans.). In P. Rabinow (Ed.), *The Foucault reader* (pp. 32–50). New York: Pantheon.

Foucault, M. (1984b). Nietzsche, genealogy, history (D.F. Bouchard, Ed.) (D. F. Bouchard & S. Simon, Trans.). In P. Rainbow (Ed.), *The Foucault reader* (pp. 76–100). New York: Pantheon.

Foucault, M. (1997). The ethics of the concern for self as a practice of freedom (R. Hurley et al., Trans.). In P. Rabinow (Ed.), *Michel Foucault: Ethics, subjectivity and truth, the essential works of Michel Foucault 1954–1984* (vol. 1, pp. 281–301). London: Penguin Press.

Fowler, L. C. (2006). *A curriculum of difficulty: Narrative research in education and the practice of teaching.* New York: Peter Lang.

Fraley, M. C., Nelson, E. C., Wolf, A. W., & Lozoff, B. (1991). Early genital naming. *Developmental and Behavioral Pediatrics, 12,* 301–5.

Frankel, A. (1979). *Once upon a potty.* Harper Collins.

Fraser, S. (1987). *My father's house: A memoir of incest and healing.* London: Virago.

Freire, P. (2005). *Pedagogy of the oppressed* (30th anniversary ed.) (M.B. Ramos, Trans.). [orig. English pub. 1970]. New York: Continuum.

Freud, A. (1971). *The writings of Anna Freud, Volume 7: Problems of psychoanalytic training, diagnosis, and the technique of therapy; 1966–1970.* New York: International Universities Press.

Freud, A. (1974). Four lectures on psychoanalysis for teachers and parents, 1930. In *The writings of Anna Freud, Volume I: Introduction to psychoanalysis: Lectures for child analysts and teachers 1922–1935* (pp. 73–133). New York: International Universities Press.

Freud, S. (1953–1974). *The standard edition of the complete psychological works of Sigmund Freud* (SE), 24 vols. (J. Strachey, Trans. & Ed., in collaboration with A. Freud, assisted by A. Strachey & A. Tyson). London: Hogarth Press and The Institute for Psychoanalysis.

Freud, S. (1899). Screen memories. SE III (pp. 303–22).

Freud, S. (1905a). Three essays on the theory of sexuality. SE VII (pp. 135–243).

Freud, S. (1905b). Jokes and their relation to the unconscious. SE VIII.

Freud, S. (1909). Analysis of a phobia in a five-year-old boy. SE X (pp. 1–149).

Freud, S. (1911). Formulations on the two principles of mental functioning, in *The Penguin Freud library (Vol. 11): On metapsychology: The theory of psychoanalysis* (J. Strachey, Ed. & Trans., A. Richards, Ed.) (pp. 35–57). London: Penguin.

Freud, S. (1914a). Remembering, repeating, and working through (further recommendations on the technique of psycho-analysis II). SE XII (pp. 145–56).

Freud, S. (1914b). On the psychology of the grammar-school boy (S. Whiteside, Trans.). In A. Phillips (Ed.) (2006), *The Penguin Freud reader* (pp. 354–7). London: Penguin.

Freud, S. (1914c). On narcissism: an introduction. SE XIV *(pp. 73–107).*

Freud, S. (1915a). Repression. SE XVI (pp. 141–58).

Freud, S. (1915b). The unconscious. SE XIV (pp. 159–215).

Freud, S. (1917a). Mourning and melancholia. SE XIV (pp. 243–58).

Freud, S. (1917b). Transference. SE XVI (pp. 431–47).

Freud, S. (1917c). Analytic therapy. SE XVI (pp. 448–63).

Freud, S. (1919). On the teaching of psychoanalysis in universities. SE XVII (pp. 169–73).

Freud, S. (1923). The ego and the id. SE XIX (pp. 19–27).

Freud, S. (1924). A note upon the 'mystic writing-pad,' in *The Penguin Freud library (Vol. 11): On metapsychology: The theory of psychoanalysis* (J. Strachey, Ed. & Trans., A. Richards, Ed.) (pp. 429–34). London: Penguin.

Freud, S. (1925). Negation. SE XIX (pp. 233–9).

Freud, S. (1933). New introductory lectures on psycho-analysis. SE XXIII (pp. 3–182).

Freud, S. (1937a). Analysis terminable and interminable. SE XXIII (pp. 209–53).

Freud, S. (1937b). Constructions in analysis. SE XXIII (pp. 255–69).

Freud, S. (1940). The psychical apparatus and the external world. SE XXIII (pp. 195–204).

Freud, S. (1948). *Inhibitions, symptoms and anxiety.* London: Hogarth Press.

Friedrich, W. N., Sandfort, T. G. M., Oostveen, J., & Cohen-Kettenis, P. T. (2000). Cultural differences in sexual behavior: 2–6 year old Dutch and American children. *Journal of Psychology and Human Sexuality, 12*(1/2), 117–29.

Gal, S. (1991). Between speech and silence: The problematics of research on language and gender. In M. diLeonardo (Ed.), *Gender at the crossroads of knowledge: Feminist anthropology in the postmodern era* (pp. 175–203). Berkeley: University of California Press.

Gallop, J. (Ed.) (1995). *Pedagogy: The question of impersonation.* Bloomington, Indianapolis: Indiana University Press.

Gallop, J. (2002). *Anecdotal theory.* London, Durham, NC: Duke University Press.

Gammage, S. (1988). The teaching of sexuality. In B. Carrington & B. Troyna (Eds.), *Children and controversial issues: Strategies for the early and middle years* (pp. 189–204). Barcombe, UK; Philadelphia: Falmer Press.

Gardner, H. (1993). *Multiple intelligences: The theory into practice.* New York: Basic Books.

Gardner, H. (1999). *Intelligence reframed: Multiple intelligences for the 21st century.* New York: Basic Books.

Garrison, J. (1997). *Dewey and eros: Wisdom and desire in the art of teaching.* New York, London: Teachers College Press.

Gee, J. P. (2005). *An introduction to discourse analysis: Theory and method.* New York: Routledge.

Gibbs, J. (2001). *Tribes: A new way of learning and being together.* Windsor, CA: CenterSource Systems.

Giguère, D. (1999). Gender gap widening among Ontario teachers. *Professionally Speaking,* June. Retrieved April 4, 2007, from http://www.oct.ca/publications/professionally_speaking/june_1999/gap.htm

Gilligan, C. (1996). *In a different voice: Psychological theory and women's development.* Cambridge, MA: Harvard University Press.

Gilbert, J. (2004). Between sexuality and narrative: On the language of sex education. In M. L. Rasmussen, E. Rofes, & S. Talburt (Eds.), *Youth and sexualities: Pleasure, subversion and insubordination in and out of schools.* (pp. 109–26). New York: Palgrave.

Giroux, H. A. (1997). *Pedagogy and the politics of hope: Theory, culture and schooling: A critical reader.* Boulder, CO: Westview Press.

Giroux, H. A. (2000). *Stealing innocence: Youth, corporate power, and the politics of culture.* New York: St. Martin's Press.

Giroux, H. A. (2010). Rethinking education as the practice of freedom: Paulo Freire and the promise of critical pedagogy. *Policy Futures in Education, 8*(6), 715–21.

Giroux, H., & McLaren, P. (1994). *Between borders: Pedagogy and the politics of cultural studies.* New York, London: Routledge.

Gitlin, A., & Labaree, D. F. (1996). Historical notes on the barriers to the professionalization of American teachers: The influence of markets and patriarchy. In I. F. Goodson & A. Hargreaves (Eds.), *Teachers' professional lives* (pp. 88–108). London, UK; Bristol, PA: Falmer Press.

Goodlad, J. I. (1990). *Teachers for our nation's schools*. San Francisco: Jossey-Bass.

Goodson, I. F. (Ed.). (1992). *Studying teachers' lives*. New York: Teachers College Press.

Google Translate (2005). Frequently asked questions. Retrieved March, 23, 2007, from http://www.google.com/help/faq_translation.html#whatis

Goss, M. A. K. (1996). Releasing the isolated warrior. *Technos, 5*(1), 22–3.

Gouveia, C. A. M. (2005). Assumptions about gender, power and opportunity: Gays and lesbians as discursive subjects in a Portuguese newspaper. In M. M. Lazar (Ed.), *Feminist critical discourse analysis: Gender, power and ideology in discourse* (pp. 229–50). London: Palgrave MacMillan.

Granger, C. A. (2002). Relief for ICT headaches: How effective is ASA? Paper presented at the conference of the Canadian Society for the Study of Education conference, Toronto. May 27. Retrieved March 24, 2003, from http://facwkst90.edu.yorku.ca/yorku/open/indexnew.cfm

Granger, C. A. (2003). Resisting the master(y) script: Teachers at play with information technology. *Proceedings of the 2002 York University Faculty of Education Graduate Conference in Education,* (pp. 4–22). Toronto: York University.

Granger, C. A. (2004). *Silence in second language learning: A psychoanalytic reading*. Clevedon, UK: Multilingual Matters.

Granger, C. A. (2007). On (not) representing sex in preschool and kindergarten: A psychoanalytic reflection on orders and hints. *Sex Education: Sexuality, Society and Learning, 7*(1), 1–15.

Granger, C. A., Morbey, M. L., Lotherington, H., Owston, R. D., & Wideman, H. H. (2002). Factors contributing to teachers' successful implementation of IT. *Journal of Computer Assisted Learning 18*(4), 480–8.

Greene, M. (1995). Choosing a past and inventing a future: The becoming of a teacher. In W. Ayers (Ed.), *To become a teacher: Making a difference in children's lives* (pp. 65–77). New York: Teachers College Press.

Grumet, M. R. (1988). *Bitter milk: Women and teaching*. Amherst, MA: University of Massachusetts Press.

Grumet, M. R. (1990). Retrospective: autobiography and the analysis of educational experience. *Cambridge Journal of Education, 20*(3), 321–5.

Grumet, M. R. (1992). Existential and phenomenological foundations of autobiographical methods. In W. F. Pinar & W. M. Reynolds (Eds.), *Understanding curriculum as phenomenological and deconstructed text* (pp. 28–43). New York: Teachers College Press.

Gubrium, J. F., & Holstein, J. A. (Eds.). (2002). *Handbook of interview research: context and method*. Thousand Oaks, CA: Sage.

Hammersley, M. (1992). *What's wrong with ethnography? Methodological explorations*. London: Routledge.

Hannafin, R. D., & Savenye, W. C. (1993). Technology in the classroom: The teacher's new role and resistance to it. *Educational Technology, 33*(6), 26–31.

Hargreaves, A., & Goodson, I. F. (1996). Teachers' professional lives: Aspirations and actualities. In I. F. Goodson & A. Hargreaves (Eds.), *Teachers' professional lives* (pp. 1–27). London: Falmer Press.

Hargreaves, D. H. (1994). The new professionalism: The synthesis of professional and institutional development. *Teaching and Teacher Education, 10*(4): 423–438.

Harper, H. (1997a). Difference and diversity in Ontario schooling. *Canadian Journal of Education, 22*(2), 192–206.

Harper, H. (1997b). Disturbing identity and desire: Adolescent girls and wild words. In S. Todd (Ed.), *Learning desire: Perspectives on pedagogy, culture, and the unsaid* (pp. 141–61). New York, London: Routledge.

Harré, R. (1993). *Social being* (2nd ed.). Oxford, Cambridge, MA: Blackwell.

Hativa, N., & Lesgold, A. (1996). Situational effects in classroom technology implementations: Unfulfilled expectations and unexpected outcomes. In S. T. Kerr (Ed.), *Technology and the future of schooling: Ninety-fifth yearbook of the National Society for the Study of Education, part II* (pp. 131–71). Chicago: University of Chicago Press.

Hausbeck, K., & Brents, B. G. (2003). The Politics of passing and coming out in auto-ethnographic fieldwork: Performing feminist research on the sex industry. Paper presented at the Western Social Science Association annual meetings, Las Vegas, NV. Retrieved December 12, 2006, from http://www. unlv.edu/faculty/brents/research/passWSSA.pdf

Hawthorne, L. (2007). An other place – Lucy Bleach: three versions of the outsider. *RealTime 77*, March 25. Retrieved April 8, 2007, from http://www. realtimearts.net/feature/Ten_Days_on_the_Island/8461

Hayano, D. (1979). Auto-ethnography: Paradigms, problems, and prospects. *Human Organization, 38*, 99–104.

Heidegger, M. (1996). *Being and time* (J. Stambaugh, Trans.). Albany, NY: State University of New York Press.

Higonnet, A. (1998). *Pictures of innocence: The history and crisis of ideal childhood*. London.: Thames & Hudson. Cited in C. Mitchell, S. Walsh, & J. Larkin. (2004), Visualizing the politics of innocence in the age of AIDS. *Sex Education: Sexuality, Society and Learning, 4*(1), 35–47.

Hollway, W. (1984). Gender difference and the production of subjectivity. In J. Henriques, W. Hollway, C. Urwin, C. Venn, & V. Walkerdine (Eds.),

Changing the subject: Psychology, social regulation and subjectivity (pp. 227–63). London: Methuen.

Hollway, W., & Jefferson, T. (2000). *Doing qualitative research differently: Free association, narrative and the interview method.* Thousand Oaks: Sage.

Holt, N. L. (2003). Representation, legitimation, and autoethnography: An autoethnographic writing story. *International Journal of Qualitative Methods, 2*(1). Article 2. Retrieved December 12, 2006, from http://www.ualberta. ca.ezproxy.library.yorku.ca/~iiqm/backissues/2_1/html/holt.html

Holt-Reynolds, D. (1992). Personal history-based beliefs as relevant prior knowledge in course work. *American Educational Research Journal, 29*(2), 325–49.

Hope, W. C. (1997). Today is a good day to begin using a computer. *Contemporary Education, 68*(2), 108–9.

Hull, K. (2002). Eros and education: The role of desire in teaching and learning. *NEA Higher Education Journal, 18* (Fall), 19–31.

Hunsberger, M. (1992). The time of texts. In W. F. Pinar & W. M. Reynolds (Eds.), *Understanding curriculum as phenomenological and deconstructed text* (pp. 64–91). New York: Teachers College Press.

Hutton, P. H. (1988). Foucault, Freud, and the technologies of the self. In L. H. Martin, H. Gutman, & P. H. Hutton (Eds.), *Technologies of the self: A seminar with Michel Foucault* (pp. 121–44). Amherst, MA: University of Massachusetts Press.

Institute of Justice and Reconciliation (CINDI). (2001). *How AIDS affects me: Children speak.* Pietermaritzburg, South Africa. Cited in C. Mitchell, S. Walsh, & J. Larkin (2004), Visualizing the politics of innocence in the age of AIDS. *Sex Education: Sexuality, Society and Learning, 4*(1), 35–47.

Irigaray, L. (1985). *This sex which is not one* (C. Porter & C. Burke, Trans.). Ithaca, NY: Cornell University Press.

Irvine, J. M. (2002). *Talk about sex: The battles over sex education in the United States.* Berkeley, Los Angeles: University of California Press.

James, A., Jenks, C., & Prout, A. (1998). *Theorizing childhood.* New York: Teachers College Press.

Jamieson, B. (2007). Male presence in teaching continues to decline. *Professionally Speaking: The Magazine of the Ontario College of Teachers.* Online edition, retrieved September 5, 2010, from http://professionallyspeaking. oct.ca/june_2007/male_teachers.asp

Jaremko, B. (2003, November 26). Sit up, shut up, line up. Letters. *Globe and Mail.* Online edition, retrieved March 15, 2007, from http://www. theglobeandmail.com/servlet/Page/document/v5/content/subscribe? user_ URL=http://www.theglobeandmail.com%2Fservlet%2FArticleNews%2F TPStory%2FLAC%2F20031126%2FWEDLETS26-6%2FTPEducation%2F&

ord=1318368&brand=theglobeandmail&force_login=true [tinyurl.com/2ts5n]

Johnson, M. J., Schwab, R. L., & Foa, L. (1999). Technology as a change agent for the teaching process. *Theory into Practice, 38*(1), 24–30.

Johnson, R. T. (2000). *Hands off! The disappearance of touch in the care of children.* New York: Peter Lang.

Jonassen, D. H. (2000). *Computers as mindtools for schools: Engaging critical thinking* (2nd ed.). Columbus, OH: Prentice-Hall.

Jones, E. (1991). Do ECE people really agree? Or are we just agreeable? *Young Children, 46*(4), 59–61.

Jones, F. H., & Jones, B. (2000). *Tools for teaching: Discipline, instruction, motivation.* Santa Cruz, CA: Fredric H. Jones and Associates.

Kadar, M. (Ed.). (1992). *Essays on life writing.* Toronto: University of Toronto Press.

Kadar, M. (1992a). Coming to terms: life writing – from genre to critical practice. In M. Kadar (Ed.), *Essays on life writing* (pp. 3–16). Toronto: University of Toronto Press.

Kadar, M. (1992b). Whose life is it anyway? Out of the bathtub and into the narrative. In M. Kadar (Ed.), *Essays on life writing* (pp. 153–61). Toronto: University of Toronto Press.

Kahn, P. H., Jr., & Friedman, B. (1998). Control and power in educational computing. In H. Bromley & M. W. Apple (Eds.), *Education/technology/power: Educational computing as a social practice* (pp. 157–73). Albany: State University of New York Press.

Kapferer, B. (1988). The anthropologist as hero: Three exponents of postmodernist anthropology. *Critique of Anthropology, 8*(2), 77–104.

Kaplan, A. (1993). *French lessons.* Chicago: University of Chicago Press.

Kaplan, C. (1991). Gender and language. In D. Cameron (Ed.), *The feminist critique of language: A reader.* London: Routledge. Cited in H. Harper (1997a), Disturbing identity and desire: Adolescent girls and wild words. In S. Todd (Ed.), *Learning desire: Perspectives on pedagogy, culture, and the unsaid* (pp. 141–61). New York, London: Routledge.

Kehily, M. J. (2002). Sexing the subject: Teachers, pedagogies and sex education. *Sex Education: Sexuality, Society and Learning, 2*(3), 215–31.

Kermode, F. (1995). Memory and autobiography. *Raritan, 15*(1), 36–51.

Kerr, S. T. (1996). Visions of sugarplums: the future of technology, education and the schools. In *Technology and the future of schooling: Ninety-fifth yearbook of the National Society for the Study of Education, part II* (S. T. Kerr, Ed.) (pp. 1–27). Chicago: University of Chicago Press.

Kincheloe, J. L. (2008). Critical pedagogy and the knowledge wars of the twenty-first century. *International Journal of Critical Pedagogy, 1*(1), 1–22.

King, N. (2000). *Memory, narrative, identity: Remembering the self.* Edinburgh: Edinburgh University Press.

Klein, M. (1946). Notes on some schizoid mechanisms. In *The writings of Melanie Klein, Volume III: Envy and gratitude and other works 1946–1963* (1984) (R. Money-Kyrle, Ed., in collaboration with B. Joseph, E. O'Shaughnessy, & H. Segal) (pp. 1–24). New York: The Free Press.

Klein, M. (1948). On the theory of anxiety and guilt. In *The writings of Melanie Klein, Volume III: Envy and gratitude and other works 1946–1963* (1984) (R. Money-Kyrle, Ed., in collaboration with B. Joseph, E. O'Shaughnessy, & H. Segal) (pp. 25–42). New York: The Free Press.

Klein, M. (1952a). The origins of transference. In *The writings of Melanie Klein, Volume III: Envy and gratitude and other works 1946–1963* (1984) (R. Money-Kyrle, Ed., in collaboration with B. Joseph, E. O'Shaughnessy, & H. Segal) (pp. 48–60). New York: The Free Press.

Klein, M. (1952b). Some theoretical conclusions regarding the emotional life of the infant. In *The writings of Melanie Klein, Volume III: Envy and gratitude and other works 1946–1963* (1984) (R. Money-Kyrle, Ed., in collaboration with B. Joseph, E. O'Shaughnessy, & H. Segal) (pp. 61–93). New York: The Free Press.

Klein, M. (1957). Envy and gratitude. In *The writings of Melanie Klein, Volume III: Envy and gratitude and other works 1946–1963* (1984) (Ed. R. Money-Kyrle, in collaboration with B. Joseph, E. O'Shaughnessy, & H. Segal) (pp. 175–235). New York: The Free Press.

Klein, M. (1963). On the sense of loneliness. In *The writings of Melanie Klein, Volume III: Envy and gratitude and other works 1946–1963* (1984) (Ed. R. Money-Kyrle, in collaboration with B. Joseph, E. O'Shaughnessy, & H. Segal) (pp. 300–13). New York: The Free Press.

Kleinfield, N. R. (2007, April 22). Before deadly rage, a lifetime consumed by a troubling silence. *New York Times.* Print edition, pp. 1, 22.

Kogawa, J. (1993). *Itsuka* (revised ed.). Toronto: Penguin.

Korenman, J. (1998, Feb. 7). The personal is political – 3 years of responses. In *'The personal is political': Origins of the phrase.* Retrieved April 5, 2007, from Academic Women's Studies List: http://www.research.umbc.edu/~korenman/wmst/pisp.html

Korthagen, F., & Kessels, J. P. A. M. (1999). Linking theory and practice: Changing the pedagogy of teacher education. *Educational Researcher (May),* 4–17.

Kristeva, J. (1994). The speaking subject is not innocent (C. Miller, Trans.). In B. Johnson (Ed.), *Freedom and interpretation: The Oxford Amnesty lectures 1992* (pp. 147–74). New York: Basic Books.

Kristeva, J. (2000). *The sense and non-sense of revolt, Volume 1* (J. Herman, Trans.). New York: Columbia University Press.

Kubrick, S. (Producer & Director). (1968). *2001: A space odyssey* [Motion picture]. Metro-Goldwyn-Mayer.

Labaree, D. F. (1997). Public goods, private goods: The American struggle over educational goals. *American Educational Research Journal, 34*(1), 39–81.

Labaree, D. F. (2000). On the nature of teaching and teacher education. *Journal of Teacher Education, 51*(3), 228–33.

Lacan, J. (1950). A theoretical introduction to the functions of psychoanalysis in criminology. (M. Bracher, R. Grigg, & R. Samuels, Trans.). *Journal for the Psychoanalysis of Culture and Society, 1*(2), 18–25.

Lacan, J. (1953). Some reflections on the ego. *International Journal of Psychoanalysis 34*, 11–17. Cited in M. Markham (1999), Through the looking glass: Reflective teaching through a Lacanian lens. *Curriculum Inquiry, 29*(1), 55–75.

Lacan, J. (1968). The mirror-phase as formative of the function of the I. *New Left Review, 51*, 71–7.

Lacan, J. (1975). *Le Séminaire, livre XX: Encore.* Paris: Seuil. Cited in S. Felman (1982), Psychoanalysis and education: Teaching terminable and interminable. *Yale French Studies, 63*(21–4).

Lakoff, R. (1975). *Language and women's place.* New York: Harper Colophon.

Laplanche, J. (1990). Psychoanalysis, time and translation. In J. Fletcher & M. Stanton (Eds.), *Jean Laplanche: Seduction, translation and the drives, a dossier* (pp. 161–77). London: Institute of Contemporary Arts.

Laplanche, J. (1992). Notes on afterwardsness. In J. Fletcher & M. Stanton (Eds.), *Jean Laplanche: Seduction, translation and the drives, a dossier* (pp. 217–23). London: Institute of Contemporary Arts.

Laplanche, J. (1999). *Essays on otherness* (L. Thurston, Trans.). London: Routledge.

Laplanche, J., & Pontalis, J.-B. (1973). *The language of psycho-analysis.* (D. Nicholson-Smith, Trans.). New York: W.W. Norton.

Larson, M. S. (1980). Proletarianization and educated labor. *Theory and Society, 9*(2), 131–75. Cited in M. Apple (1986), *Teachers and texts: A political economy of class and gender relations in education.* New York: Routledge & Kegan Paul.

Lather, P. (1986). Issues of validity in openly ideological research: Between a rock and a soft place. *Interchange, 17*(4), 63–84.

Lather, P. (1991). *Getting smart: Feminist research and pedagogy within the postmodern.* New York: Routledge.

Lather, P. (2001). Postbook: Working the ruins of feminist ethnography. *Signs: Journal of Women in Culture and Society, 27*(1), 198–227.

Lawson, T. & Comber, C. (2000). Introducing information and communication technologies into schools: The blurring of boundaries. *British Journal of Sociology of Education, 21*(3), 419–33.

Leavitt, R. L., & Power, M. B. (1997). Civilizing bodies: Children in day care. In J. Tobin (Ed.), *Making a place for pleasure in early childhood education* (pp. 39–75). New Haven: Yale University Press.

Lemke, J. L. (1995). *Textual politics: Discourse and social dynamics.* Washington: Taylor & Francis.

Lenskyj, H. (1990). Beyond plumbing and prevention: Feminist approaches to sex education. *Gender and Education, 2*(2), 217–30.

Lever-Duffy, J., & McDonald, J.B. (2008). *Teaching and learning with technology.* Boston: Pearson.

Lévi-Strauss, C. (1968). *The savage mind.* Chicago: University of Chicago Press, 1968. Cited in S. Turkle (1985), *The second self: Computers and the human spirit.* New York: Touchstone.

Levinas, E. (1987). *Time and the Other and additional essays* (R. A. Cohen, Trans.). Pittsburgh: Duquesne University Press.

Levine, A. E. (2000). The Future of colleges: 9 inevitable changes. *Chronicle of Higher Education, 47*(9). Retrieved March 24, 2007, from http://education.gsu. edu/ctl/Programs/Future_Colleges.htm

Lionnet, F. (1991). Autoethnography: The an-archic style of Dust Tracks on a Road. In D. LaCapra (Ed.), *The bounds of race: Perspectives in hegemony and resistance* (pp. 164–95). Ithaca, NY: Cornell University Press.

Little, D. (1991). *Learner autonomy I: Definitions, issues and problems.* Dublin: Authentik. Cited in R.C. Smith (2001), Teacher education for teacher-learner autonomy. In H. Trappes-Lomax (Ed.), *Proceedings of 'Autonomy in Language Teacher Education' II (The 9th IALS Symposium for Language Teacher Educators).* Edinburgh: University of Edinburgh. [CD-ROM.] Retrieved April 4, 2007, from http://www.warwick.ac.uk/~elsdr/Teacher_autonomy.pdf

Lively, V., & Lively, E. (1991). *Sexual development of young children.* Albany, NY: Delmar.

Livingstone, D. W., Hart, D., & Davie, L. E. (2001). *Public attitudes towards education in Ontario, 2000: The 13th OISE/UT survey.* Toronto: Ontario Institute for Studies in Education. Retrieved March 9, 2007, from http://www.oise. utoronto.ca/OISE-Survey/2000/report2000.pdf

Lloyd, S. L. (2005). Examining a framework of dialogue e-mails and inquiry into practice to scaffold reflective practice in preservice teachers during their early field experience. Doctoral dissertation, University of South Florida. Retrieved February 24, 2007, from ProQuest Digital Dissertations database. (Publication No. AAT 3168720).

Lorde, A. (1983). The master's tools will never dismantle the master's house. In C. Moraga & G. Anzaldúa (Eds.), *This bridge called my back: Radical writings by women of color* (pp. 98–101). New York: Kitchen Table: Women of Color Press.

Lortie, D. C. (1975). *Schoolteacher: A sociological study.* Chicago: University of Chicago Press.

Lortie, D. C. (1990). *Schoolteacher: A sociological study* (2nd ed.). Chicago: University of Chicago Press.

Lotherington, H., Morbey, M. L., Granger, C. A., & Doan, L. (2001). Tearing down the walls: New literacies and new horizons in the elementary school. In B. Barrell (Ed.), *Technology, teaching and learning: Issues in the integration of technology.* (pp. 131–61). Calgary: Detselig.

Luke, A. (1996). Text and discourse in education: An introduction to critical discourse analysis. *Review of Research in Education, 21,* 3–48.

Luke, A. (1997). Theory and practice in critical discourse analysis. In L. Saha (Ed.), *International encyclopaedia of the sociology of education.* Oxford: Pergamon.

Luke, C. (1996). Feminist pedagogy theory: Reflections on power and authority. *Educational Theory, 46*(3): 283–302.

MacDonald, C. J., Baker, D., & Stewart, S. R. (1995). Student teachers in the classroom: Associate teachers' perspectives. *McGill Journal of Education, 30*(1), 73–95.

Macdonell, D. (1986). *Theories of discourse: An introduction.* New York: Basil Blackwell.

Machado, A. (1963). CXXXVI, Proverbios y cantares Verse XXIX [1913]. In *Poesías Completas, Décima edición,* p. 158. Madrid: Espasa-Calpe.

MacKay, A. W., & Sutherland, L. I. (2006). *Teachers and the law: A practical guide for educators* (2nd ed.). Toronto: Emond Montgomery Publications.

Maddux, C. D. (1998). Barriers to the successful use of information technology in education. *Computers in the Schools, 14*(3/4), 5–11.

Maines, D. R. (2001). Writing the self versus writing the Other: Comparing autobiographical and life history data. *Symbolic Interaction, 24,* 105–11.

Malinowski, B. (1922). *Argonauts of the Western Pacific.* London: Routledge & Kegan Paul.

Malinowski, B. (1967). *A diary in the strict sense of the term* (N. Guterman, Trans.). New York: Harcourt, Brace & World.

Marcus, G. E. (1994). What comes (just) after post? The case of ethnography. In N. Denzin and Y. Lincoln (Eds.), *The handbook of qualitative research* (pp. 563–74). Thousand Oaks, CA: Sage.

Markham, M. (1999). Through the looking glass: Reflective teaching through a Lacanian lens. *Curriculum Inquiry, 29*(1), 55–75.

Martinez, K. F. (1998). Preservice teachers adrift on a sea of knowledges. *Asia-Pacific Journal of Teacher Education, 26*(2), 97–106.

Martusewicz, R. A. (1997). Say me to me: Desire and education. In S. Todd (Ed.), *Learning desire: Perspectives on pedagogy, culture, and the unsaid* (pp. 97–113). New York, London: Routledge.

Mazzei, L. A. (2003). Inhabited silences: In pursuit of a muffled subtext. *Qualitative Inquiry, 9*(3), 355–73.

McClintock, R. (2001). Experience and innovation: Reflections on emerging practice with new media in education. *Journal of Educational Computing Research, 25*(1), 95–104.

McDiarmid, G. W. (1989). Tilting at webs of belief: Field experiences as a means of breaking with experience (Research Report #89–8). East Lansing, MI: National Center for Research on Teacher Education. Cited in D. Holt-Reynolds, (1992), Personal history-based beliefs as relevant prior knowledge in course work. *American Educational Research Journal, 29*(2), 325–49.

McGill University. (2006). *Integrated studies in education: Bachelor of Education.* Retrieved February 26, 2007, from McGill University, Faculty of Education: http://www.mcgill.ca/edu-ntegrated/undergraduate/programs/#KE

McNeil, L. M. (2002). Private asset or public good: Education and democracy at the Crossroads. *American Educational Research Journal, 39*(2), 243–8.

McNulty, A. B. (2000). Preservice teachers' beliefs about teaching and learning before, during, and after the application of feminist pedagogies. Ed.D. dissertation, Texas A&M University. Retrieved July 27, 2007, from ProQuest Digital Dissertations database. (Publication No. AAT 9965847).

McWilliam, E. (1995). *In broken images: Feminist tales for a different teacher education.* New York, London: Teachers College Press.

McWilliam, E. (1996). Seductress or schoolmarm: On the improbability of the great female teacher. *Interchange, 27*(1), 1–11.

Mead, G. (1934). *Mind, self, and society from the standpoint of a social behaviorist* (C. W. Morris, Ed.). Chicago, London: University of Chicago Press.

Mebarak, S., & Mendez, L. (2001). Underneath your clothes. On *Laundry Service* [Audio recording: compact disc]. Sony Music International.

Micek, K. (2007, March 27). Parent criticizes book 'Fahrenheit 451.' *Montgomery County Courier* (Houston). Online edition, retrieved March 27, 2007, from http://www.hcnonline.com/site/news.cfm?newsid=17270600&BRD=1574&PAG=461&dept_id=532215&rfi=6

Michaels, A. (1996). *Fugitive pieces.* Toronto: McClelland & Stewart.

Miller, J. (1996). *School for women.* London: Virago.

Miller, J. L. (1988). The resistance of women academics: An autobiographical account. In W. F. Pinar (Ed.), *Contemporary curriculum discourses*. Scottsdale, AZ: Gorsuch Scarisbrick.

Miller, J. L. (1992). 'The surprise of a recognizable person' as troubling presence in educational research and writing. [Review of the book *Gender and the journal: Diaries and academic discourse*]. *Curriculum Inquiry, 24*(4), 503–12.

Miller, J. L. (2005). *Sounds of silence breaking: Women, autobiography, curriculum.* New York: Peter Lang.

Miller, N. (2002). *But enough about me: Why we read other people's lives.* New York: Columbia University Press.

Mills, C. W. (1961). *The sociological imagination.* London: Oxford University Press.

Milton, J. (2003). Primary school sex education programs: views and experiences of teachers in four primary schools in Sydney, Australia. *Sex Education: Sexuality, Society and Learning, 3*(3), 241–56.

Ministry of Education, Ontario (MOE) (1998). *The kindergarten program.* Toronto: Queen's Printer.

Ministry of Education, Ontario (MOE) (2006a). *The Ontario curriculum, grades 1–8: Health and physical education.* Retrieved April 11, 2007, from http://www.edu.gov.on.ca/eng/curriculum/elementary/health18curr.pdf

Ministry of Education, Ontario (MOE) (2006b). *The kindergarten program (revised).* Retrieved April 11, 2007, from http://www.edu.gov.on.ca/eng/curriculum/elementary/kindercurrb.pdf

Mitchell, C., Walsh, S., & Larkin, J. (2004). Visualizing the politics of innocence in the age of AIDS. *Sex education: Sexuality, society and learning, 4*(1), 35–47.

Mitchell, J. (1966). The circle game. On *Ladies of the canyon* [Audio recording: compact disc.] Scarborough, ON: Warner Brothers.

Mitchell, S. A. (1993). *Hope and dread in psychoanalysis.* New York: Basic Books.

Mitrano, B. (1981). Feminism and curriculum theory: Implications for teacher education. *Journal of Curriculum Theorizing, 3*(2), 5–85.

Morbey, M. L., & Granger, C. A. (2002). Cybercolonialism in the State Hermitage Museum, St. Petersburg, Russia: Does it matter? *Proceedings of the Electronic Imaging and Visual Arts Conference.* Moscow: Ministry of Culture of the Russian Federation.

Mountains & Plains Booksellers Association. (n/d). *Banned books.* Retrieved April 4, 2007, from http://www.mountainsplains.org/banac.htm

Murphy, S. & Gaymes San Vicente, A. (2007). *Teacher candidate practicum evaluation protocol.* Toronto: Faculty of Education, York University.

Neumann, A. (1998). On experience, memory, and knowing: A post-Holocaust (auto)biography. *Curriculum Inquiry, 28*(4), 425–42.

Nicholas, D. (1991). Childhood in medieval Europe. In J. M. Hawes & N. R. Hiner (Eds.), *Children in historical and comparative perspective: An international handbook and research guide* (pp. 31–52). Westport, CT: Greenwood Press.

Noble, D. (1998). The regime of technology in education. In L. E. Beyer & M. W. Apple (Eds.), *The curriculum: Problems, politics, and possibilities* (2nd ed.) (pp. 267–83). Albany, NY: State University of New York Press.

Noddings, N. (1992). *The challenge to care in schools: An alternative approach to education.* New York, London: Teachers College Press.

Noddings, N. (2003). *Caring: A feminine approach to ethics and moral education* (2nd ed.). Berkeley, CA: University of California Press.

Norquay, N. (1990). Life history research: Memory, schooling and social difference. *Cambridge Journal of Education, 20*(3), 291–300.

O'Brien, L. M., & Schillaci, M. (2002). Why *do* I want to teach, anyway? Utilizing autobiography in teacher education. *Teaching Education, 13*(1), 25–40.

O'Connor, K. A. (2003). *What happens to the mentoring dispositions of cooperating teachers who participate in a university course in supervision with on-site support?* Doctoral dissertation, Boston College.

Ogden, T. H. (1994a). The analytic third: Working with intersubjective clinical facts. In S. A. Mitchell & L. Aron (Eds.), *Relational psychoanalysis: The emergence of a tradition* (pp. 461–92). Hillsdale, NJ; London: The Analytic Press.

Ogden, T. H. (1994b). *Subjects of analysis.* Northvale, NJ: Aronson.

Oram, A. (1989). A master should not serve under a mistress: Women and men teachers 1900–1970. In S. Acker (Ed.), *Teachers, gender and careers* (pp. 21–34). Barcombe, UK: Falmer Press.

Organisation for Economic Co-operation and Development (OECD). (2001). *Learning to change: ICT in schools.* Paris: OECD Publications.

Pagano, J. (1988). The claim of philia. In W. Pinar (Ed.), *Contemporary curriculum discourses* (pp. 514–530). Scottsdale, AZ: Gorsuch Scarisbrick.

Paley, V. G. (2004). *A child's work: The importance of fantasy play.* Chicago: University of Chicago Press.

Papert, S. (1984). Trying to predict the future. *Popular Computing, 3*(13), 30–44.

Papert, S. (1993). *The children's machine: Rethinking school in the age of the computer.* New York: Basic Books.

Parker, I. (1992). *Discourse dynamics: Critical analysis for social and individual psychology.* New York: Routledge. Cited in A. Luke (1996), Text and discourse in education: an introduction to critical discourse analysis. *Review of Research in Education, 21*, 3–48.

Pelias, R. J. (2004). *A methodology of the heart: Evoking academic and daily life.* Walnut Creek, CA: Altamira Press.

Pendleton Jiménez, K. (2000). *Are you a boy or a girl?* Toronto: Green Dragon Press.

Petress, K. (2001). The ethics of student classroom silence. *Journal of Instructional Psychology, 28*(2), 104–107.

Phelan, A. M. (1996). 'Strange pilgrims': Disillusionment and nostalgia in teacher education reform. *Interchange, 27*(3, 4), 331–48.

Phelan, A. M. (1997a). When the mirror crack'd: the discourse of reflection in pre-service teacher education. In K. Watson, C. Modgil, & S. Modgil (Eds.), *Educational dilemmas: debate and diversity, Volume 1: Teachers, teacher education and training* (pp. 169–78). London: Cassell.

Phelan, A. M. (1997b). Classroom management and the erasure of teacher desire. In J. Tobin (Ed.), *Making a place for pleasure in early childhood education* (pp. 76–100). New Haven; London: Yale University Press.

Phillips, A. (1994). *On flirtation.* Cambridge, MA: Harvard University Press.

Phillips, A. (1998). Learning from Freud. In A. O. Rorty (Ed.), *Philosophers on education: New historical perspectives* (pp. 411–17). New York: Routledge.

Phillips, A. (1999). *The beast in the nursery: On curiosity and other appetites.* New York: Vintage.

Pinar, W. F. (1976). Self and others. In W. F. Pinar & M. Grumet (1976). *Toward a poor curriculum* (pp. 7–30). Dubuque, IA: Kendall/Hunt.

Pinar, W. F. (1981). 'Whole, bright, deep with understanding': issues in auto-biographical method and qualitative research. *Journal of Curriculum Studies, 13*(3), 173–88.

Pinar, W. F., & Grumet, M. (1976). *Toward a poor curriculum.* Dubuque, IA: Kendall/Hunt.

Pinar, W. F., Reynolds, W. M., Slattery, P., & Taubman, P. M. (2000). *Understanding curriculum: An introduction to the study of historical and contemporary curriculum discourses.* New York: Peter Lang.

Pinkman, G. D. (n/d). *How to stay awake in teacher inservices.* Retrieved April 1, 2007, from http://www.pinkman.org/jokes/SchoolsandEmployment/Schools andEmployment.htm#How_To_Stay_Awake_In_Teacher_Inservices:_Offered_ As_A_Public_Service_

Piper, D. (1997). Through the 'I' of the teacher: Towards a postmodern conception of self. *McGill Journal of Education, 32*(1), 51–67.

Pitt, A. J. (1998). Qualifying resistance: Some comments on methodological dilemmas. *International Journal of Qualitative Studies in Education, 11*(4), 535–53.

Pitt, A. J. (2000). Hide and seek: The play of the personal in education. *Changing English: Studies in Reading and Culture, 7*(1), 65–74.

Pitt, A. J. (2003). *The play of the personal: Psychoanalytic narratives of feminist education.* New York: Peter Lang.

Pitt, A. J. (2006). Mother love's education. In G. M. Boldt & P. M. Salvio (Eds.), *Love's return: Psychoanalytic essays on childhood, teaching, and learning* (pp. 87–105). New York, London: Routledge.

Pitt, A. J., & Britzman, D. P. (2003). Speculations on qualities of difficult knowledge in teaching and learning: An experiment in psychoanalytic research. *International Journal of Qualitative Studies in Education, 16*(6), 755–76.

Pomerantz, A. (2005). Using participants' video stimulated comments to complement analyses of interactional practices. In H. te Molder & J. Potter (Eds.), *Conversation and cognition* (pp. 93–113). Cambridge, UK: Cambridge University Press.

Pratt, M. L. (1977). *Toward a speech act theory of literary discourse.* Bloomington, London: Indiana University Press.

Pratt, M. L. (1999). Arts of the contact zone. In D. Bartholomae & A. Petroksky (Eds.), *Ways of reading.* New York: Bedford St. Martin's. Retrieved June 9, 2006, from http://web.nwe.ufl.edu/~stripp/2504/pratt.html

Preissle, J., & Grant, L. (1998). Exploring the ethnography of education. *Journal of Contemporary Ethnography, 27*(1), 3–9.

Prentice, A. (1977). *The school promoters.* Toronto: McClelland & Stewart.

Provenzo Jr., E. F., Brett, A., & McCloskey, G. N. (1999). *Computers, curriculum and cultural change: An introduction for teachers.* Mahwah, NJ: Lawrence Erlbaum Associates.

PyllikZillig, L.M., Bodvarsson, M., & Bruning, R. (2005). *Technology-based education: Bringing researchers and practitioners together.* Greenwich, CT: Information Age.

Ragan, S. L. (2000). 'The critical life': An exercise in applying inapplicable critical standards. *Communication Education, 49*(3), 229–32.

Reed-Danahay, D. E. (Ed.). (1997). *Auto/ethnography: Rewriting the self and the social.* Oxford, New York: Berg.

Remlinger, K. (2005). Negotiating the classroom floor: Negotiating ideologies of gender and sexuality. In M. M. Lazar (Ed.), *Feminist critical discourse analysis: Gender, power, and ideology in discourse* (pp. 114–38). Basingstoke, UK; New York: Palgrave Macmillan.

Ribeiro, O., & vanBarneveld, A. (2008). Encouraging professional development through technology use. In K. McFerrin, R. Weber, R. Carlsen, & D. Willis (Eds.), *Proceedings of Society for Information Technology & Teacher Education International Conference 2008* (pp. 1525–30). Chesapeake, VA: AACE.

Rice, J. M. (1969). *The public school system of the United States.* New York: Arno Press. [orig. pub. 1892] Cited in L. Cuban (1993a), *How teachers taught: Constancy and change in American classrooms, 1880–1990.* New York: Teachers College Press.

Rich, A. (1986). *Of woman born: Motherhood as experience and as institution.* New York: Norton.

Richardson, L. (1997). *Fields of play: Constructing an academic life.* New Brunswick, NJ: Rutgers University Press.

Richardson, L. (2001). Getting personal: Writing-stories. *International Journal of Qualitative Studies in Education, 14*(1), 33–8.

Richardson, V. (1996). The role of attitude and beliefs in learning to teach. In J. Sikula, T. J. Buttery, & E. Guyton (Eds.), *Handbook of research on teacher education* (2nd ed.) (pp. 102–19). New York: Macmillan.

Ricoeur, P. (1985). History as narrative and practice: Peter Kemp talks to Paul Ricoeur in Copenhagen (R. Lechner, Trans.). *Philosophy Today, 29,* 213–22.

Riemer, J. (1977). Varieties of opportunistic research. *Urban Life, 5,* 467–77.

Riessman, C. K. (1993). *Narrative analysis.* Newbury Park, CA: Sage.

Robertson, S. L. (1996). Teachers' work, restructuring and postfordism: Constructing the new 'professionalism.' In I. F. Goodson & A. Hargreaves (Eds.), *Teachers' professional lives* (pp. 28–55). London, UK; Bristol, PA: Falmer Press.

Rosen, H. (1998). *Speaking from memory: The study of autobiographical discourse.* Stoke-on-Trent, UK: Trentham.

Rosenwald, G. C., & Ochberg, R. L. (Eds.). (1992). *Storied lives: The cultural politics of self-understanding.* New Haven, London: Yale University Press.

Ruhlman, W. (1995, February 17). From blue to indigo. Retrieved February 6, 2007, from *The Joni Mitchell discussion list:* http://jmdl.com/library/view.cfm?id=115

Sandholtz, J., Ringstaff, C., & Dwyer, D. (1997). *Teaching with technology: Creating student-centered classrooms.* New York: Teachers College Press.

Sarason, S. B. (1996). *Revisiting 'The culture of the school and the problem of change.'* New York: Teachers College.

Sartre, J.-P. (1963). *Search for a method* (H. Barnes, Trans.). New York: Random House.

Scardamalia, M., & Bereiter, C. (1996). Computer support for knowledge-building communities. In T. Koschmann (Ed.), *CSCL: Theory and practice of an emerging paradigm* (pp. 249–68). Mahwah, NJ: Lawrence Erlbaum Associates.

Schaafsma, D. (1996). Things we cannot say: 'Writing for Your Life' and stories in English Education. *Theory into Practice, 35*(2), 110–16.

Schafer, R. (1983). *The analytic attitude.* New York: Basic Books.

Schafer, R. (1992). *Retelling a life: Narration and dialogue in psychoanalysis.* New York: Basic Books.

Schuhrke, B. (2000). Young children's curiosity about other people's genitals. In T. G. M. Sandfort & J. Rademakers (Eds.), *Childhood sexuality: Normal sexual behavior and development* (pp. 27–48). Binghamton, NY: Haworth Press.

Schwab, R. L., & Foa, L. J. (2001). Integrating technologies throughout our schools. *Phi Delta Kappan, 82,* 620–4.

Schwartz, L. (1998). Exploring silence. In A. R. Cacoullos & M. Sifianou (Eds.), *Anatomies of silence, selected papers: Second HASE International Conference on Autonomy of Logos* (pp. 184–91). Athens, Greece: Parousia.

Scott, J. (1992). Experience. In J. Butler & J. Scott (Eds.), *Feminists theorize the political* (pp. 22–40). New York: Routledge.

Scotta, C. (Producer), & Berliner, A. (Director) (1997). *Ma vie en rose* [Motion picture]. Sony Pictures.

Searle, J. R. (1969). *Speech acts: An essay in the philosophy of language.* Cambridge, UK: Cambridge University Press.

Séguin, R. (2007, March 26). Son caged in class, parents say: school board backs 'time-out area.' *Globe and Mail.* Online edition, retrieved March 26, 2007, from http://www.theglobeandmail.com/servlet/story/LAC.20070210.C AGE 10/PPVStory?URL_Article_ID=LAC.20070210.CAGE10andDENIED=1

Shakespeare, W. (1623). Twelfth Night. In S. Greenblatt, W. Cohen, J. E. Howard, & K. E. Maus (Eds.), *The Norton Shakespeare: Comedies* (pp. 660–713). New York, London: Norton.

Shields, C. (1984) *Happenstance: Two novels in one about a marriage in transition.* Toronto: Vintage.

Shilling, C. (1993). *The body and social theory.* London: Sage.

Shreve, A. (1989). *Eden Close.* Orlando, FL: Harcourt Brace.

Sigafoos, J., & Green, V.A. (2007). *Technology and teaching.* New York: Nova Science.

Silin, J. G. (1995). *Sex, death, and the education of children: Our passion for ignorance in the age of AIDS.* New York: Teachers College Press.

Silin, J. G. (2006). Reading, writing, and the wrath of my father. In G. M. Boldt & P. M. Salvio (Eds.), *Love's return: Psychoanalytic essays on childhood, teaching, and learning* (pp. 227–41). New York, London: Routledge.

Simon, P. (1990). Further to fly. On *The rhythm of the saints* [Audio recording: compact disc]. Rio de Janeiro, New York: Warner Brothers.

Simon, R. (1992). *Teaching against the grain: Texts for a pedagogy of possibility.* New York: Bergin & Garvey.

Smagorinsky, P., Cook, L. S., Moore, C., Jackson, A. Y., & Fry, P. G. (2004). Tensions in learning to teach: Accommodation and the development of a teaching identity. *Journal of Teacher Education, 55*(1), 8–24.

Smeets, E., & Mooij, T. (2001). Pupil-centred learning, ICT, and teacher behaviour: Observations in educational practice. *British Journal of Educational Technology, 32*(4), 403–17.

Sofia, Z. (1996). Contested zones: Futurity and technological art. *Leonardo, 29*(1), 59–66.

Sparkes, A. C. (2000). Autoethnography and narratives of self: Reflections on criteria in action. *Sociology of Sport Journal, 17*, 21–41.

Spender, D. (1980). *Man made language.* London: Routledge & Kegan Paul.

Spigelman, C. (2001). Argument and evidence in the case of the personal. *College English, 64*(1), 63–87.

Spindler, G., & Spindler, L. (1992). Cultural process and ethnography: An anthropological perspective. In M. D. LeCompte, W. L. Millroy, & J. Preissle (Eds.), *The handbook of qualitative research in education* (pp. 53–92). San Diego: Academic Press.

Stewart-Wells, A. G. (2000). An investigation of student teacher and teacher educator perceptions of their teacher education programs and the role classroom management plays or should play in preservice education. Doctoral dissertation, The Claremont Graduate University, San Diego. Retrieved July 27, 2007, from ProQuest Digital Dissertations database. (Publication No. AAT 9963039).

Stofflett, R., & Stoddart, T. (1992). Patterns of assimilation and accommodation in traditional and conceptual change teacher education courses. Paper presented at the Annual Meeting of the American Education Research Association. San Francisco. Cited in M. Wideen, J. Mayer-Smith, & B. Moon. (1998), A critical analysis of the research on learning to teach: Making the case for an ecological perspective on inquiry. *Review of Educational Research, 68*(2), 130–78.

Stuart, C., & Thurlow, D. (2000). Making it their own: Preservice teachers' experiences, beliefs and classroom practices. *Journal of Teacher Education, 51*(2), 113–21.

Suppes, P. (1980). The teacher and computer-assisted instruction. [Orig. pub. February 1967: *NEA Journal.*] In R. P. Taylor (Ed.), *The computer in the classroom: Tutor tool, tutee* (pp. 231–5). New York: Teachers College Press.

Tannen, D. (1991). *You just don't understand: Women and men in conversation.* London: Virago.

Taubman, P. M. (1992). Achieving the right distance. In W. F. Pinar & W. M. Reynolds (Eds.), *Understanding curriculum as phenomenological and deconstructed text* (pp. 216–33). New York: Teachers College Press.

Taubman, P. M. (2006). I love them to death. In G. M. Boldt & P. M. Salvio (Eds.), *Love's Return: Psychoanalytic essays on childhood, teaching, and learning* (pp. 19–32). New York, London: Routledge.

Theilheimer, R., & Cahill, B. J. (2001). A messy closet in the early childhood classroom. In S. Grieshaber & G. S. Cannella (Eds.), *Embracing identities in early childhood education: Diversity and possibilities* (pp. 103–13). New York: Teachers College Press.

Tillema, H. H. (1998). Stability and change in student teachers' beliefs about teaching. *Teachers and Teaching: Theory and Practice* 4(2), 217–28.

Tobin, J. J. (Ed.) (1997). *Making a place for pleasure in early childhood education.* New Haven, London: Yale University Press.

Tobin, J. J. (1997a). The missing discourse of pleasure and desire. In J. J. Tobin (Ed.), *Making a place for pleasure in early childhood education* (pp. 1–37). New Haven, London: Yale University Press.

Todd, S. (1997). Looking at pedagogy in 3-D: Rethinking difference, disparity, and desire. In S. Todd (Ed.), *Learning desire: Perspectives on pedagogy, culture, and the unsaid* (pp. 237–60). New York, London: Routledge.

Todd, S. (2003a). *Learning from the Other: Levinas, psychoanalysis, and ethical possibilities in education.* Albany: State University of New York Press.

Todd, S. (2003b). A fine risk to be run? the ambiguity of eros and teacher responsibility. *Studies in Philosophy and Education, 22,* 31–44.

Todorov, T. (2002). *Imperfect garden: The legacy of humanism* (C. Cosman, Trans.). Princeton, NJ: Princeton University Press.

Toronto District School Board (TDSB) (n/d). *Ontario Knowledge and Network for Learning* (OKNL). Retrieved March 31, 2007, from Toronto District School Board: http://schools.tdsb.on.ca/parkdaleps/OKNL/OKNLtemplateE.html

Turkle, S. (1985). *The second self: Computers and the human spirit.* New York: Touchstone.

Turkle, S. (1997). *Life on the screen: Identity in the age of the internet.* New York: Simon and Schuster.

University of British Columbia (UBC) (n/d). *Program description for B.Ed. elementary option (12 months).* Retrieved February 26, 2007, from University of British Columbia, Faculty of Education: http://teach.educ.ubc.ca/ bachelor/elementary/12-month/english/program.html

University of California at Los Angeles (UCLA) (2006). *Jumping off the bannedwagon: Reading what I want, where I want, when I want.* Retrieved March 27, 2007, from UCLA College Library: http://www.library.ucla.edu/college/nwsevnts/exhibits/banned99/index.htm

University of New Brunswick (UNB) (n/d). *General information.* Retrieved February 25, 2007, from University of New Brunswick, Faculty of Education: http://www.unbf.ca/education/programs/general.html

University of Texas at El Paso (n/d). Meeting the challenge of high quality teacher education: Why higher education must change. Paper presented at the National Conference on Teacher Quality, University of Texas at El Paso. Retrieved March 24, 2007, from University of Texas at El Paso: http://www.ed.gov /inits/teachers/exemplarypractices/b-9.html van den Berg, R. (2002). Teachers' meanings regarding educational practice. *Review of Educational Research, 72*(4), 577–625.

van Dijk, T. A. (1993). Principles of critical discourse analysis. *Discourse and Society, 4*, 249–83.

Volbert, R. (2000). Sexual knowledge of preschool children. *Journal of Psychology and Human Sexuality, 12*(1/2), 5–26.

Walker, R. (1998). *Good reasons for staying off-line.* Retrieved March 24, 2007, from ultiBASE: http://ultibase.rmit.edu.au/Articles/oct98/walker1.htm

Walkerdine, V. (1990). *Schoolgirl fictions.* London; New York: Verso.

Waller, W. (1967). *The sociology of teaching.* New York: John Wiley and Sons.

Wang, L. C. (2008). Technology integration in public schools: Generalizing from Northeast Ohio to a global setting. *International Journal of Continuing Engineering Education and Life Long Learning, 18*(4), 446–62.

Warner, J. (Producer), & Cukor, C. (Director). (1964). *My fair lady* [Motion picture]. Warner Brothers.

Warren, W. (2008). Teachers, teaching, schools and society. In T. Di Petta (Ed.), *The emperor's new computer: ICT, teachers and* teaching, pp. 1–4. Rotterdam: Sense.

Weeks, J. (1993). *Sexuality and its discontents: Meanings, myths and modern sexualities.* London, New York: Routledge.

Whatley, M. (1994). Keeping adolescents in the picture: Construction of adolescent sexuality in textbook images and popular films. In J. Irvine (Ed.), *Sexual cultures and the construction of adolescent identities* (pp. 183–205). Philadelphia: Temple University Press.

Wideen, M., Mayer-Smith, J., & Moon, B. (1998). A critical analysis of the research on learning to teach: Making the case for an ecological perspective on inquiry. *Review of Educational Research, 68*(2), 130–78.

Williams, R. (1983). *Keywords.* London: Flamingo Press.

Winnicott, D. W. (1945). Thinking and the unconscious. In *Home is where we start from: Essays by a psychoanalyst* (1990) (pp. 169–71). New York, London: W. W. Norton.

Winnicott, D. W. (1960). The theory of the parent-infant relationship. In *The maturational processes and the facilitating environment: Studies in the theory of emotional development* (1965) (pp. 37–55). New York, Madison, CT: International Universities Press.

Winnicott, D. W. (1963a). The value of depression. In *Home is where we start from: Essays by a psychoanalyst* (1990) (pp. 71–9). New York: Norton.

Winnicott, D. W. (1963b). *Sum,* I am. In *Home is where we start from: Essays by a psychoanalyst* (1990) (pp. 55–64). New York: New York.

Winnicott, D. W. (1963c). Communicating and not communicating leading to a study of certain opposites. In *The maturational processes and the facilitating environment: Studies in the theory of emotional development* (1965) (pp. 179–92). Madison, CT: International Universities Press.

Winnicott, D. W. (1965). *The maturational processes and the facilitating environment: Studies in the theory of emotional development.* Madison, CT: International Universities Press.

Winnicott, D. W. (1971). *Playing and reality.* New York: Routledge.

Winnicott, D. W. (1990). *Home is where we start from: Essays by a psychoanalyst.* New York, London: W.W. Norton.

Wodak, R. (Ed.) (1997). *Gender and discourse.* London: Sage.

Wolcott, H. F. (1987). On ethnographic intent. In G. Spindler & L. Spindler (Eds.), *Interpretive ethnography of education: At home and abroad* (pp. 37–57). Hillsdale, NJ; London: Lawrence Erlbaum Associates.

Wooffitt, R. (2005). *Conversation analysis and discourse analysis: A comparative and critical introduction.* London: Sage.

Woolf, V. (1981). *A room of one's own.* New York: Harcourt Brace Jovanovich.

Worthington, V. L., & Zhao, Y. (1999). Existential computer anxiety and changes in computer technology: What past research on computer anxiety has missed. *Journal of Educational Computing Research, 20*(4), 200–315.

York University. (2006a). An overview of the programs. Retrieved February 25, 2007, from York University, Faculty of Education: http://www.yorku.ca/foe/Programs/BEd/preservice_handbook/preservice_handbook0607/programs/overview/index.html

York University. (2006b). Practicum guide. Retrieved March 1, 2007, from York University, Faculty of Education: http://www.yorku.ca/foe/Programs/BEd/PracticumGuide/Consecutive/index.html

Young, N. (1964). Sugar mountain. On *Decade* [Audio recording: compact disc]. Toronto: Warner Brothers.

Young-Bruehl, E. (1998). *Subject to biography: Psychoanalysis, feminism, and writing women's lives.* Cambridge, MA: Harvard University Press.

Zalewski, D. (2000, October 8). Anthropology enters the age of cannibalism. *New York Times.* Online edition, retrieved December 12, 2006, from http://www.nytimes.com/2000/10/08/weekinreview/08ZALE.html?ex=1148443200&en=6b8286dedd9bd854&ei=5070

Zeichner, K. M. (1999). The new scholarship in teacher education. *Educational Researcher, 28*(9), 4–15.

Author Index

Subject Index

transparency, absence of: in education, 167, 229–30; in narrative, 56–8,
261n6; in research, 28, 33–4, 40–1, 56
trauma, traumatic events, 16–17,
62–3, 66, 79, 85, 95, 186, 202, 219
truth, 33–4, 40, 53–5, 78–80, 85, 161,
179; régimes of, 46

unconscious, the, 13, 17, 41–4, 60–8,
88, 90, 96, 187, 219, 226, 241; access
to, 43–4, 83–6; desire and, 69–70,
81, 86, 97, 238, 251, 260n8/n9,
262n10; functions of, 17, 60–2,
65, 66, 86, 219, 229–31; and language, 149–50, 184–5; and learning, 67, 184–6, 221; and narrative,
91–4, 197–8, 202–3; and sexuality,
121–7; silence and, 241–3 (*see also*
silence); and teaching, 85–6, 142,
145–9, 151–3, 157–8. *See also* psychoanalytic theory; self
understanding: fear and, 176–7; in
language, 34–5; narrative and, 53;
as partial. *See also* knowledge

University of British Columbia,
173
University of California at Los Angeles, 263n5
University of New Brunswick, 173
University of Texas at El Paso, 173
unpleasure, 17, 43, 61, 85, 122; defence
against, 119, 121–2

wishes. *See* desire; unconscious
women's work. *See* teaching, as
gendered
writing: adolescents and, 87, 108;
as delaying tactic, 92–4, 195; and
memory/remembering, 57–9,
63–4, 78–80, 91–6, 197, 238; -pad,
see mystic writing-pad; personal,
16, 27, 52–7, 166–7, 194–9, 217,
237, 239–40, 257n3, 258n2, 268n13;
as research methodology, 14, 27–8,
31–5, 228–9

York University, 169, 173, 181, 191,
209, 264n1, 266n8